The Best
AMERICAN
SPORTS
WRITING
1992

To Kirk for mike
alland

The Best
AMERICAN
SPORTS
WRITING
1992

EDITED AND WITH
AN INTRODUCTION BY
Thomas McGuane

Glenn Stout, SERIES EDITOR

HOUGHTON MIFFLIN COMPANY
BOSTON · NEW YORK · LONDON   1992

ISSN 1056-8034
ISBN 0-395-60340-4
ISBN 0-395-60341-2 (pbk.)

Printed in the United States of America

AGM 10 9 8 7 6 5 4 3 2 1

"Shadow of a Nation" by Gary Smith. First published in *Sports Illustrated*. Copyright © 1991, The Time Inc. Magazine Company. Reprinted courtesy of *Sports Illustrated*, from the February 18, 1991, issue.

"Muhammad Ali, the Mongoose, and Me" by George Plimpton. First published in *Esquire*. Copyright © 1991 by George Plimpton. Reprinted by permission of the author.

"Rodeo" by Thomas Mallon. First published in *The Yale Review*. Copyright © 1991 by Thomas Mallon. Reprinted by permission of the author.

"They Shoot Heroes, Don't They?" by David von Drehle. First published in *Tropic*, the Sunday magazine of *The Miami Herald*. Reprinted by permission of the publisher.

"Center of Gravity" by Timothy Dwyer. First published in *The Philadelphia Inquirer Magazine*. Reprinted by permission of the publisher.

"A Painter on a Planet of Blind People" by Michael Disend. First published in *Sports Illustrated*. Copyright © 1991 by Michael Disend. Reprinted by permission of the author.

"Stealth Bomber" by Joe Sexton. First published in *The New York Times Magazine*. Copyright © 1991 by Joe Sexton. Reprinted by permission of the publisher.

"A Winter Grouse" by Sydney Lea. First published in *The Virginia Quarterly Review*. Reprinted by permission of the publisher.

"For Ali, Greatness Takes Another Form" by William Gildea. First published in *The Washington Post*. Copyright © 1991 by *The Washington Post*. Reprinted by permission of the publisher.

To Dan Lufkin

Contents

Foreword

SEVERAL YEARS AGO I read a poem by David Rein entitled "A Baseball Player Looks at a Poet." In the poem, Rein explores the connection between athletics and the act of writing. From the ballplayer's perspective, Rein writes, "Every time the ball comes my way,/ In the field/ Or at the plate,/ The critics count./ Every misplay,/ Every strikout,/ Goes into my record — indelibly,/ While you come out with your slender book of poems,/ Poems which you yourself select . . ./ You *seem* to bat and field one thousand./ But what's your real average?" Rein's point is obvious. The writer, unlike the athlete, has the advantage of hindsight. The writer can edit his or her performance, the athlete cannot. Who then can blame the athlete for looking to the writer, as so often happens these days, with a jaundiced and mistrusting eye?

As I spent my time this past year reading magazines and newspapers in search of candidates for *The Best American Sports Writing 1992*, I thought a great deal about the relationship between sports and writing. For while Rein's observation is accurate, it is also incomplete. Sports and the act of writing have a great deal more in common than many suspect, and those congruencies go a long way toward explaining precisely why the writers in this series have chosen to write about sports and why so many readers are interested in what they chose to write about. If some athletes can be aptly described as poets, the reverse observation is also true.

I came to this conclusion several months ago following a conversation I had with a writer friend. He asked me why I thought that people felt so, well, *connected* to sports. As I grappled for a coherent answer, I asked him the same question. He was prepared, and paraphrased some anonymous anthropologist who stated that "all sports are in some way either aiming or chasing," both activities that were imperative to the prehistoric hunter-gatherer societies from which all modern societies have evolved. That statement, while not necessarily conclusive, seemed true enough, and our conversation went on to a heated discussion of the aimers and chasers of our favorite teams in the National Basketball Association.

Now, while that kind of observation makes some people uncomfortable, it led me to reassess my own athletic history. I was surprised to discover that it also led me to do a lot of thinking about writing.

My personal athletic résumé includes lengthy participation in baseball; less successful experiences in football and basketball; steady, if unspectacular, participation in running and other desultory exercise; total failure in hunting, fishing, skating, and billiards; and the usual basement and back yard mixture of boxing, wrestling, Ping Pong, Whiffle ball, and other familiar suspects. I have skied and played tennis precisely once each, and my golf has been limited to the miniature variety. Yet in each I had to admit that yes, aiming or chasing did seem to be a part of the sport, either directly or as a not too well disguised metaphor. Apparently, the roots of my hunter-gatherer ancestry are buried just below the ground.

But I also noted that at about the same time I stopped actively participating in most sports, I actively turned to writing. What did this mean? As a child I thought nothing of kicking a football back and forth across the back yard for the better part of a day. Even while attending college I'd skip class after lunch for the chance to play pickup softball until dusk. Today writing is the only activity I can still manage to pursue with the same voracity that once sent me scurrying after softballs at the expense of Shakespeare.

A couple of years ago I wrote a biography of the baseball player Ted Williams. Because of deadline pressures, I had to complete the entire process, both research and writing, in ten weeks. For those two and a half months I spent literally every waking moment, while not at my day job, at work on the project.

I do not think I could have done this, or at least had the confidence that I could, if not for my experience in sports. While writing the book I was after different quarry, the enigmatic personality of one of baseball's most volatile stars, but I was still aiming and chasing, and I knew how to do that. The English department had provided me with the appropriate tools, but I took my methodology from sports.

The goal of good writing may be more discrete than the goals that are so manifest in sport, but there is a very similar satisfaction when that goal is achieved. The feeling experienced by Michael Jordan after sinking an impossible shot when his game rises to that unmistakable "other level" is akin to the feeling a writer sometimes enjoys. Suddenly, after hours of research, writing, rewriting, playing basketball with the wastebasket, too much coffee and not enough sleep, the disconnected fragments of verbiage transform and the music of truth washes over the page in a single, resonant voice. As writers, this is what we chase, and this is what we aim toward. And this may be why some writers find sports so willing a subject.

The writers represented in *The Best American Sports Writing 1992* know this feeling as well as any of their subjects. The writing I selected for consideration by guest editor Tom McGuane is sports writing that completes the chase and strikes the target. The writer reaches his or her goal and the story attains, as McGuane quotes in his introduction, that "sweet spot in time."

As I surveyed, issue by issue, several hundred publications in search of those stories, I felt somewhat like a baseball "bird-dog," the lowest but most important member of baseball's scouting hierarchy. The bird-dog is a scout who searches among the unlikely on the off chance the exceptional might appear. This scout drives untold thousands of miles alone, watches hundreds of games, and evaluates countless numbers of unremarkable ballplayers, making a quick but careful appraisal of each, looking for that one player whose talent separates him from the horde and leaves all others in shadow. Finding that player sends a tremor through the bird-dog's body and justifies the long, solitary search. Discovering the best sports writing gives me the same sensation. I hope readers of this book can share that experience.

To be considered for inclusion in *The Best American Sports Writing 1992*, a story must have been published in 1991, and must have been column length (approximately 1,000 words) or longer. From my survey of hundreds of publications, Tom McGuane received only the very best. From this group Tom had the daunting task of selecting the twenty-five stories that appear.

While I read as much material as I can, I depend on publishers, editors, and writers throughout the United States and Canada for their assistance. Publications that want to make certain their contributions will be considered for the next edition should include this anthology on their subscription list. Editors, particularly the sports editors of newspapers, may submit works of merit from their own publications. The writers themselves, naturally, are also encouraged to respond. Submissions for next year's volume, with complete bibliographic references, should be received by me no later than February 1, 1993 (Glenn Stout, *The Best American Sports Writing*, P.O. Box 963, Back Bay Annex, Boston, Massachusetts 02117). Subscriptions can be sent to the same address.

My thanks go again to the staff of the Boston Public Library for making this job a little bit easier. I am also grateful to Doe Coover, Alan Andres, Steve Lewers, Larry Cooper, and Carin Goldberg for the success of this project. Robert Atwan, series editor of *The Best American Essays,* made some welcome suggestions, as did a number of other writers, editors, and friends. Guest editor Tom McGuane's enthusiastic participation and selections have resulted in a book that I believe is once again worthy of its title.

GLENN STOUT

Introduction

WHEN I WAS YOUNG, playing away the summer evenings on our neighborhood baseball diamond, I resented the late dining habits of my family. I craved a Marty Marion infielder's mitt. I struggled against my skinniness, my weakness, the speed of the ball, and the weight of the bat. I feared disgrace and the opprobrium of older boys. I worried about being picked last when we chose sides. I was ashamed that I had to choke up on the bat, and I never felt confident that I understood the regulations of the game, the austerity of each batter going single-handedly against nine defensive players. The most distinguished thing about our family was that my mother knew Birdie Tebbetts, the manager of the Cleveland Indians. At Tiger Stadium, when we contemplated the arm of Al Kaline, we were awed by his throws burning dead level from deep outfield to home plate. We enjoyed the consolations offered by religion to its adherents with a benign comprehension of our limitations. We even imitated the bizarre batting stance of Gerry Priddy as our zealotry deepened to nonsense. We chewed tobacco. We warmed up with multiple bats when we barely had the strength for one. Once in a great and reckless while we deliberately hit the Hillerich & Bradsby Louisville Slugger on its incised label to feel a crack shiver through our grip, and ran out a broken-bat single.

And then we were eighteen, out of high school, and old. None of my gang was good enough to play in college — even, say, a Dukhobor college in the Dakotas. Suddenly we were fans only. The radio with its unparalleled vividness, thanks in part to the voice of Ernie Harwell, couldn't be turned on to every game. Our time was not quite our own as it had once been. But somehow, one could get to the sports page by evening, or the next day, or to a magazine on the weekend; and there we became dependent on sports writers. It was their job, we knew instinctively, to keep the candles burning, to get the news to the faithful.

Sports for me have frequently been what the British call field sports and have involved teammates who are often not human. In my struggle over the ethics of hunting, my biggest hurdle is the notion of giving up my projects with dogs. It is one thing to have a dog as a pet and quite another as a colleague of the fields and woodlands. Feeding my cutting horse in the box stalls of strange towns, I have felt in the great, breathing, heat-filled weight of the sentient creature standing beside me a rapture of sporting partnership.

Fishing has been the unifying thread of my life. I give equal importance to the choggies and tautog I gazed at in transubstantiating delight under the dock at Sakonnet Point forty years ago and to the sea-thickened Atlantic salmon of last summer on the Grand Cascapedia of Quebec. My pantheon includes the big-time anglers of the world as well as the urban poor of Paris and Mobile and Detroit soaking worms and bread balls and cheese potions in their home waters. The real angler knows his sport transcends every limitation of economics, class, and culture. In my own hometown, fishing was the only place the doctor, the alcoholic welder, the priest, the barber, and the town bum could meet on equal footing. I vividly remember how reluctant they were to leave that superior world for the primitive, status-conscious society that surrounded it. If a rich man had any standing in that group, it was but to bribe the lighthouse keeper on Lake Erie to let him and his friends fish for pickerel under the big circling beams that attracted the bait. Fishing has the most extensive literature of any sport, though it lingers at the edge of the psychologically very odd things people do, like ferret legging and racing pigeons. It is a somewhat different world than that of, say, soccer, whose striving is more comfortable beside that of children racing across a finish line with eggs balanced in soup spoons.

It's possible to feel that sports and show business are about all that's left. Only a brief, easy-to-follow recent war interrupted our preoccupation. And sports make the better national theater. Show business aims to give us whatever we want, but sport has its own rules. The referee is going to call the fouls whether the American people want it or not. We are deeply offended by any game that is fixed, because in sport we want to see skill, bad luck, and opportunity in their roughest clothes. Sports are the national parks of chance. In a poll- and trend-driven universe, they need no other excuse. Movies, politics, all pander to the innermost twitching of our desires while sports often defy our wishes. The difference between watching a baseball game and watching a movie is very like the difference between making love with your spouse and making love with a prostitute. The sporting world is as real as weather or landscape. The unfolding of human potential is nowhere else so purely revealed.

The reader of sports writing is a strict, occasionally cruel individual. There has never been a modernist period in sports writing, much less a postmodernist spell. Anything beyond telling the sports fan what actually happened requires the heart of a lion, a jeweler's eye. Otherwise, one risks being tossed out by the reader himself. The sports page of any newspaper is truly an impact zone where writers and readers compare impressions of something they often have both seen. No one is taking anyone's word for anything. Opinions are truly earned. Fancy sports writing is some of the worst writing of any kind. Since sport has come under the scrutiny of literary persons in search of microcosms, some wistful horrors have resulted, as well as hellish impeachments of the old compact between sports and their storytellers. Sports writing is not necessarily an occasion for self-discovery, and sports writers, of all the kinds of writers there are, are the least cuddly. They are notorious for going sour with drink or age. The end of a sports writer is more like the end of Marlowe's Faust, showering curses from his cauldron, than the end of Achilles or Lord Nelson. It is sports writers' mission to bring the news from the field; they have more in common with war correspondents than they do with any other kind of writers.

What is shared, foremost, is the event. If we weren't there, the writer describes it for us. That the reader might have been there too is chastening to the writer. Often the writer tries to carry us along as though we *had* been there; and perhaps he selects and emphasizes the episodes to foreshorten the logic of his argument. It's usually about meaning. Some of our most famous sports writers have been most high-handed in telling us about significance. Perhaps the real meaning of a sports event lingers somewhere beyond the event itself, like the athlete's retirement, the sportsman's childhood in the South Bronx or Yarmouth, an aunt's view of honor, an illness. Life seems demarcated on a playing field or a trout stream, and human matters like the definition of character acquire a clarity rare in the pandemonium of modern life.

Anyone who has gone through the highlights of a year's sports writing must be impressed by its wildly uneven quality. The war between writers and editors is seen in the frequently inappropriate titles, imitations of successful movie titles or soft-drink advertisements, as well as the suddenly intrusive hand on the text, often at the end, in the form of heart-rending and odious twists. Here the corporation meets the street, and the writer, customarily, is the street. The writer, struggling from the material outward, runs up on the macro reef of the editor's overview — an overview that is, in some cases, in the interest of neither the subject nor literature.

Because of the vigorous intrusions of sports writers, their writing is almost impossible to deconstruct. Fiction has become a better expression of anonymity. But good sports writers find room for style, what Sam Johnson defined as "the last resort of a Spaniard." There is style in the approach of the immortal A. J. Liebling which consists of such knowingness as to make of oneself a part of the scene reported, entitled to shapely inside commentary. There is the Hemingway approach in which the sport — jai alai, say, or bullfighting — is like the shadows on the wall of Plato's cave, manifestations of immortality. The writer may recognize that the practitioner of sport may cross into a zone, some "sweet spot in time," that contains suggestions of immortality. There is the Ring Lardner approach, not so different from Liebling's, in which the sardonic insider is perhaps funnier, but more likely to find something over the top, unexpected sentiment or surrealistic lack of accountability. And yet, all things considered, the baseball card is still one model of good sports writing. There is always that clear-eyed reader who wants to know what actually happened.

Practitioners of the solitary sports of hunting and fishing, who are often uncomfortable with the title of "sport" at all, thinking that "art" is more in their line, as in "the art of dry fly-fishing" or "the art of upland game hunting," have been least successful when on some damp quest for meaning and most successful when seeing themselves as players. The great Izaak Walton was quite clearly a sanguine and cheery player in the grand game of angling. Hunting, even with its many deaths, has produced words to live by. Turgenev's and Ortega y Gasset's have borne undoubted greatness. But their melancholy subject has confined them to a narrower band of the human wheel than that occupied by the archers of Japan, the anglers of England and America, the single-handed sailors of France, the baseball players of Latin America, and so on. In Chekhov, one bird hunter holds out a dead woodcock to another and asks, "Aren't we a couple of great fellows?" casting an entire sport in doubt.

The base-path nimbleness of Ricky Natiel, the Hail Marys of John Elway, the roguish concentration of Sam Snead, and the edge of speed in Florence Griffith Joyner are for life, part of the upward reach of the human spirit as well as its power to cope with all things, starting with gravity and the resistance of air. The sports writer, in refraining from pouring it on too thick, takes his lift from these efforts and extends their soaring into language, that surest of all mediums in which these efforts may go on living. Language is the only place the devastation of Rocky Marciano's right hand can leave a telling impression. Film footage makes him into a pushover. In this case, a word is worth a thousand pictures.

As the human race is driven to reduce itself to exemplary citizens and icons, we study the moral wagers of drug-recovering pitchers and gambling infielders for hints about our own lives. The national dramas of Joe Louis and Max Schmeling and the balladry of American dreams implicit in a life like Joe DiMaggio's have given way to a pointillistic microcosm of our own society. The coliseum mentality of a prodigious, electronically bonded audience for sport raises, among the sensible, questions about our rapidly forming national character. Dubious "human-interest" stories attempt to resurrect our expensive gladiators from the savagery of the spectacles we have devised. Yet sport offers ancient raptures, and its best writers are like guides in old cathedrals, each possessing treasured childhood memories of the sacristy.

In my experience, the world of sport has been a bifurcated phenomenon: sport that is a spectacle, in which one takes part as a participant or as a spectator, and sport that is often a more private affair — hunting, fishing, sailing, horsemanship, flying, falconry. I think we are in some ways dealing with a language failure in listing both baseball and falconry as sports. But that is what we do. The rich soup that is the environment of the fan of team sports, with its franchises and divisions, its superstars and their agents, is very different from the sporting world occupied by the solitary angler on a woodland stream. It's a healthy exercise for the mind to comprehend their co-occupation of sport, to track Ted Williams's delicate transition from power hitter to great fisherman without somehow breaking the thread. When individuals from the second form of sport are thrust into the world of spectator sport, adding solitude to the challenges of the self, some peculiar and even shaggy monsters are the result. One thinks of the baleful lot that have been skippers of the America's Cup boats; one thinks of long-distance runners plucked from the solitude of their suffering and commitment to the spectacle of public marathons where they encounter the hopelessly overage, the Rosie Ruizes, and those dodging family histories of heart disease. The national interest in the often grotesque marathon finishes and the wall of late runners like something out of Hieronymus Bosch has much to do with frightening, mortal instruction and not much, perhaps, to do with sport; a sense less of admiration than of "there but for the grace of God go I."

Because of the stately pace of the game itself, the long, long season, the geographical dispersion of teams, and the years that some players can survive, baseball is in a better position to reflect the society in which it is embedded than any other American sport. It is a spectacle of nuances in which a player has little hope of concealing the innermost whorls of his character, and it is the sport that society has the least chance of isolating from its own defects. It is also the sport in which achievements based on character can seem the most incontrovertible. A Willie Mays, a Sandy Koufax, a Joe DiMaggio, occupies a high ground combining probity and glory, unassailable by the most determined enemy. There is even room for fully formed and complicated, not all good, characters like Ted Williams or, we may see, Pete Rose. As in great novels, the final characters of baseball are indelible. The appointments to its Hall of Fame resonate in the national imagination beyond their equivalents in other sports. The balance between the life of the individual and the life of the team is, in baseball, the most ideal. Many Americans have a baseball player in their human iconography. For me it is George Kell, the Detroit third baseman of the fifties: serious, cheerful, a bomb-proof presence in the hot corner, a hitter who approached the plate apparently oblivious of his disruptive powers. It is easy to see why conversations about baseball have as much heat as those about politics. We are talking about ourselves.

Basketball is rising as a national drama. Its tempo is better related to the present. The sheer athleticism it requires might be the most extreme of any sport. The changing, star-studded rosters remind us of the sudden turnovers of show business. Indeed, the celebrity fans of the Lakers and their out-of-town wannabes, peering at the action through their dark glasses or lounging in Italian suits, make us aware of the similarity of the two worlds. We sniffingly suspect that basketball is a sport for today and that baseball belongs to an older, earlier America, that football is at bottom an invention of the Republicans, that hockey is seminative at best, that tennis draws its talent from a nonlevel playing field. None of this, of course, is quite true.

The pitcher bent from the waist to scrutinize the signals of his catcher, the quail hunter thumbing out the seeds from a quail's crop, the quarterback detecting a misstep in the secondary, the trout fisherman watching the blue-winged mayfly unfurl its wings on the ball of his forefinger, the golfer suspending his putter like a plumb bob, the falconer casting the intense little tiercel into the wind, the tennis player repeating a self-invented mantra, the Grand Prix driver hearing a new signal etched from the valve train uproar at a hundred ninety miles an hour, the sprinter smothered by the quarter step that will separate him from the other sprinters, all have leveled their spirit at the unknown. At the core of sport is courage.

The best writing on sport springs from avidity, not detachment. It is sometimes unliterary — not archly so, as with the sardonic primitives of other forms of writing where simplicity is the result of a sharp eye on the audience. The best sports writers are swept away by their subject, sometimes to comic effect, though we patronize the outlandish or overpartisan at our own peril. The creeping presence of adulatory sports writing, borrowed from the press that serves the entertainment business, is worrisome enough, but sports writing is at its worst when the writer measures the player against his own virtue and finds the player wanting. Pete Rose and Ted Williams and Mike Tyson have been subjected to this poisonous nattering, as have many others. And yet, an athlete or sportsman usually finds an irreducibly earned stature even at the end of a blizzard of publicity.

No one sport has a greater claim on rational behavior than another. And in the modern sporting spectacles, proving who, or which team, is "better" has become marginalized except where the surfeit of events has made us into statisticians. We watch pitchers, or secondaries or goaltenders or the copings of the recently detoxified; we watch the tantrums of owners, the gambles of free agents and the heart-risking stampedes of overweight coaches. We watch and covertly subject ourselves to the same dramas. We ask ourselves if we would get to our feet and throw again like the chronically sacked quarterback. We wonder why billionaires want the headaches of owning baseball teams, or is it a love of headaches that made them billionaires? We wonder if our courage could survive a seven-game Series. We're trying to find out who we are. We turn to our writers when it all slows down, and ask, What happened? What did it mean?

Thomas McGuane

GARY SMITH

Shadow of a Nation

FROM SPORTS ILLUSTRATED

> I have not told you half that happened when I was young. I can
> think back and tell you much more of war and horse stealing. But
> when the buffalo went away the hearts of my people fell to the
> ground, and they could not lift them up again. After this nothing
> happened. There was little singing anywhere.
> — Plenty Coups, Chief of the Crows, 1930

SINGING. Did you hear it? There was singing in the land once
more that day. How could you not call the Crows a still-mighty
tribe if you saw them on the move that afternoon? How could
your heart not leave the ground if you were one of those Indian
boys leading them across the valley of the Big Horn?

It was March 24, 1983, a day of thin clouds and pale sun in
southern Montana. A bus slowed as it reached the crest of a hill,
and from there, for the first time, the boys inside it could see
everything. Fender to fender stretched the caravan of cars behind them, seven miles, eight — they had made the asphalt go
away! Through the sage and the buffalo grass they swept, over
buttes and boulder-filled gullies, as in the long-ago days when
their scouts had spotted buffalo and their village had packed up
its lodge poles and tepee skins, lashed them to the dogs and mi-
grated in pursuit of the herd.

But what they pursued now was a high school basketball team,
twelve teenagers on their way to Billings to play in a state tournament. The boys stared through their windows at the caravan.
There was bone quiet in the bus. It was as if, all at once, the boys

had sensed the size of this moment . . . and what awaited each of them once this moment was done.

In one seat, his nose pressed to the window was one of Hardin High's starting guards, Everette Walks, a boy with unnaturally large hands who had never known his father. In a few weeks he would drop out of school, then cirrhosis would begin to lay waste his mother. He would wind up pushing a mop at 2 A.M. in a restaurant on the Crow reservation.

In another seat sat one of the forwards, an astounding leaper named Miles Fighter. He too had grown up with no father, and recently his mother had died of cirrhosis. In just a few years, he would be unemployed and drinking heavily.

Not far away sat the other starting guard, Jo Jo Pretty Paint, a brilliant long-range shooter, a dedicated kid — just a few minutes before a game at Miles City, his coach had found him alone, crouched, shuffling, covering an invisible opponent in the locker room shower. In two years Pretty Paint would go out drinking one evening, get into a car and career over an embankment. He would go to his grave with a photograph of himself in his uniform, clutching a basketball.

Hunched nearby, all knees and elbows and shoulders, was Darren Big Medicine, the easygoing center. Sixteen months after Pretty Paint's death, he would leave a party after a night of drinking, fall asleep as he sped along a reservation road, drive into a ditch and die.

And then there was Takes Enemy . . .

Weeping. Did you hear it? There was weeping in the land that day. Sobs for those missing from that glorious caravan, those decaying in the reservation dust, for Dale Spotted and Star Not Afraid and Darrell Hill and Tim Falls Down, Crow stars of the past dead of cirrhosis and suicide and knife-stabbing and a liquor-fogged car wreck. Sobs for the slow deaths occurring every night a mile from Jonathan Takes Enemy's high school, where an entire squad of jump shooters and dunkers and power forwards from the past could be found huddling against the chill and sprawled upon the sidewalks outside the bars on the south side of Hardin. Jonathan's predecessors. Jonathan's pathbeaters. "Good Lord!" cries Mickey Kern, the computer-science teacher and former basketball scorekeeper at Hardin High. "How many have we lost? How *many?*"

But Takes Enemy — he would be the one who escaped, wouldn't he? That was what the white coaches and teachers and administrators at his school kept telling him. His mind was sharp, his skill immense; the destiny of all those others needn't be his. Brigham Young wanted him. Oregon State and Arizona State had sent letters. O.J. Simpson would shake his hand in New York City and present him with a crystal cup for being named Montana's Outstanding Athlete of 1984. He was six foot two, he could twirl 360 degrees in the air and dunk the ball, he could shoot from distance. He loved to take a rebound with one hand and bring it to his other palm with a resounding *slap,* make a right-angle cut on the dribble at a velocity that ripped the court wide open, then thread it with a blind running pass, an orange blur straight from the unconscious. "Watching him play," says Janine Pease–Windy Boy, the president of Little Big Horn College, the junior college on the Crow reservation, "was like watching clean water flow across rocks."

Young Indian boys formed trails behind him, wearing big buttons with his picture on their little chests. They ran onto the court and formed a corridor for him and his teammates to trot through during pregame introductions, they touched his hands and arms, they pretended to *be* him. The coaches had to lock the gym doors to start practice. Girls lifted their pens to the bathroom walls: "I was with Jonathan Takes Enemy last night," they wrote. "I'm going to have Jonathan Takes Enemy's baby." He was a junior in high school. Already he was the father of two. Already he drank too much. Already his sister Sharolyn was dead of cirrhosis. Sometimes he walked alone in the night, shaking and sobbing He was the newest hero of the tribe that loved basketball too much.

Takes Enemy felt the bus wheels rolling beneath him. The sun arced through the Montana sky. The circle was the symbol of never-ending life to the Crows — they saw it revealed in the shape and movement of the sun and moon, in the path of the eagle, in the contours of their tepees and the whorl of their dances. As long as the people kept faith with the circle, they believed, their tribe would endure. Jonathan settled back in his seat. Sometimes it seemed as if his life were handcuffed to a wheel, fated to take him up . . . and over . . . and down . . .

Somewhere behind him on the highway, his first cousin would soon be getting off his job on the reservation's road crew and joining the exodus to the ball game in Billings — *the* legendary Crow player, some people said; the best player, *period*, in Montana high school history, said others; the one who ignited his tribe's passion for high school basketball back in the 1950s and seemed to start this dark cycle of great players arising and vanishing: Larry Pretty Weasel. The one whose drinking helped drive him out of Rocky Mountain College in Billings and back to the reservation in 1958, just a few days before the NAIA's weekly bulletin arrived proclaiming him the best field-goal percentage shooter in the country.

Horns honked in the caravan behind Takes Enemy, passengers waved. In the long-ago days before white men had brought their horses or guns or cars or liquor, his people had chased buffalo in this same direction, across these same valleys, stampeding them over cliffs near the land where Billings would one day arise. This same creature whose skull the Crows would mount on a pole and make the centerpiece of their religious Sun Dance . . . they would drive over the edge of the cliff and then scramble down to devour.

The bus ascended another hill. Takes Enemy looked back at his people one more time

One winter night in 1989, the custodian at Lodge Grass High on the Crow reservation forgot to flick off a switch. When the team bus pulled into the parking lot after a road game nearly four hours away, the lights above six of the seventeen outdoor baskets that surround the school were still burning. It was 2 A.M. It was snowing. Two games of five-on-five were being played.

Somehow, in the mindless way that rivers sculpt valleys and shame shapes history, the Montana Indians' purest howl against a hundred years of repression and pain had become . . . high school basketball. Yes, the Crows' eighty-three hundred people were racked by alcoholism and poverty, 75 percent of them were unemployed, the attrition rate for those who went to college was 95 percent, and their homeland, through cheating, broken treaties and sellouts, had dwindled from the 38.8 million acres guaranteed them by the U.S. government in 1851 to the present-day 1.1 million — *however*, just let them lace on sneakers and lay their hands on a basketball. Though Indians constituted but 7 percent of Montana's population, their schools would win ten Class A, B and C state high school basketball titles between 1980 and 1990.

To the north and northwest of the Crow reservation lay the reservations of the Blackfeet, Sioux, Flathead, Assiniboine, Gros Ventre, Chippewa, Cree, Salish, Kootenai and Pen D'Oreilles; to the east lay the Cheyenne. These tribes too loved to run and shoot and jump. At tournament time in Montana, Indian teams were known to streak onto the floor for lay-up drills in war headdress, their fans to shake arenas with chants and war cries and pounding drums as their boys raced up and down the floor at speeds few white teams could sustain. Old women wrapped in blankets were known to pound the bleachers in unison with their canes, to lose their cool and swing the canes at the calves of enemy players; a few, back in the 1940s, even jabbed opponents with hat pins as the boys ran up the sidelines.

Their children spent their days shooting at crooked rims and rotting wooden backboards. Their young men drove for days to reach Indian tournaments all across America and came home to strut the dusty streets in the sheeny jackets they had won there.

Of all the perplexing games that the white man had brought with him — frantic races for diplomas and dollar bills and development — here was the one that the lean, quick men on the reservations could instinctively play. Here was a way to bring pride back to their hollow chests and vacant eyes, some physical means, at last, for poor and undereducated men to reattain the status they once had gained through hunting and battle. Crow men had never taken up the craftwork, weaving or metallurgy that males in other tribes had. They were warriors, meat eaters, nomads whose prestige and self-esteem had come almost entirely from fulfilling an intricate set of requirements — called "counting coup" — while capturing enemy horses or waging battle. A man could count coup by touching an enemy, by seizing a bow or a gun in a hand-to-hand encounter, by capturing a horse in a hostile camp or by being the pipe carrier (which signified leadership) on a successful raid. Only by counting coup, some say,

could a man marry before the age of twenty-five; only by counting coup in all four categories could he become a chief. Children
were named after the exploits of warriors; men starved themselves for days and slept alone in the mountains to invite dreams
that would guide them on raids; a woman attained honor by the
number of scalps and the war booty captured by her man, tokens
of which she brandished when she danced.

And then the white men hunted the buffalo nearly to extinc-
tion and banned intertribal warfare. "It castrated the Crow
male," says Ben Pease, a tribal elder who played basketball for
Hardin High in the 1940s. "It created a vacuum. During World
War I we still weren't citizens, so our men couldn't gain prestige
from that war. People began living off the war deeds of their
ancestors, depending on them for their status. Some Crows
fought in World War II, and for a while these men, especially
those who came back with wounds or proof of bravery, became
our leaders, and our ceremonies often revolved around them.
But time passed, and there weren't enough wars or war heroes;
there was a void that needed to be filled. In the late fifties Larry
Pretty Weasel emerged at Hardin High, and our basketball players began to be noticed in the newspapers. That continued
through the sixties and seventies; more and more of our children began to play. Something had to take war's place, some way
had to be found to count coups. It was basketball."

Old Crow rituals had warm blood and fresh drama again.
Some players tucked tiny medicine bundles — little pouches that
might contain tobacco seeds or small pieces of bone or feather —
inside their socks or tied them to their jerseys, the way warriors
once had tied them to their braids before entering battle. Some
burned cedar and prayed before big games. The same drum ca-
dence and honor songs used two hundred years ago to celebrate
the seizing of a dozen horses or the killing of three Sioux now
reverberated through gymnasiums and community halls at the
capture of a basketball trophy.

"For us, a victory in a high school basketball game is a victory
over everyday misery and poverty and racism," says Dale Old
Horn, who heads the Department of Crow Studies and Social
Sciences at Little Big Horn College. "But it's not a *real* victory. It
doesn't decrease bigotry. It doesn't lessen alcoholism. It doesn't

remove one Indian from the welfare rolls or return a single acre of our land. It gives us pseudo-pride. It hasn't led us on to greater things."

No Indian has ever played in the NBA. Only one, Don Wetzel of the Blackfeet, ever came off a Montana reservation to play for an NCAA Division I team (the University of Montana, 1967–71). Trophy cases in the lobbies of Indian schools throughout the state are filled with gleaming silver . . . and with black-bordered dedications to the dead. This is not just the Crows' tragedy. Two months after graduating from Browning High on the Blackfeet reservation in 1987, six-foot-three All-Stater Gary Cross Guns packed his car to go to a junior college in Kansas. One last night out was all he wanted. The next morning his sister went for a horseback ride. She found her brother's car and his body in Cut Bank Creek.

Wetzel, who once coached basketball at Browning and is now superintendent of schools in Harlem, Montana, could bear it no longer. In the three years since Cross Guns's death, he has traveled fourteen thousand miles and talked to twelve thousand kids, "trying," he says, "to make people see how scary this whole situation has become."

Every now and then, a lesser player left the Crow reservation and quietly, with no scholarship or fanfare, got his degree. But as best as anyone can figure, since 1970 only one prominent Crow player, Luke Spotted Bear, has received a college scholarship and graduated (from Mary College in Bismarck, North Dakota) — and Spotted Bear often felt that his people held this *against* him. "Some of them say I'm too good for them now," he says. "If possible, they don't want to be around me."

College recruiters stopped coming to the reservation, opportunities disappeared. Sean Fritzler, who averaged 29.8 points a game as a senior in 1989, shot 68 percent from the field and was valedictorian of his class at Plenty Coups High School, did not receive a letter of interest from a single university.

"Well, I tried to work with Indians," says Herb Klindt, coach at Rocky Mountain College for thirty-seven years. "I tried to keep them in college. But I got to a point where I just threw up my hands in disgust and gave up, and most of the other coaches did too."

The game that was a highway into mainstream America for
black men . . . was a cul-de-sac for red ones. Something happened to their heroes when the drumbeats died, when the war
whoops faded, when the faces in the audience were not like
theirs. Something in the Crows' love for basketball was toxic.

And along came a boy who was asked to change all that. Along
came a nice, shy kid — Jonathan Takes Enemy.

His people understood his significance. They sent him off to do
battle with all the spiritual might they could muster. Before big
games a medicine man would receive a cigarette from the Takes
Enemy family, take it outside their house just in front of the Little Big Horn River in the town of Crow Agency, light it and pray
to the Great Spirit for Jonathan.

Once, the medicine man wafted cedar smoke and an eagle
feather over the gold chain that Takes Enemy carried with him
to games for good luck. He warned Takes Enemy not to shake
his opponents' hands before a game, so they could not drain
away his power. All these steps were meant to protect Jonathan
from harm, but he couldn't quite trust them. How could he escape the reservation and take up the solitary quest for success in
the white world if he let himself think in the old way? How could
he escape the dark fate of Spotted and Not Afraid and Falls
Down if he believed that a man's destiny hung upon a puff of
smoke in the wind?

When members of the tribe invited players on Jonathan's team
to join them in sweat baths before the division and state tournaments, in order to purify their bodies and spirits in the ritual way
their ancestors had before battle, Jonathan had refused; it was
simply too hot in the sweat lodge. Jonathan's coach at Hardin,
George Pfeifer — in his first year of coaching Indians and curious about their rituals — consented to do it. On a 20-degree day
on the banks of the Little Big Horn, a powdery snow falling from
the sky, the short, stout white man followed the example of eight
Crow men and stripped off his clothes. "Go in, Brother George,"
directed one of them. Brother George got on his knees and
crawled behind them into a low, dome-shaped shelter made of
bent willows and covered by blankets. Inside, it was so dark that
Brother George could not see the hand he held up in front of his
face.

Someone poured a dipper of water over sandstones that had been heated in a bonfire for hours. Steam erupted from the rocks, hissed up and filled the sweat lodge with heat more intense than any sauna's. Sitting cheek to cheek, the men put a switch in Brother George's hand, expecting him to beat himself upon the back and legs to make it even hotter. In the darkness, he heard the others thwacking themselves, groaning and praying for his team in the Crow tongue. He gave up all pretense, flopped onto the floor and cupped his hands around his mouth to find a gulp of cooler air.

A half hour passed like this. A couple of dozen more dippers of water were poured onto the scalded rocks. At last the sweat-soaked men crawled out into the frigid daylight and promptly leapt into the icy river. Brother George's legs refused. He stood there, trembling with cold, about to be sick for three days.

"You're not going to dive in the river, Brother George?" one cried.

"No way."

"That's all right, Brother George. No goddamn magic in that."

But here was the difference: in a few weeks Pfeifer would laugh and tell anecdotes about the day that he left his world and entered another. Jonathan could not. Sometimes he felt the suspicious eyes of whites upon him, felt his tongue turn to stone, his English jumble, when he tried to express to them his feelings. He had but to utter that name to white ears — Takes Enemy — to feel his own ears begin to turn red.

All day and night as he grew up, the television had been on in his home, floating images into his head of white men who drove long cars and lived in wide houses, of Indians who were slow-witted and savage and usually, by the movie's end, dead. One day when he was in junior high, he saw a movie about Custer's Last Stand. He couldn't help himself; in his stomach he felt thrilled when the Indians rolled over the hills and slaughtered every white man. It bewildered him, a few years later, to learn that it was the Sioux and Cheyenne who had slain Custer's troops — that several Crow scouts had ridden *with* Custer. Everything was muddy, nothing ran clean. It was whites who made him speak English most of the day when he entered first grade, rather than the Crow language he had grown up speaking; whites who hung a dead coyote from the outside mirror of Plenty Coups High School's team bus; whites who sang "One little, two little, three little Indians" at his brothers when they played away games in high school. And yet it was Hardin's white athletic director and assistant principal, Kim Anderson, who sometimes drove far out of his way to make sure Jonathan made it to school in the morning; white teachers who offered him encouragement and hope when he passed them in the halls.

Sometimes he would bicycle up the steep incline to the Custer Battlefield, a mile and a half from his home, to sit alone near the markers that showed where each of the white men had fallen, and to stare off into the distance. From here the world stretched out and waited for him to touch it; from here he could see land and a life beyond the reservation. In the daydream he often had here, it would be *he* who was walking from the wide house to the long car, *he* waving a cheery goodbye to his wife and kids, *he* driving off down the well-paved road to the well-paid job, *he* acting out the clichéd American dream he saw on the TV screen. What choice had he? There no longer existed an Indian success cliché to dream of.

An hour or two later he would fly back down the hillside from the battlefield, barely needing to touch his pedals, determined to make the dream come true. It was only when the long hill ran out, when he labored back into his town, that the heaviness returned to his legs.

One evening a few months after his senior season, in which he averaged 28 points a game and shattered a Montana record by scoring 123 points in three state tournament games, his mother, Dorothy, held a "giveaway" in his honor. She was suffering from diabetes, which in a few years would force the amputation of her right leg below the knee and lash her to a kidney dialysis machine three days each week, yet she was determined to thank God and her tribe for the greatness of her son. Jonathan, her seventh surviving child (two had died shortly after birth), had been born with a crooked face and a too large nose, and so in her hospital bed Dorothy had lifted the infant above her eyes and turned all her fears for him over to God. "Here, Lord," she whispered, "raise him up, he's all yours." The Lord's day-care center turned out to be a basketball court; from the age of three, all Jonathan did was dribble and shoot. On dry, frigid days he would play for so long that the ball would chafe away his skin, and he would come home at dusk with bloody fingers for his mother to bandage. Dorothy's eyes still shone when she stared at the Mother's Day card he had drawn in crayon for her in second grade: three yellow flowers in a blue vase, a snow-capped mountain beneath the sun — and a man slam-dunking a basketball. And just look how the boy had turned out, with a face straight and well proportioned, a body long and strong, a name that the wind had carried across the Big Horn and Wolf Mountains, had whispered into the ears of the Cheyenne and Sioux, even laid upon the tongues of the paleskins. If only the boy's eyes would leave his shoes. If only the boy would stop stumbling home at 4 A.M. with the same stink on his breath as her husband, Lacey . . .

In the giveaway ceremony, Jonathan's exploits were to be celebrated in the same manner in which Crows once commemorated a successful raid. Besides all the cousins and uncles and aunts and nephews and nieces who gathered, Jonathan's other "family," his clan, was there. (There are ten clans in the Crow tribe, some consisting of as many as a thousand members; at birth one automatically becomes a member of the same clan as one's mother.) First Jonathan was to dance in a circle as singers sang his honor song, then he was to stand to the side as an "announcer" gave an account of his deeds, and finally he was to give away packages that consisted of four gifts to his clan uncles and aunts. It is a lovely ritual, one in which the hero, in a reversal of the white man's custom, showers his community with gifts in gratitude for the support and prayers that enabled him to succeed. Jonathan's family, just barely getting by on his father's meager salary as a custodian in the reservation hospital, couldn't possibly afford all these gifts, but in keeping with tradition his relatives had contributed so that the giveaway could take place.

Jonathan dreaded the stares that would be drawn to him if he wore the ritual Indian clothing, but he couldn't bear to disappoint his people. Slowly he pulled on the ribbon shirt, the buckskin vest, the colorful beaded armband and the war bonnet. They felt so odd upon him; he felt like no warrior at all. The first horse he had ever ridden had flung him from its back; the first bullet he had ever fired at an animal had slain a dirt clod far from its target. One of his great-great grandfathers, known simply as Fly, had been a powerful warrior, a possessor of six wives. Another, Red Bear, had been a medicine man so potent that he simply had to fill his peace pipe and hold it toward the sun and all the tobacco in it would burn. Their home had been the river-fed valleys and shimmering plains, their roof the sky, their walls the snow-topped mountains a week's walk away. Jonathan? His home was a cramped three-bedroom box in which as many as fifteen siblings and cousins often vied for sleeping space, sometimes on the floor beneath the kitchen table or even in the driveway, in the backseat of a car. Jonathan's bed, until he was seven, was a mattress jammed between the beds of his mom and dad.

With his family and his clan trailing behind him, he lowered his eyes and led them into the Little Big Horn College building for the giveaway. Rather than tokens of scalps or war booty captured from the enemy, Dorothy wore a huge orange shawl with large black letters stitched upon it that listed his coups: JONATHAN TAKES ENEMY, STATE CLASS A MVP, ALL-STATE 1ST TEAM, ALL-CONFERENCE 1984, CONVERSE BASKETBALL ALL-AMERICA HONORABLE MENTION, HERTZ AWARD, ATHLETE OF THE YEAR. Beneath were sewn four white stars; four is the Crows' sacred number. Jonathan was supposed to lead the assembly in a dance, but his feet could not quite bring themselves to do it. Almost imperceptibly he shifted his weight from one foot to the other, leading everyone around the room again and again in a plodding circle as the big drum pounded and the eleven singers in the center lifted their voices to his glory — and reminded him of his obligation to those around him.

> Outstanding man
> Look all around you
> Nothing lasts forever
> Look all around you
> Share your talent and knowledge

Share what? All he had to divvy up, it sometimes seemed, were self-doubt and pain. One day in ninth grade, at the end of basketball practice, his family had come to the school and told him that his sister had died at the age of twenty-four, after years of hard drinking. He turned to the wall and broke down. Just a few weeks later his girlfriend told him she was pregnant. Terrified, he dropped out of school for the rest of the year, hid from his teachers on the streets, sometimes even hid from his own family — and reached for the same poison as his sister had.

He knew the danger he was wooing. The night he learned he had made the varsity, a rare honor for a freshman, he and a few friends went out in a pickup truck to drink beer. A tribal police car pulled up to the truck. Alcohol was banned on the reservation, but Crow policemen sometimes looked the other way. "Go home," this cop ordered the teenagers, but the kid at the wheel panicked, jammed the accelerator and roared away. Suddenly, Takes Enemy, a boy who was afraid even on a sled, found himself hurtling down a curving country road at 100 mph, four police cars with flashing lights and howling sirens just behind him. One came screaming up beside the truck, trying to slip by and box the teenagers in. Instead of letting it pass, Jonathan's friend lurched into the other lane to cut the car off. The pickup truck skidded off the road, toppled onto its roof and into a ditch. Takes Enemy limped out, somehow with just a badly bruised hip.

He vowed not to drink again. He remembered how uneasy he had been as a child, awakening on the mattress between his parents' beds to see the silhouette of his father stagger into the room. Even in an alcoholic haze his father was a gentle man, but still, that silhouette was not Dad — it was a *stranger*. Then, too, there was what alcohol had done to his cousin the legend, Pretty Weasel. So many fans thronged gymnasiums to watch Pretty Weasel play for Hardin High that his team had to crawl through windows to get to its locker room. He could shoot jump shots with either hand, fake so deftly that he put defenders on their pants and, at five-ten, outjump players a half foot taller. It was almost, an opponent would muse years later, "as if you were playing against a kind of enchanted person." Pretty Weasel's younger brother Lamonte got drunk and died in a car accident. Then Pretty Weasel partied his way out of a four-year college scholarship and onto a reservation road crew.

But Jonathan couldn't keep his vow. He felt as if he were locked up in a tiny room inside his body, and it was only when he was playing basketball or drinking that he could break out of it. The first time he was drunk had been in seventh grade at Crow

Fair, the week-long celebration every August when the field on the edge of his town became the tepee capital of the world. Hundreds of tepees were erected, and Indians from far away came to dance and drink and sing with his people deep into the night. Jonathan slipped the bootlegger four dollars for a half pint of whiskey, poured it down — and out poured the talking, laughing Jonathan he had always yearned to be. His mother came and found him at the fair at 3 A.M. Dorothy, a sweet, passive woman dedicated to the Pentecostal Church, began yelling that he would end up just like his father . . . but that was all. In many homes across the reservation . . . that was all.

His sophomore year he moved in with his girlfriend and her parents, to help her bring up their baby daughter. Four months after his girlfriend delivered, she had news for him. She was pregnant again. His whole life seemed hopeless, his daydream of escaping snuffed out. Was it his fault? No matter how hard Jonathan thought about it, he could never be sure. So many things had happened to his people that *were* beyond their control, it had become almost impossible to identify those that were *not*. He watched three brothers go to college and quickly drop out. He watched all three of them take turns with the bottle.

There were no movie theaters or bowling alleys or malls on the reservation. When it became too dark to see the rim on the courts behind the elementary school, Jonathan and his friends would drive up and down the main street of Crow Agency — from JR's Smokehouse to the irrigation supply yard and back again — seeing the same people, the same mange-eaten dogs and rust-eaten cars, until the monotony numbed them. Then someone would say, "Let's go drinking." It was a ritual that had become a display of solidarity and shared values among his tribe, so much so that to say no was to mark oneself as an alien. None of the teenagers had enough money to buy liquor, but all of them had Indian wealth — relatives. Uncles and aunts, cousins and grandparents are as close to most Crows as parents and siblings are to a white child; a boy can walk into five or six houses without knocking, open the refrigerator without asking, eat without cleaning up the crumbs. Jonathan and his friends would each ask a relative or two for a buck, and all of the sharing and family closeness in which the Crows pride themselves would boomerang. Each kid would come up with three or four dollars to pitch into the pot, and off they'd go to the liquor stores that waited for them half a hiccup past the reservation borders. It wouldn't take long to see someone they knew who was of drinking age — the boys were related by blood or clan, it seemed, to *everyone*. They whisked their beer or whiskey back onto the reservation, where the statutes against juveniles drinking were less severe, and began gulping it as if they were racing to see who could sledgehammer reality quickest, who could forget his life first.

Jonathan's absences from school mounted. That was how he responded to trouble. He disappeared. His parents wanted him to get an education, but to make the house quiet for two hours each night and insist that he study, to pull him out of his bed when the school bus was rolling up the road — no, they couldn't quite do that. Each of them had dropped out after the ninth grade, but there was more to it than that. Almost every Crow parent had a close relative who had been forcibly taken from his home by white government agents in the early 1900s and sent off to a faraway boarding school, where his hair was shorn, his Indian clothes and name were taken away, and he was beaten for speaking his own language. How many Indians could chase an education without feeling an old pang in their bones?

On intelligence alone, Takes Enemy had made the honor roll in junior high, but now he fell behind in class and was too ashamed to ask the white teachers for help. He lost his eligibility for the first half-dozen games of both his sophomore and junior seasons, regained it after each Christmas and started dropping in 25 or 30 points with a dozen assists a game, leading his teammates flying up and down the floor. His coaches called it Blur Ball. His people called it Indian Ball. And his brothers, three of whom had also been stars at Hardin High, would whip the crowd to wildness, reaching back into imaginary quivers on their backs, loading their make-believe bows and zinging invisible arrows at the other teams; vibrating their hands over their mouths to make the high, shrill *wooo-wooo* battle cry that once froze frontiersmen's hearts; shouting themselves hoarse, making Takes Enemy feel as if he could simply lift up his legs and let his people's ecstasy wash him up and down the hardwood.

He scored 49 points in a state tournament game his senior year and was named the tournament's MVP. The outside walls of his house literally vanished, swathed in posters of congratulation from his fans. "A great major college prospect," said then BYU coach Ladell Andersen.

Do it, teachers urged him. Do it so *they* could once more believe in what they were doing, do it so *all* the Crow children whose eyes were on him could see how it was done. "Just *one*," they kept saying to him. "If just one great basketball player from here could make the break and succeed, it could change *everything*. College recruiters would start coming here, other kids would follow your example. You can be the one, Jonathan. You can be the breakthrough."

He was flown to BYU. He stared at the twenty-six thousand white faces strolling across campus. He stood at the top of the basketball arena and looked down, his eyes growing wider and wider, the court growing tinier and farther away. He had never heard of anyone like himself playing in a place like this; he couldn't even fathom it. "He said almost nothing the whole time," recalls Andersen. "I asked him a few questions. He was nodding his head yes when he should have been shaking it no."

The stack of letters from universities grew at his home. Jonathan never replied. His senior year was ending, his sun descending toward the hills. In the long-ago days a Crow hero could go on doing what he did until an arrow or a bullet found him, then let the breeze carry off his soul to the Other Side Camp. But in the twentieth century the hero's bullet was high school graduation — and then he had to go on living. "Where are you going to college?" people asked Jonathan everywhere he went. "He'll be home by Thanksgiving," they told each other. "Like crabs in a bucket, that's how we are," says Dell Fritzler, the coach at Plenty Coups High. "Whoever tries to get out, we yank him back down." Even Jonathan's own Indian name — bestowed upon him during his senior season after it had come to the medicine man in a dream — tugged downward at the boy. Iiwaaialetasaask, he was called. Does Not Put Himself Above Others. Go off to college? That would Definitely Put Himself Above Others. No, white people couldn't understand this; Jonathan himself could barely grasp the code: it was O.K. for an Indian to clench his teeth and compete as part of a team, especially an Indian team. But to do it alone, to remove yourself from the dozen people in your living room at midnight and go sit over a chemistry or algebra book — in many families, that tainted you. "We want our young people to go off and show the world how great a Crow can be," says Fritzler, "but as soon as someone does, as soon as anyone starts trying or studying too hard, a lot of us say, 'Look at him. He's trying to be a white man.' "

Takes Enemy's head spun. There were just too many mixed signals, too many invisible arrows from the audience whizzing by. Like most Crows, he'd been brought up not to make autonomous decisions but to take his cues from his immediate family, his extended family, his clan and his tribe. If *they* hadn't decided whether to assimilate into the white man's world or to recoil from it, how could he? And then, his two little children — he couldn't just walk away from them. The small living room he grew up in, with its sixty-five photographs of family members on the wall — a warm, happy place that the people in those pictures would flow into with no invitation, sit around sipping coffee and exchanging the sly puns and double entendres that his people excelled at, talking until there was nothing left to talk about and then talking some more — he couldn't just leave that behind. "Why?" he remembers wondering. "Why do I have to do it the white man's way to be a success in this world?" Why did all the human wealth he had gathered in his life, all the close friends and relatives, count for nothing when he crossed the reservation borders; why did material wealth seem to be the only gauge? And then his eyes and whys would turn the other way: "Why am I so important to my people? Why do *I* have to carry the hopes of the Crows?" All he had really wanted to do, ever since taking apart a stereo in the tenth grade and staring in wonder at all the whatchamacallits inside, was to go to a vocational school and learn electronics. But no, the herd was rolling, the people were waving and shouting him on, his legs were pulling him closer and closer to the ledge. He drank to close his eyes to it. One night at a school dance an administrator found out he was drunk. The next day he was ordered to take a chemical-dependency class.

Where were the people in his tribe who had lived through this? Why weren't they at Takes Enemy's door? Myron Falls Down, a prolific scorer for a Crow independent team in the 1970s, heard the rumors and wondered if he should do something. Six years earlier it had come to Falls Down like thunder through a hangover: that the addiction sucking the life from him and his people went beyond the beer they drank at night after playing ball, beyond the pills some ingested and the weed they puffed, beyond the Aqua Velva and Lysol and fingernail-polish remover some of them swilled; that *basketball,* the way the Crows were using it, had become a drug too. One morning in 1979, at the age of twenty-seven, he stood up from the bed where he slept every night with his ball. He went to the two glass-enclosed cases in the living room where his fifty trophies were displayed, and he began throwing them into cardboard boxes. "What are you doing?" cried his mother. She and Myron's nieces raced to unscrew the little figurines from their wooden bases before he could sweep all of them away. He grabbed the five jackets he had won in tournaments, loaded them and his trophies into his car, drove to the dumpster on the edge of Lodge Grass and heaved them all in. He would never take another drink or drug after that day. He would never play, or go to see, another basketball game — not even, ten years later, the junior high school games of his thirteen-year-old son. "If there was a connection between education and basketball on this reservation, there would be nothing wrong with basketball," says Falls Down, now a tribal health administrator. "But right now there is none. Basketball is an escape from reality for us. But I never did speak to Jonathan. I felt he or his family would have approached me if they wanted to hear my message."

Pretty Weasel — where was he? The man named Montana's Outstanding Athlete twenty-seven years before Takes Enemy, the one recruited by the University of Utah, Texas A&M and Seattle University, the cousin caught in this same crossfire eight years before Jonathan was born. Relatives and friends had sat at Takes Enemy's dinner table to spill their guts and offer counsel, but the man who with one look or word might have given Jonathan a glimpse at the ledger, at the remorse and relief in the soul of a man who has walked away from his greatness, had signaled nothing. Pretty Weasel stood in the shadows at basketball games, refused invitations to giveaways, belittled his own legend. "Never saw myself play," he said. "Can't picture myself being able to play with those black boys." Years later, at the age of fifty-one and no longer a drinker, he would wish that he had gotten his degree, explored the borders of his talent. "But I don't give advice," he says. "I guess I feel more like the whites do. That every man can be as good as he wants to. That every man does it on his own."

Graduation day came. Jonathan still hadn't decided. Barely, just barely, he got his diploma. As the teachers watched him carry it across the stage, Anderson, the assistant principal, turned and said, "I hope we're not looking at the first day of the end of his life."

> When the dance is over, sweetheart,
> I will take you home in my one-eyed Ford.

That sloppy man with the red-rimmed eyes and the puffy face, taller than the others . . .

That whiskered man with the slurred speech and the thick belly and the slumped shoulders, standing on the riverbank near Two Leggins Bridge . . . that's him. That's Jonathan Takes Enemy.

It's 1989. It's 3 A.M. When the bars close in Hardin, Jonathan and his friends often come here to sing and laugh and drink and dance until the sun comes up. At dawn somebody often hits somebody, and somebody's brother or cousin jumps in to help, and there's a whole pile of them in the dirt. And then they go home to sleep. There's no work for most of them to do.

But the sky's still dark, they all still feel good. They're singing "49" songs, native chants interspersed with English lyrics, sad-happy tunes to the beat of a drum. Takes Enemy still can't bring himself to dance or sing, but he's thumping out the drumbeat on a car hood. "Way-la-hey-ley, way-la-hey-ley . . . ya-hey-oh-way-la-hey . . . ," his companions croon. "When the dance is over, sweet-heart, I will take you home in my one-eyed Ford."

The dance is over. It ended four years ago, as soon as it began. Six games into Jonathan's freshman season at Sheridan College, the Wyoming school whose scholarship offer he grabbed at the last minute because it was just an hour's drive from home, he quit. It's all still a blur to him: Hiding from everyone when it was time to leave home. Reporting to college two days late and only because Anderson found him and took him there. Being stopped in the yard as he left, asked by his teary-eyed mother, "Are you *sure* you want to go, Jonathan? They aren't *forcing* you?" Trying to go from a world where it's disrespectful to look someone in the eye into one where it's disrespectful *not* to. Sitting alone in his dorm room for days, walking alone to the cafeteria, eating alone. Telling none of the white people about his fear and loneliness. Being guided by no one through the bewildering transition from reservation to white world. Knowing before his first game that something was wrong, because he had done something he could never do the night before a high school game — sleep. Knowing that the feeling he had had at Hardin — that he was on a mission, playing for his people — was gone. Returning to the reservation three straight weekends and not coming back in time for Monday practice. Two weekends later, not coming back at all. Walking away from the number one–ranked junior college team in the nation . . . but whose nation, *whose?*

"Crawled back under the blanket," said the whites. They've seen Indians do it so often that they have a cliché for it. "Every Indian that leaves has a rubber band attached to his back," says Jonathan's brother James. The Crows have seen their people do it so often that they only shrug. In some strange way, by going away to college and then by quitting, too, Takes Enemy has managed to fulfill *everyone's* expectations.

Somewhere, perhaps upon the hilltop at Custer Battlefield, his daydream still exists. More and more, he bicycles back there as if in search of it. After all, he is only twenty-four, he tells himself, his life is just beginning — or already half over, according to Crow life-expectancy charts.

His pockets are empty. He bums beer money from his dad, who has stayed clean since entering an alcohol rehabilitation program recently. No one will hire Jonathan. No one will buy him drinks at the bars in Hardin the way they did when he was in high school. Sometimes he walks out of the bars and onto the streets, sees a teacher from the school driving by and slinks into the shadows. He's not a bum, he's *not*. Twice he has been thrown into the reservation jail for drinking, lain on the floor all night in a cell with thirty other drunk men, listened to them moan and retch.

He has gained more than twenty pounds. He still plays ball,

lumbering up the floor in Indian tournaments held across the state and the country. After games the team goes drinking — and sometimes even right before them. He signs up for courses at the reservation's junior college; some he completes, some he doesn't. He has a new girlfriend, Trudi Big Hair, and two more children, Jonathan and Tashina. The four of them sleep in a small room at his parents' house, and no one ever hints that it's time he moved out. Sometimes in the morning the children jump on him in bed and shout, exploding his hangovers. He drifts back to sleep until noon, goes to a class or two, kills a few hours staring at the TV or picking up his welfare check, plays pickup basketball with his friends until dark . . . and then often starts all over again. Each time he drinks, Trudi etches an X on the calendar. Day by day, Jonathan watches his life get crossed out.

Once or twice he has gone to see his old school play. He doesn't go inside. He watches from a half-open door. It's not his court anymore, not his domain. A new hero has arisen, a boy at Lodge Grass High named Elvis Old Bull. Old Bull took his team to state titles in 1988 and 1989, was named tournament MVP both years, noticed kids beginning to dress and cut their hair like he does, heard himself called a major college prospect. He has a child, but isn't married; he skips school too much; he drinks too much; his eyes are haunted. Sometimes Jonathan feels as if there is something he could tell the boy — but no, he can't, he *can't*. Old Bull enters a rehabilitation center just after his junior season. The treatment fails. He misses far too many days of school to remain eligible for his final season, but the people need that third straight title too much, and school administrators can't quite bring themselves to sit him down. "You're going to end up just like Jonathan Takes Enemy," people in the tribe keep telling him. He leads his team to the third state title, wins his third tournament MVP trophy, then simply stops going to school. He watches his classmates graduate through eyes swollen from a car wreck from another night's drinking. And the sun arcs across the Montana sky, and the eagle wheels, and the circle remains unbroken.

Autumn 1990. The sun drops behind the Big Horn Mountains. An orange 1980 Mustang turns onto the highway and bears

north across the reservation, toward Billings. There is no caravan behind him. Takes Enemy goes alone.

His face is clean-shaven, his clothes are neat, his cheekbones
have bloomed again. He is twenty-five, but he looks like that boy
in those high school pictures once more. All summer he has
jumped rope, slipping into his back yard to do it at midnight
when no one on the reservation could see.

He presses the accelerator. Just a short visit home today; he
cannot dally. He needs to get off the reservation by nightfall and
back to his apartment in Billings, to Trudi and little Jonathan
and Tashina, back to his new life as a student and a basketball
player at Rocky Mountain College. Because when the darkness
comes and his friends come . . . "To do this," he says, "I can't be
near them. I *miss* them. But I have to be alone." He hasn't had a
drink in months. He hears that Old Bull has made a change too,
moving to Bozeman with hopes of fulfilling his high school requirements and getting a shot at college ball.

"It's *my* decision to go to college this time," Jonathan says. "I
finally realized that I was running out of time. It's not that the
reservation is a bad place. There are many good people there.
But it's just not a place where you can become what you want to
become. It's not a place where you can achieve your dreams."

Last spring he convinced Luke Gerber, the coach at Hardin
High, that he was serious. Gerber called Jeff Malby, the coach at
Rocky Mountain College, and Malby remembered how the clean
water had once flowed across the rocks. He offered Takes Enemy
a scholarship to the liberal arts college in Billings, with 810 students. So far, it fits Jonathan just right.

He passed the reservation border, glances into his rearview
mirror. He knows that some people back there are now calling
him an "apple" — red on the outside, white on the inside. He
knows what he is leaving behind, what he is losing. Knows it in
the morning when he passes his new neighbors in Billings and
they just barely nod. Knows it when it's midnight and he and
Trudi are buried in textbooks, and the apartment is silent. "It's
just too quiet here," he'll say. "We're so isolated." And when he
lies in bed at night and thinks of his sick mother, he knows it
then, too.

His eyes move back to the windshield. Ahead of him, over the rolling hills, across the sage and buffalo grass, he can just make out the soft electric glow of Billings. He's starting to get an idea of what lies this way. He's passing all four of his classes. He's averaging 19.8 points and 4.6 assists for his new team. He's just getting his bearings, but his coaches say that he'll soon establish himself as the best player in Montana and that he's destined to be an NAIA All-America before he's done.

Everything's still so new to him. Paying his own rent each month from the grant money allotted to him by the tribe and the Bureau of Indian Affairs, paying electric bills, buying his own food. Studying until 1 A.M., making sure that Trudi gets off to Eastern Montana College in the morning, that his kids get off to day care and preschool, living in the white man's world, in a hurry, on a schedule.

He wants to go back to the reservation someday and help kids to take the risk, to see both the beauty and the danger of the circle. But he may never live there again. He rolls down his car window. He listens to the air. There is no singing in the land. There is only a quiet, sad-happy song inside a young man's heart.

GEORGE PLIMPTON

Muhammad Ali,
the Mongoose, and Me

FROM ESQUIRE

A COUPLE OF months ago I drove down to Atlantic City to see the Foreman-Holyfield heavyweight championship fight. I had not been to a fight in years — not since visiting Muhammad Ali at his home in Los Angeles during the 1984 Olympics. I watched him sign autographs at his desk, the pen working laboriously across the paper. He spoke softly and very slowly, his speech slurred. He stood up to show me some magic tricks, stuffing a bright handkerchief into his closed fist and then snapping open his hand to show it wasn't there. There were others — tricks with rings, collapsible canes, a "levitation" trick in which by standing on tiptoe within his trouser legs he appeared to grow a couple of inches. Then he whispered to me that his Muslim beliefs wouldn't allow him to be deceitful, so he showed me how all the tricks worked. Walking slowly, he took me upstairs to show me his trophies, a somewhat shabby collection laid out on the floor. Parkinson's disease they said he had, and that sometimes he forgot to take his pills. Perhaps, but after that visit I never covered a fight again. Oscar Wilde wrote that each man kills the thing he loves, but in Ali's case it seemed the other way around.

Nonetheless, when the hoopla began about the Foreman-Holyfield fight — inspirationally titled the Battle of the Ages — the temptation proved too much, and I called up to get press credentials. One of the main reasons for going was that I'd get a chance to visit — as they say in the South — my idol and old friend Archie Moore, who was a head man in George Foreman's corner. Years before, in a participatory journalistic stint when he was light-heavyweight champion of the world, I had "fought" him three rounds (the last one truncated by a nervous time keeper) and predictably suffered a severe nosebleed as a result.

I drove down on the day of the fight. In Trump Plaza I spotted Muhammad Ali at a table in the coffee shop with an entourage, a number of them Black Muslims. I came up to the table with Angelo Dundee, who had been in Ali's corner in Zaire and would be in Foreman's that night. I couldn't tell if Ali recognized me. I wrote a book called *Shadowbox,* which was largely about him, and he used to call me Author, as in, "Put Author in the front seat." Dundee was crouched by his chair. Ali smiled at him slyly, the look he puts on when he does his magic tricks. "A comeback," he whispered huskily. "I'm getting ready to come back." Dundee roared with laughter. "Hey! Hey!" Down the length of the table there were perfunctory grins and nods from the Ali contingent. Ali had trouble drinking his tea. His hand was shaking. A waitress leaned over and slipped a soda straw in his cup so he could draw on it. "There," she said.

I went up to see Archie Moore in his hotel room. He was lying on the bed fully clothed, boots on, wearing a white woolen cap on which were pinned a number of pilot's wings, the kind stewardesses hand out to children. He explained they were keepsakes from trips he had taken, which were pleasant to remember and savor. He would take the cap off and look at it when he felt low.

It was good to see him The Mongoose. Most fighters have a single sobriquet. Archie's best known is the Mongoose. But there have been others — many, I have no doubt, self-improvised: the Bearded Patriarch, the Impenetrable Legend, the Relic, the Merry Methuselah, the Fistic Fable, the Antique, the Aging Tiger, the Sweet Scientist. The Mongoose, though, is his favorite, and what he teaches his students he refers to as Mongoosiana.

"What have you taught George?" I asked.

Archie yawned. "Mental gymnastics. Escapology. Mongoosiana. What a jab can really do . . . the basic punch in boxing. He can damage a man with his jab."

"Archie, what's George going to do with the money?"

I asked because Archie had put a large part of his fight money into a youth organization called Any Boy Can (AB&C), which he started in San Diego in 1965.

"George's main love is to kick a mule," Archie replied obliquely. "Then he has his church. He loves people. That's what I like about George. He's a decent man."

Archie began describing an idea he wanted to present to him. While training a Nigerian boxing team for the 1980 Olympics, Archie had become interested in the mid-continent country of Chad.

"They have hot summers there and a dearth of water," he said. "It's a parched country, and yet I have seen a waterfall with the water coming over the top by the ton. But it drifts away into a wasteland. What should be done is to build concrete pipes out of the desert sand and dig a lake to hold that water so the people can drink what is clean and healthy. That would be a nice thing for George to do."

I nodded and said that was enough reason to cheer for him.

When it got close to fight time, I thought I'd hang out in the dressing room area — a row of curtained cubicles backstage in the Convention Hall. George Foreman had the corner cubicle. I didn't have the right press credentials to be on the stage, but I managed to slip by the door guard a few times. Through a crack in the curtain I could see Foreman in his boxing trunks, lying on his side on a rubbing table. He was asleep, I was told.

Suddenly, Donald Trump appeared in the stage area. He had a considerable entourage with him. A camera crew led the way. They crouched, walking backward with their shoulder cameras aimed at Trump and his friends, including actor Kevin Costner. Two young women were in the crowd, one of them Marla Maples, a gold blonde wearing a close-fitting black cocktail dress cut high on her model's legs. Without a moment's hesitation, the ensemble bulged into Foreman's cubicle, the women included. It occurred to me that Foreman, stirring from his nap and looking up at those two from his rubbing table, must have assumed that Holyfield had belted him briefly into paradise!

I tried to get close but was stopped by the security man. "But I'm a friend . . . of Marla Maples."

He shook his head. "You haven't got the right credentials." I peered in over his shoulder. Flashbulbs were going off. It was almost unheard of — bursting in on a fighter's privacy before a major bout. He was supposed to be in a cocoon of concentration, psyching himself up, putting on a game face, as they say. And women! True, the occasional wife stays with her husband before a fight. Jean-Pierre Coopman, the so-called Lion of Flanders, not only had his wife in there with him before he fought Muhammad Ali but also a bottle of champagne. The bottle went out to the ring with him and he had a lot from it between rounds until he got knocked out in the fifth — very likely the happiest loser in boxing history. Harry Greb was another exception to the rule. A middleweight in the 1920s, he had a couple of low-class prostitutes in his dressing room before a fight. Norman Mailer (who told me this) felt that a kind of transference was involved, that Greb took some of the brutality and meanness of the streets out to the ring with him. He was renowned as the dirtiest fighter of his era.

Trump and his friends left Foreman eventually (presumably to see Holyfield), but then, literally minutes before the fighters were due out in the arena, they all returned. This time the Reverend Jesse Jackson was with them. Whether George Foreman wanted it or not, they were going to crowd into his cubicle and pray with him. The voices died down. I imagined Marla Maples standing by the fighter, head down, with her hands clasped.

I went out to the arena. I sat in a press section far from ringside, which was given over to the entertainment gentry — movie stars, athletes, television talk-show hosts, and so forth. A searchlight picked them out as their identities were intoned, one by one, over the loudspeaker system. Donald Trump received a patter of applause. Marla Maples, my backstage "friend," was not singled out. Muhammad Ali and Joe Frazier, up in the ring before the main event, got the biggest of the prefight roars. Ali, looking grand in his brown suit, went over and whispered in George Foreman's ear and then went across and did the same with Holyfield.

As for the fight itself, Foreman performed honorably, as everyone knows — certainly putting to rest the notion held by many in the far-flung press seats that the whole adventure was a sham. He kept the pressure on Holyfield, plodding steadily forward. I was reminded of Muhammad Ali's nickname for him in Zaire — the Mummy. In his slow, stiff-legged pursuit he did indeed seem the movie monster in search of his beloved tana leaves.

I kept my eye on Archie, his white hat visible as he rose at the bell at the end of each round and worked the stool through the ropes so Foreman, who invariably stands in his corner, could put a foot up on it if he had a mind to. It seemed to be Archie's only function, though on occasion I could see him reach through the ropes to knead Foreman's legs just above the ankle, a useless therapy unless there was something magical about the old guru's touch.

The next day I drove Archie up to Newark, where he planned to visit his mother, in her nineties and bedridden since losing a leg because of diabetes. He didn't have the correct address, but he said he'd be able to recognize her house; his bedroom window looked out on a cemetery. On the way he sat with his hands in his lap, slowly twiddling his thumbs. He was curiously noncommittal about Foreman's performance.

"Mongoosiana started George out pretty good," he said. "He hardly got his hair mussed" — an acute if obvious comment, since Foreman is completely bald.

I asked him about Jesse Jackson's prayer and he brightened. He said that the reverend was much taller than he'd imagined. "I'd like to train him. He'd make a hell of a fighter."

After a while I said that I was sorry about the waterfall in Chad. The championship for Foreman would have meant a lot more money to build the lake.

"Will you talk to George about it?"

"About what?"

"Helping the people in Chad."

"One day. He's a decent man. Very decent," Archie said.

"Pile of money," I said. "They say the receipts from the fight may reach over a hundred million."

"Is that so." Archie yawned, and began talking about his first fight, which was against the Poco Kid, also known as Piano-Mover Jones. "He was a furniture mover in Hot Springs, Arkansas . . . very strong . . . could lift an upright piano into the back of a truck. Knocked out a lot of people in Hot Springs. I was persuaded to go against him in a ten-rounder. I played a tune on him. I was promised seven dollars," he said without a smile. "To this day Billy Cisco, the fight promoter, owes me that seven dollars — with interest that comes to about $190,000, doesn't it?" He looked over with a smile.

"Something like that," I said. I asked him what he had been paid to fight Rocky Marciano.

"A quarter of a million."

I glanced over at Archie's hands (he had knocked Marciano down in that fight) and was reminded of A. J. Liebling's lovely conceit. The *New Yorker* boxing correspondent had once written that if you got hit on the nose by a professional prizefighter, you were linked to a kind of genealogical tree of people who had bopped each other on the nose. It stretched back to Victorian times. It also meant, because Archie had bopped me on the nose in our "fight," that I was connected not only to Marciano but to Joe Louis, back through Jack Dempsey and John L. Sullivan to Jem Mace and also to Piano-Mover Jones!

"Hey!" I said.

Once we got to Newark it took almost three hours to find his mother's house. We drove slowly up and down South Eighteenth Street, Archie peering up at the housefronts. He was fairly sure the address had a nine in it. Occasionally he got out and made inquiries. "She's an older woman with one leg." The cemetery was almost a mile in length. No luck.

A teenage kid said he had seen such a woman in the neighborhood. Encouraged, we tried two nearby cemeteries, on the off chance that Archie had the street number wrong. The kid led us there in his car. I told Archie that every time Newark came to mind I was going to think of it as a city of tombstones. He took out his suitcase and opened it up on the sidewalk, rummaging through it for papers that might have his mother's address. No luck. By this time he was a familiar figure in the neighborhood, white-capped, tapping on front doors like a traveling salesman. "I'm looking for my mother." He was recognized immediately. People in passing cars said, "Hey, Archie *Moore!*" Everyone in the vicinity, which was overwhelmingly black, had seen the fight the night before on television and they wanted Archie to reassure Foreman he had nothing to be ashamed of. I began to notice as they crowded around that although I was obviously with him, no one ever spoke to me or even glanced over. I felt invisible. Afterward I mentioned it to Archie. He nodded. "Oh, yes," he said. "It don't feel good. Any one of us can be invisible."

Finally he called home in San Diego for the address. His wife, Joan, gave him the house number. It was in a row of identical houses; we'd passed it a dozen times. Inside, Archie introduced me to his mother. He sends money every month for someone to look after her. In a small, darkened back room she was sitting in a chair watching television — very old and frail, with a fine-boned face like an Indian's. She didn't look up. On the television screen some kind of kindergarten show was on; children with their hands raised, shouting for attention. "Me! Me! Me!"

In the front room the kid who had helped us sat on the edge of a swaybacked sofa and said it was the greatest day of his life . . . to think he was with a champion.

"Yup, the Mongoose. You stick with him," I said. "He'll tell you stories. He likes the way you helped."

A few days later I called up George Foreman. He sounded very chipper. I asked him about Trump's entourage. "They just barged in," he said. He was laughing. "It was sort of swell. They weren't going to allow George to get any butterflies. But you know what was weirder? In the ring, when they announced Muhammad Ali and Joe Frazier, standing there before the fight in their nice suits, ten years out of boxing, everybody cheering, and it's O.K. that I'm in the ring, too, but what am I doing in there *boxing!*"

"What did Ali whisper in your ear?"

"He said, 'I'm praying for you,' and then he went across the ring and whispered the same thing to Holyfield."

"Playing it safe," I said. I asked about Archie Moore.

"The foundation of the whole campaign," Foreman said. He went on to say that he was paying him a million dollars.

I couldn't resist asking.

"Has he ever talked to you about a waterfall in Chad?"

"What's that?"

"It's an idea he has. I'm sure he'll talk to you about it."

The other day I ran into a friend of mine who works downtown. We got to talking about the huge amounts of money the fight had generated. He said he'd be willing to get into the ring with either one of them, or even both, if it meant that kind of payday.

"Wow! I mean, why not?"

I asked what he'd do with the money.

"Are you kidding? To start with, I'd buy a yacht."

THOMAS MALLON

Rodeo

FROM THE YALE REVIEW

AMERICAN musical memory knows there was a time when an
Oklahoman had to travel up to Kansas City if he wanted to walk
to privies in the rain and never wet his feet. By January 1990
things had progressed to the point where he could spend a week
at the rodeo without venturing outdoors between his hotel room
and an arena with fewer odors than any privy ever had: a "sky-
walk" connects the downtown Doubletree Hotel to the Tulsa
Convention Center, in which the Twentieth International Finals
Rodeo was being held atop three thousand cubic yards of
trucked-in dirt, whose lower sandy layer succeeded in absorbing
the smells.

But if IFR 20 was deodorized, it was not entirely deracinated,
as almost any ride in one of the Doubletree's elevators could remind you. One afternoon, as the car came to a gentle stop, a cowboy and his girlfriend let out a steadying *whoa* and laughed about
how their insides were flopping, and on Saturday night, on his
way to compete in the penultimate calf-roping round, Ken Bai-
ley, number 46, could be heard to exclaim, when the car stopped
a floor above the lobby, "One stop's enough for me!" In another
two hours Ken would be jumping off his speeding horse, Slick,
to rope a calf in 8.7 seconds and tie for second-fastest time of the
night.

Fans of the IFR, whose cowboys ride a circuit of over three
hundred competitions sanctioned by the International Professional Rodeo Association (IPRA), will tell you it's more real, if
less old and rich, than the National Finals held by the Profes-

sional Rodeo Cowboys Association each year in Las Vegas. The
PRCA evolved over decades and awards a lot of five-figure
prizes, but since it moved from Oklahoma City to Las Vegas four
years ago, it's been overwhelmed by the Strip. "They start the
sessions at seven so everybody can get out early enough to get to
the shows and casinos," says Dayna Cravens, who does publicity
for the IPRA and whose father, J. O. Cravens, a former bull
rider, is its president.

In its twentieth year the IFR seemed to be literally a step behind its competitor. As the finals were getting under way in
Tulsa, the city's papers were full of rumors that this would be the
last time before the event moved itself and its twenty-five thousand ticket sales to — Oklahoma City. J. O. Cravens complained
of a lack of political and business support, but wouldn't say yes
or no about moving as the rodeo opened on Thursday, January
18. So over the next several days, along with the fortunes of
hometown favorites like barrel racer Connie Cooper and saddle-
bronc rider Justin Rowe, Tulsans were following this other
drama, wondering if the city would have its confidence, just
mending after the oil glut of the 1980s, given a small new shake.
Columnist Jay Cronley in the *Tribune* said that Tulsa had every
hosting advantage over Oklahoma City except the "leadership"
needed to keep the IFR from leaving: "You start losing naturals
like the rodeo. . . . You want to live in a small town . . . ? Stick
around."

At night around the Convention Center it was easy to get the
feeling one already was living in a small town. The downtown
blocks, some of them malled over and gentrified a decade or so
ago, were now deserted with a kind of neutron-bombed thor-
oughness. Patrons of the Doubletree exchanged restaurant discoveries in a fundamental way: if you came upon any restaurant
open at night, that was news good enough to pass on, never mind
the quality of the food. Tulsa is a city of suburbs, and the IFR
seemed properly unsure how long it could expect patrons to find
their way to a downtown arena that might best be described, in
the words of a friend, as centrally isolated.

But if on opening night Tulsa's hold on the IFR seems ten-
uous, there is no doubting the larger loyalties of the crowd.
When Miss Rodeo USA 1989, Lisa Watson of Elmore City, Okla-

homa, rides out upon a white horse, carrying the American flag, thousands of cowboy hats go over thousands of hearts. "The Battle Hymn of the Republic" seems a generous choice of an opening song for a rodeo association including so many cowboys from the Confederate states, but it is quickly followed by "This Is My Country," as Lisa is ridden round by a circle of flag-carrying attendants in a spectacle that should be grotesque but is instead eerily beautiful: the other women canter, their flags flying in near darkness around Lisa, who is bathed in a white spotlight and beautiful in the manner of that string of southern Miss Americas from the 1950s.

It is hard to imagine a sports crowd displaying more genuine involvement in an event's patriotic preliminaries. One fears for one's ears, not to mention the horses' ability to stand their ground, during Miss Candi Todd's worst-ever a cappella rendition of "The Star-Spangled Banner," but the heart soars again when someone has the nostalgic wit to play — as they will on each of the following three nights — a vintage recording of "God Bless America." Careful equine choreography gives Lisa, left in solitary splendor toward the close, an opportunity to gallop all the way across the arena and disappear through the gate just as Kate Smith hits her final "home."

With lights back up, and hats back on, the flags of states and sponsors begin whirling by, each of their carriers galloping a single furious circuit, seeming to lack nothing but gray tunics and cavalry bugles. The banner of the cowboy chapter of the Fellowship of Christian Athletes takes precedence, followed by the flags of Canada (which sends one contestant) and twenty-seven states. The announcers try to kindle pockets of alphabetical enthusiasm by shouting out state nicknames that might be vaguely recalled from grade school, and the almost impolite hush that greets the flag of New York is probably attributable more to remoteness than hostility. The banner of the Acme Boot Company, sponsor of the Miss Rodeo USA pageant — another contest to be decided this week — brings to their feet the seventeen local queens vying to be Lisa Watson's successor. Miss Johnson Ford Rodeo has come from Sturgis, South Dakota, and Miss WZPR Rodeo, jointly sponsored by Jay's Auto Wrecking Service, is here from Edinboro, Pennsylvania.

The crowd, in fact, is not entirely local either. Forty-seven per-cent of it, the paper says, comes from at least forty miles away. On Friday and Saturday nights the stands will seem a little more suburban, but on this weekday opening the hats and jeans seem more like work clothes than going-out drag. Their wearers look over the parading 1988 world champions, give one more salute to Lisa, and are ready for action on what Jerry Todd (Candi's husband) has proclaimed, from the announcer's booth, "the roughest playing field in America."

Rodeo is probably the most compulsively announced sport in the world. The spectator is never out from under an amplified waterfall of statistics (Captain Crunch, a bull, is "unridden" in his last twenty-one outings), jokes, and sentiment. At each session after the first, the announcers do an endless recitation of the pre-vious one's times and scores and places, though all of this infor-mation is easily available in the patron's newspaper or program. IFR 20 requires two announcers, Jerry Todd for the timed events and Danny Newland, a former saddle-bronc rider, for the "rough stock" competitions like bareback and bull riding. Rodeo announcers are typically the subject of newspaper profiles, pro-gram feature articles, and a level of fan awareness unexperi-enced by the off-television commentators of any other sport. Danny Newland's battle with Hodgkin's disease and his off-season career of teaching agriculture in high school are written up as prominently as any stories about the competitors them-selves. *Rain or Shine,* Cyra McFadden's fine family memoir, tells the story of her father, Cy Taillon, the "Dean of Rodeo An-nouncers": "It's still difficult to pay for a drink, in a Western bar, if your last name is or once was Taillon." Cy's own life's journey from "rakehell" to respectability ran parallel to the evolution of his sport. Before Taillon began working in the 1930s,

> rodeo was used to announcers who treated the sport as a Wild West show, part vaudeville, part circus. Cy dignified it, with his ten-dollar words, his impeccably tailored, expensive suits and his insistence that the cowboys were professional athletes. When he intoned "Ladies and gentlemen," women became ladies and men became gentlemen; the silver-tongued devil in the announcer's box, as often as not a rickety structure over the chutes and open to the rain, spoke with unmistak-able authority.

For all Danny Newland's rodeo lore and info — young south-
erners tend to get interested in bull riding, Canadians in saddle
broncs — his voice is a little nasal, like a TV pitchman's. Jerry
Todd, from behind the see-through plastic bunting, seems more
in Taillon's line of baritoned professional dignity. He may bring
out the same one-liners nearly every night ("UPS couldn't have
wrapped him up any better!"; "Triple A, eat your heart out!"),
but he consistently directs his listeners' attention to the theme of
cowboy effort. Contestants are said to be "working" for the
crowd, not performing, and when Mike Pharr from Georgia
lands out of the money after missing a calf-roping throw, the
fans are reminded to pay him off anyway: "The only thing he'll
take with him tonight is what you give him, so be generous with
the applause." (Cyra McFadden says that this instruction to the
crowd originated with Cy Taillon.) Todd imagines the gloom
among two teammates who miss entirely and get a no-time — "I
wouldn't want to be in that room tonight" — and when the
crowd is distracted by a decidedly uncharacteristic fistfight in the
stands, it is reminded to watch the chutes and not "the idiots in
the stands," an injunction that brings on applause.

How, one wonders, does a rider trying to stay, for eight seconds, on an angry, bucking horse, trying to earn a purse and
keep his spinal cord whole, manage to concentrate amidst the
poorly timed burst of band music for him and the announcer's
voice, which as the horse charges out of the chute may still be
pitching straight lines to the clown or be in mid-anecdote about
some other cowboy? In fact, the riders claim not to notice any of
it. As I was told before round five by Steve Danylo, western region bare-back-riding winner, "You're so into yourself and what
you're gonna do."

What they're going to do is wait for any clatter in the chute to
die, see the rope let go, and then experience an eight-second chi-
ropractic catastrophe.

Some rodeo experts will stress the toll taken not on the back,
but on the single arm permitted to hold the rigging. If with his
free hand the cowboy touches either the horse or himself, he's
disqualified. It's that free hand, flying out and up as the horse
bucks into the arena, that a spectator's gaze is drawn to. The gesture it makes seems to say, simultaneously, "I'm O.K." and "I'm

going down, help me." The eight seconds look more like an elec-
trocution than a ride, and even after a successful one the plain-
tiveness of the waving arm is magnified by the most curiously
poignant moment in rodeo — when the dismounting rider
throws himself onto the body and horse of a pickup rider. The
strangest aspect of the event, and it's the same with saddle-bronc
and bull rides, is that even the highest-scoring cowboys, ones
who have gone the distance firm in the saddle, appear to be getting rescued.

Whatever the outcome there is little time for pride or wound
licking, and certainly, not ever, any McEnrovian tantrums. On
Friday night Troy Smithson of Spring Hill, Tennessee, is badly
thrown, enough to make one of the clowns go to his rescue. But
the next rider is already out of the chute before Smithson can be
brought off the field. At the IFR Trade Show a browser finds not
only saddles and boots and trucks and buckles, but also a display
of Niagara Lounge Chairs from Joplin, Missouri, "official therapy equipment of the 1980 and 1984 Olympics," relieving muscle spasms and back pain with Radiant Heat and the Rolla-ssage
System.

The winner of each bareback-riding round takes a victory lap,
and over several nights a few of the leaders develop a modest
celebrity. A second Troy, Troy Eaton of Bouton, Iowa, has the
unthreateningly pretty looks of a bubble-gum rock star, and during his second victory lap, on Friday, the announcer shouts, "Ma-
mas, grab your daughters!" But remoteness does not seem to go
along with rising popularity. A fan can go out to the concession
stands ringing the arena, and cowboys who've just had a big
round will be there drinking beer along with everybody else.
They're "working" for you, and this is their break.

By the time the steer wrestling begins, a front-row spectator
will be used to the particular discomforts of his position: horses
slamming into the metal bars in front of his face, clods of dirt
striking him on the nose. These are minor matters compared to
what the steer wrestlers go through in an event that makes Jerry
Todd's talk about working seem close to the literal truth. Twist-
ing a steer's neck until he's down on the ground is hard, sweaty
labor. The cowboy seems to be struggling less with a big living
creature than with an immense boiler valve. A good time will av-

erage about five seconds, but as with most hard jobs, it sometimes takes longer than you expect. On Thursday night Jimmy Dale Wisdom walks away tired and disgusted after making an 11.6. The following night Jack Wiseman, a sentimental favorite from Krebs, Oklahoma, who's qualified for all twenty IFRs ("Two generations have seen this cowboy!"), gets pinned to the ground by an upside-down steer but persists for 17.4 seconds. "A lot of men would've given up," says Todd, but Wiseman will prove smart to have stuck with it. He finishes way out of the money in this second go-round, but it's better to have a 17.4 than a no-time factored into your total for the rodeo if you want to preserve a chance of winning the five-round average — which is what Wiseman will have accomplished by Sunday afternoon.

Steer wrestlers tend toward the solid and stocky. They don't have the stringy look of the cowboy stereotype. They're bigger than the rough-stock riders, who, while hardly jockey-sized, usually have the average trim build of the first astronauts, whose vehicles couldn't accommodate six-footers. But even the big-boned ruggedness of the steer wrestlers is giving way to some modern polish. "We've got some pretty smart cowboys," says Todd, referring to Shawn David of McCloud, Oklahoma, who's come out of collegiate rodeo and holds a degree in business.

If any rodeo event can appeal to products of modern education and technocracy, it is probably team roping. Though a timed competition where good scores average around six or seven seconds, this seems the most leisurely of all the events, a matter of balletic precision and teamwork, not brute strength and single combat. The "header" must take the steer by the horns with any of the three approved head catches (figure eights are not allowed), and then the "heeler" goes for the feet. The crowd seems appreciative of the skills displayed, but Todd's assertion that this has become rodeo's most popular event seems a gross overstatement. Tom Bourne of Marietta, Georgia, was the IPRA's 1988 Rookie of the Year, and is touted for his blond good looks ("the blue-eyed wonder!") in the manner of Troy Eaton, but this is not an event that excites the crowd much. (Almost nothing, it might be noted, brings rodeo fans to their feet. Even the most harrowing bull ride going on at a far end of the arena is performed for fans who are shouting and sitting.) Team roping has been around for a long time, but they didn't even add it to the Sitting Bull Stampede up in Mobridge, South Dakota, until 1984. It may promise too much longevity to its competitors. Saddle-bronc riders last longer than bareback ones, and team ropers can go on much longer still. In fact, team roping is the golf of rodeo.

Rodeo humor is a matter of strictly regulated convention. A clown roams inactive patches of the arena at almost all times, chatting up sections of the crowd between exchanges with the announcer. Cliff "Hollywood" Harris is IFR 20's funny man, and the jokes run to the Hee-Hawish: baldness; Preparation H; swishy walking behind a saddle-bronc rider who's just dismounted. Between bursts of bull riding, Hollywood tells Danny Newland that he named his four kids Eenie, Meenie, Miney, and Fred, because he didn't want no mo'. Each night Newland asks him how he feels — the cue for someone to start a tape of James Brown's "I Feel Good," so Hollywood can drop his pants and gyrate in frilly pink underwear.

The crowd expects and gets a precisely formulaic mix of cowardice and bravado: the clown cowers, but imputes effeminacy to the hyper-macho cowboys; he quavers, but in fact quite bravely allows the bull to charge the little barrel he hides in, a one-man shelter reminiscent of a jar in the *Arabian Nights* or an air-raid manhole in Hanoi. Although removed from all the cowboy exertion and animal anger in the ring, Hollywood is not so much a foil to those things as an extension of the audience, an Everyman caught on the wrong side of the bars.

Between the steer wrestling and bull riding, Brother Taylor, the main comedy act this year, alternates his "Government Trapper" and "Matador" routines, each of which leads up to his doing battle with a small dog dressed up as a skunk or bull. Married to a trick rider and himself a former rodeo contestant, Brother Taylor delivers acts that, according to the program, are "family-oriented and keep all ages entertained." The bits are so bad that they generate more laughter each time one sees them, the elements of the cornball cocktail — Taylor's audacity and your own indulgence — growing stronger with each performance.

"Like most government jobs, that was a stinker": this comment from the announcer, after the "Government Trapper" meets up with the skunk, is the only Reaganesque political moment of IFR 20. The kind of solidarity the crowd is worked into has less to do with ideology than with regionalism and lifestyle. The intermission music goes a little way toward this with numbers like "San Antonio Rose" and "Don't Call Him a Cowboy Until You've Seen Him Ride," which warns people from New York City that the guy they think is a cowboy may have had his toughest ride in a foreign car. But there's not much musical will to fight homogenization: the themes from "Bonanza" and "Rawhide" are recognizable to anyone in the crowd over thirty, irrespective of geography, and at one point the band resorts to a peppy westernized version of "Frère Jacques." The only musical joke, played before the start of each go-round, is what seems at first, inexplicably, just an old Engelbert Humperdinck number, until — ah, got it: "Release Me."

Aside from Brother Taylor and Hollywood, the only noncompetitive entertainment is provided by S. L. Pemberton, a twenty-one-year-old Roman rider from Tennessee. "Isn't that a pretty sight?" the announcer asks, and it is. Skinny S.L. is a child's fantasy, standing on two horses with another two trotting in front of those, wearing satiny red white and blue, delighting the crowd as his whole team improbably jumps hurdles, together, like the long sine curve of a slow-flying lariat.

After the bareback riding, the Miss Rodeo USA contestants, looking more Bob Mackie than Kitty Wells, line up for a much-complimented appearance. For the next hour or so, until after intermission, spectators will see, aside from a female photographer, only one woman on the field, and that's the wife of steer wrestler Rick Chaffin. She acts as his "hazer," racing along on the other side of the steer from the one he's going after, making the animal run in a straight line so the wrestler can get a clean throw of his rope before jumping off his horse to take the animal by the horns. From that point on, spectators have to wait until the cowgirls' barrel racing to see the combination of "fast horses and beautiful women," as Jerry Todd puts it, the first time one's heard the phrase unreversed in a joke-listening lifetime.

Done well, barrel racing is fast, precise, and satisfying to watch. The rider gallops out of the gate, and then she and her horse do hairpin turns around three barrels (oil drums painted red white and blue) set up like a baseball diamond. The barrel occupying the second-base spot is the last one she has to round before charging back to the gate. Times usually fall between fourteen and fifteen seconds and are carried to three decimals on the stopwatch. Knocking down any barrel means a five-second penalty, though the rider is allowed to brush and wobble them in the manner of ski slaloming.

"I want you to make some noise!" shouts Jerry Todd. "She makes the turn, you make some noise!" Listening to this frequent, insistent encouragement, beyond anything asked for the working cowboys, one wonders if this isn't mostly condescension: a little something for the little ladies. There's some truth in that, but the prodding also has a practical side. The louder the audience cheers, the faster the horse will run. If the audience yells about equally for each cowgirl, the playing field stays relatively even.

It's the only elegant event in rodeo, the only one where the competitors' facial expressions seem readable for meaning. Unlike in the rough-stock competitions, the contestant here doesn't draw a horse by lot. She trains and travels with her own animal: Connie Cooper and her two horses, Saw Bucks and Baby Bucks, have gone seventy thousand miles through twenty-one states between the last IRF and this one. The training of the horse is particular and problematic. Dayna Cravens does some barrel racing but, she tells me, the new horse she's working with doesn't really get it yet. On Friday night when Tracy Postrach's horse messes up, you can see her give the animal an angry whack with her crop when she gets it back through the gate. "She's not a happy camper," says Todd, from his announcing booth directly above.

Tracy Postrach gets the cowgirls' Hard Luck Award that evening. There's also a Best Dressed title conferred in this event each night, and those citations tend to downgrade the exertions of the cowgirls — who have been known to require stitches after bad bangs against the barrels — to those made by the Miss Rodeo USA contestants. Next to me in the stands, a teenage boy from Tennessee named Chance, sporting traces of a never-shaved mustache, ogles their program pictures; for all the barrel racers' skill, they suffer from an unspoken sense that the event is the ladies' auxiliary one. Its placement on the program after intermission, as well as its being the evening's shortest event — no recalcitrant animals to keep rigging up in the chutes — contribute to the feeling that it lies somewhere between being one of the real, statistics-riddled competitions and part of the evening's entertainment, along with the trick riders, the clowns, the pageant.

DeBoraha Akin, a barrel racer with four children between seven and sixteen, is the first black woman to qualify for the IFR finals, and she receives some good-willed attention from the press and crowd. Asked by the *Tulsa Tribune* about other black women in her sport, she says: "There are some tough ones out there. . . . The problem is most of them stay mostly in the black rodeos. I go to some of those, but I don't understand why you wouldn't go to the main circuit events." Rodeo has a number of persisting concentric circuits — for blacks, gays, and prisoners — that show little desire or chance to ripple outward into the main ones. IFR 20 has two black cowboys, steer wrestler Clarence LeBlanc and bull rider Larry Mosley, both of whom still seem novel to the almost entirely white crowd. The announcers can exhibit a foot-in-mouth well-meaningness toward them. Danny Newland says that Mosley has a lot of grit even though he doesn't ride with "a lot of class." During a rough ride he's praised because he "keeps on keepin' on," a phrase one doesn't hear applied to anyone else. (In fact, steer wrestling may have been invented by a black cowhand, Bill Pickett. The rodeo historian Clifford P. Westermeier wrote: "As the story goes — based on tradition and hearsay, and elaborated upon in repetition — Bill, upon failing to drive a steer into a corral, became angry and leaped from his horse to the steer's head and proceeded to wrestle the animal to the ground.")

What Larry Mosley is keeping on doing is responding to "Rodeo's Toughest Challenge." This is what the announcers like to call the bull riding. It's the event that closes the show, and the one most productive of macho anecdote and legendary injury. IFR 20 makes its own contribution here: Rusty Smith of Fort Smith, Arkansas, scores an impressive 81 points in the first round, even though once he's off the bull he has to get back on his crutches: he accidentally shot himself in the foot, with a nail gun, the other day. By Saturday afternoon it's clear that no one will ride all five head he draws at IFR 20: after three rounds everyone's been thrown at least once.

I ask Lloyd Burk, Sr., the 1965 world champion bull rider and now a rodeo judge, about the worst injury he ever sustained. "This bull hit me in the face at Cooper, Texas," he tells me. "After the whistle I rode him, won the bull ridin'. He knocked all my teeth out, knocked twenty-eight teeth out, cut my lip off, broke my nose, broke my jaws, and, you know, I stayed in the hospital Thursday till Sunday, and I got out of the hospital on Sunday afternoon. Well, we was comin' home. My daddy came and picked me up, and instead of takin' me home, they had a rodeo started on Tuesday. . . . Well, he just stopped and entered me in the rodeo, put me up on Saturday night. Well, I had a hundred sixty-four stitches in my mouth, where my teeth had cut my lip off, and so, come Saturday night I borrowed me a football helmet off of a friend there who played football, went down to Ada [Oklahoma], got on the bull, and won the bull ridin', and that was the year I won the world. I went to like forty-somethin' head before they ever throwed me off another bull after I got hit in the face."

On Friday night at IFR 20, with his father watching, "Little Lloyd," Lloyd Burk, Jr., gets thrown by Tar Baby, and on Sunday has another tough break, getting thrown just before he can get through all eight seconds of what looked like a great ride. Still, he'll come in third in the average this year and finish fourth in the year-long contest for the world championship.

Even in this event, rodeo remains significantly different from bullfighting or hockey, in that the audience is not out for blood. They're not waiting for something awful to happen so much as they're waiting to see something *not* happen — come close to happening, but that's it. The "bullfighters" — not the riders, but the cowboys dressed like clowns and charged with diverting a bull's attention from the rider he's just thrown and would now like to charge — are probably the bravest men in the arena. "These are cowboy lifesavers," says Danny Newland, not putting it too strongly. And yet rodeo psychology and protocol require that the bullfighters present themselves as weak. Their mandatory motley is donned not just as a red-flag distraction for the bull, but also to emphasize the bullfighter's own position inferior to that of the rider. On the night before the first go-round, one

bullfighter tells a Tulsa television reporter that his greatest reward is to be thanked by a bull rider. A knight-page relationship
is the rule, with the curious difference that it's the page who is
looking out for the knight. According to the program, "Doug
Abbiatti has been chosen as the cowboy's protector by the IFR
bull riders eight times in his career! . . . Abbiatti has earned that
honor more times than any man in the history of the International Finals Rodeo." He is there to provide the audience with
the thrill of hairsbreadth avoidance.

"Haven't you guys got anything better to do?" A city cop, mistak-
ing me for a reporter from the major media, asks this question
in a friendly way as we watch an animal rights demonstration
gather outside the Convention Center at 4:30 on a cold Thursday afternoon. Actually, with five demonstrators present, it's just
about already gathered. Five cops, three of them on horseback,
are there to keep things in line; a news anchor and one camera-
man/interviewer are also present to provide coverage for the
evening news. The cop bets that all five demonstrators — whose
numbers have not swelled twenty minutes into the event — are
from out of state. In fact, he's wrong about that. A little conversation reveals that it is Tulsans who are carrying the signs: "Rodeos Are Shocking (Literally)" — a reference to electric cattle
prods; "Animal Cruelty Is No Sport"; "What Does It Prove
When You Beat Up a Calf?" A woman hands me an article from
the Fund for Animals newsletter: "Those Brave Cowboys, Wrestling Baby Steers."

Actually, it is not steer wrestling but calf roping that excites the
most revulsion among animal rights activists, and even if you
have an active hostility for the animal rights movement, you're
likely to find the calf-roping section of any evening's rodeo program to be the one in which you're rooting for the animal instead
of the cowboy. As Martha Brown, a soft-spoken teacher of history at Tulsa Junior College, tells me from what passes for the
picket line: "You rope a calf running at fifteen or twenty miles an
hour and throw him down. You injure them very easily at that
age. If it were done once it wouldn't be so bad, but the same calf
is used over and over and over, without medical care usually.
They're babies, after all. . . . They're in no place that they can
understand. So it seems to me it's really pretty brutal for them."

The teenaged Cyra McFadden, growing estranged from Cy Tail-lon, was "blandly disengaged" from rodeo, "except when a calf got its neck broken in the calf-roping event. On these occasions, infrequent though they were, I registered moral outrage. Rodeo was cruel, I said. This attitude my father could not tolerate, not from me, not from journalists and, most of all, not the self-righteous, lily-livered SPCA."

The calves do appear horribly frightened, and even when their necks remain unbroken, their heads snap around sickeningly. Their eyes run and their mouths shoot drool. The sound they're making isn't lowing — it's screaming — and after their feet are speedily tied they may defecate in panic. If they start struggling, the cowboys lose points, and if they can stagger to their feet within five seconds of being tied, the cowboys get a no-time averaged into their five-round score. So these calves are not going to be gently ribboned.

Tim McKee, who organized the demonstration, appears to be an all-purpose radical, with his talk about how he came to an antirodeo awareness through an antifur one, which came in turn from an environmental one: Greenpeace. He finds it interesting that barrel racing, the least objectionable rodeo event, is the only one women are involved with, and mentions that he is a recent student of "ecofeminism." One feels that if, as the song goes, he could talk to the animals, he'd bore them to death. It's not the menagerie but the millennium that's on his mind, whereas Martha Brown of NOAH (Northeastern Oklahoma Animal Helpers) seems to be in this geographically quixotic enterprise for the creatures themselves. Rodeo is not her "big priority," but she objects to more than the calf roping, reminding me that the bulls and broncs are not wild animals who are normally afraid of humans. Rodeo defenders say that the bucking straps that get them to jump and kick are placed more or less where a belt would be on a human, but foes say that the straps are squeezing the genitalia. As Ms. Brown gently puts it to me: "They're around very sensitive parts of the animals' bodies." (Clifford Westermeier has found objections to bronc riding dating back to an exhibition held in Cheyenne in 1872.)

It's hard to tell whether the new, more aggressive stance of the activists is provoking the slightest defensiveness in rodeo people. Almost each evening Danny Newland tells those folks in the audience who may have an intractable horse, one that "wakes up ornery one morning and refuses to go to work," that they shouldn't abuse him but instead contact the IPRA and see about getting him into rodeo, where his life can be extended and made useful. It's doubtful this is just a cynical pitch designed to improve the level of rough stock, but there's probably a certain public relations motive at the heart of it. On Thursday night a calf gets so banged up it can't hobble off the field even after it's been untied. One of the pickup riders has to take up the hind legs and push him back toward the gates the way you would a wheelbarrow. "We do have a veterinarian who is on standby call at all times in case any of our animals is injured," swears Newland to the fans. "We will take care of that."

The cowboys don't see anything wrong with the way the stock get treated. On the contrary, W. Bruce Lehrke, president of Longhorn Rodeo, is quoted by a *Tulsa Tribune* sports columnist as saying: "You ask just about any cowboy, and he will tell you if there is such a thing as reincarnation, he wants to come back in his next life as a bucking bronc or a bull. They have the 'Life of Riley.' " Even Martha Brown will allow how the cowboys suffer not from active cruelty as much as a "different perspective": "I think they *like* their animals."

No doubt they do. The sight of a pickup rider gentling his horse with friendly pats, reassuring him against the lights and noise and sudden bursts of activity by various species, is a sweet one. And however off-putting may seem the fate of the calves and steers, any brutality suffered by the rough stock (those straps) seems not very great, and, furthermore, it is not so much the result of a cowboy's desire to dominate as his understanding that he and the animal are equal partners in this event. It's not simply the even-steven agreement that the cowboy can hurt the horse because the horse will hurt the cowboy; there's a numerical equality established by the rules. A perfect score in bareback or saddle-bronc riding is one hundred; most cowboys who stay on total somewhere in the seventies, half from each of the two judges on opposite sides of the arena. But fifty of the potential hundred points are earned by the animal. A horse that won't buck is like a dog that won't hunt, and fans will express more displeasure over an animal's poor performance than a rider's. "At least that son of a bitch bucked," said somebody not far from me when an energetic horse followed a more contented one during the first night's saddle-bronc riding.

Bucking stock are listed by name and number in the program, and a spectator can look up their records the same way he can a cowboy's. Marijuana, number 360 from the Gene Smith Rodeo Company, is a brindle "age 7, wt. 1600; out 8; dis. 8" — which is to say, he's thrown every contestant who's been momentarily atop him. Godfather, a saddle bronc from the JS Pro Rodeo Company, an eight-year-old quarter horse weighing 1,350 pounds, is six for nine. The cover bull from the current issue of *Rodeo News* gets to take a special promenade before being auctioned off for over six thousand dollars at the bucking-stock sale held the day before IFR 20 opens.

The purpose of the day-long event is to sell broncs and bulls to local rodeo companies, the kind that make up the circuit leading IPRA cowboys to the finals in Tulsa. By the time one reaches the level of the IFR, rodeo, like most things in modern life and art, starts to be about itself. The crowd watching Rocky Top, a five-year-old sorrel gelding, buck up a snorting storm on Wednesday morning is advised that they're watching a "Saturday night ticket seller!"

As they sit in front of advertising banners for Stetson, Ford trucks, and Pepsi, cowboys in the stands videotape the proceedings with hand-held cameras. The older women, teased and permed, wear neatly pressed pantsuits; the younger ones tend toward pink sweatshirts. The auctioneer knows a lot of the bidders by name, and what they're listening to, all day, is a curious blend of hype and understatement. On the stock sheet, lots 3 through 9 are presented by their owner, Bill Moore of the Diamond M Rodeo Company: "As I have sold my indoor arena, I will sell the remainder of my bulls. All of these bulls are outstanding bulls." The pitch often takes the form of straight-faced humor: "Boys, y'all count your money. I can't stay here all day. Boys, y'all asleep there?" All a young longhorn needs "is some groceries and a little time." After the announcer's laudations, the animal's angry bucking, and the auctioneer's amplified tongue-trills, the gavel goes down with a kind of sigh, allowing everyone involved to catch breath and return to modest reality. Then the auctioneer will say nothing more than the simple truth: "I sold a bull."

The stock sale showcases animals less on the basis of their vital, measurable statistics than their personalities and life histories. "Here's an old campaigner," says auctioneer Sam Howry, of lot 267, Band Wagon, a horse that's seen "about every finals that's been," has in fact "been all over the world." He comes "out of the north country" — Jim Crothers's rodeo company in Gypsum, Kansas — and in his advanced age is recommended as a practice horse. The crossbred bulls being auctioned seem easily the angriest, and anger is a prize virtue. Lot 55, a six-year-old Bradford cross, is "a big stout rodeo rascal." Bidders and spectators in the stands are asked: "Don't you like that crooked-horned bull? Mercy, mercy." The Reverend B. Thomas is on his way to New York after a crowd-pleasingly scary show of stuff. He gives the bullfighters a lot of attention and gouges a piece out of the clown's barrel with his horn. He's as good as lot 23, in fact, a brindle modestly described in the list of available animals as a six-year-old who "bails out and bucks hard, hooks a little" and is "hard to ride" — but who excites Sam Howry to happy heights of commercial appreciation: "Here's the rodeo-est bull we've had in here! . . . He's a Saturday night bull!"

The clowns and bullfighters work the stock sale for nothing. They, too, are on display for local rodeo companies who might want to hire them. If they do well here, the bullfighters will get their IPRA cards on Friday. When a bull goes after one of them hard, the announcer hardly knows whether to hype the animal or the man, settling for a soft sell of the bull: "He will tend to scoop 'em up."

Martha Brown objects when events she finds cruel are historically justified, as if tradition itself were a reason to sanction them. The first professional rodeo is thought to have been held in Prescott, Arizona, in 1888; according to Matt Kohlman, in the special Sitting Bull Stampede issue of the Mobridge, South Dakota, *Tribune*, although the sport's origins are imprecise,

> the cattle drives of the late 1800s definitely played a major part in its development. When ranch outfits met on the trails or at towns, riding and roping exhibitions would often take place as the cowboys bet their scant wages on the outcome.
> Usually conducted in the wide open prairie without fences or corrals, the contests provided a welcome relief to the hard life of the trail.

Clifford Westermeier links rodeo to fiesta, noting that the word "rodeo" originally meant "to round up the cattle for branding, or to take them to the cattle market, which was often held during a fiesta." The movement from trail to ranch to city occurred over several decades, and by 1936 the cowboys were beginning to organize themselves into what would eventually become the PRCA. "Because they [were] slow in organizing," Matt Kohlman said, "they called themselves the Cowboys Turtle Association."

If pro rodeo is cut off from the ranching labors that brought it into being, it keeps going by constantly extending its own bloodlines. This is a family sport, not in some PG sense of the term, but literally. It is hard to find anyone competing at the IFR who is unrelated to someone else in rodeo. Tulsa's Connie Cooper, the world champion barrel racer, had an aunt in the same sport and a father who rode bulls. DeBoraha Akin jokes to the *Tulsa Tribune* that she took up barrel racing to get on the good side of her rodeoing father-in-law. Tracy Postrach may have taken Friday's Hard Luck Award in the barrel racing, but by Sunday afternoon her brother Terry is the world champion calf roper. Mika John Calico's mother is the arena secretary, and his father is a judge. There are so many Foremans who team rope that on opening night Jerry Todd imagines that, back home, "Poor old Mama Foreman's legs are all scraped up." On a couple of nights, even S. L. Pemberton is joined by his trick-riding ten-year-old sister, Jaclyn, named, one suspects, for a Charlie's Angel.

Lloyd Burk, Sr., did not come out of a rodeoing family. He tells me that back in 1953 his high school basketball coach offered to pay his entry fees into a "little old FFA rodeo" if Lloyd would go ride a bull. "This thing throwed me so high that a bird could've built a nest in my hat before I hit the ground." But the next week he won $165 in merchandise at another rodeo in Sulphur: "Britches, shirts, clothes, boots, hats. . . . I got my mama some stuff, my daddy stuff, and I got [the coach] stuff, and I got his wife clothes. Back then, you know, you could buy a lot of clothes and stuff for a hundred sixty-five dollars. And that's how I started ridin' bulls, on a bet."

For Lloyd Burk, Jr., bull riding was a birthright. Little Lloyd was born one day when Lloyd Senior was at a rodeo in Jonesboro, Arkansas, and by the time he was six he was getting up on calves. Five years later he started going to rodeos, and "for lots of years" after that he rode bulls with his father. Lloyd Senior is pretty sure his son will win a world title someday: "He rides real good. He's got a lot better style than I got." But rodeo is "about all he knows." On Tuesdays and Wednesdays Lloyd Junior works at the livestock auction in Ada, and by Thursday he's off to a rodeo.

Lloyd Senior says that "a man can make a good living rodeoing today." Entry fees and purses are a lot higher than they were thirty years ago, and the circuit runs year-round, not just the six or seven months it used to. Still, it's clear that very few cowboys are getting rich here. According to Danny Newland, "Downtown" Jason Brown figures he can wait to make $50,000 a year with his marketing degree; right now he can have a better time making $25,000 riding saddle broncs. The championship standings going into IFR 20 had Mika John Calico, the leader in bull riding, with a total of $21,745 for 1989 and Lloyd Burk, Jr., in sixth place, with just $8,653. Four days later, Little Lloyd would be up to $10,603, and Calico, the world champion, would have added less than $200 to his total. To get these sums IPRA riders may get up on between fifty and seventy animals. The PRCA circuit has more money, more rodeos, and more self-supporting cowboys, but according to Steve Danylo, the regional bareback-riding champion, who's a construction worker during the week: "In rodeo, as long as you break even or a little bit above, you're doing good." Dayna Cravens tells me about the IFR cowboys who work at American Airlines there in Tulsa.

A bull rider can go on until he's thirty-five or so, according to Lloyd Burk, Sr., who, in good health at forty-nine, still gets up on one every now and then. But mostly he judges now: in 1990 he's got contracts to work twenty-seven rodeos. Cy Taillon's son, Terry, went in the same way from saddle-bronc riding to judging to announcing. Perhaps the most unexpected thing about rodeo is that it gives the people who work in it a chance to age gracefully.

On Friday afternoon, IFR's "Old Timers" gather at the Park Plaza for their reunion. Dayna Cravens, who grew up with these people, introduces me around before the event gets going. I ask her father, J.O., if the IFR is really leaving Tulsa. He'll only tell me that there are two rumors every year: that they'll have a full house and that they're pulling out of the city.

The women walk with video cameras between tables holding finger food and Lite beer as the event gets under way in the highly structured manner of a rodeo go-round. Even here, the master of ceremonies is constantly announcing. The nostalgia is formal: people go up to the mike and complete for a prize in storytelling. They're asked to keep the stories "rodeo-related." A plaque goes to the Most Deserving Old Timer, and another to the oldest clown present — "and I'm sure that pertains to comedy acts and things like that," says the emcee. The Mark Trophy Company, donor of the plaques, is thanked like any other sponsor. Some of the reminiscences involve particular animals, and Buck Crofts takes the storytelling honors after ending with a sentimental one about two friends who are gone — a tale in keeping with the invocation mentioning those who have gone "to ride a much higher range."

The Cowboy Chapter of the Fellowship of Christian Athletes is present not just with their first-into-the-ring banner at each session of the rodeo, but with prayer meetings throughout the week and testimonial literature available at the trade show. The Cowboy Chapter was conceived at a 1974 rodeo in Denver by Wilbur Plaugher, a rodeo clown, and Mark Schricker, a contestant. It now claims four thousand members and boasts of having "distributed over 130,000 Cowboys Bibles throughout the world." Allen Bach, a 1979 team-roping champion, writes that for a time he "put roping first instead of my relationship with the Lord. If I had put into my Christian walk what I put into rodeo, and read the Word like I practiced roping, I'd be a better example today. I didn't need to stay a baby Christian for twelve years." A small blue pamphlet asks contenders if they'd rather be a "Rodeo Winner or Soul Winner": "Would you rather lay up a hoard of worldly treasures to dust and rust and mold in the short time we are here on earth, or would you lay up a multitude of treasures in heaven by working for God and leading others to do the same?" This seems especially sincere in light of what the figures say about the chance of making any kind of extravagant living through the IFR.

The undisputed king of IFR competition, Dan Dailey, who has qualified in four different events, won seventeen world championships, married a Miss Rodeo USA, and is still competing in IFR 20, is the Cowboy Chapter's most attractive spokesman. He has the kind of good looks and bland dignity that make you think of him as a potential Republican candidate for the Senate, a kind of Steve Garvey who may not be too good to be true. But for all his formidable skills he seems completely lacking in any of the rough-edged, dirt-covered, hot-damn colorfulness that might make Danny Newland shout, as he sometimes does, "Wild and Western!" If Dailey's sport were women's tennis, he'd be Chris Evert, a champion for sure, but one who has professionalized himself into a higher, stainless-steel order of being. It's no surprise that he's been nicknamed the Bionic Cowboy. One thinks that he — with the addition of one of those college diplomas held by some competitors like "Downtown" Jason Brown — must represent the future of the rodeo cowboy.

Still, one doesn't yet have to look too far to find the tobacco-spitting, shit-kicking rodeo model, the kind that's still going to be given a jolt by the Doubletree's elevators. Greg Wheeler, a bareback rider from Kellyville, Oklahoma, is the son of Earlene Wheeler and Bobby Wheeler, a rodeo veteran who, while feeling no pain at the Old Timers' Reunion, steps up to the mike to tell the story of how maybe twenty or so years ago, out on the circuit with a very young Greg, he spent a night in a Missouri jail after being a little disorderly. The next morning, when both he and Greg were standing in court, the head-shaking magistrate asked the boy his birthday. "September third," replied Greg. "What year?" asked the judge. "Well, shit," answered Greg, "every year."

Like Tulsa's boom-and-bust economy, five days of rodeo expand and contract: stretches of boredom are separated by eight-second bursts of excitement. It is, like track and field, a sport of repetitions, one giving rise only sparingly to individual dramas. Before the final, Sunday afternoon round gets started, most of the world championships, dependent on the year-long money totals, have already been decided; the only suspense, and it's minor, is to see who will win the round and the five-day average. Attendance seems the lowest of any session, and the hoof- and horn-pocked banners give the arena a tired atmosphere. Even the crowning of Miss Rodeo USA, when it finally comes, before the last steer-wrestling round, seems anticlimactic: Miss Nicki Barefoot's new tiara-ringed Stetson doesn't seem much different from what she already had on. Still, the repetitions have their pleasures — even if they only involve catching sight of Brother Taylor's assistant holding the "skunk" she's got to set loose, or hearing someone in the stands, wishing to be the one who brings forth the sound of James Brown, shout: "Hey, Hollywood, how do you *feel?*" Actually, Hollywood, still in his pink underwear, started looking a little tired yesterday.

But the real moment of IFR 20 is about to come. It will last, of course, for eight seconds, and be provided by Justin Rowe of Tulsa, during the last round of saddle-bronc riding.

With his custom-made monogrammed black and white shirt, Rowe seems more dandified than his competition, and he's in the enviable position of being not only the hometown favorite but second only to Dan Dailey himself in the year-long trail of bank deposits leading to the world championship. Last night he seemed to get a suspiciously lucky break: needing 81 points to stay in first place for the five-day average, he came up with 82, on a ride that seemed less spectacular than Mike Hemann's, though that one earned only a 76 and some boos for the judges. The scoring does at times seem arbitrary. On Thursday night, for example, Tim Smith of Miami, Oklahoma, rode a saddle bronc with the kind of elegance the sport usually makes impossible to display, and came up with only a 69. Maybe it was the forward dismount that kept him low on points. Still, when Rowe comes out of the chute on Sunday afternoon, one is past being blindly faithful toward the judges' abilities.

But there he is, stunning the crowd on a horse that's bucking to high heaven, beating the air with his free arm, mastering all around him with a steady, slicing control. It's a gorgeous, hard ride and he's raising the roof, taking the crowd, which realizes what it's seeing, up into its own roar of pleasure. It's the best thing anyone has watched in five days. In fact, it's the best saddle-bronc ride the Tulsa Convention Center has *ever* seen, an arena record — 90 goddamn points.

And a little while later he's out by the concession stands, just talking to somebody near the beer line, and you want to shake his hand.

The last thing the crowd sees each night is a riderless bull, let out of the chutes not to try and throw a cowboy, but just to disport himself as threateningly as he can in the presence of the bull-fighters. This little bit of closing business by the best of the bulls — *"Close your rodeo with this bull!"* — seems designed to let the animal have the last word, and to prepare the arena for its desertion by the riders.

On Sunday afternoon Steve Danylo told me he planned to hop a plane back to Arkansas before the last round of bull riding was finished, and a couple of hours after that all the living creatures of the IFR were moving on from Tulsa. At around 5:30 you could find a rodeo family in one of the deserted downtown parking lots, packing things into a pickup — garment bag, attaché case, bucking rope. In the back of the Convention Center, lot 360, the brindle called Marijuana, the big stout rodeo rascal ridden in the first round by Mika John Calico, the world champion, was loaded up behind the bars of his truck, ready for his next move with the Gene Smith Rodeo Company.

In fact, the IFR was leaving Tulsa for good. The next morning a press release from J. O. Cravens would announce that the twenty-first finals would take place next January in Oklahoma City, partly because of its "twenty years' experience hosting the PRCA's National Finals Rodeo" — before, that is, the PRCA moved to Vegas. Like the training wheel on a bicycle, the smaller circuit was chasing the larger one.

Rodeo, like country music, is stuck on itself. Both of them have to be, because they depend on a sense of cultural disappearance. Each asserts that it's as strong as ever in these rootless, rushed, and misguided times, but the only way such defiance works, and gives its hearers poignant pleasure, is for them to know the pro-claimant *is* embattled, slowly but certainly fading. When the an-nouncer says goodbye each night to the crowd, his valediction is meant to sound robust, but his chosen emblem can't help being elegiac: "Good night, God bless you, and remember, as long as there's a sunset, there'll be a West."

DAVID VON DREHLE

They Shoot Heroes, Don't They?

FROM TROPIC

HISTORY LOOKED like this to Walter Bingham, a writer for *Sports Illustrated:*

"It was Sunday, Oct. 1, 1961, at Yankee Stadium in New York, the fourth inning of the last game of the season. The clock on the scoreboard read 2:42 when Roger Maris came to bat for the second time in the game. There was no score, one out and no one on base. Pitching for the Boston Red Sox was Tracy Stallard, a tall 24-year-old right-hander with a 2–6 record. The first time up, Maris had hit Stallard's first pitch, a good sinker, deep to left field, but the ball had been caught.

"Now Stallard threw a fast ball high and outside that Maris took for a ball. From all over the stadium, but especially from the packed right-field stands, Maris' home run territory, came the low rumble of boos. Stallard threw another fast ball, this time low and inside, and again there were boos. Stallard's third pitch was a third fast ball — 'a strike,' he said later, 'knee-high on the outside corner of the plate.' Maris swung and from the instant of impact there was no doubt in the mind of anyone (including two Cincinnati pitchers in a front-row box) that he had just hit his 61st home run of the season, more than any other player in the history of the game. The ball rose toward the right-field stands, just to the right of the Yankee bullpen some 360 feet from home plate, and fell about six rows deep into a wild confusion of grappling fans. It was caught on the fly by a 19-year-old Brooklyn boy named Sal Durante who was immediately escorted with his precious souvenir — a California restaurant man had offered $5,000 for the ball — to the Yankee dressing room.

"Maris circled the bases slowly to a standing ovation from the crowd of 23,000. Yogi Berra, waiting to hit, was the first to shake his hand, followed by the Yankee batboy and a jubilant fan. Maris disappeared into the dugout, but when the applause continued he reappeared on the dugout steps, his hat in his hand, a delighted smile on his face. When he tried to sit down once more his teammates refused to let him, pushing him back into view. Again, he waved his cap at the crowd. At that moment the Yankee management flashed a message on the scoreboard: MARIS' 61 HOMERS BREAK RUTH'S 1927 RECORD FOR A SEASON.

"There was little new for Maris to say to the mob of reporters who surrounded him after the game. 'I'm happy . . . good feeling . . . the greatest,' were the expectable answers to the expectable questions. In the Boston clubhouse Stallard, who had lost the game to the home run, 1–0, was far from despondent. 'I'll tell you this,' he said. 'My price just went up to the banquet circuit.' "

It was, in its realm, a feat of tremendous heroism. In the field of baseball, which has meant so much to so many, where the home run epitomizes excellence and domination, Roger Maris reconfigured all notions of the possible, setting a standard for power unchallenged across thirty subsequent seasons.

More than that, Maris did what he did in the face of unimaginable pressure. "Of all the records in sports, none is more honored, none more renowned, than the 60 home runs Babe Ruth hit in 1927," *Sports Illustrated* pronounced as Maris mounted his assault. No god of sports has ever fired the passions and captured the imagination of Americans as Babe Ruth did; he was the brightest star of the nation's favorite game. His name was etched on nearly every page of baseball's record books, as a hitter and as a pitcher, and of all his records, the mark for home runs in a single season was the one that crystallized his colossal achievements. It was known simply as "Ruth's record," though he held so many, and the phrase became a staple in the American lexicon — as much a part of the contemporary culture, baseball historian Bill James has written, "as Jimmie Dean, sock hops, Hank Williams and Marilyn Monroe."

The dearest triumph of baseball's greatest player: this was the mark matched and surpassed by Roger Maris. Mickey Mantle, the Hall of Famer — Maris's better on the baseball field in every respect but this one — has said of the record: "What Roger did that year, hitting 61 home runs, doing it under incredible pressure . . . was simply the greatest single feat in the history of sports. I believe that. I'll argue that with anybody."

And yet, when we gaze back over the broad green spaces of baseball history, when we survey three decades played out between the clean, white foul lines, we find scarcely a trace of the man who broke the game's greatest record. It was the strange fate of Roger Maris to be less than his accomplishment, to be — by some weird calculus — *diminished* in the eyes of the world by his success, crushed under the weight of what he had done. Baseball fans may recall that a Detroit slugger, Cecil Fielder, made a bid last season to hit 50 home runs. In the buildup to the final game of the year — in which Fielder bravely clobbered homers 50 and 51 — much was made of the fact that he would be the first man to hit so many since Cincinnati's George Foster tallied 52 in 1977. Hardly a murmur was heard, however, about the man who soared past 60.

A poet, viewing history, once called it "the lengthened shadow of a man," evoking the image of heroes upon whom the sun is always shining, whose shadows thus are vivid and ever expanding as time tracks its course, until at last the shade they cast tinges everything that comes after them.

The shadow of Roger Maris is evanescent, fleeting and enigmatic; like a shadow cast on a cloudy day of bitter cold which appears for a moment when the sun ekes faintly through the gray, then vanishes before we can measure it; returns still paler, then lapses into uncertain memory. The sun never smiled on Maris long enough for his shadow to be fixed.

Out of his heroic feat no hero was produced. A strange fate, indeed. For what makes a hero if not heroism?

He made his way to destiny's door from Fargo, North Dakota, a small city isolated on the vast prairie at America's heart. Fargo was, and still mostly is, a place where sturdy shoes and a warm winter coat were a good deal more valued than the latest Paris fashions, a place where parents frequently reminded their children that actions speak louder than words. What a person did in Fargo mattered a lot more than what he said about it.

Roger Maris was a quiet, serious boy, prematurely intense. Athletically gifted from the start, he let his feats on the gridiron and the baseball diamond do his talking. Off the field, he could be blunt. When he went out for the football team at Fargo High, Maris demanded to join his older brother Rudy in the backfield. The coach refused. So the Maris boys transferred to a Catholic school, Bishop Shanley High, where Roger's running gave eloquent testimony to the rightness of his judgment. In one game for Shanley, he returned four kickoffs for touchdowns — still a national high school record.

However, when Shanley, led by the Maris defectors, beat Fargo High in Rudy's senior year, Roger Maris first discovered that actions, just like words, can be taken the wrong way. The townspeople were angered by his disloyalty rather than dazzled by his skill.

Bud Wilkinson, the great Oklahoma football coach, recruited Maris to play for the powerhouse Sooners, but college held no appeal. Instead, Maris signed a contract to play baseball for the Cleveland Indians. He cut a fine figure as a ballplayer: six feet tall, with blond hair and an iron jaw and 195 pounds well concentrated in his legs, chest and arms. Cleveland promoted him to the big leagues in 1957, and he turned in a respectable rookie season. But when the Indians suggested he hone his skills playing winter ball in Latin America, Maris refused, and the following year the club was happy to trade him to the lowly Kansas City Athletics.

His reputation for quiet stubbornness preceded him. Bob Cerv, a genial slugger for the A's, was called into manager Harry Craft's office and told he would be rooming with Maris on the road. "I want you to find out what makes him tick," Craft said.

"So I did," Cerv says. "It didn't take Roger very long to figure something was up. One day he looked at me and asked, 'What the hell are you doing?' I guess I was asking too many questions. I said, 'Skip told me to find out what makes you tick.'

"Well, he looked at me a minute, then he said, 'Hell, I like a guy who tells the truth.' And we got along fine after that."

Maris posted a .273 batting average with 21 home runs for the

A's in 1959. Craft, his manager, said Maris reminded him of the young Joe DiMaggio in the field. Maris was happy in Kansas City — the town felt comfortable to a boy from Fargo — and when news came late that year that he had been traded as part of a package deal to the mighty Yankees (a deal that included Marvelous Marv Throneberry, future clown prince of the hapless New York Mets, and Don Larsen, the only man to pitch a perfect game in the World Series), Maris announced, spontaneously and petulantly, "I don't want to go to New York."

That's just the way Maris was. Ask him a question, he gave you an answer. Like the Camels he smoked before and after ball games, Maris was unfiltered. New Yorkers didn't necessarily understand this; then, as now, naïveté baffled them; they tended to think everyone was shrewd and calculating. Maris was neither, and proudly so. A tough old New Yorker, Big Julie Isaacson, met him at the airport, took one look at his rough crew cut and white buck shoes, and growled: "Listen, kid, Yankee ballplayers don't dress like you. You got these Pat Boone shoes, they gotta go." Maris went out and bought two more pairs.

But he was not immune to the Yankee grandeur. No one could be. Over thirty-nine seasons before Maris arrived in New York, the Yankees had played in twenty-three World Series and won seventeen of them. There's a glimpse, perhaps, of his feelings — romanticized, admittedly — in the pages of a boys' novel that was ghostwritten under his name after the 1961 season. The main character, Billy Mack, is a barely disguised version of Maris himself. In the opening scene of *Slugger in Right*, Billy Mack arrives for the first time at Yankee Stadium:

"As he walked slowly along, Billy's mind flashed back through the years . . . back to the day he had first dreamed of becoming a ballplayer with the Yankees. He remembered how he had first learned about Babe Ruth from a book; then how he had, in childish enthusiasm, proclaimed to one and all that one day he would play Ruth's position on the Yankees. Now he was actually in the park where the Babe had played and had led the Yankees to so many championships."

The Yankees saw in Maris the possible next link in their forty-year chain of otherworldly outfield superstars, a line of succession that was inaugurated by Ruth, who gave way to the elegant DiMaggio, who was in turn succeeded by Mantle. At his best,

Mickey Mantle was as good as anyone who ever played the game, but he was fragile. In those days, it was the Yankee way to plan for every eventuality, and Maris was at the heart of their plan for Mantle's possible collapse.

Maris, at twenty-five, had the look of a future All-Star. He was, by the standards of the time, big and fast, he had a good arm and — most importantly — he was a left-handed pull hitter, which meant his power zone corresponded perfectly with the short right-field fence in Yankee Stadium.

Appearances were immediately translated into reality. In 1960, his first season with the Yankees, Maris led the league in runs batted in and slugging percentage and finished second in home runs, with 39 to Mantle's 40. He won the Gold Glove for his outstanding defense in right field, the only American Leaguer in nearly a decade to out-field Detroit's majestic Al Kaline at that position. At season's end, the baseball writers voted him Most Valuable Player in the American League.

But those 39 homers were as nothing compared to The Record. A man could hit 39, then half again as many, and still not rattle Ruth's monument. Thirty-nine homers did not rank in the top seventy-five single-season performances. In four major league seasons, Maris had 97 home runs — an admirable total, but nothing to presage the coming astonishment. There were those who honestly believed Ruth's record would *never* be broken by *anyone;* in over thirty years, the closest any player had come was 58. Moreover, *if* the record was to be broken, it was generally believed that Mickey Mantle would be the one to do it (or if not Mantle, perhaps the magnificent Willie Mays).

No evidence exists to suggest that the idea of assaulting Ruth's record ever crossed the mind of Roger Maris until he was already well down the path. Some men are born great, some achieve greatness, and some have greatness thrust upon them.

The Yankees of 1961 have been called the finest baseball team ever to take the field. Their starting nine included three future members of the Hall of Fame — Mantle, pitcher Whitey Ford and Yogi Berra, who moved that season from catcher to left field. They had more power at the plate than any team before or since; the third, fourth, fifth, sixth and seventh men in their batting order all hit more than 20 home runs that year. Ford won twenty-five games and lost just four for the best record of his career. Berra's replacement behind the plate, Elston Howard, had the best batting average (.348) in the league. Their infield included slugger Bill Skowron at first, five-time Gold Glove winner Bobby Richardson at second, former Rookie of the Year Tony Kubek at shortstop and Clete Boyer, an electrifying defensive player, at third. The Yankees won 109 games and the World Series that season, leaving a dazzling Detroit Tigers squad in their dust.

Yet the season opened dismally, with five losses in the Yankees' first ten games. Mantle was the only thing to cheer about in the early going; he carried the team, and Maris was among the dead weight. By game thirty, the Yankee management was so concerned about Maris's performance they dispatched him to an eye doctor, who prescribed drops that caused an allergic reaction. In a funk, Maris told a friend, "I doubt if I'll ever hit more than twenty-five or thirty homers a year."

Maris was frequently in a funk. When the affable Whitey Ford was elected player representative for the Yankees, he jokingly put Maris "in charge of grievances." It takes so much intensity, so much inner drive and competitiveness, to be among the finest in any endeavor, but even among baseball's best, Maris stood out as a man wound awfully tight. By the middle of May, Maris was miserable and his numbers were in the toilet. He was hitting .215 with three homers and eleven runs batted in.

Then *boom!* — he was on fire. Seventeen games: 12 home runs. And he stayed hot. After eighty-two games (one game past the halfway point of the season), Maris had 33 home runs; Ruth, in his record year, had 27 after the same number of games. "It seems like every hit Maris gets is a home run," said Yankees manager Ralph Houk.

Only then did it begin to dawn on the watching world that something marvelous might be in the making. "I bet you lie awake at night thinking how you're going to break Ruth's record," a reporter ventured.

"Listen," Maris fired back, "I don't think about the record, and I'm surprised I've got as many homers as I do." He wasn't the only one. Surprise was universal, and the only thing that kept the baseball world in joint that summer was that Mickey Mantle, the Expected One, was right with Maris, matching him homer for homer. By mid-July, it was Mantle 36, Maris 35.

Funny how we neglect the things we cherish until they come under attack. When Ruth hit 60 home runs, he broke his own record of 59. Many fans imagined that the Babe would push the record still higher. But as years turned into decades and the mark remained intact, it took on the glow of an impossible barrier. The invincibility of Ruth's record became a central part of baseball's mythology.

Now, as the 1961 season moved into its second half, the myth was threatened. Ford Frick, the commissioner of baseball, decided something must be done. Ruth's record required special protection.

Frick latched on to the fact that the American League had added two new teams that year, forcing an extension of the season from 154 games to 162. In July, he decreed that if Ruth's record was to be broken, it must be broken within 154 games. If the record was broken beyond the 154-game limit, the new standard would be stigmatized by "a distinctive mark" in the records books. This would later become known among baseball fans as "the asterisk."

Ford Frick was very close to Babe Ruth: he was Ruth's ghostwriter among other things. But in rushing to defend the Babe's legacy, he did more than merely expose a personal bias; he reflected a national devotion. "The commissioner has strong backing in this attitude," *The Sporting News* declared admiringly. Sports writers were polled on their reaction to the ruling, and endorsed it 2 to 1.

The decision was not embraced by everyone, however. *Sports Illustrated* called Frick's decree "a foolish, pathetic little statement, foolish because it makes so little sense, pathetic because it will be ignored. . . . A season is a season, no matter how many games are played, and if Mantle hits 61 home runs this year, the answer to the question of who hit the most home runs in a season will be Mickey Mantle."

Or Roger Maris. *Sports Illustrated* didn't bother to mention that possibility. But Maris quietly pressed ahead, matching Mantle blow for blow. After an August 6 doubleheader, the score was 43–43. The pressure was building. Maris did not succumb: at the first of September, he had 51 homers to Mantle's 48.

Never in the history of baseball . . . never in the history of sports . . . had there been anything like the mania that gathered around Maris and Mantle, squeezing tighter and tighter through the month of September until it was, very nearly, a death grip. Some of the excesses may seem commonplace to us now, inured as we have become to assaults on records: Henry Aaron chasing Ruth's career homers mark, Pete Rose closing in on Ty Cobb's career hits record, Rickey Henderson running down Lou Brock's career steals total. In 1961 it was all new.

The handful of reporters assigned to the Yankees grew to a dozen, then to a score, then to several score. Photographers recorded nearly every move the two men made; it was hard not to be distracted by the explosion of shutters at each swing of their bats. The *New York Post* ran a five-part series on Roger Maris, calling him "a throwback to Superman." The *Chicago Sun-Times* performed a nearly microscopic comparison of the eyes and hands of the two sluggers. Journalists arrived from as far away as Japan.

On the floor of Congress, North Dakota Senator Milton Young rose to announce that "Roger Maris, a North Dakota farm-raised boy, hit two more home runs today. We expect him to break the world's record by quite a few." And why stop at Congress? One sports editor "dispatched" a reporter to heaven to get an exclusive from the Babe himself. (Ruth, it was reported, thought Maris was more likely to break the record than Mantle. Like Ruth, Maris batted lefty in a park designed for left-handed power. Perhaps it's true what they say about perfect vision in Paradise.)

"It is possible," Walter Bingham wrote, "that someday Roger Maris will be able to walk across a street without shaking a dozen hands, speak a simple sentence without being quoted from coast to coast or swing a bat without having his picture taken. But last week, such privacies were not possible. Everywhere he went, he was engulfed in a fury of excitement."

Maris's 51 home runs at the beginning of September put him well ahead of Ruth, who had 43 at the same point in 1927. But the key to Ruth's record was the incredible performance he turned in during the last month of the season, when he homered 17 times. Anyone setting out to surpass Ruth's record had to keep from being swallowed up by that tidal wave. Hack Wilson was drowned at 56 in 1930. Jimmie Foxx in 1932 and Hank Greenberg in 1938 reached 58 before being submerged. Mantle himself said several times during the 1961 season that whenever he thought about breaking the record, all he had to do was ponder Ruth's 17 in September to bring himself down to earth.

Roger Maris needed a 10-homer month to pass the Babe. In other words, he had to maintain the blistering pace he had set for himself, even as the grind of game after game, day after day, mile after mile of travel, press swarm after press swarm, sapped his energy and concentration. And American League pitchers weren't likely to give him a lot of fat ones to hit; one writer speculated that pitchers might start rolling the ball to the plate when Maris was at bat. Ten home runs in a month, under suffocating pressure. Devotees of baseball statistics may recognize this as more than twice the average monthly output of Hall of Famer Stan Musial; some 40 percent more than the average monthly production of Ted Williams, that epic and beautiful slugger.

In the first week in September, the Yankees played a series against Detroit that turned out to be the end of the pennant race. Maris and Mantle — they were by now known as the M&M Boys, or simply M&M — helped decide the matter with a pair of homers each. Ushers rushed onto the field with ropes after each game to clear a path for the M&M Boys through the adoring fans who spilled from the stands.

It seemed that nothing mattered in the whole world but the race to catch Ruth. The fine points of the game were lost in the clamor for home runs. Against Cleveland, Maris laid down a perfect bunt to score Tony Kubek for what turned out to be the winning run, then hit number 55 in his next at-bat. After the game, baffled reporters demanded to know why he had bunted when he could have been swinging for the fences.

Maris was baffled by the question. "Because I wanted to win the game," he said.

Two things happened in the middle of September that, in the bright light of history, turned out to be pivotal. First, Mickey Mantle came down with a virus. Mantle's career had been a long string of injuries and illnesses, which he overcame by treating the fragility of his body with contempt. Enfeebled by the virus, he sought out a doctor of marginal repute for a powerful pick-me-up. Dr. Feelgood took aim at Mantle's butt and drove the needle down to the bone. An infection set in, and soon the slugger was in a hospital bed with an oozing abscess, done for the season. The second pivotal occurrence was a mini-slump for Roger Maris. He went eight games without a home run.

The effect of the first event was to leave Maris horribly isolated. All season long, he had been able to dodge a good deal of pressure by playing in Mantle's substantial shadow. Mantle was no master of the press, but he had nearly a decade's worth of experience under the microscope to sustain him, and he had learned the art of the amusing one-liner. Maris was twenty-six, inexperienced with the press and utterly artless in conversation. Never was the difference between them more pronounced than at the end, when Mantle dropped out of the race. Reporters swept in for comments, and Mantle fended them off with a little joke about the record Babe Ruth and Lou Gehrig set in 1927 for the most home runs in a season by a pair of teammates. Ruth hit 60 and Gehrig 47.

"I've caught my guy," Mantle said, referring to Gehrig. "Now it's up to Roger to get his."

Maris was all alone. And he couldn't hit the ball out of the park. The reaction of the press and the fans was instantaneous. He'd have a three-hit and see nothing in the headlines but his failure to club a home run. He'd swing violently at the ball and hear nothing but questions about whether he was chasing bad pitches. Maris began to despair that nothing he could do was right. One night it got so bad he holed up after the game in the trainer's room, off limits to the press, talking to his brother.

He was crucified. MARIS SULKS IN TRAINER'S ROOM AS FUTILE NIGHT CHANGES MOOD, the *New York Times* headlined. "How does Maris feel?" the *Times* reporter asked. "Well, he didn't say. Maris wouldn't say anything."

"If there is a slight sound of triumphant laughter from above, Babe's ghost is chortling," wrote Joe Trimble of the *New York Daily News*. "Maris secured himself in the trainer's quarters of Tiger Stadium . . . looking like a culprit trying to hide."

It was crazy. Here was a twenty-six-year-old kid from Fargo with 56 home runs, fifth-best total in baseball history with two weeks left in the season, and the papers said he was sulking, called him a culprit, had Ruth mocking him from the great beyond. "I can't take it anymore, Mick," Maris said to Mantle.

"Rog, you've got to," Mantle answered.

Maris broke out of his slump, but he couldn't get a break. He hit number 57 in Tiger Stadium. Al Kaline, a gentle man much beloved by the press, picked up the ball as it bounced off the upper deck and tossed it into the Yankee dugout so Maris could have it for a souvenir.

"Don't you think it was a nice gesture for Kaline to get the ball for you?" Maris was asked.

"I appreciate it. But I guess anyone would have done it."

An ingrate.

The next day he hit number 58. No one but Ruth had ever hit more. "It means an awful lot. It's something to think about," Maris said.

An inarticulate bumpkin.

With three games left before Frick's deadline, the Yankees headed to Baltimore, where the stray winds of hurricane Esther were moaning toward home plate. King Kong couldn't hit the ball out in that wind. In the first two games, Maris had no homers.

A choker.

The day of the 154th game, the wind was howling again. In his second at-bat, Maris smashed the ball into the teeth of the gale. It rose on a low line to right, rose, rose, then settled into the stands — number 59.

He went to the plate two more times, failing to homer both times. After the game he said: "Commissioner Frick makes the rules. If all I'm entitled to is an asterisk, then it will be all right with me. I'm the luckiest hitter in baseball history. I had my chance and I didn't quite make it."

In the many years since Maris played, a huge industry has sprung up trading in arcane analysis of baseball history and statistics and performances, a multimillion-dollar enterprise that endlessly generates ever more detailed encyclopedias and abstracts and computer programs. Probably the most immense project turned out by this industry is a seven-pound volume called *Total Baseball,* which — after all its data crunching and combing of trivia — sums up the strange story of Roger Maris with this simple sentence:

If he'd hit 59, he'd have been a hero.

It's a remarkable thing to say, and entirely true. If Maris had stalled at 59, if he had left undisturbed the ghost of Babe Ruth, if he had stopped just short of the summit, he would be remembered today as an intense, private man who strove valiantly and failed. Those gracious words — "I'm the luckiest hitter in baseball history. I had my chance and I didn't quite make it" — would be quoted fondly as an example of inspiring humility. Few things are as admired in this world as grace in defeat.

But Maris was not defeated. He pushed ahead to hit his 60th and 61st home runs. The mere mortal rushed headlong into Ruth's temple and left with the Mighty One's most cherished possession. It was as if Prometheus, a mere Titan, had once again stolen fire from Zeus, king of the gods.

Roger Maris could play baseball. In 1960 and 1961, he played baseball about as well as it can be played. Over two seasons, he racked up 100 home runs, scored 230 runs, hit safely 300 times, batted in 254 runs and earned a Gold Glove on defense. He became one of the only nine players in history to win the Most Valuable Player award in two consecutive seasons.

Roger Maris was not an adroit celebrity, however. When America's mythmakers draped the cloak of heroism around his shoulders, he let it fall in a heap to the floor. Roger Kahn, author of *The Boys of Summer,* followed Maris for several weeks at the end of the 1961 season, an experience he recounts in his recent *Games We Used to Play.*

Over the phone, Kahn reminisces about the downfall of Roger Maris. "You never got the feeling he enjoyed the attention," Kahn says. "But basically, he was very cooperative. He never denied anybody access. He didn't curse anybody out. He answered every question he was asked. The problem was, some people didn't like the answers."

Kahn recalls some of the questions Maris endured. From a reporter for *Time* magazine: "Do you play around on the road?"

Maris didn't. What he did on the road was go to Mass every Sunday. What he did was visit sick kids in the hospital, never bothering to alert the press. To the man from *Time* he said simply, "None of your fucking business."

Another guy asked, "Who's your favorite female singer?" and when Maris said he didn't have one, followed up with, "Is it all right if I put down Doris Day?"

"How can you put down Doris Day when I just told you I don't have one?" Maris snapped.

"You have to remember, this was in the days before the media blitz," says Kahn. "You might call it the dawn of the media blitz. The Yankees did nothing to protect Roger; they had no experience with this kind of thing."

Earlier Yankees mastered their own publicity, he says. "Joe DiMaggio ran a brilliant PR operation out of Toots Shor's restaurant. Casey Stengel knew the circulation of every newspaper that ever covered the Yankees. If Arthur Daley or Red Smith called from the *New York Times,* he'd give them all the time in the world, but if the guy called from the Albany *Knickerbocker News,* it was a different matter."

In his long career on the field and in the broadcast booth, Tony Kubek has seen a lot of ballplayers under a lot of pressure. He wrote a book about the Yankees' glorious season in which Maris figures prominently, called *Sixty-One.* He says: "I don't know if there's ever been an athlete under more intense pressure for a longer period of time than Roger Maris. I remember Roger talking for hour after hour after hour with the press. And this was a guy who had to be pushed out of the dugout to tip his hat after he hit his 61st home run. It wasn't something that he enjoyed or that came naturally.

"The Yankees didn't organize a single press conference the whole season. Nowadays, you have Nolan Ryan answering a half-hour of questions a week, period, with provisions for another half-hour if he pitches a no-hitter. Roger was completely on his own."

It was like leaving a pipe fitter in charge of laser surgery. The art of celebrity is a precise and delicate art; Maris was an artless man. Or rather, his art was in his actions, in his compact, lightning swing, his violent slides into second to break up the double play. Not in his speeches. Roger Kahn remembers being flabbergasted when, near the end of the 1961 season, he had to introduce Maris to Red Smith, the dean of New York's sports writers. Maris had no idea who Smith was — and he didn't care.

Maris tried letting his actions on the field speak for him. It didn't work. Eventually, he simply stopped trying.

Spring training, 1962. Jimmy Cannon, the irascible and influential sports columnist, strode to the batting cage and demanded an exclusive interview with Maris. Maris said he was trying to practice. Cannon punished the offense with a vicious column, titled "Roger the Whiner." Other writers rushed to Cannon's side. "If it weren't for sports writers, Roger Maris would probably be an $18-a-week clerk at the A&P back in Missouri," wrote Tommy Devine in the *Miami News*. Quite a thing to say about a man who had just hit 61 home runs.

That same spring, a photographer asked Maris to pose for a photo alongside Rogers Hornsby, a nasty old man who was, in his day, one of the finest hitters baseball has ever seen.

"Let's get the two rajahs together," the photographer said.

Maris was stunned. The previous season Hornsby had gone out of his way to belittle Maris and denounce the assault on Ruth's record. "Roger Maris couldn't carry Babe Ruth's jock," Hornsby had said.

Maris looked at the photographer and said, "Fuck Rogers Hornsby."

Simple. Direct. Disastrous.

Then there was the ultimate, irreversible shortcoming of Roger Maris: he failed to hit 61 homers again. In 1962 he smacked 33, which would have led the league in six of the past thirty seasons. He was booed nearly every time he took the field.

The boos finally got to him in 1963. A fan was heckling Maris from the right-field stands in Minneapolis; Maris turned and shot out his middle finger. The exasperated gesture became one of the most talked about events of the season.

"Other players have done worse, and protests have been minor. With Maris, it became a national issue," wrote Robert Creamer, the author of a splendid biography of Ruth. "Why? . . . Because he has proved to be such an unsatisfactory hero."

There was a time — gone, but not long gone — when the world was obsessed with achievements: *higher, stronger, faster,* the Age of Great Aspirations. In those days heroes walked the earth, cloaked in simple magnificence. From some hidden wellspring in the soul of the age, sublime challenges issued ceaselessly. A solo flight across the trackless Atlantic Ocean. A trek to the top of Everest. There were doctors who theorized that the four-minute barrier for the mile run was so deeply woven into the fabric of nature that a man would fall dead if he burst through the wall. They seemed impossible, these goals.

They seemed impossible, that is, until a hero rose up to conquer them. Glory, laud and honor fell to those who met each new challenge. A giddy thing it was to be alive in the Age of Great Aspirations, and this public giddiness forgave any shortcomings the heroes might have. Of those who broke the records, shattered the limits, did the impossible, little else was required. Once Charles Lindbergh had flown the Atlantic, it hardly mattered that he became an apologist for Hitler. His heroism was secure. Once Babe Ruth had hit 60 home runs, no one remarked when he drunkenly disrupted the funeral home where his noble teammate Lou Gehrig was laid out in his coffin.

Roger Maris grew up in that era, a time when a single glorious deed could speak louder than a lifetime of ill-chosen words. Things changed, however, and Maris, perhaps more than anyone else, was punished by the new paradigm. Today he stands out as one of the last men to punch through a seemingly insuperable barrier — along with the early astronauts — for in the years since 1961, science and technology and a general jadedness have virtually erased any notion of the impossible. Achievements that would have seemed miraculous in the Age of Great Aspirations now strike us as almost mundane. Then, records and barriers were things to be reverenced and marveled over. Now they are made to be broken. A man could dance a jig over the virgin dust of Mars and not stir a fraction of the awe that greeted Lindbergh when he landed outside Paris.

When Maris wasn't looking — when nobody was looking — someone rewrote the rule book. The fact that an athlete had broken a great record, instead of being cause for celebration, became a disturbing indication that the world had slipped its moorings.

But we never lose our need for heroes. And so, as the glory of achievements has diminished, the demand on our heroes to be "satisfactory" as celebrities has increased, in a lockstep equation. As we care less for what people *accomplish*, we care more about how they *appear*. Judge Wapner of *The People's Court*, we learn, is the most admired jurist in America. We reverence the image over the deed. A poll of schoolchildren today is likely to find that the person they admire most in the world is Madonna, the greatest manipulator of public images of our time.

Or perhaps the children would say Norman Schwarzkopf. No

matter. The general himself is a sign of the topsy-turvy nature of the New Heroism. Historians may one day examine the hero-making of Norman Schwarzkopf and marvel at the strangeness of it. For nearly six months, the general commanded a truly remarkable buildup of forces thousands of miles from home. His logistical achievement in moving half a million troops to a distant desert in so little time, fully supplying and deploying them, ranks among the great military feats of all time.

It is scarcely mentioned by Schwarzkopf mythmakers.

Instead, what made Schwarzkopf a hero was the Mother of All Briefings. A television performance! Clad in his camouflage, mugging for the cameras, the general recounted a plan of attack that he had little to do with developing. It was mapped out by a group of officers-in-training at a college in Kansas. Television analysts and newspaper reporters had been describing it in detail for months. Of all the Gulf War accomplishments, the strategy of the attack was perhaps the smallest.

Schwarzkopf was crowned a hero not for his genuine achievements but for his on-camera demeanor. In war, the forge of epic heroes, the identification of celebrity with heroism became complete.

Roger Maris eventually left the Yankees, a chorus of jeers ringing in his ears. The 1965 season was a bitter one: Maris chipped a bone in his wrist and struggled through a painful year as one doctor after another insisted nothing was wrong. In interviews, Yankees management implied Maris was faking injuries, giving fans and writers another reason to hate him. By the time the bone chip was discovered and surgically removed, Maris has lost the power in his wrists that is so crucial to a long-ball hitter.

He also lost his will to play ball. He planned to quit at the end of the 1966 season. Then August Busch, owner of the St. Louis Cardinals, enticed him into the National League with the promise of a Budweiser distributorship after he retired — basically a guarantee of lifetime economic security.

To Maris's surprise, the St. Louis fans greeted him with cheers and applause, and he answered them gratefully with the brand of baseball he was born to play. Talk to the men who played baseball with Maris and they will fill you with stories of his fielding, his bunting, his baserunning. The home runs, they will tell you, distracted from the subtler, more rounded excellence of his game. Distracted the fans, and distracted Maris. With the Cardinals, in the twilight of his career, he briefly reasserted himself as an all-around player.

The opening game of the 1967 season painted the picture. Maris hit a ground ball to advance a runner in his first at-bat, stretched a single into a double in his second appearance, and bunted for a base hit on his third trip to the plate. A veteran ballplayer, his head down and his knees churning, straining toward first to beat out a bunt — could this be Roger Maris, the sulky slugger?

The fans gave him a standing ovation.

"The people were cheering for me," he said. "It was strange hearing it."

By then, however, it was too late. Though Maris was still good enough to start in right field for a team that won back-to-back pennants, he was not good enough to make the world forget what had gone before.

Now and then, a fan will wonder aloud whether Maris belongs in the Hall of Fame. Some of the men who played with him and against him — men like Mantle, Bob Cerv, Rocky Colavito — say he belongs in Cooperstown. Certainly he was better than a number of players who have been honored. His two greatest seasons, 1960 and 1961, were of the highest caliber. In twelve years in the big leagues, he played in seven World Series, scoring more Series' runs than all but five players in history.

But the bottom line simply does not add up. Maris retired with 275 home runs and a career batting average of .260. He never won a second Gold Glove. He scored 100 runs in a season only once. He struck out more than he walked.

And so it is that most players remember him with a certain sadness, and use words like "underrated" to describe him. The word captures, in simple language, their sense of a great player trapped in a low-gloss persona. When he broke Ruth's record, Maris was expected to be superhuman; when he was not superhuman, he was judged to be a failure. He was crushed by the weight of what he had done.

If he'd hit 59, he'd have been a hero.

Some Maris haters have made a virtual art of running down his stunning performance in 1961. They point out that the American League had expanded, which meant more pitchers, which meant that some guys who should have been in the minor leagues were playing in the majors. They theorize that the ball must have been livelier than usual. They say Maris couldn't have done it without Yankee Stadium's short right-field fence. Or they blame the batting order: Maris hit before Mantle, the theory goes, so pitchers were afraid to walk him.

But the fact is that the major leagues have expanded by an additional eight teams since 1961 and no one has hit more than 52 home runs in a year. Maybe the ball *was* livelier; 1961 was an unusual year for homers across the American League, with the Yankees setting the all-time mark for home runs by a team. The record they broke, though, was the one set by Ruth's 1927 Yankees. Maybe the Babe was hitting a souped-up ball himself. As for the short right-field fence: it was built for Babe. If it explains away Maris, why wouldn't it explain away Ruth? Fact is, it *doesn't* explain away Maris, who hit 31 of his 61 homers on the road.

Maris batted ahead of Mantle; Mantle batted ahead of Yogi Berra, who retired with just three fewer career home runs than the great DiMaggio; Berra batted ahead of Elston Howard, who batted ahead of Bill Skowron. There has never been such a nightmare for opposing pitchers. Maris wasn't the only guy in baseball who got a boost from the man hitting behind him.

There's something small and mean-spirited at the heart of this exercise, picking away at Maris's record like a scab. If any old chump can hit 61 homers, how come no one else has?

Roger Maris did have the satisfaction of seeing Ford Frick's ruling fall into disgrace. With each passing year, the decision to end the home run race at 154 games became more ridiculous. For one thing, it was based on an error: because of a quirk in the rain-out rule, Ruth's Yankees actually played 155 games in 1927. For another thing, the ruling was tinged by dishonesty. If Frick's genuine intention was to equalize the conditions faced by Maris and Ruth, he should have counted balls that bounded over the fence as home runs for Maris. That's the way they were counted in Ruth's day. Maris bounced at least two out of the park in 1961. They counted for doubles. If he had been batting alongside

Ruth in 1927, those two balls would have given Maris the record in 151 games.

Most of all, Frick's ruling was plain unfair. Since 1961, scores of records have been set by players who played out their careers during the era of the 162-game season. Only Maris bears a stigma.

For his audacity in stealing fire from Zeus, Prometheus was chained to a mountainside and condemned to have his liver perpetually devoured by a vulture. It's sorrowful to think of him there, that overachieving Titan, feeling his guts being torn away hour after hour.

Clete Boyer tells the story of Roger Maris in the years after his retirement, secure in his family and with a prosperous beer distributorship, painstakingly poring over films of himself as a player. He searched his own batting stance, his grip, the sweep of his swing. He riddled over the grainy images for an answer to the questions he had pondered over and over again. Where did his power come from? Where did it go?

What went wrong?

Perhaps the answer was not on film. Perhaps it was locked away in the mind of Roger Maris, a small voice off in a corner warning him urgently of the perils of audacity. Maris learned too late that he was not cut out to be a hero in an upside-down time. He felt too sharply the vulture at his guts. It is easy to imagine that Maris spent the years after 1961 trying to atone for his presumption, to give back the fire he had stolen.

Cancer consumed him in 1985. Roger Maris was buried under Fargo's icy December earth. Mickey Mantle, haunted by the specter of his father's early death, avoided funerals for thirty-four years. He showed up to bury Roger Maris. Bobby Richardson delivered the eulogy.

It was a cloudy day of bitter cold. The aging men who, on a sun-dappled Sunday in a distant October, watched Maris do the impossible shivered helplessly in their dark suits.

The sun eked faintly through the gray, then disappeared. As the mourners turned from the bare grave and headed to their cars, no shadows followed them.

TIMOTHY DWYER

Center of Gravity

FROM THE PHILADELPHIA INQUIRER MAGAZINE

FROM THE MOMENT you step out of the plane, your senses are assaulted by the armies of misery. What's that smell? Rotting human waste and smoldering wet leaves, and while you're sniffing, random flies are rocketing up your nostrils and lighting in your eyes. Only a moment has passed and balls of sweat are rolling down the small of your back as you try walking from the plane, which is a little dicey because a morning rain has turned the runway into cake batter. The air hangs like a wet towel and it takes all the energy you can muster to keep swatting away the flies that are now swarming all over you, and suddenly your eyes adjust to the equatorial sunlight and you see thousands of people standing before you, staring.

They are more bones than flesh and they are dressed in rags or nothing at all and they are staring at you anxiously because you have just stepped out of an airplane and an airplane to them means one of two things: they will be either fed or bombed. And as they stand there waiting to see which it will be this time, a murmur rises among them as they realize that this plane has brought neither food nor bombs, but a brother.

Manute Bol unfolds his endless legs with the dignity of a great Dinka chief, ducks under a wing and comes face to face with their naked despair. An old woman steps out of the crowd, and then two more, and together they walk up to him with tears in their eyes. One puts a hand to her shrunken bosom and pounds her heart with an exaggerated beat. She is weeping and shaking her head in disbelief.

Manute touches her shoulder gently and speaks to her in his native Dinka tongue, which only speeds her pounding hand and her tears. Then he looks up and speaks in English: "She is from my village. She knew me when I was growing up. Now she lives here."

She is swathed in rags, and skin hangs off her cheekbones like frostbitten leaves. He is wearing a fresh cotton jersey and designer jeans and a fine gold watch that catches the sun and passes it on in little beams of light. "They can't believe I'm here," he says, again in English.

Here is Pochala, in the southern Sudan, a land once ruled by tribal chiefs and ancient traditions, a land where death is now king.

Manute Bol has returned to this place to help his people. He is a basketball millionaire, rich beyond comprehension to villagers who measure wealth in ears of corn. He has come back to witness the horror of their foodless lives so he can return to his adopted home in the United States and spread their story and raise money to send them beans and grain.

But he has returned for another reason, too: when he left eight years ago, Manute left his heritage, his family, his identity as a Dinka. He was born to a noble family of cowherders; his grandfather, rich and mighty by the standards of his people, had fifty-seven wives and too many cows to count. War has made everyone poor, but Manute's relatives have maintained their status by taking prominent roles in the fight.

By coming back, by reaching out for the shoulder of the woman weeping in front of him, by embracing the orphans of famine, Manute was doing much more than staging a public relations homecoming. He was setting out to reclaim his nobility.

The village where he grew up is gone, destroyed in the civil war that has smoldered in the Sudan for the last eight years. Since Manute came to the United States in 1983 to play basketball at the University of Bridgeport and then in the NBA, he has stayed out of the politics of his homeland. It was a practical decision. His heart was with the Dinka-dominated rebels in the south, but the Muslim government in the north controlled his passport (and thus his career). He was also afraid. He still had family in the

Sudanese capital of Khartoum, and he didn't know what would happen to them if he publicly took the rebels' side.

This year he changed his mind. He met rebel leader John Garang in Washington and was shocked by Garang's account of how bad things had gotten back home. People had been driven from their villages and had sought refuge in Ethiopia. In June and July, civil war there had forced them back to the Sudan, where they gathered in shelterless villages and waited with sinking hope as the rainy season turned the tiny runways to swamps and they were forced to eat grass and bugs to survive.

Manute had felt some pressure from his family to do something. His cousins have been fighting in the bush for six years without coming out to see their families. His uncle Justin Yaac Arop, an obstetrician trained at the University of London, is a high-ranking officer in the rebel army and a top political adviser to Garang.

Manute could not fight like his uncles and cousins and play in the NBA, too, but he could help their cause — not only by making his support public but also by raising money for the refugees of the south. Last spring, he formed a fund-raising group and began making arrangements to visit one of their camps. His plan was to videotape his visit and use the footage to persuade people to donate.

When the 76ers' season ended, he took his wife and children to his off-season home in Cairo. Then, in July, he kissed them goodbye, packed up his custom-made suits and NBA sweats, and checked into a $300-a-night suite atop the Nairobi Safari Club hotel to wait for the details of his trip to be ironed out.

Hundred-dollar hightops and a megasalary have not made him a Western man. In Nairobi, surrounded by cousins, playing pickup basketball, speaking Dinka, he was more relaxed than he's ever been in an NBA locker room. Still, he was a fistfighter when he was young, his cousins said, partly because he was defensive about his freakish height and partly because he just had a bad temper. And that ornery streak, mixed with one part princely heritage and one part American celebrity, makes for an explosive personality. Impatience is a Western disease, and Manute has picked up a good dose.

Time passes indefinitely in Africa. When someone says something will take a few minutes, it really means hours. And though Manute's trip had been arranged well in advance through rebel contacts in Washington, when he arrived in Nairobi he found that there was no plane to take him to the Sudan. No one in the rebel organization was surprised that their counterparts in Washington had failed to tell them of Manute's trip, and no one seemed to share his sense of urgency. No problem — there would be other planes and other days.

So for seven straight days Manute sat in his suite, a captive of Dinka bureaucracy. His phone rang constantly and meetings were convened several times a day, the meetings led to promises that the trip was only hours away, and the hours became days and room service was called and meals were taken and waiters came and went constantly smiling at the big man in bed, whose only escape from African time was two hours of basketball daily at a local gym. Each day as he woke up to more phone calls and more discussions and more reassurances and more staying put, he got a little more on edge.

And then, after all promises had been broken and all hope collapsed, he got on a shoebox of a plane and flew to his past, to this place.

Word of his arrival spreads quickly through the camp, and more and more people make their way to the edge of the runway to get a glimpse of him. Teenage boys armed with fresh switches stand between the growing crowd and the plane to keep them from overwhelming the seven foot seven pilgrim.

Two leaders step forward to greet him, one a teacher and the other a local representative of the Sudanese Rescue and Relief Association (SRRA), a humanitarian arm of the rebels.

Like most of the top rebel leaders, both men are Dinkas. Each one in turn places his right hand on Manute's left shoulder and exchanges greetings in Dinka. The language sounds singsongy and is punctuated with tongue clucks, which mean "yes" or "O.K."

They take their hands back and then speak English. "We were not expecting you," says the rebel representative. "We were not told you were coming."

Three other men make their way toward the plane. They

stand tall, well over six feet, obviously Dinkas. Scars line their ebony foreheads, the result of a traditional Dinka ceremony that celebrates their manhood by cutting lines into their heads. It gives them a fierce look, but it is deceptive. They go right for Manute, who breaks into a wide smile — one of few smiles of the day — when he sees them. This time, they forgo the hand-on-the-shoulder greeting and exchange a series of palm slaps and belly laughs while speaking excitedly in Dinka.

"I used to play ball with these guys," Manute says in English. Then he looks at their tattered clothes and sunken cheeks and his smile disappears. His friends haven't played basketball in years. They recently finished a walk of many miles from their refugee camp. It took two weeks because it was the rainy season and the swamps and rivers were swollen to a murderous level.

"Many, many people died because the walk was too difficult," says the teacher. "Others were swept away when we crossed the rivers. And now we are here and there is no food. We get fifty grams of beans a day, sometimes every other day. We used to get eight hundred [in Ethiopia]. Sometimes there isn't enough, and only those who are most in need get the food. Also, there are eighty-nine hundred orphans. They are the worst off because they have nobody to look after them. They live an hour's walk from here. They come here once a day to get their food."

The teacher asks Manute if he would like to take a tour of the camp. There are times when Manute has the look of a child in his eyes, part fear, part innocence — just as he has now — but he nods his head yes. Someone pulls out a bullhorn and parts the crowd with a command in Dinka. Manute walks away from the plane with his head pointed down. He walks like this out of habit, for he must always look down into the face of whoever speaks to him, but the posture gives him a humble appearance. When he reaches the edge of the crowd, he is swallowed by three or four hundred people, all of whom want to touch him.

For the next four hours he walks through the camp, always with hundreds of people around him, pushing to get close to him, reaching out to him, grasping for one of his massive hands, as if his touch can somehow lift them out of their desolation.

*

The suite at the Nairobi Safari Club was full of Dinkas. It was after noon and Manute was still in bed. He appeared to be naked beneath a sheet that was pulled up to his waist. A business suit was folded over a chair, and a pair of red bikini briefs was dangling over the bedroom door like drying laundry.

"What's up, dude?" he said, his traditional English greeting.

It was Wednesday, and Manute had arrived from Cairo the night before. Six other men were in the room, most of them his cousins, others acquaintances who would become a fixture of his Nairobi entourage — guys who would answer the phone, call room service and get the door. Manute was in a good mood, looking forward to his visit to the Sudan.

In fact, he was eager to go, since he had scheduled a trip to another refugee camp in Mozambique for the following Tuesday. He had to be in and out of the Sudan by then. But he was confident that it would take only two or three days because the SRRA office in Washington told him the trip was all set up. That seemed to be all he needed.

The rebel movement comprises three wings — the army, the political organization and the SRRA, which coordinates food and other relief efforts in the southern Sudan. Since the rebels control most of the south, you must get an entrance visa from the SRRA. Neither the SRRA nor the rebel army has its own airplanes, so the SRRA depends on international relief organizations like the International Red Cross, the World Lutheran Federation, and the United Nations for transportation. The dependence, however, is mutual: relief planes can't enter rebel-held areas without SRRA permission.

On his first day in Nairobi, Manute got a suggestion of the week to come. Someone had neglected to inform SRRA headquarters in Nairobi of his trip. A plane on Wednesday? Impossible. Perhaps Friday. Yes, there was a plane on Friday, but there were only two empty seats. Manute had been promised five. The following Tuesday was the earliest five seats could be found. Manute got all this bad news on Wednesday afternoon, by phone, as he lay in bed apparently naked, surrounded by his Dinka cousins.

The tall man was not pleased. First, he spit out a ten-minute diatribe in Dinka accompanied by much arm waving, and followed that with an explosion in English. "These people are bull-shit," he fumed. "We're not dealing with them anymore. I'm pay-ing three hundred dollars a night for this room and I got to sit here till Friday. That's bullshit. The man at the SRRA office is bullshit. The chairman [John Garang] told me everything was arranged. This is bullshit. I'm here to raise money for them and they treat me like this!"

Jane Mulavi, the woman who runs the SRRA office, was deter-mined to make clear to Manute that he would not get home with-out dealing with her first. She curtly informed him that everyone would need an SRRA-issued visa to enter the rebel-occupied Su-dan. And everyone — even Manute Bol — would have to come to the SRRA office outside Nairobi to fill out the form. Manute tried to impress her by mentioning his friendship with John Gar-ang, but she repeated that he would not go without getting a form from her.

"I don't need no paper to go into Sudan," he seethed. "I got a Sudanese passport. What do I need a visa for? This is bullshit. I'm not going anywhere. If they want me to fill it out, they can bring it here."

The doorbell rang and a waiter entered carrying a tray of Ken-yan beer. There were already a half-dozen empty beer bottles scattered around the room, apparently from the night before. Someone suggested that Manute relax and have a beer. "I don't like Kenyan beer, it's bullshit!" he yelled. "I'm a Heineken man!"

On Wednesday afternoon, the twin-engine Aero Commander was in pieces on the hangar floor. "Broken wing," said the pilot, an American mercenary who makes several trips a week into the rebel-occupied Sudan. The pilot, who asked that his name not be used, charters his plane according to the politics of cash flow. He flew reconnaissance missions in Vietnam, and that experience serves him well, since he has to stay out of the way of the Su-danese air force — a small cadre of Soviet MiGs and a few high-altitude transport planes that are used periodically to drop bombs on rebel areas.

"I think the wing will be stronger than it was before," said the pilot, searching through his red toolbox for a wrench. But he couldn't possibly get the plane in the air before Tuesday.

This plane on the hangar floor was the one that the SRRA was trying to get to take Manute Bol into the Sudan. Manute is afraid of flying. I decided not to tell him about the plane.

The teacher: his title is director of education for the village, but there is little teaching going on in Pochala these days. "At present the priority is actually food," says Mechak Ajang Alaak. Then, like a good teacher, he makes a list of the camp's priorities: "Number one is food. Number two is medicine. Number three is shelter — tents, sheets and blankets. Number four is tools and equipment. Number five is material for clothing."

Water, he says, is also a problem. Though the Akobo River is a few hundred yards away and it is full of fish, there are no nets to catch the fish. So people starve. And the water is not clean, so people drink it and get sick. Why do they drink the dirty water? "You cannot talk of what is clean, but what is available," says the teacher.

The temperature is about 90 degrees and the air is dead humid, but he is wearing a down jacket. The teacher, like everyone else in the camp, wears everything he owns. Mechak Ajang Alaak is not a missionary. He is stuck here like everyone else. His belly is empty and he worries about when he will eat next, not what he will teach. He is not certain he will ever teach again, for that matter. "The future is something you cannot determine now," he says.

The doctor: he is not feeling well. He had bad diarrhea. But each day, he goes to his clinic under the big tree, where he sees five hundred people a day. Once, he had a house and a car and a good private practice. Now, like everyone else in Pochala, he has nothing. He was chased from his village by government troops.

"The main cause was that they thought I was cooperating with the rebels and they would kill me," says Bellario Ahoy Ngong.

"Were you cooperating?"

He smiles and says only, "I am now."

Each day, he does what he can for the sick without benefit of medicine or equipment. A stick lady lies shivering under a blanket; a boy has an open, running sore on his ankle the size of a grapefruit. "Tropical ulcer, we call them," says the doctor. "We are at an emergency state," he says quietly. "All of the health problems you can imagine are with us." Then he goes back to his patients under the tree.

The priest: he is called Father Dominic. He wears a beret and spectacles. He, too, is sick. Rheumatism. There is much work here for a priest, he says. He says it is not difficult for him to convince those stuck here that they must not lose their faith in God.

"That is the only thing they have left is their faith," he says. "I tell them that there is a story in the Bible about food and desperation. It is when Christ turns the rocks into bread."

It is the bombs that Father Dominic has a hard time explaining. Ten days before Manute arrived, the government bombed Pochala. At first, people thought the planes were dropping food and they did not seek shelter. When they heard the bombs, they panicked. Luckily, the bombers were not accurate. No one was hurt.

Many of the villagers have asked Father Dominic how the government could be so cruel as to bomb them, since they are already starving. "I just tell them it is the policy of a tyrannical government."

How do you explain that in terms of their faith? he is asked. How can you convince them that God loves them or even cares about them if He allows this to happen to them?

Father Dominic shrugs his shoulders. He says he has no answer.

It was late in the afternoon before Bol finally got out of bed Thursday. He was dressed in Washington Bullets sweats, ready to go play some basketball with a local industrial team. His suite was still thick with Dinkas. I had brought him his SRRA visa application, but Bol was still in a snit about it.

"I'm not filling it out," he said, and then let go with a gale of Dinka to his cousins.

"You have to fill it out," I said, "or they will not let us go."

"No," he said, and disappeared into the bathroom.

"You want to come this far and then not be able to go because you won't fill out a form?" I shouted. "Fill it out!"

"You fill it out," he snapped. "You know my name."

It was like talking to a spoiled child or, worse, a spoiled professional athlete, someone who was used to getting his way and getting everyone to do everything for him.

"Manute, I'm not your fucking secretary. Now fill out the fucking form!"

His cousins waited for Mount Manute to blow. They had seen it many times before. Fighting among boys is a part of the Dinka tradition, a part of growing up. Even after Manute left his village, for a school in Khartoum with a basketball program, he would fight anyone who teased him about his height. Then he would throw rocks as they ran from him. But I didn't know about his famous temper. His cousins filled me in later.

Manute surprised everyone when he came out of the bathroom laughing. "Dude, you're crazy," he said to me and offered his palm for a low five. "O.K.," he said, "I'll fill it out."

I tossed the form and a pen at him. He struggled to read the questions, which were in English. "Occupation?" he said. "What should I put?"

"Basketball player," I said.

"B-A-S — how do you spell it?" he said.

Now I knew why he hadn't wanted to fill out the form. He has trouble reading and writing English. He's barely literate, I thought. But then I realized it was not a question of literacy. Dinka was his language, not English. He was not bilingual, but his English — written and spoken — was far better than my second-language skills.

Now I was embarrassed. I realized just how far Manute Bol had come since he had left the Sudan nine years ago. I took the form and finished filling it out. I'm sure he would have done the same for me if it had been in Dinka.

"We have to bring it back to the office tomorrow morning," I said. "We'll pick you up at eight-thirty."

"O.K., dude," he said. "My uncle is having a party for me tomorrow. All my family will be there. He wants you to come." He didn't wait for an answer. He just went back to speaking Dinka to his cousins.

The next morning, there was no answer at his door. Manute, like all NBA players, works mostly at night. He goes to bed late and sleeps in.

Finally he opened the door a crack, a sleeping giant. "What's up, dude?" he said testily. "I'm sleeping."

I reminded him of our appointment at the SRRA office. "I'll meet you there," he said, and slammed the door shut.

A while later, he called the SRRA office and asked for me. "I'm sorry," he said. "I was up, then fell asleep again. Can you give me directions to SRRA?"

When he showed up in a cab half an hour later, Jane Mulavi was stalking the office, as usual, in a gaily colored dress and bare feet. She greeted him with the cool eyes of an accountant. She still had not found a flight for him.

"The Red Cross will not take you on their planes," she said.

"Why?" he shouted.

"That's a good question," she said.

"*WHY?*" he shouted again, louder.

She just shrugged her shoulders and smiled.

"They say they don't want to take me because they work with the Sudan government and if they take me they will get in trouble with the Sudan government. Right? Right?"

She nodded yes.

"*So why couldn't you tell me that?*" he shouted.

She just smiled.

Manute was arrested in Khartoum in 1989 by the Sudan government. He was held for about eight hours before being released. "They said I was helping SPLA [the rebel army]," he said. "They were wrong. I was living in San Francisco then and raised money for something called Airlift for Africa. We sent food and blankets to Nairobi and they were for all of Sudan." He has not been back to Khartoum since. "They will throw my ass in jail if I go," he says.

Manute was supposed to meet the head of the SRRA that morning to make the final arrangements for his trip. But after he had waited two hours, Jane Mulavi told him that the man had left the office and would not be able to meet with him. She said she had not been able to find a plane.

"This is bullshit," Manute fumed. "Let's go."

Another trip to the hangar, without Manute, to check on the plane with the broken wing.

Now there were two wings on the plane but no seats, and one engine was still in parts on the hangar floor.

"I might be able to fly by Sunday," the pilot said with a straight face. "But I'd like to take it for a test flight first to see if the wing is going to hold together before I take anyone anywhere. All I have left to do, really, is get the wing painted and put the engine back."

I told him the SRRA had told Manute they were trying to hire his plane to take him to the Sudan tomorrow.

"Oh really?" he said. "That's interesting. Nobody's talked to me yet."

Manute's uncle Justin Yaac Arop lives in a duplex on the outskirts of Nairobi. It was a sweltering winter day. All the women were sitting outside under a carport. Though there was a stove in the kitchen, all the cooking was being done over an open fire in the back yard.

Only men were allowed in the house. The older men sat around a coffee table in the living room, and the younger men sat in two rows of chairs that had been set up in the dining room.

Manute sat at the head of the coffee table. Whenever another man arrived, he stood up and shook his hand. "Welcome," he said each time, in English. "Have a seat."

There were no empty seats in either room, but somehow each man's position in the family was silently appraised, and then someone gave up his seat. Most of the men sitting around the coffee table were veterans of the civil war.

"Before today," said a man sitting next to me, "I have not seen my family in seven years. I have been in the field."

He is Manute's uncle, but not one of his "close" uncles, not one he knows well. His name is Daniel Alcot, and he has three children. His wife was outside cooking, and his children were playing. He was drinking Kenyan beer.

"There was a lot of crying," he said of his family reunion, "a lot of clapping and hugging together. Photos were taken immediately. My children were very happy to have me back, but the small one cannot know me, only through photographs."

He said that after a few weeks at home, he would return to the bush to fight some more. How long would he continue to fight? "Until the war is over," he replied matter-of-factly.

All the men at the table were pleased that Manute had decided to visit the war zone. "It is important that he see his brothers and the children and see their pathetic state," said Alcot. "That in itself is important."

The table of uncles agreed that Manute was better off playing basketball and raising money than he'd be joining the rebel army. They said he would not make a good soldier. "He is too tall to be a soldier," one said. "He would be too big a target. The trees are too short for him to hide behind."

Manute did not laugh.

For the next hour, all the uncles discussed in Dinka Manute's problem in getting a flight. Manute said in English, "I'm not dealing with SRRA anymore. I went to meet the head of SRRA and he left the office without seeing me. How can he treat me like that?"

Another long discussion in Dinka followed. Then Manute said, "They say my Uncle Justin is talking to the chairman [John Garang] at this moment to straighten this out. That's why he is not here."

Everybody stood when Uncle Justin entered.

"Don't worry," he said. "I have just come from a meeting with the chairman, and he understands the importance of your trip. You will go." But Uncle Justin said he did not know when we would go or how we would get there. "Don't worry," he said. "The chairman is working on it."

Then it was time to eat. The women set up a gigantic buffet. "In Africa, the men always go first," said one uncle. All the men lined up and filled their plates. After them, the women came inside and took what was left. They ate outside with the children.

There is a surprise for Manute at the camp. He has met many cousins and friends from his youth, even men he played basketball with in Khartoum before the civil war began. He did not expect to see that many people. But neither did he expect to find the best man from his wedding, Bol Nyuon.

"When I tell my wife that I came here and met Bol, she is not going to believe it," Manute says. He and his best man keep looking at each other and saying nothing. There is nothing Manute can do for him. He cannot take him away; there is no room on the plane. So they look at each other and say nothing other than that they cannot believe they have met here in this place.

"I wanted to come here for a very long time so bad," Manute finally says. "Then to see all these cousins and nephews and uncles, I didn't know there would be so many of them here."

We are sitting in a tent now with the local rebel commander. He produces a metal fragment and says it is what's left of one of the bombs that was dropped ten day before we arrived.

"They just bombed this place?" Manute says, surprised. He told the SRRA repeatedly that he did not want to visit anywhere dangerous. "I have to be able to come back from wherever I go," he said.

Manute takes the fragment in his hand. "We have to convince people that people are dying here," he says, the anger rising in his throat, "that people are dying and need help. I did not know they had bombed this place. There are little babies here being bombed by a government. It's not right. They let them die by hunger and it's all right, but bombing little babies?"

Bol, the best man, stands at the entrance of the tent, staring at his cousin Manute. Manute catches his look and says again, "My wife will not believe I met you here."

Saturday afternoon, and Manute was just getting out of bed. He had stayed at his uncle's well past midnight and then gone to a Nairobi disco with his cousins.

"My uncle must not know that we went out after we left his house," Manute said. "My uncle used to like to go out when he was younger, but now he doesn't go out anymore and he doesn't want us to go out, either."

All the cousins laughed at having put one over on Uncle Justin.

A short time later Uncle Justin arrived at the hotel suite. He said arrangements had been made for a flight the next morning at 6 o'clock.

Manute promised to go to bed early.

At 1 A.M. the pilot phoned me: "You get another day of vacation. I took the plane up today and wasn't happy with it. Maybe we can go Monday."

At noon Sunday, there were more Dinkas than usual in Manute's suite. "I think we will go tomorrow," he said.

A waiter arrived with a tray full of Kenyan beers and Coca-Colas. One cousin grabbed a bottle of soda and opened it with his teeth. He did this several more times.

"We're going to the soccer game today," Manute announced, and dispatched a cousin to come up with nine tickets.

The Sudan was playing Kenya in a match to decide who would go to the African Games. One cousin said he would cheer for Kenya rather than support a team that was part of the Sudanese government.

"I'm supporting Sudan," Manute said. "I'm Sudanese."

Manute said he needed something to eat and something else to "get warm" for the game. He had eaten nine pancakes for breakfast, but now he was hungry again. He ate a club sandwich and had a couple of sherries chased with Kenya beer.

"I'm warmed up now," he said.

Traffic was heavy on the way to the stadium. "I have never seen so many cars pass a Mercedes," Manute said to the cab driver. "What's the matter, you don't know how to drive? If I was driving I would go down the side of the road and pass everyone."

The cab driver looked at the big man beside him and seemed ready to drive down the shoulder. "I'm just kidding, man," Manute said.

The game had started by the time Manute got to his seats down by the goal. But Manute would not sit. "These are not our seats. We paid two hundred shillings for these seats. We must be at mid-field. Let's go."

Everyone followed Manute to a gate at mid-field. "Let me ask you. In the States, if you pay two hundred dollars for a ticket, do you sit next to someone who paid one hundred? No! Thank you very much! Hey!" He shouted to a police officer at the gate. "Our seats are in here."

The office opened the gate, and Manute Bol walked down the seats until he found an empty one in the third row. As he walked the crowd recognized him and stood up and cheered. Manute waved and sat down.

The Sudan lost, 2–1.

By 10 P.M. the entourage, which had split up to eat and pack, had heard nothing from the pilot. Monday was the last day Manute could go. Everyone assumed the trip was off.

But at 12:30 Manute called. "The pilot just called me. We're leaving at 6 A.M. Can you call and wake me up?"

It was still dark when Manute went to the airport. We walked out to the tarmac, where there were several small planes. "Which one is ours?" he said.

I pointed it out.

"Where? That small one? No way, man. Too small. Where am I going to sit? A limousine is bigger than that plane. No way."

It looked big to me. But I had seen it in pieces just two days before.

He wanders the village always surrounded by children. He simply goes where the crowd takes him. He walks past three men squatting over half a dozen ears of corn. "This is the village marketplace," someone explains. He walks past a boy of four whose head is swollen to the size of a pumpkin, a head so heavy that the boy cannot hold it up himself, his sister must help. "It started swelling when he was one year old," a village elder explains. "No doctor can tell us what is causing it, and it won't stop."

Manute walks past an elderly woman lying in the middle of a grassy plot, naked, insanity in her eyes, bones outlined on her skin. He visits the clinic and then several grass huts where women hold half-dead infants to shrunken breasts. "I can't believe the kids," Manute says. He touches as many hands as he can and takes special care to pat the head of every child who works up the courage to approach this giant brother, this famous Dinka countryman, the great basketball player who left them all behind, became even richer than his grandfather and then still cared enough to come home.

He is one of them after all, isn't he? Then you look at Manute Bol and the little-boy look has captured his brown eyes and you realize that he must be thinking the very obvious, very horrible and very humbling thought: if he were a foot shorter, chances are he would be either living in a place like this or out fighting in the bush, a soldier in an endless civil war.

A three- or four-year old girl grabs Manute's hand and holds

on. He looks down and holds on tight until the girl's hand is replaced by another little hand, and then another and another.
With each passing moment, Manute looks more and more
drained.

And when it is time to leave, a thousand people gather in a
circle around him. He speaks in a voice so soft it hardly carries
ten feet. Clearly he is no public speaker, so uncomfortable and
unsure of what to say. But the naked and ragged people strain to
hear his words. One small boy stands in Manute's long shadow,
holding a cardboard model of a Red Cross relief plane, his connection to the outside world. Now he has another in Bol the basketball giant, and he drops the plane to his side and listens.

"I am not happy to be here today," Manute tells everyone, first
in Dinka and then in English, for the benefit of the crew that is
recording his visit. "But I will be happy to bring this videotape
back and try to help you." Though he speaks for about fifteen
minutes, he cannot come up with any message of hope for his
people. Only this: "Just ask God to get you through today and
tomorrow and then start again."

Spontaneous applause. Manute looks toward the ground and
moves his feet uneasily. It is time to go.

Just before he gets back on the plane, he gives away a jacket
someone let him borrow for the day and a couple of bottles of
water. He can do no more than that.

And as the plane leaves the muddy runway, Manute Bol sits
back in his seat and closes his eyes tight. He says he doesn't want
to talk at all, but a moment later he can't help himself: "Did you
see those kids? I can't believe those little kids." He lifts a giant
hand to his forehead, partially covering the four deep lines left
from the ceremony marking his passage from boyhood. Manute
was fourteen when he was cut to the bone, but he could not cry.
That's part of the ceremony. Now, there are no tears either.

"I can't believe that," he says, over and over again like a
stricken prince. "I'm dead," he says finally, closing his eyes. "I
feel dead."

MICHAEL DISEND

"A Painter on a Planet of Blind People"

FROM SPORTS ILLUSTRATED

JOE DURSO has been the greatest one-wall handball player for nearly a decade, but he's just as well known for his ferocious verbal assaults against his opponents. For both those reasons everybody wants to tear him down.

Today he's playing a pickup game against Abdul from Albania, a hotshot high schooler in New York City, where handball was once the preeminent adult participation sport. With his pencil mustache and cresting pompadour, Abdul comes off like another young Brooklyn stud on the rise. His mission: to whack Joe Durso and become Boss of All Handball Bosses.

This drama unfolds last summer on the municipal handball courts in Coney Island, where people drink lime rickeys and egg creams on the boardwalk, a knish toss from the center of the one-wall handball universe. Sea gulls whirl in crazy patterns overhead. In contrast to the urban rubble all about, the courts are as clean and white as altars. All the regulars are there to watch the match.

Durso, thirty-five years old at the time, is ultrafit and has male-model looks. At six foot one he is the tallest champ ever in a sport in which close-to-the ground guys are thought to have the edge — a concept backed up by the stature of most previous one-wall champs. Durso lets Abdul build an 8–2 lead and then, reluctantly, gets interested.

"Your death will be slow and excruciatingly painful," Durso

taunts Abdul, beginning the torrent of facile abuse that is his trademark.

Durso leaps, meets a ball in mid-flight, seems to plunge to the right and then, with a feathery stroke, taps the ball to the left corner. It strikes the wall about two inches above the court, hangs there, and rolls out flat. Unplayable. Abdul can only stumble helplessly after it.

Durso does variations on this theme until the score is tied. The mocking smile never leaves his face. He doesn't sweat or even breathe hard.

"You can see he's crushed," Durso says, laughing. "He's demoralized. All he wants to do is crawl under the boardwalk and cry."

"He's disasterizing the kid," says Stevie the Judo Man, one of Durso's cronies. "I ain't storybooking it. Joe is the da Vinci of handball."

Durso grins wolfishly at Abdul. Crouching into a sidearm serve, he snaps the ball into the far right corner so hard that the challenger doesn't even run for it. His dominance assured, Durso starts creating three-dimensional aerial patterns composed of ball-hitting-wall, ball-riding-air-currents. The effect is breathtaking. Stars and trapezoids magically are drawn, only to vanish. Then come other, even more complex, shapes as Durso wills them. The blue ball is his paintbrush. The looming wall his canvas. Elaborate masterpieces are created, vanish and are recreated in seconds.

"I'm like Jackson Pollock, submerged in my own creation," Durso boasts loudly.

"Sounds like a rock star who cleans pools," cracks a spectator.

The fans gawk as Durso, stationary in the middle of the court, sends Abdul on futile chases along the perimeter. Durso lifts the ball, changes its velocity, drops it in front of himself and whams unreachable angle shots with either hand. He finally cracks Abdul's composure with an array of velvety underhand taps, and he finishes the game with a precise crosscourt push shot for his twenty-first point, a shot that leaves the Albanian gasping. Abdul stalks off the court, fuming.

"Did you see that?" Durso asks, laughing. "Was it godlike? Olympian? Tell me the truth. It's like I'm a gyroscope! Spin me around and I never fall. Albert Einstein couldn't compute the physics of these shots. Nobody wants any part of me. It's pure pain."

Nobody laughs or applauds the world's foremost living one-wall player. Joe Durso has been trampling other players' egos on Surf Avenue for almost two decades, and as a result he is a man who inspires, at best, mixed emotions.

"He's head and shoulders above the players of today," says Howie Eisenberg, an eight-time one-wall national champion (six of those are doubles victories) and the former one-wall commissioner of the United States Handball Association. "There's no question that Joe Durso has been the best player for the last eight years or so."

Among Durso's detractors are many of the tanned Brooklyn oldies who haunt the courts to schmooze in the sun and the salt air. The menagerie includes Red Face Benjy, Pat the Butcher, Louie Shoes (he never plays in sneakers), Abe the Ganef (which translates from Yiddish as "thief," but implies a more or less lovable rascal). They tell you that handball by the sea is a healthy way of life. They tell you that Durso wouldn't last against the Depression-era players back in one-wall's golden age. They tell you that the way Durso behaves on the courts leaves a lot to be desired.

Morris Levitsky, the grizzled park historian who usually refs the money games, appraises Durso dourly. "Anybody involved with handball has a childish mind," says Levitsky.

A childish mind never stopped anyone from becoming a celebrity in America. But Durso — the holder of seventeen national one-wall titles, including ten singles titles, the last four in a row outdoors — is not a player in the wealth-and-fame department. In a mainstream sport he might be a legend, recommending orange juice and sneakers for a price, squiring starlets in and out of gossip columns. But this is *handball,* light-years off the sports-media and money loops. So Durso is stuck in Brooklyn, teaching math at David A. Boody Junior High, chatting up stray maidens on the boardwalk and performing arcane athletic wonders on the court while the world looks the other way.

Aficionados say handball is an elite sport, a game in which being ambidextrous is not merely an advantage, it is virtually a requirement. And it is the only game in which you *dive* headfirst on concrete. Like boxing, it's too painful for most people. If you get good at handball, you're in an elite within an elite.

If you get *great,* if you transcend the genre, you're a Steve Sandler, the king of one-wall handball from the late sixties to the mid-seventies. Sandler won *fifteen* national singles titles. He was so feared then that he had to play many games one-handed, lefty, just to get a match. Or you're a Joe Durso.

That status won't get you recognized in airports. As far as can be determined, the Betty Ford Center is devoid of addicted millionaire handball players.

After the game with Abdul, free as usual of media pressure, Durso breaks for lunch with Stevie the Judo Man. Sniffing the salt air and the aroma of cotton candy, Durso swings his eleven-year-old sports car up Surf Avenue. The streets are full of teen-agers; they are horsing around and shouting boisterously, maybe even menacingly. Durso turns back and cruises past the bumper-car arcade, the roller coaster, the dingy pizza parlors and the dark bars. He stops at a light. Nearby is a run-down shooting gallery. For a buck, a visitor can shoot an array of small animals clanking in and out of range on unseen belts. Hit anywhere near the target and a metal coyote snaps his head back and howls, "Owwwwwooooooooo! Oww Oww Owwwwwooooooooo!"

Durso looks at the coyote, perhaps sees something of himself in it, shudders and drives on.

He parks in front of Lulu's deli, in Brighton Beach. These days Brighton Beach is called Little Odessa. In the shadow of the elevated train tracks, where mobsters once carried tommy guns, hordes of Russian immigrants now troop in and out of stores carrying shopping bags filled with salamis as big as baseball bats, jars of pickled Danubian salad, loaves of crisp bread. On the sidewalk, a fiddler plays unfamiliar melodies.

"It's like I'm a painter on a planet of blind people," says Durso as he dips the end of a kasha knish in mustard. "My talent is almost like a curse. I achieved greatness in something that the world can't appreciate. The fact that I got supergreat just adds to the pathos. If I'm playing a guy who I know is unworthy, where's my motivation? If I play hard, I'm acknowledging that he's worthy for me to play against, which I can't do. Does McEnroe play pickup games in the park? Did Ali have street fights?"

Durso is shirtless, his torso bronzed. Some Russian girls in tight silk dresses eye him from the next table. He winks at them. They blush.

"While guys are just struggling to make points," he continues, "I'm way beyond that. I *know* I'm going to make the points. It's *how* I make them. It's a whole new level of being. What makes what I do trivial is the fact that handball is not in the American consciousness. That makes *me* look trivial. No matter how good *I* get, I can't get good enough to overcome the fact that the sport is not well known. I guess I must have the need to be loved."

Back at the courts, Durso stands in front of the handball doyens and stretches out his arms. "Who's the best who ever lived?" he asks. "Who towers over this game like the Colossus of Rhodes?"

The veterans snort and follow Durso with their eyes as he begins tracking a pretty blonde with a small white dog on a leash. In moments he is charming her, and she sways with laughter. The white dog nips at Durso's feet.

Rivalries are as bitter as those of a prison yard. The glory days of one-wall are long gone, and even then there was no money in it. But with thousands of concrete courts in playgrounds — plus a limitless supply of flat factory, warehouse, theater and garage walls — new blood always rises. Especially in black and Latino neighborhoods, where the game is having a resurgence. However, the ball of choice among the younger set is a racquetball — which is far easier on the palms than the smaller, harder handball. Durso is not so much of a purist that he refuses to play "big ball" handball.

Last summer, the comer was Buddy Gant, a spindly-legged black ace who dominated the courts on West Fourth Street in Greenwich Village, where the game is mostly big ball.

"When you going to play Buddy?" a Surf Avenue handball maven asks Durso between cigar puffs. "I got large cash on the guy."

"They'll stick your Gold Card in the coffin with you," says Durso. "It won't be long now."

A kingdom, however small, must be defended. Especially if your identity exists solely within its borders. Durso has a law degree, but he has not yet passed the New York State Bar exam.

Meanwhile, he spends his days at the handball courts — whipping two players at once using just his left hand and spotting them ten points — checking out the women and lamenting the fame that has eluded him.

"Where else can I go?" he asks.

Even the old masters, the stars of yesteryear, can't shake the game. They've gone on to raise families, retire, move to other states. But in their minds, they never leave Surf Avenue. And come the end of May, many of them will probably be there physically as well. Unlike previous years when the national tournament stretched out over several weekends, this year it will be a frenetic four-day affair held over Memorial Day weekend.

After eviscerating a pair of sullen Puerto Rican boys in a two-on-one match, Durso leans against the wall and waxes philosophic. "The *point,*" he says, "is that losing is a habit. I like to lose the least amount that I can. Which is paradoxical because I probably lose more than anybody in the park. Out of boredom. But I never lose when I don't *want* to lose."

"That's enough to him. Let's get on to something worthwhile," says Ruby Obert, a grinning, extremely fit white-haired gent in a warm-up suit.

Durso's eyes pop, and his face contorts into half smile, half rage. "Tell us who you were," he says. "Who *were* you, Ruby?"

Obert, one of the best all-around doubles players who ever lived, is enshrined in handball's Hall of Fame out in Tucson. He and his brothers, Carl and Oscar, were dominating forces in the sport from the mid-fifties to the early seventies, collecting ninety-two championships among them — an impressive feat even after you take into account that three separate organizations (YMCA, AAU and USHA) awarded championships. Obert doesn't flinch at Durso's jibe.

"Joe," he shouts back, "you're the transcendental manifestation of a cerebral aberration."

"Look at me," cries Durso. He angrily punches a ball at the wall. "Do I look thirty-five? Not an ounce of fat." Nodding in the direction of Obert, Durso says, "He wouldn't get a shot, the poor devil."

Obert, the unofficial mayor of these courts, is not about to back down: 'Hey Joe, can two of you beat one of you? Can you beat yourself with a ten-point lead? I gave Joe a hockey puck last week. He's still trying to open it. . . . That's a nice head you got on your shoulders, Joe. Too bad it's not on your neck."

"When I lose, it takes on epic proportions," says Durso, turning Obert's allusion neatly into a willing acceptance of his own mythic status.

Still, the obscurity of any handball championship has weighed heavily on players before Durso. Outside New York, few states have one-wall courts. Great handballers like Joe Garber, Moe Orenstein and Vic Hershkowitz remain unknown, and even the legendary Sandler was once heard to say, "Being the game's best player gives me the right to sit in the Bowery with the bums."

An air of mourning seems to surround the sport and its partisans. For Durso, who has devoted his life to handball, the mourning has turned to bitterness.

"One reason is that he doesn't have competition to develop his game," says Eisenberg, who now plays three-wall along the beach in Venice, California. "You grow up wanting to be a handball champ, like I did, and then find out you picked the wrong sport."

The long foyer of Durso's apartment in the Bay Ridge section of Brooklyn is adorned with T-shirts from scores of handball tournaments. They hang from wire hangers like flags at half-mast. Durso walks down the hall on this summer afternoon, knocks lightly, then enters the bedroom where his eighty-three-year-old grandmother, Geraldine Durso, lies propped up by pillows. She smiles radiantly when she sees him. A home nurse gives Joe the once-over as he fluffs up his grandmother's pillows.

"Do you love me, Grandma?" he asks.

"I love you, Joseph."

He closes the door softly behind him. "She's dying of bone cancer," he says. It is a simple statement of fact: in three months, Geraldine will be dead.

They lived together in the small apartment for many years. Geraldine was the light of Durso's life after he was a year old, when his parents sent him to live in Point Pleasant, New Jersey, with his grandparents. Durso has seen very little of his parents since then, and their absence hasn't made his heart grow fonder.

Durso's grandfather, also named Joseph, died when Durso

was ten, and Geraldine moved back to Coney Island with her grandson. In excellent physical shape from exploring Point Pleasant's beaches, construction sites and boatyards, Durso played and ran outside from morning to night.

"I never hung around or watched TV like kids do today," he says. "I really think I developed an extra-big heart muscle or something."

As for sports, Durso was attracted only to handball, a game in which he didn't have to rely on anyone else.

"I don't really look for the love of audience," he says. "I don't expect the love of audience. In the same way I never looked for or expected the love of my parents. I didn't look for it then, and I don't play for it now. In a way it's freed me so I don't have to obey the conventions. I do what I want. And if other people don't like it . . ."

Durso's room is decorated with trophies and framed photos of athletic male and female bodies. There are posters of David Bowie and Bruce Lee in action. Durso shows scrapbooks documenting his career.

"Do you like these?" he asks, proudly indicating several unpainted replicas of Greek statuary that he picked up for twenty dollars apiece. On a VCR he plays a video pastiche he has made of Laurence Olivier doing Shakespeare, Bruce Lee demolishing foes, and Joe Durso in tournament play on the Surf Avenue courts. Durso studies the performances with equal intensity.

"Idealized form, that's what I'm into," he says. "That's what Olivier is, and Bruce Lee. And that's what I try to be. I can *transcend* that way. Bowie is an idealized rock musician. Ayn Rand had an idealized philosophy of how life should be. Conan the Barbarian is an idealized tough guy."

All of which leads to Durso's approach to handball. "It's like the shadow world of Plato," he says. "There's somewhere an idea of the sublime volley. I try to reveal that. Ballet is supposed to be visual poetry. The visual beauty is pretty, and I try to be physically graceful. I'm not trying to make the *point* alone."

Durso looks around the small, cluttered room with its narrow bed, and suddenly seems sad. "This game is all about *I'm better than you.* It's not like a painting where you're trying to communicate some principle. It's just *I'm better than you.* It's a childish, stupid thing. But people do it because they've got nervous energy or misplaced sexual tension. Maybe I have more than anyone else. It's an ego confrontation. I'm very good at that."

Durso is silent. He switches off the TV sound and watches images of himself with that long reach, scoring points. Leaping. Vaulting. Spinning. Then, as if responding to an inner signal, he softly goes down the hall to check on Geraldine.

JOE SEXTON

Stealth Bomber

FROM THE NEW YORK TIMES MAGAZINE

To BE in the game without being in the collective consciousness of the opposition. It is a one-man, clandestine operation Brett Hull launches again and again in the course of a night in the National Hockey League.

Hull, the pitiless scoring machine for the St. Louis Blues, likes to slip onto the ice while the play is ongoing, to lose himself amid the fast-paced, often randomly evolving action and to find the patch of open ice everyone else has momentarily forgotten.

"I believe that when you are most out of the play, you are the furthest in it," says Hull in a characteristically thoughtful assessment of his style. "My whole game, in fact, is based on deception. I'm there, and then I'm not. I don't do a lot because I don't want to be noticed. I don't want to be seen. I barely raise my arms when I score. I don't want people mad at me for making them look stupid. I don't want them looking for me."

And so, night after night for the past three seasons, Hull has dodged detection well enough to make his name an almost everyday occurrence in the NHL box scores. The son of the legendary Hall of Famer Bobby Hull, twenty-seven-year-old Brett has led the league in goal scoring for the last two years and is on pace to do it again this season. But while Bobby, the man regarded as the finest left wing in NHL history, played the game with unceasing aggression, his son's approach is far more surreptitious — passive, low-key, even Zen-like.

"There comes that moment when I have lost myself and only the play finds me," says Hull, who last season captured the Hart

Trophy, the NHL's Most Valuable Player award. "And I have nothing but confidence in my ability to bury that puck in the net in that moment."

Of course, a full moment to execute is a rare extravagance in the NHL; split seconds are the more common allotment of performance time. Hockey is, after all, not a sport that can easily be deconstructed. It is a game of instant instincts, ruled by those capable of spontaneous acts of creativity, of sudden, authoritative action.

"Other than the power play, it's all ad lib," Hull says.

Brett Hull is a master of minimalist improvisation. His shot, a high-voltage combustion of forearms and leg torque, is his entire act: passing, skating and checking are not what hockey fans pay to see him do. And he doesn't require a lot of time or terrain to unleash his salvos. Bobby Hull insists his son could get his shot off in a bird cage.

"I have raised cattle, and I know a thing or two about genetics," says the fifty-two-year-old Hull. "And I can tell you the biggest contribution I've made to Brett's success is providing him with the genes to do what he does so well."

Adam Oates, the St. Louis center who has conspired to set up a fair percentage of Hull's goals over the last three seasons, refrains from genetic observations other than to say: "Hey, I don't know what else he's got of his dad's, but take a look at his forearms. From the elbows down, he is his old man."

From the neck up, he is anything but, the son being as cavalier about his talents as the father was obsessive, the son scoring goals as if by absentminded accident while the father scored with a palpable force of will, the son cultivating his image as gifted goof-off whereas the father offered himself up as the tireless, toothless embodiment of hard work.

"Maybe I've got his genes, but I definitely don't have his personality," Brett says of the oft-made comparison with his father, who'd vanished from his life for the better part of a decade. "You talking to the laziest man alive. I'm not into expending physical energy. I'm into expending mental energy."

Such habits developed early in Brett Hull's life, much to the changin of his impatient, already famous father. As a kid growing up in Winnipeg, Manitoba, Brett asked to play goaltender because it meant he wouldn't have to skate, regularly took a seat on the bench during warm-ups to avoid unnecessary exertion and managed to keep a smile on his face throughout an entire game no matter how bad or bloody — giving rise to early speculation that he wasn't tough enough for his father's violent sport.

But today Hull is, without question, the most feared sniper in hockey, a danger not only from almost all distances but also from the most preposterous angles. He can pile-drive a slap shot through a goaltender from sixty paces, whip a puck into the net with a flash of his wrists or shovel in a stray rebound like the most practiced garbage collector. His 72 goals in 1989–90, his third full season in the NHL, set a season's scoring record for a right wing. But Hull quickly outdid that mark with 86 last season, a breathtakingly consistent binge that fell only 6 goals shy of Wayne Gretzky's revered 1981–82 record of 92. And it amounted to 28 more than his father scored in his most productive year.

"Sure, he shoots the puck a zillion miles an hour, and maybe his slap shot is nastier than his dad's, harder than there has ever been," says John Vanbiesbrouck, the veteran goaltender for the New York Rangers. "But let's get real. Brett Hull's shot is all about release."

Hull's prodigious talent for putting the puck in the goal has made him, along with Gretzky of the Los Angeles Kings and Mario Lemieux of the Pittsburgh Penguins, one of the elite performers of the game. "It's so special to score goals — it's the home run," says Ron Caron, the Blues general manager, whose acquisition of Hull from the Calgary Flames in 1988 in return for a backup goaltender, Rich Wamsley, and a veteran defenseman, Rob Ramage, ranks as one of the most lopsided trades ever. "The red goal light is on, the arms are in the air, the people are out of their seats. Brett Hull has that dimension, and he's opened it full throttle. It's a gift not given to too many."

The physical package the gift comes in is less than formidable. At five feet ten inches and 205 pounds, Hull looks less like a hockey player than a dissolute fraternity brother on spring break. And as a skater, he exhibits all the finesse of a Zamboni ice scraper. "On the ice, my dad was like a thoroughbred," Hull once said. "I'm more like a train. I chug."

It's a train that runs on its own deadly schedule. "He could be called a floater, but then he'll float back into scoring areas just when the puck happens to be arriving," says E. J. Maguire, the former assistant coach of the Chicago Blackhawks. "And at that point, of course, he can shoot the puck — not only through the net but through the end of the building. He's never a threat until the puck is within a circle of five feet of him. The entire thing is exasperating. It still blows people's minds."

Even Brett Hull's. Derided early on as a loafer, drafted late out of the University of Minnesota at Duluth and then traded prematurely, Hull can, even now, sound confused about the legitimacy of his own talents and suspicious of the ferocity with which his fame has exploded around him.

"I never thought I had any great genius in the game,"Hull says matter-of-factly. "I could score goals, and that's all I've ever been able to do. I can't do anything else."

The lacerating analysis is no sooner out of his mouth than the smirk is on his lips. Perhaps the self-disparagement is a legacy from childhood, a reflexive defense against the unforgiving up-braidings of his father. Regardless of its origins, Brett Hull continues to insist that he is nothing special — an ordinary athlete, an ordinary guy — even if deep down he doesn't completely believe it.

"I've got a reputation as a lazy, mostly unskilled player, without the great competitive edge — and it looks like it'll never leave mc," Hull says, his eyes showing resignation more than hurt. "It's undeserved."

But the knock is still powerful, and the ache of doubt and fear continues to reverberate even as the nets fill with goals, the bank accounts with enormous deposits. There is the four-year $7.1 million contract, the promotional deals unmatched in hockey by anyone but Gretzky, and yet there are still moments when Hull stares at his hands — which, in the words of one NHL executive, are as "big as dinner plates" — and acknowledges the tremble.

"It scares the hell out of me, the thought that I'll never again score as many, never again score," he says. "What am I going to do then?"

Bobby Hull presses his eyes closed, his memory gears grinding, his thoughts hurtling in reverse — past the recent images of awards banquets and photo ops, through the void of his ten-year absence from his son's life, around the physical and emotional debris of a terrible divorce and back to his first remembered vision of Brett on ice.

"It was in Winnipeg," recalls Bobby Hull, who joined the Winnipeg Jets after a fabled fifteen-year career as a Chicago Blackhawk. "He was perhaps seven, and he couldn't skate. He'd stand there with his sweater hanging down past his knees. The referee would have to pick him up and lug him to the other end of the ice when the action moved. Then, he'd plop him down in front of the goal. He'd never move."

Soon enough, he'd almost never miss.

"He had the best action in his hands that I've ever seen," Hull says of Brett, the third-oldest of his five children and the only one to play in the NHL. "He was a piece of work as a kid, walking around with his fly undone, his jacket open, his shoes sliding off, snot coming out of his nose. You didn't understand if he was interested in the game. He never showed any enthusiasm. But the deal was — he was always there. Kids come up with excuses, kids cry that they are hurt or sick or tired. Brett, whatever was going on in his mind, was always there. You could always count on him."

And then you could always rely on him for a couple of goals.

"The kid who did the least work and scored the most goals," Bobby says, sitting in a Toronto hotel room, his smile thin, his hands upturned. "I'd sit in the stands and watch him play, yelling at him what to do, screaming that he had to go get the puck, force the play, take it on his own initiative and do something. He didn't listen. And then he'd score a goal. Then two. Usually three. He'd skate by me each time, a tremendous grin on his face. He'd make quite a loop of it on the ice."

Bobby Hull's memory tape ends, the images dissolving at the point when he disappeared from his younger children's lives in the aftermath of the bitter divorce eleven years ago from his wife, Joanne. The headlines in Canada's newspapers screamed of physical abuse, huge monetary awards, claims and counterclaims of everything from infidelity to bankruptcy. Bobby Hull, the mythic figure in Canada's national sport, who had so long distinguished himself as one of the game's most charismatic ambassadors, was portrayed as a man out of control.

"He was an abusive personality," says Hull's former wife, Joanne Robinson, who moved her four sons and one daughter from Winnipeg to Vancouver, British Columbia, in 1978 and remarried in 1982. "He was an abusive husband, physically and mentally. It pains me to talk about it all again, and it's a shame that Brett should have to recount it all, too. That child is one of the world's special creatures, and the force of his personality was, in many ways, the glue that held our family together. He's made his peace with his dad. That he could forgive him is a blessing. That he could forget, I think, would be asking too much."

Bobby Hull was born in Pointe Anne, Ontario, "a town," he says, "of five hundred people and six hundred dogs." Hull's father — known as the Blond Flash during his brief minor league career — was a laborer at the Canada Cement Company Plant No. 5. Bobby, the eldest boy in a family of eleven children, spent his days breaking pitchforks in bales of hay and hockey sticks on the ice, developing some of the most famously cabled arms in hockey history.

"I'd wake up early, build the fire in the kitchen and go out to the rink to bang pucks off the boards for hours," Hull recalls."The neighbors used to beg my father to make me wait at least till 7 A.M. before doing it.

"As a kid, I never walked from here to there, I didn't trot from here to there. I ran. And I couldn't wait for winter. My father would sometimes find me in the heat of summer standing in the house with my equipment on, sweating crazily. I just wanted the feel of it. Hockey became an obsession."

Hull, whose often random experimentation with slap shots unleashed from curved rather than straight-edge stick blades both traumatized and revolutionized the sport, crashed and burned his way through sixteen NHL seasons. With a fusion of indefatigability and quiet malevolence, Hull scored a career total of 610 goals, notching more than 50 in a season five times. "I played all over the ice," he says. "I went and got the puck. I tried to be constructive. I can't fathom results coming of anything but hard work."

Full of grit and yet capable of astonishing grace, Bobby Hull was a swift-skating left wing who manufactured goals with his sheer mania for work, as well as his volcanic blast of a slap shot.

And if he lost the majority of his teeth plowing through defenses, he never lost face. One of the enduring pictures of the Golden Jet, as he was known, showed Hull, his jaw recently wired shut to correct a break, refusing to surrender in a brutally one-sided fight with Montreal's John Ferguson, a primitive player who did most of his NHL scoring with his right hand. Blood ran in rivers off Hull's face, and yet he stood in and hung on.

Joanne McKay, a figure skater in the nightly show at the Conrad Hilton Hotel in Chicago in the sixties, couldn't help falling for Bobby Hull when he suddenly appeared, his face stitched, his clothes stylish, one afternoon at practice and bent to hand her a skate guard. "He was handsome, dashing, charismatic," she remembers.

But for Brett, Bobby was an ordinary father, worthy of worship but also a source of worry, gone too much of the time and often too tough when he was around. Bobby recalls sitting on three-year-old Brett's chest, forcibly lacing the first pair of skates on his frightened son and laughing at the boy's frantic flops to safety.

"I find it hard to believe anyone has incredibly vivid memories from before the age of five or six," Brett says now."I don't have any recollections of staring through smoke at Chicago Stadium and seeing him kill someone with a slap shot. He was a normal dad who did something special. He wasn't much of a teacher when it came to hockey. He wanted us to watch him and to do what he did. He was a typical dad. Nothing was good enough."

And then, for Brett, fourteen, nothing was all there was. "A violent divorce," Brett says, his sighing shrug announcing no desire to elaborate. "My parents hated each other."

The antagonism was evidently so consuming that Bobby Hull chose to exclude several of his children, along with his former wife, from much of the next decade of his life. According to Brett's mother, Bobby never called his son, never wrote. His rare personal appearances at home often as not ended up messily, the police required at least once.

"I often wonder whether it was any deprivation at all, not having a father around," Joanne says. "Brett was fairly well used to not having a dad because Bobby wasn't ever around that much to begin with. But I went to see a psychologist when we moved to

Vancouver. He helped me understand what the size of the loss must have been for Brett. It was a dual blow — the loss of a father and the loss of a great sports figure for a kid who loved the sport himself."

Bobby Hull, who adamantly refuses to discuss the divorce, its emotional aftershocks or his own behavior, will say only that his former wife's version of events is incomplete. He says he believes that his children, with their skewed understandings of the circumstances, are in ways like victims of a cult.

"I didn't want to cause them any more anguish by trying to pump them full of the truth," he says.

Brett, whose words about the family tumult are spare and calculatedly unemotional, appears uninterested in assigning blame or mucking around in uncomfortable talk about damage or hurt. "I never said I wouldn't have liked him around," Brett Hull says of his father. "But it didn't affect me that he wasn't."

The singing struck opposing players as nothing short of eerie when they first heard it. Teams would be lined up for a face-off against the Blues, and there would be this *singing*. Their triple takes left them staring at Brett Hull, his mouth moving, his blond hair streaming down his neck, croaking like a member of the Beach Boys.

"Guys used to swear he'd do it — right there on the ice, right then in the game's final minute or whenever," E. J. Maguire says. "The guy would carry entire tunes."

While Hull's singing is far from another talent, it underscores his remarkable ability to relax and to disarm the opposition.

"High-strung is not what I would call him," says a smiling Adam Oates, who, besides setting up many of his goals, is Hull's closet friend. "And what I find amazing is that he went from nothing to star faster than anyone I've ever heard of. With Gretzky, people understood the guy was going to be great from the time he was fifteen. Brett went from nothing to God in what amounts to an instant."

It's been an apotheosis during which he has made no known enemies. In fact, Hull's chutzpah without hubris — not to mention the ripple effect his huge contract has had on league salaries in general — has made him one of the best-liked players in the

NHL among the players themselves. In a vote by his peers last season, Hull was named the sport's most dominant performer, winning in a landslide over Gretzky.

"He's got a face you can't hate," says Chris Chelios, the notorious defenseman for the Chicago Blackhawks. "And so he's got a face that's hard to punch."

Hull, in turn, is a practicing pacifist on the ice, refusing to fight and even proclaiming himself loath to cheap-shot an opponent. "I'm not going to fight anyone," he says. "When I chase defensemen into the corner in the course of a game, I'm telling them I'm behind them and to move it. I don't want to hurt anyone."

Hull's life off the ice also reflects the easygoing side of his personality. He is unmarried, unhurried about becoming so. His golf game and the fortunes of the World Wrestling Federation appear to arouse his greatest passions. "Hey, listen, I'm having a great deal of fun being me," says Hull, who lives with his longtime girlfriend, Allison Curran, and makes his offseason home in Duluth. "No one, in fact, is enjoying it more than me."

Hull's position in the locker room of the Blues unchallenged, his stature in St. Louis mythically outsized. Coached by Brian Sutter, a disciplinarian and evangelist for selfless team defense, the Blues must rely excessively on the talents of their right winger for offense, his 86 goals last season accounting for nearly one third of the team's entire output. The chemistry seems to work. Last season, the Blues had the second-best record in the NHL, defying the conventional wisdom that bad things happen to teams that build themselves around a single scorer.

Hull is not a creator or distributor in the fashion of Gretzky but a finisher, and he is the first to acknowledge his dependence on the skills of others. "He tortures himself with fears about whether other players are jealous of him, of his output, of the way the game plan is designed for him," Oates says. "But we've made our pact. He's to put the puck in the net because no one else we have will. He's accepted it, done it and handled it with dignity."

Bobby Hull's return to his son's life was slow and, to any number of observers, slightly cynical. He wasn't to be found, after all,

when Brett, at seventeen, couldn't find a reason to continue playing a game in which he seemed to have no future.

"I had nowhere to go in the sport," Brett Hull says of that time
in 1981 when his hockey playing was confined to beer league
games. "I convinced myself to forget it. I was out of shape. I
didn't care. I figured I'd finish high school. I had no thoughts."

There was to be no word from his father for years. There was
no encouragement from Bobby when Brett, on a whim and a
prayer, accepted an invitation to play Tier II junior hockey, no
reaction when Brett, unpolished but unstoppable, scored 105
goals in his second season in Penticton, British Columbia.

Except for only one or two occasions, there was no proud father in the stands at Duluth when, as a freshman and sophomore, Brett scorched the Western Collegiate Hockey Association. There was no companionship or comfort to help Brett
make it through that awful first minor league season in the Calgary organization, which he termed "my worst nightmare of self-
doubt and zero self-esteem."

Mike Sertich, the coach at Duluth, recalls, "He had big-time
hurts about his situation with his dad. There were resentments
to acknowledge, to deal with. He had to let go of them."

For once, Brett Hull's release wasn't quite so quick. But over
the years, as his father's visibility in his life increased with the
rising level of his fame, Brett has learned to accept it all — the
joint photos, the mutual appearances at charitable events, even
Bobby's less than generous characterizations of his game — with
equanimity and sometimes a little humor. In one of his several
appearances on *Late Night with David Letterman,* Hull didn't hesi-
tate to zing his old man about his missing teeth and strangely reappearing hair.

"In his mind," says the Blues' Ron Caron, "I think he wonders
whether he should respect his dad. But with age, I think he has
accepted realities he wasn't able to before."

Brett says in succinct summation: "There's no love lost.
There's a distance."

It is a fluid geometry of attack the St. Louis Blues enact on their
power play, when the extra man is their advantage and the presence of Hull is their trump card. Oates, the center, slides back to

the blue line, and from there directs a deployment that is ultimately designed to find Hull unguarded for the critical fraction
of a second he needs to unload. Because of his right-handed
shot, Hull is most lethal from the left face-off circle, and his 29
goals on the power play last season were tops in the NHL.

"People rip him for being a sad skater," Oates says. "But put a
puck in front of him, and suddenly there's no skater in the universe who can go get it quicker."

Sertich draws a distinction between Hull and Gretzky. "People
have long said that it is as if Gretzky sees the game at a different
speed," he observes. "Well, with Brett, it is as if he sees the goal
in a different light. The net is higher, larger, wider. It's pretty
magical."

This gift has dramatically lowered the quality of life for many
a goaltender. "He's got goalies so intimidated that they do the
stupidest things," Oates says. "Guys try so hard to figure out how
to stop him, they don't do what they normally would. It's really
almost pathetic."

Never more so than when Hull emerges from his apparently
aimless, intentionally anonymous wanderings and takes a clear
path to the goal.

"Brett, in on a goaltender, can slow it down to a walk," Bobby
Hull notes. "I went in and blasted away, never looked at the goaltender's feet or made any in-depth studies. Brett waits and waits,
the goaltender puts his weight on one skate, and *boom*, it's over —
buried past the pad he for a second couldn't move."

Inevitably, a kind of paranoia grips the goalie, clouding his
thinking and coloring his behavior. "Bobby Hull hit me in the
head with one of his shots," recalls Lorne (Gump) Worsley, the
former goaltender for the New York Rangers and Montreal Can-
adiens. "Took me a couple of minutes to get back on my feet, of
course, and there's no question he could drill them. But that
wasn't what scared you. If goaltenders were afraid of being hurt,
they wouldn't have been out there at all.

"No, what goaltenders are afraid of is being scored on," Worsley continues. "Against guys like Bobby Hull or his son, you find
yourself standing there waiting for them to leave the ice, then
waiting for them to come back on. And when they are on, even if
they don't have the puck, they are going to get it, and you know
it. Thank God they only come on once in a while."

Hull's stays on the ice, though, can seem interminable, even if his presence is so confoundingly imperceptible. "There is an idea, a sort of plan about what's going to happen, but there is no calculation," Hull says. "My brain thinks totally opposite to everyone else. I take the step looking for the goal, and that may mean the step is this way when everyone else is going that way. I have an unbelievably vivid imagination."

SYDNEY LEA

A Winter Grouse

FROM THE VIRGINIA QUARTERLY REVIEW

As FORECAST, last night brought this slight layer of snow. Today will be my final one to hunt grouse: the feed is vanished, the game cover skinny, the scent worse and worse.

I have, of course, the flu.

In recent years the first storm, the last day of my season and this sickness have so perfectly coincided that I've come to believe more than ever in the body's power of recall. My chest tightens, my eyes burn — they know how to mark an anniversary. I should lie in bed and recover, but there are other things to re-cover. To cover again. The covers . . .

"Colder than a frog's mouth," a neighbor says as we stamp by the general store's gas pumps. Across the common, Old Glory, blown straight as a plank. "Take two men to hold on one man's hat today," the neighbor adds; I've heard it before, but am happy to hear it again. Habit becomes me. Yes, it'll be bad scent in such a gale, and bad hearing; after all the explosive years, my ears aren't much even in a still woods.

Yet I'm happy, the world so crisp and hard-edged I might be in some museum of the Beautiful, a commemorative place. Death of a season, but I am like a person who, at the term of a bountiful life, may recognize death as the imperative that kept him keen to the bounty itself.

I know. All over the globe, desperate or despicable people un-sheathe the billy, unfurl the electric lead, approach the cell. Oth-ers somewhere contemplate throw weight. Still others — the last of the bottle sucked down — turn on wife or child in a rage that's

incomprehensible, even to themselves. Not logical, exactly, this
dream of available bliss that I vaguely pursue as I set off along
Route 113, yet there it is. It's there even as through my truck
window I read the late history of nearby woods where I used to
shoot, where new "country estates" dot the hills. I must range
farther each year, so much closing down around me.

Still, my mood is affirmative — never mind the No Hunting
posters on every tree; never mind that this will likely be my last
hunt in the Gore, which has been bought by the ski industry;
never mind that soon the winter sports enthusiasts will put up
even more posters, hoping to save the wildlife they'll never see.
(*Two thousand* condos planned in the Gore, each owner a friend
to game . . .)

I bump my rig out of sight on the creamery lane. Just a cellar
hole here now. I remember the proprietor's name: Hazen Flye.
I remember the year he died — how trim he left the place, how
soon it moldered, how soon the game flocked back to reclaim it.
Instant ruin, full of romance.

Annie shrinks and moans as I slip on the bell collar, her usual
charade of suffering; then she races across the rough ghost of a
meadow to loose her bowels. I step into the cover a few feet to
wait. A woodcock, diehard loiterer, whistles up and hovers above
me. I stare at him there along my barrels, then watch his long
flight over the road. When Annie comes back, she locks on the
little bird's scent. *Gone,* I call to her.

This is a three-hour cover if you work it all. I have small faith
that I'll move many partridge, smaller still that I'll get decent
points, almost none that I'll hear wings. But somehow I mean to
cover every inch.

Behind the creamery, land plummets down a steep lane of
haw and blasted apple. I follow. A blaze flares from a trunk
where a buck has hooked, and here and there his cuff marks and
the orange dribble of his rut show as I wobble downhill. Jesus,
I'm weak. It's going to be a real struggle coming out, but I'll
worry about that then.

The only sign of feed is a solitary thorn apple in a clump of un-
tracked snow — perfectly red, perfectly shaped and displayed. I
behold it a moment.

I move on, pausing frequently in fealty to my sickness and in order to pick up the sound of the bell. What a wind! More than once, I blow my lungs out on the whistle, so that the dog (close by after all) skulks, confused. What is bothering me?

Nothing, really. The sky is that near purple I'd sooner associate with February than November. No cloud softens the prospect, but that seems part of the general rightness this morning — rude as barbed wire, lovely.

Was that a grouse's flush? I don't know. I think so, but it may have been merely the hurtle of air. When I come on Annie, I think she has that slightly offended look she wears when a partridge has flown and no shot been fired. Has she been pointing all this time?

I toot her on, losing the sound of her in an instant, noisy as I am, crunching past the abandoned hunter's shack, tripping once on a downed alder and crashing. I smile to recall the rage such accidents used to induce, how once I stood throwing forearm shivers at a hornbeam, as if that would avenge the indignity of my pratfall. You're a grown-up now at least, I think. For better or worse . . .

No grouse among the grapevines below the shack. Why would there be, the grapes burst or bitten or buried long since?

I should take my usual route west through the remaining cover, but I'm beset by odd curiosity to explore new ground, the likelihood of killing anything remote as it is. Younger, I'd have scoffed at the notion of exploring on the last day, especially in a zone the skiers had doomed. Maybe this morning I seek a farewell that's inclusive. I don't know, I don't know.

I push on to a wide brook. Now where does *it* come from, go to? Bizarre territory: high grass waves tawny in the wind. I squint hotly at a small patch around me, watching the near stalks riffle, ignoring the snowy ridges to north and south. *This might be Africa, a lion crouched in that stuff, big tail flicking, dark stare on his face.*

A hallucination of wonder, however, not terror.

Water leaving me no choice, I do turn west and follow the brook along its ice-beaded ledges. Annie rushes past — I can hear the bell for once, and can just make out her color in the lion-cover. She stops dead forty yards on. What the hell? I scrooch to the ground; it would be soft in a softer season, and I can believe that some maverick woodcock might drop to it for a brief, disenchanting spell; but surely I saw the autumns's last woodcock up where I came in, wished him well, willed him southward.

Thus it's carelessly that I amble to the point, and in complete surprise that I behold the flush. The bird crosses the brook in the frank light, scales into larches whose last needles tumble in cascades. I have not thought to raise my gun.

I know that this winter I'll see the grouse again in mind, almost black against that drift of gold. It's true what they say about fish, I think, by sudden association — you remember The One That Got Away. I have not fired at this partridge, but somehow I've also had *him* on a line. I think just now I pray, if wordlessly, that the snow stay fluffy, that no fox paw through an overnight crust, that till melt the bird keep busy on high limbs decked in fat, nourishing buds . . .

Perfect, perfect, perfect, I whisper as I swish through the wavy stuff beside this pristine stream. Once I stop at water's edge to watch a wild brook trout dart under the cutback. Perfect, that deep green jacket, those vermilion dots, that shearwater shape.

I don't comprehend my sudden electric expectation, but it has nothing to do with grouse. I can't yet know that within the hour I will see God, or more accurately, will understand that I've been in His presence right along. Indeed, my thoughts as I break out of the strange savannah are not epical but domestic: of my tall wife, chuckling over some piece of humor we shared last night; of the children too, each a treasure. Have you had such moments, when the clutter and strife that befall the happiest of families seem never to have been? If not, I wish them on you.

I turn north again, into the blow, against the swell of that hill I tripped so dreamily down at the start. The dog begins to make game — straight up, of course. I must labor to follow, the flu like a flatiron in my chest, each breath a bubble of phlegm, my legs no firmer than jam.

No. I must stop and sit, and I do, facing downhill, and to hell with a bird! I'll find another; if not today, then . . .

My tracks in the snow dust retreat into jackfirs. I follow them there with my eyes. I could rise and retrace them, seeing much on the way of what I've already seen this morning. But not all. To see it all, I must do what I'm doing, close down my burning lids and recreate it. An impulse as of tears, not unpleasant, stirs at the back of my throat. If I sat long enough, letting go, the mind's backtrack would take me through that strange yellow grass, across the frozen bottom by the dead hunter's camp, back up the hawthorn lane to the creamery's cellar cavity where I flushed the woodcock; but it would also lead me back through a thousand other thickets, up and down a thousand sidehills, around slough and slough, over the knobby apples that a thousand grouse have pecked at. I'd come on the points of five beloved dogs. I'd come on myself, maybe flailing my wrath against that ironwood or casting down the empty shotgun, having missed an easy straightaway. And I'd come on men (especially my father and three others) who are ever my age in vision, but who are gone now, all but one. Gone, or as that one puts it, "used up."

Behind me, in wind's momentary lull, a grouse rattles away; I'm sure of it this time. Annie has been pointing, not twenty yards distant. Now she takes two steps, the bell barely clinking, and pauses. I whistle her ahead; she starts her hunt again, never daunted. I get up and puff to the knoll's top, my gun shouldered, melancholy settled on me like a huge affirmation . . . which of course it is: after all, is it not signs of life that make us mourn their passing, that joy and fullness to which we now and then have had access?

I can't know that my dog, who's so busy, so much in her prime, will be eaten up with cancer four months from now, that she'll die in my arms on a table at the clinic, that the vet — a good man, but stiff — will fumble for words to console this weeping fool, and will fail to find them.

I pause in the creamery meadow. The dung that Annie left as I waited under that hovering woodcock has already hardened. It marks where she started, and now, so soon after, she paces back and forth by the pickup, wanting me to take her someplace where the action's livelier. She's just a dog, after all, and a young one at that.

Not that I'm so old myself. I'm in good shape, ordinarily in perfect health, and this side of fifty. Not young and not old, then, but between. This is not a physical matter alone, I'm thinking, as at the wheel I ponder which dirt road to follow. The easterly one, which my doctor would recommend, takes me directly home. The westerly will take me to the Gore's far side and another big cover. But there's a third road that runs north for fifteen miles and then winds homeward. At twenty, flu be damned, I'd have ordered myself through that other big patch. In a different mood, I might still be dismayed or angry at myself for not doing so now, for not *being* twenty anymore. At sixty (if there are still places to hunt), I may in a similar circumstance choose the home road. But just now I'm in middle way, as they say, and that seems — in accord with the day's judgments — a good place.

This little middle-road tangle is almost square and sits in the center of a timber yard, ancient and vast. The loggers cut all the surrounding highland pine and oak, and there was nothing but ledge under the topsoil: the whole ridge is turned to bone, its only growth a few maple whips. Why they left this square down below I don't know. Was there no market for the cedars that loom now over the sumac, witch hazel and barberry I'll stagger through? At the northwest corner of the square they also left a hedge that juts uphill like the handle on a pot. A freshet runs through it in spring, but in fall you can hike up its bed, as I always do, because of a certain day in 1976.

There were three of us. We knew, we know, one another's moves by heart: I handle the dog, Joey to my right and Terry to my left. I was running Gus then, a real ranger, and he had spilled out of the usual cover and come on point in the hedgerow. Joe crossed the brook bed, Terry staying on the east edge, and I walked up the middle. The grouse had nowhere to go. There were six of them, and we got them all.

We have religiously tramped the row's full length ever since, though we've never found another partridge there, for whatever his conservation ethic — and ours is acute — each hunter wants just one time to see the dream of annihilation come true. If he stays at it, it will come true — just that once and never again. Yet the urge to retrace such a path of dream and memory won't be resisted.

I am nothing but aching joints and hot gasps by now, but I walk the path to its difficult uphill end. Of course I flush nothing. Annie obligingly works the strip, then breaks from it downhill toward the "real" cover. She is a rocket over the granite, with its spare adornments of cane maple, lichen, ground pine. Head high, she cuts across the rough, unseeable wind. I watch

her grow smaller, and somehow whiter, as she approaches the
thicket below. At the last moment, I blast the whistle and she
wheels without breaking stride. I regard her in the frame of the
larger landscape: black softwood at cover's edge, two knolls behind it with their stark poplar fringes. And in this instant, the air
is invisible no longer, but possesses a shine, like paint in the halos
of quattrocento saints.

It is a blasphemy, even to those of us whose faith is uncanoni-
cal, to have said that I would this morning see God. But it is in
any case not God I claim now to see so much as what Paul calls
His power and glory, evident "in the things that have been
made."

I pass in this fever of mine through what's left of the cover,
slowly, and ever more so as I near the road. There will be no
game in these last hundred or so feet — there never is — but I
mean to protract the sense of a perfect end. The winter will be
long, and what may be beyond it?

Annie already stands by the truck's door, anxious again to try
the birds somewhere else. She doesn't know that the hunt and
season are done for. I hear her whine excitement, mouth gaped
in a yawn whose climax is a vibrato squeal. The wind's still broad
and urgent, second growth around me tossing, clicking.

I look up, as we have been taught to do in such moods, and
there in a dead elm, for no reason at all, unless it be the one I
surmise, sits the last grouse I'll see this year with a scattergun in
my hand. I begin to raise the Winchester, speculating on which
direction the bird will take when it flies. But it continues to sit,
chiseled, stationary.

How long do I behold that grouse? I don't know. But the gun
comes down and I break it, momentarily feeling the shapeliness
of shotshells before I slip them into my vest.

If this were a true vision, I'd report that from that limb a voice
thunders, demanding, *What manner of man art thou?* Indeed,
though it makes no sound that an outer ear could hear, I imagine
I do hear that voice. Perhaps to that exact extent this is — all of
it — as true a vision as I believe, my gun cased, my dog crated,
my truck following the snow-smeared lane back eastward.

Back to where I've come from today — home and heat and
family, and the young year's white coming months.

WILLIAM GILDEA

For Ali, Greatness
Takes Another Form

FROM THE WASHINGTON POST

"ALI, ALI, ALI, ALI, ALI, ALI."

The chant reverberated outside the packed second-floor room, echoing down the narrow hallway of time. It was the sound of Zaire, of Manila, of Madison Square Garden. It was the sound of three hundred children in the heart of Harlem welcoming the man they learned of from their elders if not from their history books. They knew him to be the most famous fighter of all time. They knew him to be much more: maybe the most recognizable man on earth and one who had stood up for *them*.

They knew the legend, but they didn't know the man. They'd been told not to expect Ali the fighter, the brash butterfly who stung like a bee and stood over a feared foe shouting, "Get up and fight, sucker." Ali was the greatest. They were told of the ravages of Parkinson's syndrome, also called Parkinsonism, and cautioned that Ali had the condition, but that his mind was fine. He just wouldn't dance like the butterfly among them. But still, he was the greatest. They'd see.

The neurological condition sometimes causes Ali to slur words or speak unintelligibly, to walk and gesture stiffly, to move slowly. He has a tremor. He may respond to questions only after a pause. He's said to get the message immediately but needs time to articulate the response. His condition is said to be stable and expected to continue. People wonder, Is he going to die soon? No, doctors have said, not from this.

But for those who watched him in wonder when he was young, it can be shocking to see Ali for the first time in a long time. He's the ultimate measurement of their own humanity, an unsettling vision of a cruel twist of life. How bitterly ironic, the man who was the "talkingest" recently taking speech therapy.

When he is introduced before heavyweight title fights, his moves in the ring — his kisses tossed as if from a trance, his short walk from one fighter to the other — seem to require all his effort, where once they took none.

His words made people laugh, but the look on his face now is enough to make them cry. Yet as changed as he is, Ali in a way remains unchanged. Once, the surface was the show, beneath it the meaning. Now, the surface can be a shade drawn on clear thoughts and convictions.

Friends say he is happy. He understands everything going on around him. He can do most things anyone can do. Some days are better then others. If he tires, he also has extraordinary energy; he is said to have taken 147 plane flights in 1990. Ali still amazes.

He still elicits passionate emotions. Love is foremost. Another, spawned in his boxing afterlife, is concern. To those who feel this for him, he'd say these words, clearly spoken in the quiet morning of his hotel suite, where he was still dressed in a white terry-cloth robe:

"Thank you for being concerned. My condition is in Allah's hands. I accept it. I love it. It's a trial, a test. I was the greatest heavyweight of all time. Known all over the world. Now He's trying me to see if I can accept it. Nothing happens without Allah's will.

"If everything was perfect, me with my wealth and fame, it would cause envy and jealousy," he said. "People are envious of people with everything. Now they feel sorry for me. Wish me well. See I'm human. Now things are balanced."

It's as if he's up against the ropes in Zaire, being pounded but winning anyway. "Twenty-five years fighting, ten years in retirement, there's still interest in what I'm doing." Looking down to a reporter's notebook, he said, "You're still writing about me."

He could still hold a person with his charm, almost as surely as he took a child into his hands during his visit to Our Children's

Foundation, Inc., an education and counseling center for children and their families on Manhattan's 125th Street. He sat her on his knee briefly. Then he watched children perform African dances for him, applauding, it seemed, when everyone else did.

At length, he walked slowly to a microphone and addressed the children. He spoke slowly, and their eyes were on him: "The sun has a purpose. The moon has a purpose. The rain has a purpose. The snow has a purpose. Cows have a purpose. . . . You were born for a purpose. You have to find your purpose. Go to school. Learn to read and write. If you can't read a test, you can't get a driver's license. . . . What is your purpose, your occupation? Find your purpose. . . . What do you have to find?"

"Purpose," they shouted.

He'd given the speech before, but Ali hadn't expected to give it then. "I didn't know I was going there," he said the next day. He'd given the talk extemporaneously.

Ali, who will be fifty in January, sat on a boulder near the top of a hill where he once trained, at Deer Lake in Pennsylvania's Pocono Mountains. Painted on the boulder was the name of the late Sonny Liston, the man Ali screamed down at in 1965 to get up off his back. Now Ali obliged photographers, posing atop the boulder. Sitting up there in khaki blouse and slacks and white Reeboks, fists up, Ali rekindled the memory of his standing above the one he called the Ugly Bear. That was before his 1967–70 exile from boxing for refusing to be inducted into the army.

Ali and a temporary entourage had ridden a silver and blue charter bus two and a half hours from New York to the complex of cabins. The group included Ali's fourth wife, Lonnie, thirty-four, who married him in 1986; his friend of almost thirty years, Howard Bingham; Ali's spiritual teacher, the gentlemanly Jeremiah Shabazz; other friends and newspaper writers; photographers and television crews.

Ali sometimes closed his eyes on the bus as it crossed New Jersey farmland, then climbed into the Pennsylvania hills. At other times, he acted like the old Ali, jumping from his seat to bear-hug Shabazz and tickle him. Shabazz played along, yelling, feigning pain. "He can't stand it," shouted Ali. "He can't stand it."

The journey's purpose was to publicize a recently published comprehensive oral history by Thomas Hauser, *Muhammad Ali: His Life and Times.* In quoting two doctors, Hauser confirms what has long been suspected — that boxing caused his condition. "Still," Hauser concludes, "the most important aspect of Ali's health is that it's not as bad as many people believe."

Earnie Shavers was along on the bus ride. On September 29, 1977, Ali retained his title against Shavers, but took much punishment while winning a fifteen-round decision. Shavers was one of the hardest-hitting heavyweights ever. Later that day, when Ali introduced him to the children in Harlem, he said of Shavers, "He hit me so hard he jarred my kinfolk in Africa."

Bald and big, Shavers spoke quietly in front of three buildings: the small cabin in which Ali once slept, the middle-sized structure that was his dining area, the largest one that held his ring. Shavers wore a black suit and white jersey. The big man's card read: "Earnie D. Shavers, Knock-Out Evangelist, Phoenix, Az."

"He was my idol," said Shavers. "I wanted to win and I didn't want to win. I liked him. But I had a family to feed. What could you do? I knew him as a friend. He would let me train here scot-free. I knew he was a good man. He couldn't psyche me because I knew him well."

Shavers seemed to believe that their fight took a toll on Ali but remained consoled that it wasn't the only one. "Over a long period of time," said Shavers, "we all contributed. . . . It seems to affect us more than it does him."

Ali's eyes shone in the early afternoon sun as he stood in front of another cabin, this one painted white. "This is the mosque," said Ali. "It's too small. We're going to build a larger one."

He greeted Muslim friends, some of whom live on the property that he said will be the home of the Washington-based Muhammad Ali Saving Our Future Foundation, Inc. "This is the second half of my life," said Ali. "Boxing was just the start." He said he prays five times a day, and envisions a big mosque and an Islamic youth camp on the property he still owns. Hauser writes that most of Ali's holdings are in real estate, including the one in Berrien Springs, Michigan, on which he lives.

Hauser said that although Ali had given him complete editorial control of the book and facilitated many interviews, the author deleted the specifics of Ali's finances from the original manuscript at Ali's request. "He said, 'It's really nobody's business,' " said Hauser, but mentioned that Ali lives "comfortably." Ali stands to profit from the book, but Hauser would not disclose the financial arrangement.

Another of Ali's friends suggested that this day's trip to Deer Lake was bittersweet because he knew Ali could feel there the absence of his longtime cook, Lana Shabazz, and the poet Drew "Bundini" Brown, both dead. "He missed going into that kitchen and seeing her in there," said the friend, "and although he argued with Bundini sometimes, he loved Bundini."

Ali entered the building where he used to spar, but this time he went in to pray. A woman named Afriyie, from Philadelphia, prepared a vegetarian lunch of "clemburgers" (cracked wheat marinated with herbs and spices plus assorted vegetables in whole wheat pita), nori rolls (sushi wrapped in seaweed) and fruit salad. Lonnie walked the grounds, sharing her husband's dream for it.

She's known Ali since 1962 when their families were neighbors in Louisville. "She's a good lady," said Bingham. "She's an educated lady; she has an M.B.A. Her bottom line is seeing that he's cared for and loved."

Lonnie said that being married to Ali was "never boring," although sometimes difficult because "he belongs to the people and I'm a private person." What irritates her are depictions of Ali as "incapacitated." Walking along, she said, "He's not what he was twenty years ago, but he's functioning completely."

On the mountain, Darrell Golphin, who is blind, played a silver-colored flute for Ali and the guests. He began with "America the Beautiful," then played what he described as a spiritual song, "Brighten Up the Corner Where You Live."

"I played it for Ali because he definitely brightens up the corners," said Golphin. "Whatever corner you find yourself in the world, you ought to be able to brighten it up."

At times, the plaintive sound of the flute was the only sound on the hill.

The bus took Ali to Harlem. When he came downstairs from his visit with the children, the sidewalk was packed with people who spilled into the street and surrounded the black limousine that awaited him. People reached to touch him.

On the ride down Broadway toward his midtown hotel, Ali sat in the back left corner of the car. Two writers sat next to him. On the facing seat were a third writer, Bingham and Lonnie.

Ali pushed a button and lowered his window and the breeze came in. People looked in in amazement. At a red light, two men stopped their car next to Ali's and looked over. "Muhammad Ali. Muhammad Ali. Hey, champ. Champ. Muhammad Ali."

Another few blocks and Ali's eyes closed. He began snoring. The snoring grew louder. "He dropped off just like that," said Lonnie. Bingham agreed, Ali was tired. Eyes still closed, Ali punctuated the snoring with a quick left jab. "He has flashbacks," said Lonnie. "It's mostly Frazier."

Ali jabbed again. Seated up against his shoulder, a reporter could feel the strength of his body and the size of his arm. He always was stronger then many thought. He's six foot three and looks to be about 240 pounds, not that much above fighting weight. Then Ali threw a right uppercut in the air. The man on his right was jostled.

Bingham hastened to call off Ali's practical joke. "Ali, wake up. Wake up, Ali." Bingham grabbed Ali's knee.

Ali's eyes opened and a smile parted his lips. "I did that on *Candid Camera,*" he said.

He would have changed things if he could, said Bingham. "I would have had him quit a lot earlier. Just launch into a lot of other things. Commercials. Endorsements. Movies." Bingham was having breakfast of a muffin and tea in a hotel dining room. "He had the name. He had the face. Ali could have been president of the world. Does that make sense?"

But no one would, or could, call a halt. Some believe Ali simply loved the ring spotlight too much to step out of it. But he took severe punishment toward the end of his career. Seventeen of his last twenty fights lasted at least ten rounds; five went twelve rounds, one went fourteen, eight went fifteen. Finally, he couldn't fight back against Larry Holmes. In the end, December 11, 1981, he lost a decision in Nassau to Trevor Berbick. Boxing for Ali was over, finally and too late.

When would Bingham have stopped it all?

"Maybe after the Manila fight."

That was October 1975.

Bingham met Ali in the spring of 1962. A photographer for the *Sentinel,* a Los Angeles newspaper, he was assigned to cover Ali, then known as Cassius Clay, before a fight in Los Angeles. "I'd never heard of him. I covered him at a news conference. Then I was driving by the corner of Fifth and Broadway and his brother and him were watching the girls go by. I asked them if they wanted a ride. . . . They said O.K. I took them by the bowling alley, by my mother's house, just introduced them to people. That happened for most of the next ten days. They were offering me money but I never accepted any.

"Then he'd call me up. On New Year's Day [1963] he called: 'Hey, how would you like to hang out with us for a while.' He sent me tickets for the next Sunday. I'd never been on an airplane before. He met me at the airport [in Miami]. Then Ali and his brother and me drove in his pink Cadillac to Kentucky, to his mother's house. Then we drove to Pittsburgh [where Ali fought Charlie Powell]. I had never been in cold weather. He bought me earmuffs, long underwear."

Bingham, who is black, said that early on he had "a lot of problems" being Ali's friend "because I wasn't a Muslim." But Bingham and Ali's friendship proved to transcend religion.

"Being a photographer, the thing that hurts me is the facial thing." The muscle rigidity caused by Parkinson's syndrome affects the face as well. "I shoot pictures of him, but it's not like the old days. Some days it's really good. Then I tell him, 'Oh, Ali, it looks good.' "

Ali keeps "going, going, going," said Bingham. "I believe if Ali would get his rest, take his medicine, exercise like he should, he'd be fine." But there's no stopping him, just like there was no stopping him as a fighter.

"Islam is his purpose now, propagating the religion," said Bingham. "That's all he wakes up for every day."

Ali spends hours daily signing pamphlets about Islam that he later distributes. "When we go upstairs," said Bingham, "he'll be signing pamphlets."

So it was. Up in the sitting room of his corner suite, Ali sat at a round, marble-top table signing pamphlets: "Introducing Islam,"

"How I Came to Islam," by Yusuf Islam (Cat Stevens) and "Is Jesus Really God?"

"You," he said, looking up at the reporter. The day before on the bus he's played the cricket trick on him, sitting one row behind and across the aisle and reaching forward to snap his fingers to make a mysterious sound, then quickly settling back as the man turned his head. Another reporter said no way did it sound like a cricket anymore.

Ali motioned the visitor to sit at the table next to him. He revealed a briefcase filled with pamphlets. Then he lifted the lid of a suitcase on the floor. It, too, was filled with pamphlets. He slid a copy of the Bible onto the table, opening it to find documentation for his beliefs. "Getting into something heavy," he said, smiling. "This is heavy."

He found one passage in Exodus, although he had trouble finding Exodus. "Boxing ain't nothin' to this," he said.

He knew his purpose. "My purpose is that I was the first big black celebrity who spoke the truth and stepped up for his people."

Now he's Allah's messenger. "I can't change you. God changes the soul. My job is just to give the message. God's job is to change the heart. . . . There are no more challenges [in boxing]. [But] I have a challenge. The challenge is my health condition." He wishes he could do more as a messenger.

"I get nervous. I'm shaking. The way I'm talking." He looked to Bingham across the room. Ali wondered how he looked on the *Today* show that morning. It had been taped two days before.

"The way they had it, with the old fight film, it was good," said Bingham.

"Did they show me how I used to talk?"

"No," said Bingham. "They showed how great you are. You know, 'I'm a bad man.' "

"That was thirty years ago," said Ali softly.

Ali said it took courage to go on the show, that his pride almost kept him off. He didn't want people to see the difference in him then and now.

"But the Bible says, if you've got one ounce of pride, you cannot enter paradise. I thought about that. I'm shaking now, see." He pulled up his right hand. "People see that. So pride keeps you away. I'm trying to kill that pride."

A full breakfast was placed in front of him. He talked as he ate.

"I never turned down an interview. I never turned down an invitation. I never run down on people. All are equal under Allah.

"Every day I go to bed I ask myself, 'If Allah judges me just on the day, would I go to heaven? If today is my whole life, will I go to heaven?' I've done that for the past ten years. I could have gone to heaven every day.

"Before I came to Islam, I chased women. My biggest weakness was pretty women. . . . But God sees you. He knows. I know He knows. He knows I know He knows."

Ali, dancing still, was not to be guided into a discussion about boxing. "Naturally" he missed the late Liston. That was it.

"Five hours a day I pre-sign these," he said, going back to the pamphlets. "At any airport, I'll meet a hundred people. Standing in line."

Bingham spoke up. "Ali will not go into a lounge and wait. The airline people want to take him to a lounge and wait."

"If a plane is two hours late," said Ali, "I'm happy because I get two hours to pass these out.

"Changing planes. One stop. I used to hate that. Now I'm happy with changeovers." He said the pamphlets in his suitcase were in stacks of hundreds. "Three thousand pamphlets with me," he said. "They all know me. I don't have time to sign. I just hand 'em out. Two, three hundred on a corner. Man, Allah's blessed me."

The visitor slid his chair back to leave. Ali had to get dressed for his noon book-signing appearance, although he didn't mention he had to. In fact, he said, "Don't say I sent you away. You left."

Then, with a laugh, "You know, I charge now for interviews. Fifty dollars."

There was a pause. "Twenty?" he said.

He laughed. He was still, as he used to say, pretty.

The line at the bookstore extended along Fifth Avenue, turned a corner, stretched through an arcade and disappeared around another corner. The crowd on the wide sidewalk out front shifted en masse toward the black limo when it pulled up. Ali got out. "He's here! He's here! Ali! Ali! Ali!"

The advertisement in the window said he would sign books from noon to 1:30. At 1:30, the line still had no end. It was a stream of people, most pouring out deeply felt greetings — a kiss, a handshake — as they approached the table where he sat, handing out labels signed in advance for them to stick into their books. With each, he gave a pamphlet on Islam.

One of his eight children, Miya, nineteen, surprised him by lining up and appearing before him. His eyes grew wide in delight as she bent to kiss his cheek.

About 2:00, a store employee carried a hand-printed sign to the front window and covered the part of the advertisement that said noon to 1:30. It read: HE'S STILL HERE.

He was still there at 3:30 when a halt was called. The publishing people said they'd never seen anyone like Ali who'd stay so long past his commitment. They thought he was still the greatest.

BRYAN WOOLLEY

Glory Denied

FROM THE DALLAS MORNING NEWS

IT NEVER entered his mind that they had done anything special, Coach Don Haskins says, but few who saw the game would ever forget it. For the first time, an all-black team had played an all-white team for the NCAA national basketball championship. The black men had won. History had been made. The Texas Western Miners had changed college basketball forever.

But that was 1966. The march from Selma to Montgomery had happened only a year before, and the struggle for the rights of black people still held the country in turmoil. Civil rights workers still were being shot. Arsonists still were torching black churches. Governor George Wallace still was defying a school desegregation order in Alabama. A congressional committee was investigating the Ku Klux Klan. The Georgia legislature was refusing to seat a newly elected black representative named Julian Bond. Rioting had broken out in a Los Angeles neighborhood called Watts. And Dr. Martin Luther King, Jr., was promising to take the civil rights movement northward to Chicago.

A lot of people in the country didn't like the kind of history that the team from Texas had made. "I was so young and näive," Mr. Haskins said as the 1966 Miners were gathering earlier this month to celebrate the twenty-fifth anniversary of their victory. "I hadn't thought of it as putting an all-black team on the court. I was simply playing the best players I had. It's what I had done all year. Then we came home and the hate mail started pouring in. Thousands of letters, from all over the South."

The letters were only the beginning of his bitter time. Mr. Haskins and his team would remain subjects of intense controversy in newspapers, magazines and books for more than a decade after they brought the championship trophy home to El Paso. So deep was Mr. Haskins's pain that a dozen years after the greatest athletic triumph in his own life and the history of his school, he would say, "If I could change one thing about my coaching career, I'd wish we came in second in 1966."

On the night of March 19, 1966, the Texas Western College Miners walked onto a court in College Park, Maryland, to play the University of Kentucky Wildcats in the final game of the NCAA tournament.

Kentucky had compiled a record of twenty-three wins and only one loss during the regular season. It was ranked number one in the nation. On the previous evening, in the game that most coaches and sports writers thought would really determine the championship, the Wildcats had beaten the nation's number two team, Duke. If the Wildcats beat the Miners, as almost everybody expected, they would give Kentucky and its legendary sixty-four-year-old coach, Adolph Rupp, their fifth national championship.

Texas Western College — now the University of Texas at El Paso — was a small group of buildings perched on a desert hillside a few hundred yards from the narrow Rio Grande and Mexico. Six thousand students were enrolled there. The Miners' thirty-six-year-old coach was in his first college job. Until the 1965–66 season, no one in big-time college basketball had paid much attention to Texas Western. In its entire history, it had won only one NCAA tournament game. Since none of the major basketball schools had bothered to recruit any of Mr. Haskins's players, the eastern and midwestern press early in the season had dismissed them as "castoffs," "unknowns" and "nondescripts."

But the Miners also had compiled a 23–1 record during the regular season, and when the tournament started, they were ranked number three in the country. After an easy victory over Oklahoma City University in their first tournament game, they had nipped Kansas and Cincinnati, both in overtime, and had beaten Utah in the semifinals to get a crack at the title.

"I run into people who remember that game, and they still

think I went to an all-black school," said one of the players, Willie
Worsley, at the team's twenty-fifth reunion. "I always have to explain what Texas Western was, and what UTEP is, and where it
is, and what we were all about."

Texas Western wasn't an all-black college. Far from it. A large
percentage of the small group of black students on campus had
been recruited for their skills at basketball, football and track. El
Paso, where a majority of the citizens are Hispanic — El Paso is
across the Rio Grande from Mexico's fourth-largest city — had
comparatively few black residents. So did the vast, nearly empty
desert region around it.

Yet eleven years earlier, in 1955, Texas Western had been the
first all-white college in Texas — indeed, in the entire old Con-
federacy — to admit black students. And in 1956 it had recruited
its first black athlete, a basketball player named Charlie Brown,
years ahead of any other school in Texas or the South.

These steps were taken without fanfare and without incident.
Because El Paso is isolated from the other big Texas cities by several hundred miles and most of Texas Western's athletic opponents were southwestern and western schools that had never
been segregated, almost nobody east of the Pecos noticed, and
almost nobody west of the Pecos cared. "We were so insulated out
here in El Paso that we barely knew all that racial stuff was going
on in other places," said David Palacio, one of the 1966 players.
"We heard about it, I guess, but we didn't think about it. We
weren't really conscious of the race thing until we started to win
in the playoffs. Then it started to surface. It was kind of in the
air. Until then, it had never occurred to me that, hey, we've got
five black guys who are starting."

Nor were the Miners really an all-black team. Of the twelve
men who were on the squad, four — Togo Railey, Jerry Armstrong, Louis Baudoin and Dick Myers — are white, and Mr. Palacio is Hispanic. All had played in games during the season, and
Mr. Armstrong had been instrumental in the semifinal game,
coming off the bench to shut down Utah's star shooter, Jerry
Chambers.

They and the seven black players were a close-knit group. "We
used to drink wine in the dorm together because we didn't have
the money to go out," Mr. Palacio said. "We used to play a lot of

cards. It was friendship, pure friendship. I don't remember a single instance of race being an issue or a problem among us."

But the team's five starters and two best backup players — Bobby Joe Hill, Orsten Artis, David Lattin, Willie Cager, Harry Flournoy, Nevil Shed and Mr. Worsley — are black, and they were the only players who got into the game against the Wildcats, the only Miners seen on TV.

Kentucky had never had a black player. Neither Mr. Rupp nor any other coach in the Southeastern Conference had ever recruited one.

Midway through the first quarter, with the Miners leading by a single point, Mr. Hill stole the ball, dribbled down the court and made an easy lay-up. As Kentucky was bringing the ball back up the court, Mr. Hill stole it again, dribbled down the court and made another easy lay-up, giving the Miners a five-point lead. The Wildcats never recovered. Texas Western won, 72–65.

"It wasn't even as close as the score indicates," Mr. Artis said. "At one point we led by seventeen. Our easiest games in that tournament were the first one, against Oklahoma City, and the last one, against Kentucky."

After the game, the Kentucky players — minus their coach — went to the Miners' locker room and congratulated them. "There wasn't any racial thing as far as the two teams were concerned," Mr. Artis said.

The next day, ten thousand delirious fans turned out at El Paso International Airport to welcome the only team from Texas ever to win the NCAA Division I national basketball championship. Mr. Cager made a speech: "From all of us to all of you, number one was the best we could do." The crowd went wild. There was a parade through the town.

"It wasn't until later on," Mr. Shed said, "that we started realizing that this team had opened the doors, not just for blacks but for all minorities, to have an opportunity to play ball at some of the top-notch schools around the United States. What was so beautiful about it was that the very next year things began to open up."

Soon even Mr. Rupp would recruit a black player. But he was a sore loser. "I hated to see those boys from Texas Western win it," he told the press. "Not because of race or anything like that, but because of the type of recruiting it represents." He hinted that several of Mr. Haskins's players had done sinister deeds in the past and that Texas Western had practiced recruiting most foul. A number of sports writers fell in behind him.

"The title really should belong to Kentucky," wrote an Iowa columnist. "I have heard that one of the top Texas Western players had been charged with a major crime at one time." Since Texas Western was an independent, he wrote, "they can do about as they please in recruiting. They can take rejects from other schools and make them immediately eligible. A school with such low ethics should not be allowed to compete for a national title. Rather it should be in the NBA [pro basketball] playoffs."

Mr. Rupp's hometown newspaper editorialized that "there is no disgrace in losing to a team such as was assembled by Texas Western after a nationwide search for talent that somehow escaped the recruiters for the Harlem Globetrotters."

As Mr. Rupp got older, his loss to Texas Western seemed to gnaw more and more exquisitely, and his pronouncements about his opponents grew more and more lurid. In a 1975 interview, he said the biggest disappointment of his long career had been losing to "all those ineligible players."

"They were a bunch of crooks," he said. "One was on parole from Tennessee State Prison. Two had been kicked out of a junior college in Iowa. Texas Western was suspended by the NCAA for three years after that."

In fact, Mr. Lattin transferred from Tennessee State University, not the state prison. Mr. Hill and a player on the Texas Western freshman team — not the championship squad — transferred from Burlington (Iowa) Junior College. There were no ineligible players on the team. Texas Western had never been suspended by the NCAA. Indeed, the NCAA investigated the allegations after the 1966 tournament and gave the school a clean bill of health.

"I didn't like us being called misfits, criminals and convicts," Mr. Shed said at the reunion. "My mother and father worked hard to bring me up, to make sure that I represented myself with a well-mannered attitude. The people who did that to us didn't really know us. If they had taken the time to look into what 'those seven blacks' were all about, they would have found some pretty impressive guys."

But the most serious damage was done in 1968, when *Sports*

Illustrated published a five-part series titled "The Black Athlete." Part three, the centerpiece of the series, titled "In an Alien World," was devoted entirely to the University of Texas at El Paso (the name of the school had been changed a year earlier) and its alleged exploitation of black athletes.

"One might suppose that a school which has so thoroughly and actively exploited black athletes would be breaking itself in half to give them something in return, both in appreciation for the achievements of the past and to assure a steady flow of black athletes in the future," wrote its author, Jack Olsen. "One might think that UTEP, with its famed Negro basketball players, its Negro football stars and its predominantly Negro track team would be determined to give its black athletes the very squarest of square deals. But the Negroes on the campus insist this is not the case — far from it."

Mr. Olsen went on to describe UTEP and El Paso as a kind of racist hell in which the athletes labored in virtual slavery. The article outraged almost everyone connected with the university. El Paso and UTEP perhaps hadn't achieved a racial paradise during the turbulent sixties, but with its heavily Hispanic population and its location on an international border, El Paso had for more than a century been a racially tolerant city — certainly more tolerant than the rest of Texas and much of the country.

The athletes said that statements attributed to them in the article had been taken out of context and twisted. UTEP President Joseph Smiley ordered an internal investigation of all the school's intercollegiate athletic programs. The investigating committee found no major racial injustices but recommended a few small reforms, most having nothing to do with race.

Mr. Olsen and *Sports Illustrated* stood by their article, however, and that made recruiting very hard for Mr. Haskins. "Every coach in the country had a copy of that article in his back pocket," he says, "and whenever a black player would indicate an interest in UTEP, they would yank it out and say, 'You don't want to go to El Paso. It's a horrible place.' "

In 1975, Neil D. Isaacs, a college professor, published a book called *All the Moves: A History of College Basketball.* Relying entirely on the *Sports Illustrated* article, he cited the 1966 Texas Western team as the best example of the abuse of black athletes in Amer-

ica. "There was little in the way of social rewards for them in El
Paso," he wrote. "None of them was ever awarded a degree from
Texas Western, and they feel that they have lived out the full
meaning of exploitation."

A year later, one of America's most famous authors added a
few licks of his own. In *Sports in America,* James A. Michener described the 1966 Miners as "a bunch of loose-jointed ragamuf-
fins" who had been "conscripted" to play basketball in El Paso.

"The El Paso story is one of the most wretched in the history
of American sports," he wrote. "I have often thought how much
luckier the white players were under Coach Adolph Rupp. He
looked after his players; they had a shot at a real education; and
they were secure within the traditions of their university, their
community and their state. They may have lost the playoff, but
they were the winners in every other respect, and their black opponents from El Paso were losers."

Years before Mr. Michener's book was published, eight of the
1966 squad — the five whites plus Mr. Shed, Mr. Flournoy and
Mr. Cager — had received their UTEP degrees.

Mr. Lattin had left early because he was drafted by the pro
basketball Phoenix Suns. "He had a year of eligibility left, but I
encouraged him to go," Mr. Haskins said. "There was a lot of
money in it for him, and I kept thinking, What if he plays another season for me and ruins a knee or something?"

The remaining three players — Mr. Artis, Mr. Hill and Mr.
Worsley — had racked up between 78 and 115 semester hours of
credit before they dropped out of school to take jobs.

Mr. Michener, who often brags of the amount of research that
goes into his massive books, later admitted in a letter to Dr. Mimi
Gladstein, a UTEP English professor, that his investigation of
the 1966 Miners had gone no further than the *Sports Illustrated*
article.

Today Mr. Shed is the director of intramural athletics at the University of Texas at San Antonio. Mr. Lattin is in public relations
in Houston. Mr. Flournoy is a sales executive for a baking company in California. Mr. Hill is senior buyer for El Paso Natural
Gas in El Paso. Mr. Myers is vice president of a clothing manufac-
turing company in Florida. Mr. Palacio is vice president of Co-

lumbia Records in California. Mr. Atis is a detective on the police force in Gary, Indiana. The others — Mr. Armstrong, Mr. Baudoin, Mr. Cager, Mr. Railey and Mr. Worsley — are teachers and school administrators in Texas, Missouri, New Mexico and New York.

Mr. Haskins is one of the winningest coaches in the game. During his thirty seasons at Texas Western/UTEP, his teams have won six Western Athletic Conference championships. Five teams have played in the National Invitational Tournament and thirteen in the NCAA tournament. But 1990–91 was a bad year for Mr. Haskins and the Miners. Crippled by injuries and the scholastic ineligibility of a key player, the Miners didn't make it to the NCAA tournament. It was the first time in eight years that they hadn't been there. And the NCAA is investigating UTEP's basketball program for possible recruiting violations.

As their twenty-fifth anniversary reunion began, on the eve of the Miners' last home game of the 1991 season, the coach and players greeted one another like brothers and talked deep into the night, recalling their days of glory. It was the third time over the years that they had gathered to relive what they had done. They are still a close-knit group.

"We won some games while all you guys were here," Mr. Haskins told them, "but the thing that makes me the happiest is that each and every one of you has turned out to be a fine citizen and a good person and all of you are doing well. That's the most important thing of all."

He's in the twilight of his career. He has mellowed, he said, and is no longer bitter. It's finally sweet to have won.

"It was all a long time ago," he said. "A lot of bridges have been crossed. The entire country has come a long way in the way people think. Tomorrow night, I'm going to start my best five, regardless. And that's what I was doing then."

PETER GAMMONS

The Throes of
Tossing a Baseball

FROM THE BOSTON GLOBE

DAVE ENGLE was hitting fungoes as a coach for the Tucson Toros
last week when a young catcher from another team asked to talk
to him privately. "The kid knew I had the problem," says Engle.
"He didn't think anyone really knew about it yet, so he needed to
talk. He's desperately trying to find out what to do before people
notice. It gets around and he goes haywire and a private hell becomes public."

Engle knows about going haywire. He is thirty-five and could
still be catching and making millions. Instead, he is a $20,000-a-
year coach in Tucson because he couldn't throw a baseball back
to the pitcher.

"What's more natural than playing catch?" Engle says. "Yeah,
well, nothing's tougher when you go haywire."

It happened to Steve Blass, who less than two years after being
the World Series MVP couldn't pitch to a batter. Joe Cowley sim-
ilarly went from a twelve-game winner with the Yankees in 1986
to not being able to come within two feet of the plate. In March
1979, the Red Sox' two best prospects, Bobby Sprowl and Steve
Schneck, threw pitches up onto screens and hit batters in the on-
deck circle. Steve Sax once could not pick up a ball and throw it
seventy-five feet from his position at second base to the first baseman. Anyone who has watched Mets catcher Mackey Sasser the
last couple of years has seen his throwing problems. Intentional
walks and throwing to bases have become serious problems for

Matt Young after two years of obscurity and one year in front of
no one in Seattle. Darrell Johnson was out of baseball for a year
because of it. Jerry Moses almost had to give it up. Mets catcher
Phil Lombardi had to quit. "That was my boyhood dream," Lombardi told the *New York Times,* "and I was going to the park feeling sick to my stomach."

Harvey Dorfman, a psychologist — and former coach, counselor and teacher — who works with the Oakland Athletics, is a
lighthouse for any troubled player from any organization and
has coauthored (with Karl Kuehl) "The Mental Game of Baseball." He has talked to thousands of players. One, a 98-mph-
throwing kid named Steve Gasser, couldn't hit the wall of Dorfman's house in Prescott, Arizona.

"These problems almost always can be traced to some trauma,"
says Dorfman. "Ray Fosse had the problem. He couldn't throw
the ball to the pitcher. A couple of years ago we started talking,
and he traced it back to its inception. He was a rookie. Luis Tiant
was the ace of the Cleveland staff. Ray made a couple of throws
that were off. Tiant stuck his glove in front of his face and said,
'Throw the ball here, [expletive].' Ray related how it became imperative to hit Tiant's glove. He told himself, I *have* to do this. It
becomes a life-threatening situation; breathing stops and the
brain makes it so, physiologically, you can't throw the ball.

"But it all goes back to trauma, and traumatic memory forces
one to replicate the experience. Put a board three feet wide down
in your living room and you can walk down it fine. Put it across
the Grand Canyon and feel your legs. Well, to Ray Fosse or Steve
Gasser, Steve Blass or Bobby Sprowl, they feel as if they're falling
into the Grand Canyon on every throw.

"The more you think about it, the worse it becomes, and negative advice continually makes things worse. I know a pitcher
who has the problem who constantly wakes up from a dream
where he has thrown a ball in the bullpen that is wild, gets out
on the field and the game is stopped while the ball is retrieved
and everyone looks at him. He wakes up with this dream every
night."

Bobby Sprowl doesn't remember how many innings or how
many runs he allowed that March afternoon in 1979 in Daytona

Beach. "I guess I've tried to block some of that out," Sprowl says. "But I remember the pitch that hit the tarp two thirds of the way up to the press box. And that I never should have gone out there."

Sprowl, now the pitching coach at his alma mater, the University of Alabama, claims he doesn't believe it was the trauma of being thrown into the Red Sox' collapse and the Boston Massacre that caused him to go haywire. But he does come under Dorfman's category of being rushed with unrealistic expectations. Sprowl was supposed to be the phenom savior, thrust into the fray against Joe Morgan's recommendation. After a decent start in which he lost, 4–1, to Jim Palmer in Baltimore, Sprowl was asked to stop a Yankee sweep on September 10; he never made it out of the first inning. "I didn't pitch that badly, I wasn't *really* wild," Sprowl says.

But the first time he threw batting practice the next spring, he began to have problems throwing strikes. Three veteran players became angry. Rick Burleson flung down his bat and walked out. Another whom Sprowl refuses to identify yelled to a coach, "Get this [expletive] minor leaguer out of here. This is supposed to be the big leagues and this [expletive] is going to kill someone." Reminded that Sprowl indeed had pitched in the big leagues in September, the player said, "*That* was big league pitching?"

Sprowl was a nervous sort who fidgeted with his hands, contrary to minor league coach Johnny Podres's report to Don Zimmer that Sprowl "has ice water in his veins." He lacked social self-confidence and, as his room at the Holiday Inn was next to this reporter's, often came next door to chat at night. "I don't understand what's happening," he said one night. "It's embarrassing, and players act as if I'm embarrassing them."

Sprowl recalls that it kept unraveling. "I couldn't throw the ball to a catcher, I couldn't breathe properly," he says. "Guys were telling me that I was gripping the ball too tight. Everyone had a different idea. I remember trying to throw to a target I drew on a wall; I not only hit the target, but I could have thrown it through the wall. But put a catcher and a hitter out there . . .

"When I started taking abuse from teammates, it got more and more frustrating. At first I tried telling hitters I was just missing, but they wouldn't listen. Oh well, at least I got back to the big leagues. I wasn't hopeless. I know this: I watch Mackey Sasser on TV and I feel for him. God, I feel for him."

After going all the way back to Winter Haven, Florida, Sprowl was included in the deal for Bob Watson and eventually appeared in nineteen games for the Astros from 1979–81. He never won a game.

"After that spring, he never threw the ball as hard and had the great slider he had in the minors," says Bruce Hurst, who after successful work with Dorfman in 1983 tried to get Sprowl to talk to him. "Bobby Sprowl was awesome before he went haywire. But after that, he never threw the ball with abandon again. People ask me who was the best of our little lefty group — John Tudor, Bobby Ojeda or me. I tell them, 'Bobby Sprowl was the best left-hander the Red Sox developed since Mel Parnell.' But just as he was close to being developed, the wires got crossed."

Says Sprowl, "Kevin Saucier scouts this area, so I see him a lot. The same thing happened to him. We talk about what happened, but neither of us really knows. Every once in a while I'll be throwing batting practice, and I start thinking in the back of my mind what happened. But I'm O.K. I love what I'm doing.

"When I was coaching junior college, I had a kid who developed this problem. I talked to him about my problem and told him to just go to the bullpen and throw and throw and throw until it became natural again. He overcame it and is in the minors. I had another kid this year at 'Bama that the Yankees drafted; I don't think he will overcome it. I try to help."

"It's hard for Sprowl to help because he never identified the cause of his problem," says Dorfman. "He's thirty-five right now. He'd probably still be in the big leagues."

Sprowl was not alone that spring of 1979. The best young pitcher in the Red Sox' organization was Schneck, a twenty-three-year-old right-hander who was the Double A pitcher of the year with a 15–7, 2.15 record; his 2½-season minor league ERA was 2.13.

"I had put tremendous pressure on myself, as I'd believed my press clippings about making the club," says Schneck. "I went to Puerto Rico near the end of the winter season to be completely ready to make the team, and right at the end I had some problems with feeling at the tips of my fingers."

Was it psychosomatic?

"I don't know," he says. "It all happened so fast. Everything went haywire, and I had no feeling in my fingertips. But I don't know which came first."

Schneck's fastball skittered and ran in and out of the strike zone. Spring training 1979 started out harmless enough. "I was having trouble throwing the ball over the plate and had some trouble with the feeling, but I wasn't awful or anything," he says. "I had some trouble throwing strikes a couple of times in BP, and some veterans started yelling at me. It crushed me. I mean, here I was a kid, nervous, with all sorts of expectations and pressures, and I felt humiliated.

"Right before the games were to start, I was throwing in the bullpen and having trouble hitting Bob Montgomery's glove. He finally said 'Kid, I'm not going to move. If you can't throw it over the plate here, I'm going to let it go.' As Zimmer, Al Jackson, writers and fans watched, the balls kept rolling away. Then when I warmed up for my first appearance against the Tigers, the same thing happened. Montgomery kept letting the balls go by him. Only this time there were six thousand people in the stands, and I felt as if every one of them was watching me. It was the worst experience of my life, and I remember it as if it were twenty minutes ago." All Monty was trying to do was help Schneck concentrate, but . . .

"A week later, they had me warming up on the left mound in the two-mound bullpen in Winter Haven," recalls Schneck. "The pitcher on the right mound — Joel Finch, I think — had a batter in the right handed batter's box. I hit the guy in the head."

Three weeks after that, Schneck was sent down to work with the kids who hadn't made the Winter Haven or Winston-Salem rosters and would play in the extended spring program until June. He started against Harvard, and after walking the first six hitters, he wound up for the first pitch to the seventh hitter. He hit the batter in the on-deck circle and left the mound.

"I tried throwing with my eyes closed, and I threw strikes O.K." says Schneck. "During the extended spring, Eddie Popowski and Rac Slider did everything they could to restore my self-confidence and esteem, but when I got to Pawtucket, I was never the same." He was 8–13 with a 4.67 ERA and led the league with 101 walks in 143 innings. "The next spring, I was throwing balls up on backstops, and I told Ed Kenney I didn't know if I could go through it again." He tried a comeback in the Detroit system but had the same problem and retired.

Schneck now works with former Pawtucket outfielder Barry Butera running a baseball school in New Orleans. One of their pupils was Will Clark, who works out with them occasionally in the winter. "Schneck has as good stuff as anyone in the National League," says Clark.

Schneck, who has a bunch of no-hitters for Triple-A Sporting Goods in a semipro league, talked to Hurst about coming back and thought about a tryout with the Mets but changed his mind.

"I don't know if I could do it in front of crowds now," says Schneck. "One part of me wants to try it again, but the other part recalls what I went through. Some things you can't erase from one's memory."

Blass would prefer that he not have a disease named after him. He is a broadcaster with the Pirates now, an outgoing, insightful, gregarious man who also prefers not to talk about what he went through. He is remembered for Steve Blass disease more than his extraordinary pitching, which included eighty-one wins over five years, including a 2–0 shutout in the seventh game of the 1971 World Series. After that Series, he was 19–8. And after that, his record reads:

| 1973 Pittsburgh | 3–9 | 9.81 ERA | 84 BB 27 K |
| 1974 Charleston | 2–8 | 9.74 ERA | 103 BB 26 K |

"He was a little wild in spring training in 1973, but no one noticed," says Pirate coach Milt May, who caught Blass's first two starts that year. "He walked five or six in his first start. Nothing I noticed. Then in his next outing, he was facing the Braves. He went 3-and-0 on Ralph Garr leading off, and the fourth ball was behind him. Then three more fastballs, way out of the strike zone, to Marty Perez. I called for a slider. He threw it *behind* Perez. Then I knew something was haywire.

"It got worse and worse. But you know what's weird? Warming up in the bullpen, he always had his same great stuff, right on the black. Put a batter up there, and he couldn't throw it close."

John Curtis still recalls the day Blass threw a pitch that landed

in the stands halfway between third and home in a spring training game in 1974 in which Blass walked the first eight batters.

Blass told Roger Angell — who retold Blass's tale in the unforgettable piece "Gone for Good" (republished this spring in Angell's *Once More Around the Ballpark*) — that he doesn't to this day
know what happened. But he vividly recalled the spring of 1974:
"We have a custom in the early spring that calls for pitchers to
throw five minutes of batting practice every day. Well, the day
before the first workout, I woke up at 4:30 in the morning. I was
so worried that I couldn't get back to sleep — and this was just
throwing to pitchers. I don't remember what happened that first
time, but I know that I was tense and anxious every time I went
out."

Angell quoted former Pirate pitcher and broadcaster Nellie
King: "I think there's a lost kid in Steve. I remember after the
1971 World Series he said, 'I didn't think I was as good as this.'
He seemed truly surprised at what he'd done. The child in him
is such a great thing, and maybe suddenly he was afraid he was
losing it. It was being forced out of him. Being good up here is *so*
tough — people have no idea. It gets much worse when you have
to repeat it: 'We know you're great. Do it again for me.' Pretty
soon you're trying so hard, you can't function."

Dorfman brings up Dale Murphy. Now, Murphy has been a
great player, but he was legend. There was the spring training
game when he was catching and tried to throw to second, and
center fielder Barry Bonnell caught it on the fly. Or the time he
hit his pitcher in the derriere in Richmond.

"It was so bad that he couldn't throw the ball to the third baseman after a strikeout," says Pirate coach Gene Lamont. "He'd
wind up, and the left fielder would race over behind the third
baseman, catch the ball and relay it to the shortstop."

"Murphy had the pressures of being the future of the entire
Braves franchise," says Dorfman, who has spent countless hours
with Murphy, baseball's ultimate gentleman. "He finally had to
get to a position where he could throw. He went from catcher
to first and finally relaxed in the outfield. I've worked with
Brad Komminsk, who underwent a similar buildup and pressure
later. I'll guarantee you some of those buildups Sparky Ander-

son has laid on people has hurt some." One very nice person named Chris Pittaro was ruined by being Sparky's "best rookie I've ever seen" when he moved Lou Whitaker to third base for forty-eight hours.

"Some players are bothered by having to repeat success," says Dorfman. For instance, when Sonny Siebert won his seventeenth game the first week of September 1971, he didn't want to pitch the rest of the way, saying, "If I win twenty, they'll expect me to do it again." Dorfman says, "That isn't as uncommon as you'd think. I've worked with one former major league pitcher who says that every time he won, he'd go get drunk, wasted. If he lost, it was normal." Bruce Swango got $100,000 in the early 1950s and couldn't pitch in front of crowds.

"There's nothing funny about any of these problems," says Dorfman. "These are human beings with human conditions."

In March 1985, Engle was twenty-eight years old and a pretty good player on the rising Minnesota Twins. He'd batted .305 and .266 the previous two seasons while converting from the outfield to catcher. He'd made the 1984 All-Star team. He had grown up with baseball, as his father not only was Ted Williams's high school catcher but also ran the Ted Williams Camp in Lakeville; father and son drove cross-country from San Diego every June to Lakeville. "Baseball was my life," says the Tucson coach.

"I was catching batting practice and threw a ball back to the pitcher — normally," says Engle. "But it ticked the top of the screen in front of the pitcher and broke his nose. After that, I started occasionally flipping the ball — high in the air, so it came down like a parachute over the screen. Only I started doing it more and more, and before I knew it, I was throwing that way.

"One day Billy Gardner forced me to come out and make hundreds of throws; I threw thirty or forty balls into center field, I felt humiliated, and it got worse. Calvin Griffith called me into his office and aired me out, saying that I was making the pitchers work too hard catching my throws and it was costing them velocity and strength at the end of games. The great thing was that I played for one of the great teams of all time, and my teammates — especially Tom Brunansky, Gary Gaetti and Kent Hrbek — did everything they could to help me. At first, sure, they made fun of me; but as soon as they realized that it was serious, they rallied behind and beside me.

"It started to get worse as the season went along, and I think the day it all went haywire was against Oakland. I lobbed the ball back to the mound, and Alfredo Griffin stole third. That was the beginning of a nightmare. It got so I felt as if I were climbing up a rock on a mountain, and when I approached the top there was a rattlesnake. Every throw became life-threatening.

"It still haunts me, too. I dream about it. I wake up at night thinking about it. Every once in a while I'll be catching someone in BP and it'll come back. Or I'll be throwing BP and I have trouble. I figure it cost me a minimum of five million dollars, maybe more, when I see Rick Cerone and Jamie Quirk still catching."

The Twins unloaded him after the 1985 season, and he bounced from Detroit to Nashville to Montreal to Milwaukee and finally, last year, Oklahoma City.

"I still enjoy the game, and I love working with these kids," Engle says. "But I hope I get over this sometime. I hope I can sleep right again."

In 1988, the Dodgers had the fifth pick in the country and selected a right handed pitcher from Cal State, Los Angeles, named Bill Bene. The following year, Bene — who'd always had wildness problems — went off the deep end. They tried to use him in an extended spring simulated game; he hit the first batter and broke his hand. Then they tried having him throw with an inflatable doll in the batter's box.

"That got reported and all it did was publicly humiliate the poor kid," says Dorfman. Bene's 1989–90 record in Vero Beach, Bakersfield and Salem: 1–14, 8.86 ERA, 152 walks, 83 innings. One night last summer he threw five straight pitches off the backstop.

Sasser, who works with Dr. Allan Lans, the Mets' psychologist, goes through a series of bizarre motions trying to throw the ball back to the mound. He double-pumps, then leans back. Tim McCarver says many umpires try to help him by letting him lean back on them, but the arc of his throws has resulted in stolen bases and humiliation. Broadcaster Fran Healy relates to Sasser, because he went through the same thing in Kansas City.

"Throwing the ball back to the pitcher is not the real problem," says Lans. "The real problem may have a multitude of causes." Some are complex, involving fear of failure or parental expectation. Some involve other expectations, and can be traced — like Fosse's — right to the field.

Steve Sax understands how the night can torment a player with this problem. "I'd wake up in the night sweating, worried, thinking about the problem," says the second baseman. "I remember Tommy Lasorda screaming at me: 'You can hit .290. How many big leaguers can do that? You can steal forty bases. How many big leaguers can do that? *But do you know how many millions of broads can play catch — and you can't?*' But he hadn't been through this."

Right out of Dorfman's book, Sax can trace his famous throwing problems back to a traumatic experience in 1983. "We were playing a game against Montreal in April, and I took a relay in the outfield," Sax recalls. The runner stopped at third, but I stupidly whirled and threw to the plate. The ball bounced past the catcher, and the run scored. It cost us the game. That got it started. All of a sudden, I was afraid to throw. I don't know what it was. I know I had put a lot of pressure on myself with the buildup as the next great Dodger player, the future batting champion and stuff like that. But by the All-Star break I had twenty-six errors and never slept. I was in a snowball rolling through hell.

"They tried to tell me it was a mechanical thing; of course, it wasn't. I just decided to go out there every day and try to work on it until my proper throwing became motor-mechanical again. I'd take a sanitary [stocking], tie it across my face and throw blindfolded. I worked it out. One thing: it never affected me on double play balls where I had no time to think, and eventually I overcame it. Now, I want the ball hit to me. But I wouldn't wish that problem on anyone. And I'm sure the causes are different in every case."

Sax deserves to be remembered not for having the problem but for working it out. "Some guys disguise it," says Sax. "I didn't want to. I wanted it addressed."

Steve Garvey was one who successfully disguised his throwing phobia. But in the 1974 World Series, the A's knew he would

never field a bunt and throw to another base, so every time someone was on base, they bunted to Garvey. Part of that was Los Angeles. If Garvey hadn't been able to throw in Boston, New York
or Philadelphia . . .

Dorfman refuses to discuss Matt Young's problems, "because I
worked with him." All he will say is, "Matt had one very bad incident in L.A.," that "Matt's a very sad story" and "You'll never
know how much the pressure of the contract eats at him. That's
a tough thing to live with." In fact, in spring training, it so bothered San Francisco's Bud Black that he sat down with Dorfman
to talk out the pressures of his expectations. "Remember, the
guys most affected are usually responsible, good and intelligent,"
says Dorfman. "Most feel the more they talk, the more people
notice."

Young had throwing problems when he signed with the Mariners. "I used to tell him not to throw to first base on a ground
ball, and *never* to pick anyone off," says A's scout Jeff Scott,
Young's rookie league manager. But somewhere along the line,
it became a mental thing. Last year, he made three times as many
errors as Cal Ripken and hit two first-base coaches. He couldn't
give intentional walks normally.

Early in the season, Young had few chances and usually
grabbed a ground ball and sprinted toward first. But then came
an intentional walk that went haywire. One night he threw several warm-up pitches against the screen. Then came a couple of
wild throws . . .

It astounds baseball people that the Red Sox apparently knew
nothing of Young's problems when they committed $6.35 million
to him, especially in the home of the leather-lungs, where every
game is a life-or-death matter.

But it isn't funny, because if Young didn't care, he wouldn't
have the problem. It wasn't funny when it happened to Joe
Sparma in the late 1960s, starting as an inability to throw to bases
and ending up, as Jim Leyland remembers, "with a pitch off a
lightpole." Or when a great Texas pitching prospect named Jim
Gideon couldn't warm up. Or when veteran catcher Johnny Edwards had to carry the ball to the pitcher. Or when Dick Radatz
threw twenty-one straight balls in an exhibition game.

"Maybe the best way to be is to believe ignorance is bliss," says

Dorfman. "Maybe it's best not to feel responsibility, to not care or be smart enough so even traumatic memory can take effect." Maybe it's best to have what Philip Roth called "infantryman's heart." Or what John Keegan called "the face of battle." That is, the most common parts of heroism from medieval wars to Vietnam were drugs and alcohol that prevented men from going haywire.

For many, the trait that makes a man heroic and an athlete victorious is what you would not want in your son. Would Dave Engle and Bobby Sprowl sell their souls — that which makes them *human* — to be rich and great and famous?

WILLIAM NACK

O Unlucky Man

FROM SPORTS ILLUSTRATED

> Someday they're gonna write a blues song just for fighters. It'll be
> for slow guitar, soft trumpet and a bell.
> — Charles (Sonny) Liston

IT WAS already dark when she stepped from the car in front of
her house on Ottawa Drive, but she could see her pink Cadillac
convertible and Sonny's new black Fleetwood under the carport
in the Las Vegas night.

Where could Charles be? Geraldine Liston was thinking.

All through the house the lamps were lit, even around the
swimming pool out back. The windows were open too, and the
doors were unlocked. It was quiet except for the television playing in the room at the top of the stairs.

By 9:30 P.M. on January 5, 1971, Geraldine had not spoken to
her husband for twelve days. On Christmas Eve she had called
him from St. Louis after flying there with the couple's seven-
year-old son, Danielle, to spend the holidays with her mother.
Geraldine had tried to phone him a number of times, but no one
had answered at the house. At first she figured he must be off
roistering in Los Angeles, and so she didn't pay his absence any
mind until the evening of December 28. That night, in a fitful
sleep, she had a vision so unsettling that it awakened her and sent
her to her mother's room.

"I had the worst dream," Geraldine says. "He was falling in the
shower and calling my name, 'Gerry, Gerry!' I can still see it. So
I got real nervous. I told my mother, 'I think something's wrong.'
But my mother said, 'Oh, don't think that. He's all right.' "

In fact, Sonny Liston had not been right for a long time, and not only for the strangely dual life he had been leading — spells of choirboy abstinence squeezed between binges of drinking and drugs — but also for the rudderless, unfocused existence he had been reduced to. Jobless and nearly broke, Liston had been moving through the murkier waters of Las Vegas's drug culture. "I knew he was hanging around with the wrong people," one of his closest friends, gambler Lem Banker, says. "And I knew he was in desperate need of cash."

So, as the end of 1970 neared, Liston had reached that final twist in the cord. Eight years earlier he was the undisputed heavyweight champion of the world — a six-foot-one-and-a-half-inch 215-pound hulk with upper arms like picnic roasts, two magnificent, fourteen-inch fists and a scowl that he mounted for display on a round, otherwise impassive face. He had won the title by flattening Floyd Patterson with two punches, left hooks down and up, in the first round of their fight on September 25, 1962; ten months later he had beaten Patterson again in one round.

Liston did not sidestep his way to the title; the pirouette was not among his moves. He reached Patterson by walking through the entire heavyweight division, leaving large bodies sprawled behind him: Wayne Bethea, Mike DeJohn, Cleveland Williams, Nino Valdes, Roy Harris, Zora Folley et al. Finally, a terrified Patterson waited for him, already fumbling with his getaway disguise, dark glasses and a beard.

Before the referee could count to ten in that first fight, Liston had become a mural-sized American myth, a larger-than-life John Henry with two hammers, an 84-inch reach, 23 knockouts (in 34 bouts) and 19 arrests. Tales of his exploits spun well with the fight crowd over beers in dark-wood bars. There was the one about how he used to lift up the front end of automobiles. And one about how he caught birds with his bare hands. And another about how he hit speed bags so hard that he tore them from their hinges, and ripped into heavy bags until they burst, spilling their stuffing.

"Nobody hit those bags like Sonny," says eighty-year-old Johnny Tocco, one of Liston's first and last trainers. "He tore bags up. He could turn that hook, put everything behind it. Turn and snap. Bam! Why, he could knock you across the room with a jab. I saw him knock guys out with a straight jab. *Bam!* In the ring, Sonny was a killing machine."

Perhaps no fighter had ever brought to the ring so palpable an aura of menace. Liston hammered out danger, he hammered out a warning. There was his fearsome physical presence; then there was his heavy psychic baggage, his prison record and assorted shadows from the underworld. Police in three cities virtually drove him out of town; in one of them, St. Louis, a captain warned Liston that he would wind up dead in an alley if he stayed.

In public Liston was often surly, hostile and uncommunicative, and so he fed one of the most disconcerting of white stereotypes, that of the ignorant, angry, morally reckless black roaming loose, with bad intentions, in white society. He became a target for racial typing in days when white commentators could still utter undisguised slurs without Ted Koppel asking them to, please, explain themselves. In the papers Liston was referred to as "a gorilla," "a latter day caveman" and "a jungle beast." His fights against Patterson were seen as morality plays. Patterson was Good, Liston was Evil.

On July 24, 1963, two days after the second Patterson fight, *Los Angeles Times* columnist Jim Murray wrote: "The central fact . . . is that the world of sport now realizes it has gotten Charles (Sonny) Liston to keep. It is like finding a live bat on a string under your Christmas tree."

The NAACP had pleaded with Patterson not to fight Liston. Indeed, many blacks watched Liston's spectacular rise with something approaching horror, as if he were climbing the Empire State Building with Fay Wray in his hands. Here suddenly was a baleful black felon holding the most prestigious title in sports. This was at the precise moment in history when a young civil rights movement was emerging, a movement searching for role models. Television was showing freedom marchers being swept by fire hoses and attacked by police dogs. Yet, untouched by image makers, Liston steadfastly refused to speak any mind but his own. Asked by a young white reporter why *he* wasn't fighting for freedom in the South, Liston deadpanned, "I ain't got no dog-proof ass."

Four months after Liston won the title, *Esquire* thumbed its nose at its white readers with an unforgettable cover. On the front of its December 1963 issue, there was Liston glowering out from under a tasseled, red and white Santa Claus hat, looking like the last man on earth America wanted to see coming down its chimney.

Now, at the end of the Christmas holiday of 1970, that old black Santa was still missing in Las Vegas. Geraldine crossed though the carport of the Listons' split-level and headed for the patio out back. Danielle was at her side. Copies of the *Las Vegas Sun* had been gathering in the carport since December 29. Geraldine opened the back door and stepped into the den. A foul odor hung in the air, permeating the house, and so she headed up the three steps toward the kitchen. "I thought he had left some food out and it had spoiled," she says. "But I didn't see anything."

Leaving the kitchen, she walked toward the staircase. She could hear the television from the master bedroom. Geraldine and Danielle climbed the stairs and looked through the bedroom door, to the smashed bench at the foot of the bed and the stone-cold figure lying with his back up against it, blood caked on the front of his swollen shirt and his head canted to one side. She gasped and said, "Sonny's dead."

"What's wrong?" Danielle asked.

She led the boy quickly down the stairs. "Come on baby," she said.

On the afternoon of September 27, 1962, Liston boarded a flight from Chicago to Philadelphia. He settled into a seat next to his friend Jack McKinney, an amateur fighter who was then a sports writer for the *Philadelphia Daily News*. This was the day Liston had been waiting for ever since he first laced on boxing gloves, at the Missouri State Penitentiary a decade earlier. Forty-eight hours before, he had bludgeoned Patterson to become heavyweight champion. Denied a title fight for years, barred from New York City rings as an undesirable, largely ignored in his adopted Philadelphia, Liston suddenly felt vindicated, redeemed. In fact, before leaving the Sheraton Hotel in Chicago, he had received word from friends that the people of Philadelphia were awaiting his triumphant return with a ticker-tape parade.

The only disquieting tremor had been some other news out of

Philadelphia, relayed to him by telephone from friends back home, that *Daily News* sports editor Larry Merchant had written a column confirming Liston's worst fears about how his triumph might be received. Those fears were based on the ruckus that had preceded the fight. The *New York Times*'s Arthur Daley had led the way: "Whether Patterson likes it or not, he's stuck with it. He's the knight in shining armor battling the forces of evil."

Now wrote Merchant: "So it is true — in a fair fight between good and evil, evil must win. . . . A celebration for Philadelphia's first heavyweight champ is now in order. Emily Post probably would recommend a ticker-tape parade. For confetti we can use shredded warrants of arrest."

The darkest corner of Liston's personality was his lack of a sense of self. All the signs from his past pointed the same way and said the same thing: dead end. He was the twenty-fourth of the twenty-five children fathered by Tobey Liston, a tenant cotton farmer who lived outside Forrest City, Arkansas. Tobey had two families, one with fifteen children and the other with ten; Charles was born ninth to his mother, Helen. Outside the ring, he battled his whole life against writers who suggested that he was older than he claimed he was. "Maybe they think I'm so old because I never was really young," he said. Usually he would insist he was born on May 8, 1932, in the belly of the Great Depression, and he growled at reporters who dared to doubt him on this: "Anybody who says I'm not thirty is callin' my momma a liar."

"Sonny was so sensitive on the issue of his age because he did not really *know* how old he was," says McKinney. "When guys would write that he was thirty-two going on fifty, it had more of an impact on him than anybody realized. Sonny didn't know *who* he was. He was looking for an identity, and he thought that being the champion would give him one."

Now that moment had arrived. During the flight home, McKinney says, Liston practiced the speech he was going to give when the crowds greeted him at the airport. Says McKinney, who took notes during the flight, "He used me as sort of a test auditor, dry-running his ideas by me."

Liston was excited, emotional, eager to begin his reign. "There's a lot of things I'm gonna do," he told McKinney. "But one thing's very important: *I want to reach my people.* I want to reach them and tell them, 'You don't have to worry about me dis-gracin' you. You won't have to worry about me stoppin' your progress.' I want to go to colored churches and colored neigh-borhoods. I know it was in the papers that the better class of col-ored people were hopin' I'd lose, even prayin' I'd lose, because they was afraid I wouldn't know how to act. . . . I remember one thing so clear about listening to Joe Louis fight on the radio when I was a kid. I never remember a fight the announcer didn't say about Louis, 'A great fighter and a credit to his race.' Remember? That used to make me feel real proud inside.

"I don't mean to be sayin' I'm just gonna be the champion of my own people," Liston continued. "It says now I'm the world's champion, and that's just the way it's gonna be. I want to go to a lot of places — like orphan homes and reform schools. I'll be able to say, 'Kid, I know it's tough for you and it might even get tougher. But don't give up on the world. Good things can hap-pen if you let them.' "

Liston was ready. As the plane rolled to a stop, he rose and walked to the door. McKinney was next to him. The staircase was wheeled to the door. Liston straightened his tie and his fedora. The door opened, and he stepped outside. There was no one there except for airline workers, a few reporters and photogra-phers and a handful of PR men. "Other than those, no one," re-calls McKinney. "I watched Sonny. His eyes swept the whole scene. He was extremely intelligent, and he understood imme-diately what it meant. His Adam's apple moved slightly. You could feel the deflation, see the look of hurt in his eyes. It was almost like a silent shudder went through him. He'd been delib-erately snubbed.

"Philadelphia wanted nothing to do with him. Sonny felt, after he won the title, that the past was forgiven. It was going to be a whole new world. What happened in Philadelphia that day was a turning point in his life. He was still the bad guy. He was the personification of evil. And that's the way it was going to remain. He was devastated. I knew from that point on that the world would never get to know the Sonny that I knew."

On the way out of the airport after a brief press conference, Sonny turned to McKinney and said, "I think I'll get out tomor-row and do all the things I've always done. Walk down the block and buy the papers, stop in the drugstore, talk to the neighbors. Then I'll see how the *real peoples* feel. Maybe then I'll start to feelin' like a champion. You know, it's really a lot like an election, only in reverse. Here I'm already in office, but now I have to go out and start campaignin'."

That was a campaign that Liston could never win. He was to be forever cast in the role of devil's agent, and never more so than in his two stunning, ignominious losses to Cassius Clay, then beginning to be known as Muhammad Ali. In the history of boxing's heavyweight division, never has a fighter fallen faster, and farther, than did Liston in the fifteen months it took Ali to reduce him from being the man known as the fiercest alive to being the butt of jokes on TV talk shows.

"I think he died the day he was born," wrote Harold Conrad, who did publicity for four of Liston's fights. By the nearest reckoning, that birth would have been in a tenant's shack, seventeen miles northwest of Forrest City and about sixty west of Memphis. Helen had met Tobey in Mississippi and had gone with him to Arkansas around the time of World War I. Charles grew up lost among all the callused hands and bare feet of innumerable siblings. "I had nothing when I was a kid but a lot of brothers and sisters, a helpless mother and a father who didn't care about any of us," Liston said. "We grew up with few clothes, no shoes, little to eat. My father worked me hard and whupped me hard."

Helen moved to St. Louis during World War II, and Charles, who was living with his father, set out north to find her when he was thirteen. Three years later he weighed two hundred pounds, and he ruled his St. Louis neighborhood by force. At eighteen, he had already served time in a house of detention and was graduating to armed robbery. On January 15, 1950, Liston was found guilty of two counts of larceny from a person and two counts of first-degree robbery. He served more than two years in the Missouri State Pen in Jefferson City.

The prison's athletic director, Father Alois Stevens, a Catholic priest, first saw Liston when he came by the gym to join the boxing program. To Stevens, Liston looked like something out of *Jane's Fighting Ships*. "He was the most perfect specimen of manhood I had ever seen," Stevens recalls."Powerful arms, big shoulders. Pretty soon he was knocking out everybody in the gym. His hands were so large! I couldn't believe it. They always had trouble with his gloves, trouble getting them on when his hands were wrapped."

In 1952 Liston was released on parole, and he turned pro on September 2, 1953, leveling Don Smith in the first round in St. Louis. Tocco met Liston when the fighter strolled into Tocco's gym in St. Louis. The trainer's first memory of Liston is fixed, mostly for the way he came in — slow and deliberate and alone, feeling his way along the edges of the gym, keeping to himself, saying nothing. That was classic Liston, casing every joint he walked into, checking for exits. As Liston began to work, Tocco saw the bird tracks up and down Liston's back, the enduring message from Tobey Liston.

"What are all those welts from?" Tocco asked him.

Said Liston, "I had bad dealin's with my father."

"He was a loner," Tocco says. "He wouldn't talk to nobody. He wouldn't go with nobody. He always came to the gym by himself. He always left by himself. The police knew he'd been in prison, and he'd be walking along and they'd always stop him and search him. So he went through alleys all the time. *He always went around things.* I can still see him, either coming out of an alley or walking into one."

Nothing was simpler for Liston to fathom than the world between the ropes — step, jab, hook — and nothing more unyielding than the secrets of living outside them. He was a mob fighter right out of prison. One of his managers, Frank Mitchell, the publisher of the *St. Louis Argus,* who had been arrested numerous times on suspicion of gambling, was a known front for John Vitale, St. Louis's reigning hoodlum. Vitale had ties to organized crime's two most notorious boxing manipulators: Frankie Carbo and Carbo's lieutenant, Frank (Blinky) Palermo, who controlled mob fighters out of Philadelphia. Vitale was in the construction business (among others), and when Liston wasn't fighting, one of his jobs was cracking heads and keeping black laborers in line. Liston always publicly denied this, but years later he confided his role to one of his closest Las Vegas friends, Davey Pearl, a boxing referee. "He told me that when he was in St. Louis, he worked as a labor goon," says Pearl, "breaking up strikes."

Not pleased with the company Liston was keeping — one of his pals was 385-pound Barney Baker, a reputed head-cracker for the Teamsters — the St. Louis police kept stopping Liston, on sight and without cause, until, on May 5, 1956, three and a half years after his release from prison, Liston assaulted a St. Louis policeman, took his gun, left the cop lying in an alley and hid the weapon at a sister's house. The officer suffered a broken knee and a gashed face. The following December, Liston began serving nine months in the city workhouse.

Soon after his release Liston had his second run-in with a St. Louis cop. The officer had creased Liston's skull with a nightstick, and two weeks later the fighter returned the favor by depositing the fellow headfirst in a trash can. Liston then fled St. Louis for Philadephia, where Palermo installed one of his pals, Joseph (Pep) Barone, as Liston's manager, and Liston at once began fighting the biggest toughs in the division. He stopped Bethea, who spit out seven teeth, in the first round. Valdes fell in three, and so did Williams. Harris swooned in one, and Folley fell like a tree in three. Eddie Machen ran for twelve rounds but lost the decision. Albert Westphal keeled in one. Now Liston had one final fight to win. Only Patterson stood between him and the title.

Whether or not Patterson should deign to fight the ex-con led, at the time, to a weighty moral debate among the nation's reigning sages of sport. What sharpened the lines were Liston's recurring problems with the law in Philadelphia, including a variety of charges stemming from a June 1961 incident in Fairmount Park. Liston and a companion had been arrested for stopping a female motorist after dark and shining a light in her car. All charges, including impersonating a police officer, were eventually dropped. A month before, Liston had been brought in for loitering on a street corner. That charge, too, was dropped. More damaging were revelations that he was, indeed, a mob fighter, with a labor goon's history. In 1960, when Liston was the number one heavyweight contender, testimony before a U.S. Senate subcommittee probing underworld control of boxing and revealed that Carbo and Palermo together owned a majority interest in him. Of this, Liston said, he knew nothing. "Pep Barone handles me," he said.

"Do you think that people like [Carbo and Palermo] ought to remain in the sport of boxing?" asked the committee chairman, Tennessee Senator Estes Kefauver.

"I wouldn't pass judgment on no one," Liston replied. "I haven't been perfect myself."

In an act of public cleansing after the Fairmount Park incident, Liston spent three months living in a house belonging to the Loyola Catholic Church in Denver, where he had met Father Edward Murphy, a Jesuit priest, while training to fight Folley in 1960. Murphy, who died in 1975, became Liston's spiritual counselor and teacher. "Murph gave him a house to live in and tried to get him to stop drinking," Father Thomas Kelly, one of Murphy's closest friends, recalls. "That was his biggest problem. You could smell him in the mornings. Oh, poor Sonny. He was just an accident waiting to happen. Murph used to say, 'Pray for the poor bastard.'"

But even Liston's sojourn in Denver didn't still the debate over his worthiness to fight for the title. In this bout between good and evil, the clearest voice belonged to *New York Herald Tribune* columnist Red Smith: "Should a man with a record of violent crime be given a chance to become champion of the world? Is America less sinful today than in 1853 when John Morrissey, a saloon brawler and political headbreaker out of Troy, N.Y., fought Yankee Sullivan, lammister from the Australian penal colony in Botany Bay? In our time, hoodlums have held championships with distinction. Boxing may be purer since their departure; it is not healthier."

Since he could not read, Liston missed many pearls, but friends read scores of columns to him. When Barone was under fire for his mob ties, Liston quipped, "I got to get me a manager that's not hot — like Estes Kefauver." Instead, he got George Katz, who quickly came to appreciate Liston's droll sense of humor. Katz managed Liston for 10 percent of his purses, and as the two sat in court at Liston's hearing for the Fairmount Park incident, Liston leaned over to Katz and said, "If I get time, you're entitled to ten percent of it."

Liston was far from the sullen, insensitive brute of the popular imagination. Liston and McKinney would take long walks between workouts, and during them Liston would recite the complete dialogue and sound effects of the comedy routines of black comedians like Pigmeat Markham and Redd Foxx. "He could imitate what he heard down to creaking doors and women's voices," says McKinney. "It was hilarious hearing him do falsetto."

Liston also fabricated quaint metaphors to describe phenomena ranging from brain damage to the effects of his jab: "The middle of a fighter's forehead is like a dog's tail. Cut off the tail and the dog goes all whichway 'cause he ain't got no more balance. It's the same with a fighter's forehead."

He lectured occasionally on the unconscious, though not in the Freudian sense. Setting the knuckles of one fist into grooves between the knuckles of the other fist, he would explain: "See, the different parts of the brain set in little cups like this. When you get hit a terrible shot — *pop!* — the brain flops out of them cups and you're knocked out. Then the brain settles back in the cups and you come to. But after this happens enough times, or sometimes even once if the shot's hard enough, the brain don't settle back right in them cups, and that's when you start needing other people to help you get around."

So it was that Liston vowed to hit Patterson on the dog's tail until his brain flopped out of its cups. Actually, he missed the tail and hit the chin. Patterson was gone. Liston had trained to the minute, and he would never again be as good a fighter as he was that night. For what? Obviously, nothing in his life had changed. He left Philadelphia after he won the title, because he believed he was being harassed by the police of Fairmount Park, through which he had to drive to get from the gym to his home. At one point he was stopped for "driving too slow" through the park. That did it. In 1963 he moved to Denver, where he announced, "I'd rather be a lamppost in Denver than the mayor of Philadelphia."

At times, in fact, things were not much better in the Rockies. "For a while the Denver police pulled him over every day," says Ray Schoeninger, a former Liston sparring partner. "They must have stopped him a hundred times outside City Park. He'd run on the golf course, and as he left in his car, they'd stop him. Twenty-five days in a row. Same two cops. They thought it was a big joke. It made me ashamed of being a Denver native. Sad they never let him live in peace."

Liston's disputes were not always with the police. After he had

won the title, he walked into the dining room of the Beverly Rodeo Hotel in Hollywood and approached the table at which former rum-runner Moe Dalitz, head of the Desert Inn in Las Vegas
and a boss of the old Cleveland mob, was eating. The two men
spoke. Liston made a fist and cocked it. Speaking very distinctly,
Dalitz said, "If you hit me, nigger, you'd better kill me. Because
if you don't, I'll make one telephone call, and you'll be dead in
twenty-four hours." Liston wheeled and left.

The police and Dalitz were hardly Liston's only tormentors.
There was a new and even more inescapable disturber of his
peace: the boisterous Clay. Not that Liston at first took notice.
After clubbing Patterson, he took no one seriously. He hardly
trained for the rematch in Las Vegas. Clay, who hung around
Liston's gym while the champion went through the motions of
preparing for Patterson, heckled him relentlessly. Already a minor poet, Clay would yell at Liston, "Sonny is a fatty. I'm gonna
whip him like his daddy!" One afternoon he rushed up to Liston,
pointed to him and shouted, "He ain't whipped nobody! Who's
he whipped?" Liston, sitting down, patted a leg and said, "Little
boy, come sit in my lap." But Clay wouldn't sit; he was too busy
running around and bellowing, "The beast is on the run!"

Liston spotted Clay one day in the Thunderbird Casino,
walked up behind him and tapped him on the shoulder. Clay
turned and Liston cuffed him hard with the back of his hand.
The place went silent. Young Clay looked frightened. "What you
do that for?" he said.

" 'Cause you're too —— fresh," Liston said. As he headed out
of the casino, he said, "I got the punk's heart now."

That incident would be decisive in determining the outcome
of the first Liston-Clay fight, seven months later. "Sonny had no
respect for Clay after that," McKinney says. "Sonny thought all
he had to do was take off his robe and Clay would faint. He made
this colossal misjudgment. He didn't train at all."

If he had no respect for Clay, Liston was like a child around
the radio hero of his boyhood, Joe Louis. When George Lois,
than an art director at *Esquire,* decided to try the black-Santa
cover, he asked his friend Louis to approach Liston. Liston
grudgingly agreed to do the shoot in Las Vegas. Photographer
Carl Fischer snapped one photograph, whereupon Liston rose,

took off the cap and said, "That's it." He started out the door. Lois grabbed Liston's arm. The fighter stopped and stared at the art director. "I let his arm go," Lois recalls.

While Liston returned to the craps tables, Lois was in a panic. "One picture!" Lois says. "You need to take fifty, a hundred pictures to make sure you get it right." He ran to Louis, who understood Lois's dilemma. Louis found Liston shooting craps, walked up behind him, reached up, grabbed him by an ear and marched him out of the casino. Bent over like a puppy on a leash, Liston followed Louis to the elevator, with Louis muttering, "Come on, git!" The cover shoot resumed.

A few months later, of course, Clay handled Liston almost as easily. Liston stalked and chased, but Clay was too quick and too fit for him. By the end of the third round Liston knew that his title was in peril, and he grew desperate. One of Liston's trainers, Joe Pollino, confessed to McKinney years later that Liston ordered him to rub an astringent compound on his gloves before the fourth round. Pollino complied. Liston shoved his gloves into Clay's face in the fourth, and the challenger's eyes began burning and tearing so severely that he could not see. In his corner, before the fifth round, Clay told his handlers that he could not go on. His trainer, Angelo Dundee, had to literally push him into the ring. Moving backward faster than Liston moved forward, Clay ducked and dodged as Liston lunged after him. He survived the round.

By the sixth, Clay could see clearly again, and as he danced and jabbed, hitting Liston at will, the champion appeared to age three years in three minutes. At the end of that round, bleeding and exhausted, he could foresee his humiliating end. His left shoulder had been injured — he could no longer throw an effective punch with it — and so he stayed on his stool, just sat there at the bell to start round seven.

There were cries that Liston had thrown the fight. That night Conrad, Liston's publicist, went to see him in his room, where Liston was sitting in bed, drinking.

"What are they sayin' about the fight?" Liston asked.

"That you took a dive," said Conrad.

Liston raged. "Me? Sell my title? Those dirty bastards!" He threw his glass and shattered it against the wall.

The charges of a fix in that fight were nothing compared with what would be said about the rematch, in Lewiston, Maine, during which Liston solidified his place in boxing history. Ali, as the young champion was now widely called, threw one blow, an overhand right so dubious that it became known as the Phantom Punch, and suddenly Liston was on his back. The crowd came to its feet in anger, yelling, "Fake! Fake!"

Ali looked down at the fallen Liston, cocked a fist and screamed, "Get up and fight, sucker! Get up and fight!"

There was chaos. Referee Joe Walcott, having vainly tried to push Ali to a neutral corner, did not start a count, and Liston lay there unwilling to rise. "Clay caught me cold," Liston would recall. "Anybody can get caught in the first round, before you work up a sweat. Clay stood over me. I never blacked out. But I wasn't gonna get up, either, not with him standin' over me. See, you can't get up without puttin' one hand on the floor, and so I couldn't protect myself."

The finish was as ugly as a Maine lobster. Walcott finally moved Ali back, and as Liston rose, Walcott wiped off his gloves and stepped away. Ali and Liston resumed fighting. Immediately, Nat Fleischer, editor of *The Ring* magazine, who was sitting next to the official timer, began shouting for Walcott to stop the fight. Liston had been down for seventeen seconds, and Fleischer, who had no actual authority at ringside, thought the fight should have been declared over. Walcott left the two men fighting and walked over to confer with Fleischer. Though he had never even started a count, Walcott then turned back to the fighters, and incredibly, stepped between them to end the fight. "I was never counted out," Liston said later. "I coulda got up *right* after I was hit."

No one believed him, of course, and even Geraldine had her doubts. Ted King, one of Liston's seconds, recalls her angrily accusing Sonny later that night of going in the water.

"You could have gotten up and you stayed down!" she cried.

Liston looked pleadingly at King. "Tell her, Teddy," he said. "Tell her I got hit."

Some who were at ringside that night, and others who have studied the films, insist that Ali indeed connected with a shattering right. But Liston's performance in Lewiston has long been perceived as a tank job, and not a convincing one at that. One of Liston's assistant trainers claims that Liston threw the fight for fear of being murdered. King now says that two well-dressed Black Muslims showed up in Maine before the fight — Ali had just become a Muslim — and warned Liston, "You get killed if you win." So, according to King, Liston chose a safer ending. It seems fitting somehow that Liston should spend the last moments of the best years of his life on his back while the crowd showered him with howls of execration. Liston's two losses to Ali ended the short, unhappy reign of the most feared — and the most relentlessly hounded — prizefighter of his time.

Liston never really retired from the ring. After two years of fighting pushovers in Europe, he returned to the United States and began a comeback of sorts in 1968. He knocked out all seven of his opponents that year and won three more matches in 1969 before an old sparring partner, Leotis Martin, stopped him in the ninth round of a bout on December 6. That killed any chance at a title shot. On June 29, 1970, he fought Chuck Wepner in Jersey City. Tocco, Liston's old trainer from the early St. Louis days, prepared him for the fight against the man known as the Bayonne Bleeder. Liston hammered Wepner with jabs, and in the sixth round Tocco began pleading with the referee to stop the fight. "It was like blood was coming out of a hydrant,"says Tocco. The referee stopped the bout in the tenth; Wepner needed fifty-seven stitches to close his face.

That was Liston's last fight. He earned $13,000 for it, but he would up broke nonetheless. Several weeks earlier, Liston had asked Banker to place a $10,000 bet for him on undefeated heavyweight contender Mac Foster to whip veteran Jerry Quarry. Quarry stopped Foster in the sixth round, and Liston promised Banker he would pay him back after the Wepner fight. When Liston and Banker boarded the flight back to Las Vegas, Liston opened a brown paper bag, carefully counted out $10,000 in small bills and handed the wad to Banker. "He gave the other $3,000 to guys in his corner," Banker said. "That left him with nothing."

In the last weeks of his life Liston was moving with a fast crowd. At one point a Las Vegas sheriff warned Banker, through a mutual friend, to stay away from Liston. "We're looking into a drug deal," said the sheriff. "Liston is getting involved with the wrong people." At about the same time two Las Vegas policemen stopped by the gym and told Tocco that Liston had recently turned up at a house that would be the target of a drug raid. Says Tocco, "For a week the police were parked in a lot across the street, watching when Sonny came and who he left with."

On the night Geraldine found his body, Liston had been dead at least six days, and an autopsy revealed traces of morphine and codeine of a type produced by the breakdown of heroin in the body. His body was so decomposed that tests were inconclusive — officially, he died of lung congestion and heart failure — but circumstantial evidence suggests that he died of a heroin overdose. There were fresh needle marks on one of his arms. An investigating officer, Sergeant Gary Beckwith, found a small amount of marijuana along with heroin and a syringe in the house.

Geraldine, Banker and Pearl all say that they had no knowledge of Liston's involvement with drugs, but law enforcement officials say they have reason to believe that Liston was a regular heroin user. It is possible that those closest to him may not have known of his drug use. Liston had apparently lived two lives for years.

Pearl was always hearing reports of Liston's drinking binges, but Liston was a teetotaler around Pearl. "I never saw Sonny take a drink," says Pearl. "Ever. And I was with him hundreds of times over the last five years of his life. He'd leave me at night, and the next morning someone would say to me., 'You should have seen your boy, Liston, last night. Was he ever drunk!' I once asked him, 'What is this? You leave me at night and go out and get drunk?' He just looked at me. I never, ever suspected him of doing dope. I'm telling you, I don't think he did."

Some police officials and not a few old friends think that Liston may have been murdered, though they have no way of proving it now. Conrad believes that Liston became deeply involved in a loan-sharking ring in Las Vegas, as a bill collector, and that he tried to muscle in for a bigger share of the action. His employers got him drunk, Conrad surmises, took him home and stuck him with a needle. There are police in Las Vegas who say they believe — but are unable to prove — that Liston was the target of a hit ordered by Ash Resnick, an old associate of Liston's with whom the former champion was having a dispute over money. Resnick died two years ago.

Geraldine has trouble comprehending all that talk about heroin or murder. "If he was killed, I don't know who would do it," she says. "If he was doing drugs, he didn't act like he was drugged. Sonny wasn't on dope. He had high blood pressure, and he had been out drinking in late December. As far as I'm concerned, he had a heart attack. Case closed."

There is no persuasive explanation of how Liston died, so the speculation continues, perhaps to last forever.

Liston is buried in Paradise Memorial Gardens, in Las Vegas, directly under the flight path for planes approaching McCarran International Airport. The brass plate on the grave is tarnished now, but the epitaph is clear under his name and the years of his life. It reads simply: A MAN. Twenty years ago Father Murphy flew in from Denver to give the eulogy, then went home and wept for an hour before he could compose himself enough to tell Father Kelly about the funeral. "They had the funeral procession down the Strip," Murphy said. "Can you imagine that? People came out of the hotels to watch him pass. They stopped everything. They used him all his life. They were still using him on the way to the cemetery. There he was, another Las Vegas show. God help us."

In the end, it seemed fitting that Liston, after all those years, should finally play to a friendly crowd on the way to his own burial — with a police escort, the most ironic touch of all.

Geraldine remained in Las Vegas for nine years after Sonny died — she was a casino hostess — then returned to St. Louis, where she had met Sonny after his parole, when he was working in a munitions factory. She has never remarried, and today works as a medical technician. "He was a great guy, great with me, great with kids, a gentle man," says Geraldine.

With Geraldine gone from Las Vegas, few visit Sonny's grave anymore. Every couple of minutes a plane roars over, shaking the earth and rattling the broken plastic flowers that someone placed in the metal urn atop his headstone. "Every once in a while someone comes by and asks to see where he's buried," says a cemetery worker. "But not many anymore. Not often."

JAMES KILGO

Mountain Spirits

FROM THE SEWANEE REVIEW

THE MAN who told me how to find Bascomb Creek had lowered
his voice to keep from being overheard by the people standing
near us. "It's hard to find but it's easy to fish," he'd whispered,
"and it's jumping with trout. Just keep it to yourself." That
sounded too good to be true, but as soon as I got home I called
my friend Charlie Creedmore. At five o'clock the next Saturday
morning we were driving north toward Rabun County. At first
light we crossed the concrete bridge over Bascomb Creek, pulled
over at a wide spot in the gravel road and climbed out. Charlie
headed upstream while I made my way south through the dim
woods. After walking for perhaps twenty minutes I stepped into
the water and began fishing back toward the bridge. My skepticism had been well founded. The canopy was too low for easy
casting, and because of drought the water was warm and shallow,
the pools few and far between. I waded fast, eager for a pool I
could cast to, and before I knew it I was back at the bridge. It was
not yet eight o'clock.

Between me and the bridge, and several terraces above my
head, lay a wide inviting pool. Streams of water spilled from it,
splashing down to where I stood. I climbed slowly, careful not to
spook any fish it might hold. Then, at eye level, on shelved stone
around the pool, I saw the trash: Styrofoam fast-food containers,
empty cans labeled Niblets, beer cans, and the plastic six-pack
rings they had come in. I could almost see the crowd that left it,
craning their necks at the hatchery truck on the bridge above,
eager for its bounty of washed-out rainbows. Keep it to yourself,
the man had said.

At least a dozen trout had survived the last onslaught. They were schooled near the bottom — eight- and ten-inchers they looked like — hanging still in the cold lower layer. Tin cans glinted through the depths.

I congratulated myself a little on having the decency not to cast to those harried fish, though in fact I doubted that they would take a fly. I thought of the thermos of coffee in the Blazer, said to hell with fishing, and climbed through the littered woods toward the road. Near the top I came upon a blind TV, set upright among the hemlocks. The road itself looked like a garbage dump. I laid my fly rod across the hood of the Blazer and poured myself a cup of coffee. Amidst the trash across the road fluttered strips of toilet paper.

I did not want to think that mountain people had made this mess. I wanted to believe that mountain people behaved like the stout old craftsmen I had read about in the *Foxfire* books, that treasure of Appalachian lore collected right here in Rabun County by Eliot Wigginton and his high school students. I knew better than that, of course. The *Foxfire* project was itself a response to the threat of commercial development.

Many years earlier I had taught a young man who had been part of Wigginton's first group of student folklorists. I remembered well a quart jar of white likker he brought me one Monday morning. "That's what they call it," he said. "White likker. And that right there is the best in Rabun County."

The jar had lasted three years because I drank it slowly, saving it for those times when I needed an antidote against the banalities of the world I lived in.

I turned to look again at the broken TV in the woods. Its doleful stare from out of the hemlocks reminded me of a colleague who lost his composure one day over the stupidity of a program his children were watching. Before his rage spent itself, he had hauled the family set out into the country and shot it to pieces with a deer rifle. After the fact he had been a little embarrassed, but he explained to me that he'd had to do it, had to accomplish its destruction with his own hands. In the long run, though, it did no good. By the time he got back home, a neighbor, having heard that his children were deprived of television, had donated one of hers.

I at such times took a ritual sip from the fruit jar. The bite of that mountain corn — like good medicine — reminded me that in Rabun County at least people were still living in a world crafted by their own hands. But that had been fifteen years ago; the jar was long since empty and I had not tasted any since.

As I began to unseat the reel from my fly rod, I heard a car coming, tires on gravel, approaching the bridge. But it wasn't a car. It was an old pickup, dead paint blue, and it pulled to a stop directly across the road from me, scattering trash. I became uncomfortably conscious of my fly-fishing vest, Orvis zingers dangling down the front, laminated landing net hanging from the back. I wished I had taken it off. Intent on the rod I ignored the truck.

A door opened, slammed shut. Someone was coming. I glanced — a local it was, sleeveless shirt unbuttoned, black hair greased down solid. Thick glasses magnified his eyes, but the detail that bothered me most was the frames — opaque green and plastic, dime-store glasses. I had often berated city folks ignorant enough to assume that everyone in Rabun County is as depraved as the two perverts in James Dickey's *Deliverance,* but this fellow at best looked like the kind who would dump his broken TV in the woods. I wondered where Charlie was, what was taking him so long. The man was not walking straight toward me so much as sidling in my direction, and while his face was set my way his eyes seemed fixed, sure enough, on the television set behind me. A bad burn was healing on the back of one hand.

"You going or coming?" he asked.

"Just waiting on my buddy," I said.

"What you fishing with?"

For the first time in my life I hated having to say "fly rod."

The man glanced at it, muttered an obscenity.

"I couldn't do nothing with 'em," I said. "Y'all getting ready to try 'em?"

"You ever hear about old Towse?"

The senselessness of the question disturbed me more than anything that had happened yet. "No," I said, "I don't believe I have." I unjointed the sections of my rod, anxious for Charlie.

"I thought you might have heared about old Towse."

The man was close enough now for me to smell the whiskey on his breath. I had a feeling that a lot depended on the answer I gave. "No. You'll have to tell me about him."

"Coon dog. You want a drink?"

As early as it was, I chose what seemed the prudent course. "I believe I might."

The man led me across the road. As we approached the pickup, he spoke to his companion, who was concealed behind the glare of the windshield. "Monroe, reach me that bottle."

While Monroe was bestirring himself, I noticed a revolver on the dash — an unholstered nickel .38, every visible chamber loaded. I could picture it sliding hard from one side to the other as the truck swung through hairpin curves.

Monroe climbed out on the far side — an older man with a puffy, pocked face, wearing overalls and a soft-looking old baseball cap. Without a word or nod of greeting he offered the bottle across the hood — a fifth of liquid as clear as vodka, but the remains of a label suggested that its original contents had been quite different. A blue and red can of RC Cola followed.

Rabun County white likker, I thought, but who knows how bad this stuff might be. As afraid as I was to drink it, I was more afraid not to. Besides, I wanted to hear the story. If this homemade product fell short of my memory of the student's gift, I would say, "That's good, thank you, but I'm afraid it's a little early in the day for me."

It was good. I mean it tasted right as far as I could tell, serious but smooth, no barbed wire in it, and a flavor unlike that of any commercial sourmash I had ever drunk. I declined the RC and took another swallow.

"They's a Church a God preacher over in Walhally put out a bluegrass song on him," the one with glasses said.

On Towse, he meant.

"And they tell me a feller up in Franklin made a ballad about him too, but I ain't heared that one."

"Can you sing the Church of God one?" I asked.

"I ain't got my guitar. You remember the words to it, Monroe?"

"I can't keep 'em straight."

"Damn if he wont a good one. Trail didn't get too cold for Towse."

"I didn't think there were that many coons up here."

"It ain't. Not like it used to be. Where you from?"

I told them I lived in Athens. The one with glasses, whose

name was Roy, said they used to hunt around Athens — down in Jackson County — a world of coons down there. He asked was I with the university. Somewhat surprised, I said yes. He figured that must be a good job. Monroe said a cousin of his had a daughter went to the university, he thought I might have known her, named Tami Bascomb, works for a bank in Atlanta now. I started to explain that the university was much larger than most people realized, but Roy passed me the bottle and Monroe said, "They ain't near the game in these mountains they used to be."

"I thought the deer and turkeys were coming back," I said.

"Too much goddamn, Atlanta," Monroe said. "Used to, a man could feed his family just on hunting and fishing, plant a garden, maybe run a little likker on the side. Right up yonder in that cove one day I killed four pheasants and thirteen gray squirrels."

"Is that right?" I asked, careful to conceal my skepticism. By pheasant Monroe meant ruffed grouse. I had hunted the bird enough to know that four in one day, in these steep wooded hills, required a combination of remarkable luck and exceptional wing shooting.

"Shore did. Shot three on the ground and one in the air. And thirteen gray squirrels." Monroe held his fist to his face. "I had me a string of stuff this long."

"The thing about Towse," Roy said, "he wouldn't give up on no coon. You take a normal dog, a old coon'll lose him, swim the river on him, run on rock — rock'll not hold his scent, see. But Towse'd stay on his ass — rock, water, what have you. He run a coon one night up in a rock clift." Roy took a pull on the bottle, chased it with RC, passed the bottle to me. "That's what done him in."

I had to ask Roy to explain what he meant by a rock clift.

"Why, it's kindly like a hole."

"A hole in the ground?"

"No. It's where you have a clift in the rock." He paused, then continued, "Hell, it's just a rock clift, is what it is."

I featured a deep cleft in the face of a cliff. "And Towse did what? Ran a coon into the rock clift?"

"That he did. Time we got there, the hole was done caved in, all them dogs a-running round, a-climbing rocks, barking treed. My brother said, 'I don't see Towse.' The old man said, ' 'Cause he's in there with 'at coon is why.' You remember that, Monroe?

And shore 'nough, you could hear him; over all them other dogs, you could hear him way down in that rock clift, a-killing that coon."

Somewhere in Roy's account Monroe had begun to talk. Intent on Roy, I had picked up only snatches, enough to realize that his comments had nothing to do with Towse. He was talking about fishing as far as I could tell, but Roy seemed not to mind; he didn't even slow up. The two men were as oblivious to each other as two radios tuned to different stations, turned up loud. Trying to hear what both were saying was frustrating. If I could stop Monroe with a question, maybe Roy could finish his story. "*What* kind of trout?" I asked.

"Speckled trout."

Roy was saying something about the cave-in, something to do with a slab-sided bitch that was down in there with Towse, but Monroe went right on. "Damn near rare as a chestnut tree anymore. Hatchery fish is what done it. Used to, speckled trout was all you'd catch."

Roy was still talking — not competing with Monroe, just telling his story. But I was interested also in this mysterious speckled trout. "I'm not familiar with that fish," I said.

"Generally he'll not go more'n six inches. And real bright. Orange and red and black and white and speckled."

"You mean a brook trout?"

"No. A speckled trout. Old-timey, original fish. Catch him in the morning, he'll not rot on you like these here goddamn stocked fish. He's the best eating fish they is. Meat's right pink. I caught forty-three one day, on up Bascomb Creek here."

Roy had stopped to take a drink and had not yet recovered his voice.

"What did you catch them on?" I asked, thinking, corn probably.

"Sawyers. Sawyers and waust grubs."

I had to ask what he meant by sawyers.

"Fat white worms. You find 'em in a old rotten log. Best bait they is. That and waust and hornet grubs."

I wondered how one acquired wasp and hornet larvae, especially during the summer when nests are active, but Monroe did not regard that as a matter requiring explanation.

"You need to cook 'em first. Bake 'em in the oven about forty-five minutes, get 'em right tough. That way they'll stay on your hook. Used to, it'd take my daddy three days to get ready to go a-fishing, three days to gather up his bait. But when he went he by God caught 'em. All speckled trout too.

"It's best to wait for a good hard pour to dingey up the creek. It come up a hell of a rain the day I caught them forty-three. I found me a stooping tree to get up under and waited for it to quit. Time it did I caught the fire out of 'em."

"Was Bascomb Creek named after some of your people?"

"I imagine it was, but I couldn't tell you just exactly who. My granddaddy owned from the bridge here clear up to the headwaters on Hogpen Mountain. But it was Bascomb Creek before his time. They used to be a world of Bascombs all up through here. I reckon we was all kin one way or another."

"Did your granddaddy sell his land to the Forest Service?"

"A right smart of it, he did. And what little bit the government left, goddamn developers got. You know Blue Mountain Ski Resort? Got that off my granddaddy's old sister and her not knowing no better."

"It's got to where now a man can't afford to keep his own place," Roy said.

I was afraid the end of his story about Towse had been swallowed up in Monroe's lament for speckled trout, as the dog himself was buried beneath the rock slide. But surely there was more to it than just a dead coon hound, or why would Roy have asked a stranger if he'd heard about old Towse? That might have been the whiskey, of course, but people didn't make ballads out of what I'd heard so far.

"Goddamn Atlanta," Monroe said.

"Florida too," Roy added.

"They say these tourists spend a lot of money up here," I suggested.

"Shit." For once they spoke in unison. Roy said he was yet to see the first green dollar of it hisself, and Monroe said: "You want to see that tourist money, look at all this trash strowed up and down the road. People got no self-respect."

I did not believe that tourists from Atlanta and Florida had driven through the national forest throwing garbage from their windows, and I didn't think Monroe did either, but somewhere in his comment was an association of one with the other that was worth thinking about.

"Same thing with likker. Used to, a man took pride in making whiskey, but this goddamn radiator likker they're selling now kill you. I've seen some would peel the paint off a car. They was a fellow up here at Scaly one night spit out a mouthful against the door of a pickup truck, it run down the side, took the paint right with it."

"How do they use a radiator?"

"Condenser. Instead of a worm. Then they'll put potash in on you, Irish taters, no damn telling what all. Possum fall in and drown, they don't give a damn, run it anyway. I'd not touch a drop that I didn't know who made it. Not like it is now."

I was somewhat comforted by Monroe's implicit endorsement of the product we were drinking. "I guess you know who made this then?"

Monroe paused for a second. Then he said, "Yeah, I do."

"I wasn't asking who. I'm just glad you know it's good."

'I guaran-goddamn-tee it's good," Roy said. "This here ain't nothing but pure corn." He thumped the bottom of the bottle to make it bead. "Same as it's always been."

"I guess y'all's ancestors must have passed it down — the right way to make it, I mean — father to son."

Roy said, "That they did."

He took a swallow. "The bitch come out after four days. We thought it was her that caused the slide . . ."

"Generally is," Monroe interjected.

"She was a slab-sided bitch to start with, and after four days in that hole she was poor enough to squeeze through. But Towse was too stout through the shoulders."

"What kind of dog was he?"

"Half redbone and half bluetick and half bulldog. Eighteen days in that hole, he was, and him without nothing but that coon to eat. We like to never got him out."

"What did you do? Dig him out?"

"Blowed him out with dynamite. Case and a half, quarter stick at a time."

I accepted the exaggeration as an appropriate tribute to the dog. I accepted it as I accepted their whiskey, with pleasure. "Good Lord. How much rock did you have to blast through?"

"Forty foot."

"And he was still alive."

"Just barely. You remember when he come up out of there, Monroe? All bowed up and caved in, he was, but he by God walked out on his own. Course he never heared too good after that. My daddy just retired him, let him lay up by the stove for as long as he lived, which won't but about another year. But he was one more tough son of a bitch in his prime, won't he, Monroe?"

"He was that. How old was you when your daddy started you at his still?"

"Had me toting jars when I was eight."

It crossed my mind to wonder if Roy's people might have been the ones who had made the whiskey the student had brought me years before. I told them about that — "the best in Rabun County" — and admitted that I'd been curious ever since about the way it was made.

For the first time that morning Monroe laughed. "Why? You ain't aiming to start one up your own self, are you?"

Before I could answer, Roy took over. "Whiskey ain't something you can just lay out the making of like you can a house and expect somebody to come along and read how and then do it. It takes a man that respects corn to do it right. Corn's got it own nature, see. You run it before its time, before them old dogheads go to rising, or sun it too fast or cook it too hot, why it'll not be fit to drink. Making whiskey's more a matter of caring how good instead of how much. A man that don't plan to drink his own likker, I damn shore don't want none of it myself."

"You drink it right," Monroe said, "good likker'll not hurt you. Drink all you want, get up the next morning, eat what they put before you, sausage and eggs and cathead biscuits. I know a preacher drinks it. He don't what you'd call regular drink now, but he will take a sup or two of an evening. Says it makes him rest better. You want some more?"

I decided Charlie could drive us back to Athens.

"They's a Church a God preacher over here to Walhally made up a bluegrass song about old Towse," Roy said. "Put it out on a record. He deserved it too. He was a uncommon dog."

*

Charlie came walking out of the woods not long after that, as disappointed in Bascomb Creek as I had been. The bottle was almost empty, but we hung around the front end of Roy's pickup long enough for him to have a taste. I asked if they cold sell me a bottle to take home, but they said no, the one we'd drunk was all they had.

I rode back to Athens as high on Roy's story as I was on his whiskey. To make the story mine I tried to tell it to Charlie while Roy's words still rang in my head, but it didn't work. In my telling, the story went flat — just another Old Blue tale with appropriate exaggeration. Then it hit me: to tell it right you had to have someone to do Monroe's part. For the two men had been telling the same story all along — I could see it now — two men with nothing better to do that morning than hang around the hood of a pickup truck with a fifth of white likker in a recycled vodka bottle and an audience who must have looked to them like he might understand what they had to tell.

PAUL SOLOTAROFF

The Power and the Gory

FROM THE VILLAGE VOICE

HALF THE WORLD was in mortal terror of him. He had a sixty-inch chest, twenty-three-inch arms, and when the Anadrol and Bolasterone backed up in his bloodstream, his eyes went as red as the laser scope on an Uzi. He threw people through windows, and chased them madly down Hempstead Turnpike when they had the temerity to cut him off. And in the gym he owned in Farmingdale, the notorious Mr. America's, if he caught you looking at him while he trained, you generally woke up, bleeding, on the pavement outside. Half out of his mind on androgens and horse steroids, he had this idea that being looked at robbed him of energy, energy that he needed to leg-press two thousand pounds.

Nonetheless, one day a kid walked up to him between sets and said, "I want to be just like you, Steve Michalik. I want to be Mr. America and Mr. Universe."

"Yeah?" said Michalik in thick contempt. "How bad do you think you want it?"

"Worse than anything in the world," said the kid, a scrawny seventeen-year-old with more balls than biceps. "I can honestly say that I would die for a body like yours."

"Well, then you probably will," snorted Michalik. "Meet me down at the beach tomorrow at six A.M. sharp. And if you're like even half a minute late . . ."

The kid was there at six A.M. pronto, freezing his ass off in a raggedy hood and sweats. "What do we do first?" he asked.

"Swim," grunted Michalik, dragging him into the ocean.

Twenty yards out, Michalik suddenly seized the kid by his scalp and pushed him under a wave. The kid flailed punily, wriggling like a speared eel. A half minute, maybe forty-five seconds, passed before Michalik let the kid up, sobbing out sea water. He gave the kid a breath, then shoved him down again, holding him under this time until the air bubbles stopped, whereupon he dragged him out by the hood and threw him, gasping, on the beach.

"When you want the title as bad as you wanted that last fucking breath," sneered Michalik, "then and only then can you come talk to me."

For himself, Michalik only wanted two things anymore. He wanted to walk on stage at the Beacon Theater on November 15, 1986, professional bodybuilding's Night of Champions, and just turn the joint out with his 260 pounds of ripped, stripped, and shrink-wrapped muscle. And then, God help him, he wanted to die. Right there, in front of everybody, with all the flashbulbs popping, he wanted to drop dead huge and hard at the age of thirty-nine, and leave a spectacular corpse behind.

The pain, you see, had become just unendurable. Ten years of shotgunning steroids had turned his joints into fish jelly and spiked his blood pressure so high he had to pack his nose to stop the bleeding. He'd been pissing blood for months, and what was coming out of him now was *brown*, pure protoplasm that his engorged liver hadn't the wherewithal to break down. And when he came home from the gym at night, his whole body was in spasm. His eight-year-old boy, Steve Junior, had to pack his skull in ice, trying to take the top 10 percent off his perpetual migraine.

"I knew it was all over for me," Michalik says. "Every system in my body was shot, my testicles had shrunk to the size of cocktail peanuts. It was only a question of which organ was going to explode on me first.

"See, we'd all of us [professional bodybuilders] been way over the line for years, and it was like, suddenly, all the bills were coming in. Victor Faizowitz took so much shit that his brain exploded. The Aldactazone [a diuretic] sent his body temperature up to one hundred twelve degrees, and he literally melted to death. Another guy, an Egyptian bodybuilder training for the Mr. Universe contest, went the same way, a massive hemorrhage from head to toe — died bleeding out of every orifice. And Tommy Sansone, a former Mr. America who'd been my very first mentor in the gym, blew out his immune system on Anadrol and D-ball [Dianabol], and died of tumors all over his body.

"As for me, I couldn't wait to join 'em. I had so much evil in me from all the drugs I was taking that I'd go home at night and ask God why he hadn't killed me yet. And then, in the next breath, I'd say, 'Please, I know I've done a lot of terrible things — sold steroids to kids, beaten the shit out of strangers — but please don't let me go out like a sucker, God. Please let me die hitting that last pose at the Beacon, with the crowd on its feet for a second standing O.' "

Michalik's prayers might better have been addressed to a liver specialist. Two weeks before the show, he woke up the house at four in the morning with an excruciating pain beneath his rib cage. His wife, Thomasina, long since practiced at such emergencies, ran off to fetch some ice.

"Fuck the ice," he groaned. "Call Dr. Ludwig."

Dr. Arthur Ludwig, a prominent endocrinologist who had been treating Michalik on and off for a number of years, was saddened but unsurprised by the call. "Frankly," he told Michalik, "I've been expecting it now for ages. Your friends have been telling me lately how bad you've been abusing the stuff, especially for the last five years."

That he certainly had. Instead of cycling on and off of steroids, giving his body here and there a couple months' recuperation, Michalik had been juicing pretty much constantly since 1976, shooting himself with fourteen different drugs and swallowing copious amounts of six or seven others. Then there was all the speed he was gulping — bennies, black beauties — to get through his seven-hour workouts, and the handful of downs at night to catch four hours of tortuous sleep.

There, at any rate, Michalik was, doubled over in bed at four in the morning, his right side screaming like a bomb had gone off in it.

"You'd better get him to New York Hospital as fast as you can," Ludwig told Michalik's wife over the phone. "They've got the best liver specialist on the East Coast there. I'll meet you in his office in an hour."

At the hospital, they pumped Michalik full of morphine and took a hasty sonogram upstairs. The liver specialist, a brusque Puritan who'd been apprised of Michalik's steroid usage, called him into his office.

"See this?" he pointed to the sonogram, scarcely concealing a sneer. "This is what's left of your liver, Mr. Michalik. And these" — indicating the four lumps grouped inside it, one of them the size of a ripe grapefruit — "these are hepatic tumors. You have advanced liver cancer, sir."

"I do?" grinned Michalik, practically hugging himself for joy. "How long you think I've got?"

"Mr. Michalik, do you understand what I'm telling you?" snapped the doctor, apparently miffed that his news hadn't elicited operatic grief. "You have cancer, and will be dead within weeks or days if I don't operate immediately. And frankly, your chances of surviving surgery are —"

"Surgery!" blurted Michalik, looking at the man as if he were bonkers. "You're not coming near me with a knife. That would leave a *scar*."

The doctor was with perfect justice about to order Michalik out of his office when Ludwig walked in. He took a long look at the sonogram and announced that surgery was out of the question. Michalik's liver was so compromised, he would undoubtedly die on the table. Besides, Ludwig adjudged, those weren't tumors at all. They were something rarer by far but no less deadly: steroid-induced cysts, or thick sacs of blood and muscle, that were full to bursting — and growing.

He ordered Michalik strapped down — the least movement now could perforate the cysts — and wheeled upstairs to intensive care. The next twenty-four hours, he declared, would tell the tale. If, deprived of steroids, the cysts stopped growing, there was a small chance that Michalik might come out of this. If, on the other hand, they fed on whatever junk he'd injected the last couple of days — well, he'd get his wish, at any rate, to die huge.

Michalik knew it was the liver, of course. He might have been heedless, but he was hardly uninformed. In fact, he knew so much about steroids that he'd written a manual on their use, and

gone on the *Today* show to debate doctors about their efficacy.
Like the steroid gurus of southern California, Michalik was a
self-taught sorcerer whose laboratory was his body. From the age
of eleven, he'd read voraciously in biochemistry, obsessed about
finding out what made people big. He walked the streets of
Brooklyn as a teenager, knocking on physicians' doors, begging
to be made enlightened about protein synthesis. And years later
he scoured the *Physicians' Desk Reference* from cover to cover,
searching not for steroids but for other classes of drugs whose
secondary function was to grow muscle.

Steroids, Michalik knew, were a kind of God's play, a way of
rewriting his own DNA. He'd grown up skinny and hating himself to his very cell level. According to Michalik, his father, a des-
potic drunk with enormous forearms, beat him with whatever
was close to hand, and smashed his face, for fun, into a plate of
mashed potatoes.

"I was small and weak, and my brother Anthony was big and
graceful, and my old man made no bones about loving him and
hating me," Michalik recalls. "The minute I walked in from
school, it was, 'You worthless little shit, what are you doing home
so early?' His favorite way to torture me was to tell me he was
going to put me in a *home*. We'd be driving along in Brooklyn
somewhere, and we'd pass a building with iron bars on the windows, and he'd stop the car and say to me, 'Get out. This is the
home we're putting you in.' I'd be standing there, sobbing on the
curb — I was maybe eight or nine at the time — and after a while
he'd let me get back into the car and drive off laughing at his
little joke."

Fearful and friendless throughout childhood — even his
brother was leery of being seen with him — Michalik hid out in
comic books and Steve Reeves movies, burning to become huge
and invulnerable. At thirteen, he scrubbed toilets in a Vic Tanny
spa just to be in the presence of that first generation of iron
giants — Eddie Juliani and Leroy Colbert, among others. At
twenty, stationed at an Air Force base in Southeast Asia, he ignored sniper fire and the 120-degree heat to bench-press a
cinder-block barbell in an open clearing, telling the corps psychiatrist that he couldn't be killed because it was his destiny to
become Mr. America. And at thirty-four, years after he'd forgot-

ten where he put all his trophies, he was still crawling out of bed at two in the morning to eat his eighth meal of the day because he *still* wasn't big enough. As always, there was that fugitive inch or two missing, that final heft without which he wouldn't even take his shirt off on the beach — for fear that everyone would laugh.

And so, of course, there were steroids. They'd been around since at least the mid-1930s, when Hitler had them administered to his SS thugs to spike their bloodlust. By the fifties, the eastern bloc nations were feeding them to school kids, creating a generation of bioengineered athletes. And in the late sixties, anabolics hit the beaches of California, as U.S. drug companies discovered that there was a vast new market out there of kids who'd swallow anything to double their pecs and their pleasure.

The dynamics of anabolic steroids have been pretty well understood for years. Synthetic variations of the male hormone testosterone, they enter the bloodstream as chemical messengers and attach themselves to muscle cells. Once attached to these cells, they deliver their twofold message: grow, and increase endurance.

Steroids accomplish the first task by increasing the synthesis of protein. In sufficient quantities, they turn the body into a kind of fusion engine, converting everything, including fat, into mass and energy. A chemical bodybuilder can put on fifty pounds of muscle in six months because most of the 6,000 to 10,000 calories he eats a day are incorporated, not excreted.

The second task — increasing endurance — is achieved by stimulating the synthesis of a molecule called creatine phosphate, or CP. CP is essentially hydraulic fluid for muscles, allowing them to do more than just a few seconds' work. The more CP you have in your tank, the more power you generate. Olympic weightlifters and defensive linemen have huge stockpiles of CP, some portion of which is undoubtedly genetic. The better part of it, though, probably comes out of a bottle of Anadrol, a popular oral steroid that makes you big, strong, and savage — and not necessarily in that order.

Over the course of eleven years, Michalik had taken ungodly amounts of Anadrol. If his buddies were taking two 50mg tablets a day, he took four. Six weeks later, when he started to plateau, he jacked the ante to eight. So, too, with Dianabol, another brutal oral steroid. Where once a single 5mg pill sufficed, inevitably he was gulping ten or twelve of them a day, in conjunction with the Anadrol.

The obstacle here was his immune system, which was stubbornly going on about its business, neutralizing these poisons with antibodies and shutting down receptor sites on the muscle cells. No matter. Michalik, upping the dosage, simply overwhelmed his immune system, and further addled it by flooding his bloodstream with other drugs.

All the while, of course, he was cognizant of the damage done. He knew, for instance, that Anadrol, like all oral steroids, was utter hell on the liver. An alkylated molecule with a short carbon chain, it had to be hydralized, or broken down, within twenty-four hours. This put enormous stress on his liver, which had thousands of other chemical transactions to carry out every day, not the least of which was processing the waste from his fifty pounds of new muscle. The *Physicians' Desk Reference* cautions that the smallest amounts of Anadrol may be toxic to the liver, even in patients taking it for only a couple of months for anemia:

WARNING: MAY CAUSE PELIOSIS HEPATIS, A CONDITION IN WHICH LIVER TISSUE IS REPLACED WITH BLOOD-FILLED CYSTS, OFTEN CAUSING LIVER FAILURE. . . . OFTEN NOT RECOGNIZED UNTIL LIFE-THREATENING LIVER FAILURE OR INTRA-ABDOMINAL HEMORRHAGE OCCURS. . . . FATAL MALIGNANT LIVER TUMORS ARE ALSO REPORTED.

As lethal as it was, however, Anadrol was like a baby food compared to some of the other stuff Michalik was taking. On the bodybuilding black market, where extraordinary things are still available, Michalik and some of his buddies bought the skulls of dead monkeys. Cracking them open with their bare hands, they drank the hormone-rich fluid that poured out of the hypothalamus gland. They filled enormous syringes with a French supplement called Triacana and, aiming for the elusive thyroid gland, *shot it right into their necks.* They took so much Ritalin before workouts to psych themselves up that one of Michalik's training partners, a former Mr. Eastern USA, ran out of the gym convinced that he could stop a car with his bare hands. He stood in the passing lane of the Hempstead Turnpike, his feet spread shoulder-width apart,, bracing for the moment of impact — and got run over like a dog by a Buick Skylark, both his legs and arms badly broken.

Why, knowing what he knew about these poisons, did Michalik continue taking them? Because he, as well as his buddies and so many thousands of other bodybuilders and football players, were fiercely and progressively addicted to steroids. The American medical community is currently divided about whether or not the stuff is addictive. These are the same people who declared, after years of thorough study, that *steroids do not grow muscle*. Bodybuilders are still splitting their sides over that howler. Michalik, however, is unamused.

"First, those morons at the AMA say that steroids don't work, which anyone who's ever been inside a gym knows is bullshit," he snorts. "Then, ten years later, they tell us they're deadly. Oh, now they're deadly? Shit, that was like the FDA seal of approval for steroids. C'mon, everybody, they *must* be good for you — the AMA says they'll kill you!

"Somehow, I don't know how, I escaped getting addicted to them the first time, when I was training for the Mr. America in 1972. Maybe it was because I was on them for such a short stretch, and went relatively light on the stuff. Mostly, all it amounted to was a shot in the ass once a week from a doctor in Roslyn. I never found out what was in that shot, but Jesus, did it make me crazy. Here I was, a churchgoing, gentle Catholic, and suddenly I was pulling people out of restaurant booths and threatening to kill them just because there were no other tables open. I picked up a three-hundred-pound railroad tie and caved in the side of some guy's truck with it because I thought he'd insulted my wife. I was a nut, a psycho, constantly out of control — and then, thank God, the contest came, and I won it and got off the juice, and suddenly became human again. I retired, and devoted myself entirely to my wife for all the hell I'd put her through, and swore I'd never go near that shit again."

A couple of years later, however, something happened that sent him back to the juice, and this time there was no getting off it. "I'd bought Thomasina a big house in Farmingdale, and filled it with beautiful things, and was happier than I'd ever been in my life. And then one day I found out she'd been having an affair. I was worse than wiped out, my soul was ripped open. It had taken me all those years to finally feel like I was a man, to get over all the things my father had done to me . . . and she cut my fucking heart out."

Michalik went back to the gym, where he'd always solved all his problems, and started seeing someone we'll call Dr. X. A physician and insider in the subculture, for two decades Dr. X had been supplying bodybuilders with all manner of steroids in exchange for sexual favors. Michalik hit him up for a stack of prescriptions, but made it clear that he couldn't accommodate the doctor sexually, to the latter's keen disappointment. The two, however, worked out a satisfactory compromise. Michalik, the champion bodybuilder who was constantly being consulted by young wannabes, directed some of them posthaste to the tender governance of Dr. X.

"They had to find out sooner or later that the road to the title went through Dr. X's office," Michalik shrugs. "Nobody on this coast was gonna get to be competition size unless they put out for him — that, or they had a daddy in the pharmaceutical business. The night Dr. X first tried to seduce me, he showed me pictures of five different champions that he said he'd had sex with. I checked it out later and found out it was all true. Nice business, isn't it, professional bodybuilding? More pimps and whores than Hollywood."

Michalik didn't care about any of that, however. Nor did he care if he went crazy or got addicted to steroids. "I didn't care if I fucking died from 'em. All I cared about was getting my body back. I was down to one hundred fifty pounds, which was my natural body weight, and no one in the gym even knew who I was. Big guys were screaming at me, 'Get off that bench, you little punk, I wanna use it!' Three months later, I'm two hundred pounds and bench-pressing four hundred, and the same guys are coming over to me, going, 'Hey, aren't you Steve Michalik? When did you get here?' And I'd tell 'em, 'I've been here for the last three months, motherfucker. I'm the guy you pushed offa that bench over there, remember?' "

By that third month, he recalls, he was hopelessly hooked on steroids, unable to leave the house without "gulping three of something, and taking a shot of something else. I'd get out of bed in the morning feeling weak and sick, and stagger around, going, 'Where's my shit?' I was a junkie and I knew it and I hated myself for it. But what I hated much, much more was not getting to Dr. X's office. He had the *real* hot shit — Primobolan, Parabolin — that you couldn't get anywhere else. They were so powerful you felt them *immediately* in your muscles, and tasted them for hours on your lips. My heart would start pounding, and the blood would come pouring out of my nose, but he'd just pack it with cotton and send me on my way.

"Suddenly, all I was doing was living and dying for those shots. I was totally obsessed about seeing him, I'd have terrible panic attacks on the subway, my brain would be racing — was I going to make it up to his office before I fell down? I was throwing people out of my way, shoving 'em into poles, practically knocking the door down before we pulled into the station.

"Understand, there was no justification for the things I did; not my wife's affair, not what had happened to me as a kid — nothing. I was an adult, I knew what I was doing, at least at the beginning, and when you add it all up, I deserve to have died from it.

"But I want you to understand what it's like to just completely lose yourself. To get buried in something so deep that you think the only way out is to die. Those ten years, it was like I was trapped inside a robot body, watching myself do horrible things, and yelling, 'Stop! Stop!' but I couldn't even slow down. It was always *more* drugs, and *more* side effects, and *more* drugs for the side effects. For ten years, I was just an animal on stimulus-response."

He flew to London in the fall of 1975 for the Mr. Universe show, already so sick from the steroids and the eight meals a day that he could scarcely make it up the stairs to the stage. "I had a cholesterol level of over 400, my blood pressure was 240 over 110 — but, Jesus Christ, I was a great-looking corpse. No one had ever seen anything like me on stage before, I had absolutely *perfect* symmetry: nineteen-inch arms, nineteen-inch calves, and a fifty-four-inch chest that was exactly twice the size of my thighs. The crowd went bazongo, the judges all loved me — and none of it, not even the title, meant shit to me. Joy, pride, any sense of satisfaction — the drugs wiped all of that out of me. The only feeling I was capable of anymore was deep, deep hatred."

Michalik went home, threw his trophy into a closet, and began training maniacally for the Mr. Olympia show, bodybuilding's most prestigious event. He'd invented a training regimen called "Intensity/Insanity," which called for *seventy* sets per body part instead of the customary ten. This entailed a seven-hour work-out and excruciating pain, but the steroids, he found, turned that pain into pleasure, "a huge release of all the pressure built up inside me, the rage and the energy."

And with whatever rage and energy he had left, he ran his wife's panicked lover out of town, and completed his revenge by impregnating her "so that there'd be *two* Steve Michalik's in the world to oppress her." Spotlessly faithful to her for the first ten years of their marriage, he began nailing everyone he could get his hands on now, thanks in no small part to his daily dosage of Halotestin, a steroid whose chief side effect was a constant — and conspicuous — erection. He was also throwing down great heaps of Clomid and HCG, two fertility drugs for women that, in men, stimulate the production of testosterone.

"Bottom line, I was insatiable, and acting it out all over the place. I had girlfriends in five different towns in Long Island, and one day I was so hormone-crazed I fucked 'em all, one right after the other. Suddenly, I saw why there was so much rampant sex in this business, why the elite bodybuilders always had two or three girls in their hotel room, or were making thousands of dollars a weekend at private gay parties. In fact, one of my friends in the business, a former Mr. America, used to get so horny on tour that he'd fuck the Coke machine in his hotel. Swear to God, he'd stick his dick right in the change slot and bang it for all he was worth. I'm telling you, my wife saw him do this, she can vouch for it. He fucked those machines from coast to coast, and even had ratings for them. I seem to remember the Chicago Hyatt's being pretty high up there on the list."

Hot, in any event, off his win in the Mr. Universe, and absolutely galactic now at 250 pounds, he was the consensus pick among his peers to put an end to Arnold Schwarzenegger's reign as Mr.

Olympia and begin a five- or six-year run of his own. He had
even prepped himself to follow Ahnuld into show business, taking two years of acting lessons and a year of speech at Weiss-
Baron Studios in Manhattan. One of the networks approached
him about hosting a science show. George Butler and Charles
Gaines filmed him extensively for *Pumping Iron,* the definitive
bodybuilding flick that put Schwarzenegger on the map in Hollywood.

And then, driving himself to the airport for the Mr. Olympia
show that November, Michalik suddenly ran into something bigger than steroids. A tractor-trailer driver, neglecting to check his
mirror, veered into Michalik's lane on Route 109 and ran right
over the hood of his Mustang. Michalik was dragged twenty
yards into an embankment; the Mustang crumpled up around
him. When they finally sawed him out of it two hours later, he
had four cracked discs and a torn sciatic nerve, and was completely paralyzed from the waist down.

The bad news, said the surgeon after a battery of X-rays, was
that Michalik would never walk again. The good news was that
with a couple of operations, the pain could be substantially miti-
gated. Michalik told him to get the fuck out of his room. For
months he lay in traction, refusing medication, and with his free
arm went on injecting himself with testosterone, which he'd had
with him in a black bag at the time of the accident, and which the
hospital had so thoughtfully put on his bedside table.

"It was hilarious. The idiot doctors kept coming in and going,
'Gee, your blood pressure seems awfully high, Mr. Michalik,' and
I'd just lay there with a straight face and go, 'Well, I *have* been
very tense, you know, since the accident.'

"Meanwhile, for the one and only time in my life, the steroids
were actually helping me. They speeded up the healing, which is
actually their medical purpose, and kept enough size on me so
that the nurses used to fight over who was supposed to wash me
every day. I started getting a little sensation back in my right leg,
enough so that when the doctor told me he'd send me home if I
could stand up, I managed to fake it by standing on one leg."

There, however, the progress halted, and Michalik, unspeak-
ably depressed, lay in bed for a year, bloating on steroids and
chocolate chip cookies. He got a call from the TV people, telling

him that they'd hired Leonard Nimoy to replace him on the science show. He got another one from the producers of *Pumping Iron*, informing him that he'd been all but cut out of the film. Worst of all, his friends and training partners jumped ship on him, neither calling nor coming by to see him.

"So typical of bodybuilders," he sneers. " 'Hey, Michalik's crippled, I gotta go see him — nah, it's Tuesday, chest-and-back day. Fuck him.' But the *real* reason, I think, was they couldn't stand to see one of their own hurt. In order to keep on doing what they're doing — the drugs, the binge eating, the sex-for-money — they've gotta keep lying to themselves, saying, 'I can't be hurt, I can't get sick. I'm Superman. Cancer is *afraid* to live in my body.' "

About the only person who didn't abandon him was his kid brother, Paulie, an adopted eight-year-old who utterly worshiped Michalik. "He used to come into my room every day and massage my legs, going, 'You feel anything yet? You feel it?' He's stubborn like me. He just refused to give up, he kept saying, 'You're a *champion*, Steve, you're my hero, you're gonna be back.'

"And then one day we're watching TV, and a pro bodybuilding show comes on. This was 1978, and the networks had started up a Grand Prix tour to cash in on the fad after *Pumping Iron.* I'm watching all the guys and just going crazy, wishing I could just get up on stage against 'em one more time, and Paulie goes, 'You *can* do it, Steve. You can come back and whip those guys. I'll help you in the gym.' "

Aroused, Michalik called an old friend, Julie Levine, and begged him for the keys to his new gym in Amityville. The next night, he got out of bed at 2 A.M. and scuttled to the window, where Paulie assisted him over the sash. Crawling across the lawn to his wife's car, Michalik got in the driver's seat and pushed his dead legs back, making room for his little brother beneath the steering wheel. As he steered, Paulie worked the gas and brake pedals with his hands, and in this manner they accomplished the ten miles to Amityville.

In the gym, Paulie dragged him from machine to machine, helping him push the weight stacks up. Michalik's upper body responded quickly — muscle had remarkable memory — but his legs, particularly the left one, lay there limp as old celery. After several months, however, the pain started up in them. Sharp and searing, it was as if someone had stuck a fork in his sciatic nerve.

Michalik, a self-made master of pain, couldn't have been happier if he'd hit the lottery.

"The doctors all told me it would be ten years, if ever, for the nerve to come back, and here it was howling like a monster. I kicked up the dosages of all the stuff I was taking, and started *attacking* the weights instead of just lifting 'em. Six months later, the pain was so bad I still could barely straighten up — but I was leg-pressing seven hundred and eight hundred pounds, and my thighs were as big as a bear's."

And a year after that, he walked on stage in Florida, an unadvertised guest poser at the end of a Grand Prix show. The crowd, recognizing a miracle when it saw one, went berserk as Michalik modeled those thirty-four-inch thighs, each of which was considerably wider than his twenty-seven-inch waist. Schwarzenegger, in the broadcast booth doing color for ABC, was overwhelmed. "I don't believe what I am seeing," he gasped. "It's Steve Michalik, the phantom bodybuilder!"

There Michalik should have left it. He was alive, and ambulatory, and his cult status was set. Thanks to Arnie, he would be forever known as the Phantom Bodybuilder, a tag he could have turned into a merchandising gold mine, and retired.

But like a lot of other steroid casualties, Michalik couldn't stop pushing his luck. He had to keep going, had to keep *growing*, testing the limits of his skeleton and the lining of his liver. If he'd gotten galactic, he figured, on last year's drugs, there was no telling how big he could get on this year's crop. A new line of killer juice was coming out of southern California — Hexalone, Bolasterone, Dehydralone — preposterously toxic compounds that sent the liver into warp drive but which grew hard, mature muscle right before your very eyes. Sexier still, there was that new darling of the pro circuit, human growth hormone, and who knew where the ceiling even *began* on that stuff?

Instead of pulling over, then, Michalik put the hammer down. He joined the Grand Prix tour immediately after the show in Florida and began the brutal grind of doing twelve shows annually. Before the tour, top bodybuilders did five shows a year, tops — the Mr. Olympia, the Night of Champions, and two or three others in Europe — which gave them several months to recuperate from the drugs and heavy training. Now, thanks to TV, they had to do a show a month. The pace was quite literally murderous.

"Not only did guys have to peak every month, they had to keep getting *better* as the year went on. No downtime, no rest from the binging and fasting — you could see guys turning green from all the shit in their systems. As you might expect, some of them were falling by the wayside, one guy from arrythmia, another guy from heart attacks.

"As for me, all I knew was that I was spending every dime I had on drugs. It cost me $25,000 that first year just to keep up, and that was *without* human growth hormone, which I couldn't even afford. The sport had become like an arms race now. If you heard that some guy was using Finajet, then *you* had to have it, no matter what it cost or where you had to go to get it. It actually paid to fly back and forth to France every couple of months, where you could buy the crap off the shelves of some country pharmacy and save yourself thousands of bucks.

"Needless to say, those five years on the tour were the most whacked-out of my life. My cognitive mind went on like a permanent stroll, and I became an enormous, lethal caveman. The only reason I didn't spend most of that time in jail was because two thirds of the cops in town were customers of mine. They belonged to my gym, and bought their steroids from me, and when I got into a little beef, which was practically every other day, they took care of it on the QT for me.

"Once I was on Hempstead Turnpike, on my way to the gym, when some guy in a pickup gave me the finger. That's it, lights out. I chased him doing ninety in my new Corvette, and did a three-sixty in heavy traffic right in front of him. I jumped out, ripped the door off his truck, and caved in his face with one punch. The other guy in the cab, who had done nothing to me, jumps out and starts running down the divider to get away from me. I chased him on foot and was pounding the shit out of him on the side of the road when the cops pulled up in two cruisers. 'Michalik, get outta here, ya crazy fuck,' they go, 'this is the last goddamn time we're lettin' you slide.' "

Word quickly got around town that Michalik was to be avoided at all costs. That went double for the wild-style gym he opened, which did everything but hang a sign out saying, STEROIDS FOR SALE HERE. There were plaques on the walls that proclaimed, UP

THE DOSAGE! and pictures not of stars but of twenty-gauge syringes.

As for the clientele, it ran heavily toward the highly crazed. There was the seven-foot juice freak who stomped around muttering, "I'll kill you all. I'll rip your guts out and eat them right here." There was the mob hit man who drove up in a limo every day and checked his automatic weapons at the door. There was the herpetologist who came in with a python wrapped around him, trailing a huge sea turtle, for good measure, on a leash. There was the former Mr. America who was so distraught when his dog died that he had it stuffed, and dragged it around the gym from station to station.

"I had every freak and psycho within a 300-mile radius," Michalik recalls. "At night, there'd be all these animals hanging around outside my gym, slurping protein shakes and twirling biker chains — and every single one of 'em was afraid of me. That was the only way I kept 'em in line. As crazy as they all were, they knew I was crazier, and that I'd just as soon kill 'em as re-enroll 'em."

If that sounds like dubious business practice, consider that a year after opening, Michalik was so successful that he had to move to a location twice the size. But for all the money he was making, and for all the scams he was running — selling "Banana Packs," a worthless mixture of rotten bananas and egg powder, as his "secret muscle formula" for $25 a pop; passing himself off as a veterinarian to get cases of human growth hormone at wholesale for his "clinical experiments" — he was still being bankrupted by his skyrocketing drug bills.

The federal heat had begun to come down on the steroid racket, closing out the pill-mill pharmacies where Michalik was filling his scrips. The national demand, moreover, for the high-octane stuff — Hexalone, Bolasterone, etc. — was going through the roof, which meant that Michalik, like everybody else, had to get on line, and pay astronomical prices for his monthly package from Los Angeles.

Constantly broke, and going nowhere fast on the Grand Prix tour — "where in the beginning I'd been finishing third or fourth in the shows, by 1983 I was coming in like eleventh or twelfth" — Michalik began caving in emotionally and physically. He'd come home from the gym at night, dead-limbed and nauseous, and suddenly burst into tears without warning. Cut off from everyone, even the stouthearted Thomasina, who had finally thrown up her hands and stopped caring what he did to himself, he sat alone in a dark room, hearing his joints howl, and dreamed about killing himself.

"I was just lost, gone, in a constant state of male PMS — the hormones flying around inside, my mood going yoyo. I just wanted an end to it; an end to all the pain I was in, and to the pain I was causing others.

"I mean, of course I had tried to get off the drugs, and always it just got worse. The depression got deeper, the craving was incredible, and those last couple of years, I was worse than any crackhead. As crazed as I was, I'd've killed to keep on going, to get my hands on that next shipment of Deca or Maxibolin."

As for his body, it was finally capitulating to all the accumulated toxins. By 1983, he was bleeding from everywhere: his gums, kidneys, colon, and sinuses. The headaches started up, so piercing and obdurate that he developed separate addictions to Percodan and Demerol. And worst of all (by Michalik's lights), his muscles suddenly went soft on him. No matter how he worked them or what he shot into them, they lost their gleaming, osmotic hardness, and began to pooch out like $20 whitewalls.

His last two years on the tour were a run-on nightmare. He almost dropped dead at a show in Toronto, collapsing on stage in head-to-toe convulsions; the promoters, disgraced, hauled him off by the ankles. There was a desperate attempt in 1985, after his cholesterol hit 500, to wean himself from steroids once and for all. His testosterone level plummeted, however, his sperm count went to zero, and all the estrogen in his body, which had been accruing for years, turned his pecs into soft, doughy breasts. Such friends as he still had pointed out that his ass was plumping like a woman's, and tweaked him for his sexy new hip-swishing walk.

He ran to one endocrinologist after another, begging them for something to reverse the condition. To a man, each pointed to Michalik's liver reading and showed him out of his office. Leaving, he had the distinct feeling that they were laughing at him.

And so, after weighing his options — a bleak, emasculated life off steroids or a slam-bang, macho death on them — Michalik emphatically chose the latter. He packed a bag, grabbed his weight belt, and caught a plane for L.A., winding up for nine months in the valley, where all the chemical studs were training.

Just up the freeway, a cartel of former med students were minting drugs so new they scarcely had names for them yet. The stuff ran $250, $300 a bottle, but pumped you up like an air hose and kept you that way. It also made you violently sick to your stomach, but Michalik didn't have time to worry about that. He simply ran to the bathroom to heave up his guts, then came back and ripped off another thirty sets.

His hair fell out in heavy clumps; a dry cough emanated from his liver, wracking him. Every joint was inflamed; it was excruciating even to walk now. But at night, in bed and in too much pain to sleep, it cheered him to think that he would finally be dead soon, and that it would take eight men to carry his casket.

He came back to New York in the fall of 1986, on his last legs but enormous and golden brown. All along, he'd targeted the Night of Champions, to be held that November at the Beacon Theater, as his swan song. It was the Academy Awards show of bodybuilding. Everyone would be there, all the stars and cognoscenti, and it would consolidate his legend to show up one last time, coming out of a coffin to the tune of Elton John's "Funeral for a Friend." Of course, it would *really* help matters if he could drop dead on stage, but that seemed to much to hope for. All that mattered, finally, was that he go out with twenty-five hundred people thundering their approval, drowning out, once and for all, his old man's malediction that he'd never amount to shit.

And then, two weeks before the show, he woke up at four in the morning with his liver on fire, and that was the end of all that.

Happily afloat on morphine and Nembutol, Michalik drifted for seventy-two hours, dreaming that he was dead. In the course of those three days, however, his extraordinary luck held up. The huge cysts in his liver stabilized and began to shrink, though they'd so eviscerated the organ already that there was practically nothing left of it. Short of a transplant, it would be months before he could so much as sit up and take nourishment. His bodybuilding career, in any case, was finished.

When Michalik awoke in intensive care, he was inconsolable. Not only was he still unaccountably alive, his beautiful body was dissolving and going away from him. His muscles, bereft of steroids and the five pounds of chicken he ate a day, decomposed and flowed into his bloodstream as waste. In three weeks, he lost more than 100 pounds, literally pissing himself down to 147 from a steady weight of 255.

Predictably, his kidneys began to fail, functioning at 60 percent, then 40, then 20. His black hair turned gray, and the skin hung off him in folds. His father came in and told him, with all his customary tact, that he looked like an eighty-five-year-old man.

In the few hours a day that he was lucid, Michalik wept uncontrollably. Out of the unlikeliest materials — bad genes, a small bone structure, and a thoroughly degraded ego — he had assembled this utterly remarkable thing, a body that no less than Arnold Schwarzenegger once venerated as the very best in the world. Now he was too weak to lift his head off the pillow. He lay there inert for months and months, the very image, it seemed to him, of his old man's foretelling.

"I was just like Lyle Alzado, who I went to high school in Brooklyn with: weak and broken-down, leaning on my wife to keep me alive. She came and fed me every day through a straw, and swiped the huge bunch of pills I was saving to kill myself. To thank her for still being there after everything, I sold the gym and gave her all the money from it. I didn't want any of it, I didn't want anything. I just wanted to lie in bed and be miserable by myself. I was so depressed I could hardly move my jaws to speak."

Finally, by the spring of 1988, he'd recovered sufficiently to get out of bed for short stretches. Possessed by the sudden urge to atone for his sins, Michalik called every promoter he knew, begging them to let him go on stage in his condition and dramatize the wages of steroids. Surprisingly, several of them agreed to the idea. They brought Michalik out, a bag of bones in a black shirt, and let him turn the place into a graveyard for ten minutes.

"All these twenty-year-olds would be staring up at me with their jaws hanging open, and I'd get on the mike and say, 'You think this can't happen to you, tough guy? You think you know more about steroids than I do? Well, I wrote the book on 'em, buddy, and they *still* ate me up. I'm forty years old and I'm finished. Dead.'"

The former proselytizer for steroids got some grim satisfaction out of spreading the gospel against them. He dragged himself out to high schools and hard-core juice gyms, using himself as a walking cautionary tale. But whatever his good works were doing for his soul, they weren't doing a damn thing for his body. He still woke up sick in every cell, poisoned by the residue of all the drugs. The liver cysts, shrunk to the size of golf balls but no further, sapped his strength and forced him to eat like a sparrow, subsisting on farina and chicken soup. His hormones were wildly scrambled — a blood test revealed he had the testosterone level of a twelve-year-old *girl* — and it had been two years since he'd had even a twinge of an erection. Indeed, his moods were so erratic that he had his wife commit him to a stretch in a Long Island nut bin.

"I wasn't crazy, but I didn't know what else to do. All day long I just sat there, consumed with self-hatred: 'Why did you do this? Why did you do that?' I mean, even when I was huge, I never had what you would call the greatest relationship with myself, but now it was, 'You're *weak!* You're *tiny!* You're *stupid!* You're *worthless!*' — and what the hell was I going to say to shut it up? The only thing I'd ever valued about myself was my body, and I'd totally, systematically fucked it up. My life, as you can probably guess, was intolerable."

It was here, however, that fate stepped in and cut Michalik a whopping break. Halfway across the world, an Australian rugby player named Joe Reesh somehow heard about Michalik's plight and called to tell him about a powerful new detox program. It was a brutally arduous deal — an hour of running, then five hours straight in a 180-degree sauna, for a minimum of twenty-one days — but infallibly, it leeched the poisons out of your fat cells, where they'd otherwise sit, crystallized, for the rest of your life.

Utterly desperate, Michalik gave it a shot. He could scarcely jog around the block that first day, but in the sauna, it all started coming out of him: a viscous, green paste that oozed out of his eyes and nostrils. By the end of the first week, he reports, he was running two miles; by the end of the second, his ex-wife verifies, his gray hair had turned black again. And when he stepped out of the sauna after the twenty-third and final day, his skin was as pink and snug as a teenager's. Liver and kidney tests confirmed the wildly improbable: he was perfectly healthy again.

"Everything came back to me: my sense of humor, my lust for life — hell, my lust, *period.* Don't forget, it'd been almost three years since I'd gotten it up — I had some serious business to take care of. But the greatest thing by far was what *wasn't* there anymore. All the biochemical hatred I'd been walking around with for twelve years, it was like that all bled out of me with the green stuff, and I had this overpowering need to be with people again, especially my son, Stevie. I had tons of making up to do with him, and I've loved every minute of it. It kills me that I could've let myself get so sick that I was ready to die and leave him."

Michalik went to his wife and told her he was going back to bodybuilding. It was his life, his art, he couldn't leave it alone — only this time, he swore on heaven, he was going to do it clean. She understood, or at least tried to, but said she couldn't go through with it again: the 2 A.M. feedings, the $500-a-week grocery bills. They parted amicably, and Michalik returned to the gym, as zealous and single-minded as a monk. In the last two years he's put on 60 pounds, and looks dense and powerful at 225, though he's sober about the realities.

"There are *nineteen-year-olds* clocking in now at two sixty-five," he says, shaking his head. "The synthetic HGH [human growth hormone] has evolved a new species in five years. By the end of the decade, the standard will be three-hundred-pounders, with twenty-three-inch necks that are almost as big as their waists.

"But all around the country, kids'll be dropping dead from the stuff, and getting diabetes because it burns out their pancreas. I don't care what those assholes in California say, there's no such thing in the world as a 'good' drug. There's only bad drugs and sick bastards who want to sell them to you."

Someone ought to post those words in every high school in the country. The latest estimate from a *USA Today* report is that there are half a million teenagers on juice these days, almost half of whom, according to a University of Kentucky study, are so naïve they think that steroids *without exercise* will build muscle. In this second stone age, the America of Schwarzkopf and Schwarzenegger, someone needs to tell them that bigger isn't necessarily better. Sometimes, bigger is deader.

KAREN UHLENHUTH

Bird-to-Bird Combat

FROM KANSAS CITY STAR MAGAZINE

BIRD-WATCHING can be dog-eat-dog.

Louis Banker is proof of that. Twelve years ago, Banker was a relentlessly competitive debate coach at Fort Osage High School in Independence, Missouri. He had driven his team to six state championships, and desired nothing so much as a national trophy to add to his collection. Then, in 1979, a heart attack nearly killed him. Banker's doctor advised him to retire, lower his blood pressure, take up a relaxing hobby. You know, like bird-watching.

Now Louis Banker, Type A debate coach, has been transformed into Louis Banker, Type A birder.

Banker, seventy, is the sort of bird-watcher who, upon hearing a report of a rare bird sighting anywhere in North America, will immediately stop chasing the squirrels from the finch feeders outside his dining room windows and take the next plane — to Newfoundland, the Rio Grande Valley, or California — and proceed to beat the bushes for the blue-footed booby or the yellow-faced grassquit.

Since this obsession overtook Banker, he has traveled three times to Attu Island, at the western tip of the Aleutians. To power birders, Attu is nothing less than a shrine. Each spring, dozens of the faithful gather there to pray that the Bering Sea will churn out storms violent enough to hurl birds out of their normal migratory path through Asia. Birders mounted on bikes and equipped with two-way radios search the island for rare birds, and broadcast alerts when they find them. "Then," said

Banker, "you pedal as fast as you can in the direction of the bird."

Banker has also trudged over Alaskan tundra in pursuit of the bristle-thighed curlew, and slogged through a blizzard and minus 5 degrees in Newfoundland in search of the dovekie.

His obsession has paid off. According to the American Birding Association, as of December 31, 1989, Banker had seen and identified 744 approved species of North American birds, placing him in a tie for twenty-first place in an ABA list of people who keep count of such things.

It hasn't been easy for Banker, especially these last few years as he's neared the top of the heap, where the time, expense and inconvenience required to log each additional species escalate dramatically.

"Once you get above seven hundred birds, they start getting really *tough*," he said.

According to the birding association, about 850 bird species show up in North America, although many of them are seen only one or two days a year.

"I'm down to those kinds of birds," Banker griped. "It takes a heckuva lot of luck."

But the obstacles notwithstanding, Banker doesn't dare slacken his pace. "It's like the Red Queen in *Alice in Wonderland*," he said. "You have to run very fast to stay in the same place. You may add a lot of birds and end up twenty-first again next year. Or some dirty so-and-so may pass you."

It was in defense of his standing that, at 4 A.M. one Saturday in December, Banker sat in the Amoco truck stop at the Kearney, Missouri, exit of Interstate 35.

At five feet six inches and 130 pounds, Banker is a hummingbird of a man. He flits more than walks, and there's a nervous intensity about him, heightened, no doubt, by his taste for stimulants.

As he sat at the counter, waiting for his traveling companion to arrive, the smoke from his Now cigarettes mingled with the steam from his favorite nectar — strong black coffee. Banker was fretting. Maybe he should have arranged this meeting for 3:30 A.M. In less than four hours, the sun would split the horizon, and Banker was afraid he would miss the show.

On the weekend after Thanksgiving, the North American Rare Bird Alert — a telephone hotline run by the Houston Audubon Society, and the source of most rare bird tips — had begun reporting the sighting of a yellow grosbeak at a cracked-corn feeder in a back yard outside Elkhart, Iowa.

Now the yellow grosbeak, a tropical bird, is elusive enough in its normal range, which spills just north of the Mexican border. But to find one in Iowa, feeding among snowdrifts, is both extraordinary and suspect. When Banker heard about the sighting, his first impulse was to strap chains on his Cheverolet Blazer's tires and rush up there, despite the foot of snow that had just fallen.

But then he thought about The Committee. The dreaded Committee.

This bird-listing business depends on trust. For the most part, the ABA accepts birders' claims without question. But when it receives reports of very rare sightings, the birding association turns to The Committee. Composed of ornithologists and other scientists, The Committee rules on whether a bird was correctly identified, and whether it arrived at the reported location through its own power or whether, say, a bird-cage door was left open.

Not surprisingly, The Committee has ruffled more than a few power birders, who contend that The Committee is too quick to dismiss birds as "escapees" simply because they are rare.

"That really irritates us," Banker said. "We say these birds are innocent until proven guilty!"

The Committee caused a sensation several years ago when it raised questions about the reported sighting in south Texas of a crane hawk, a bird normally found only in Mexico. Hundreds of birders reported having seen it, but The Committee demanded documentation — which can take the form of photos, a written description of appearance and behavior, or taped bird calls. After three years of deliberation, the ABA recently deemed the sighting legitimate.

Although Banker figured that this alleged yellow grosbeak would go to trial before The Committee — and in all likelihood be found guilty — he decided to go to Elkhart anyway. After all, James Huntington, number thirty on the ABA list, would be there. And Sandy Komito, number two, would be flying in from Fair Lawn, New Jersey.

There was, quite simply, too much at stake.

A few bird-watchers were already stationed behind their binoculars in the garage of Dean and Diane Mosman when Banker arrived at 8 A.M. Clearly, the Mosmans are birders: their ranch house is distinguished by nearly a dozen feeders, nineteen purple martin houses, and eighty bluebird boxes.

The first to arrive were the Iowans, from Marshalltown and Ottumwa and Des Moines. They would be joined by the Minnesotans and Missourians, Illinoisans and Nebraskans.

And of course by North America's number two power birder, Sandy Komito — the man who spotted 727 species in a single year. That fact clearly irritates Banker, who spent nine years racking up that many species.

"Only Sandy and God know how much he spent that year," Banker said sourly.

Between Komito and Banker, this bird listing is unpleasant business. They despise each other, and make no secret of it. Komito calls Banker "a vicious man." Banker describes the New Jerseyite as having "toxic waste on his shoes."

When the Mosmans alerted the Houston hotline of their grosbeak in late November, they didn't expect the steady stream of binoculared guests. "Every time we come home, we find a note on the door," Diane Mosman said.

The early birders that morning gathered in the Mosman garage and huddled around two windows with a view of the feeder where the grosbeak had been seen.

In their hiking boots, parkas, turtlenecks and knit caps, they alternately peered out the windows and paced back and forth, looking like expectant fathers in the waiting room of a very chilly maternity ward.

Then Diane Mosman appeared at the door. She'd called the next-door neighbor. "She says it's up there, if a *few* of you want to go up there," Mosman said.

No one offered to stay behind. Immediately, all six people trotted down the dirt road.

At the neighbor's driveway, they began creeping on tiptoe, spying one feeder, then another, through their binoculars.

"There it is," someone whispered.

All heads shifted.

"It's in the tree."

There! A splash of extravagant lemon yellow stood out among the December Iowa grays, whites and browns.

"Oh, what a bird," someone murmured.

"Oh yes, *yes*," said another.

"Is this a lifer for you, Louie?"

"Yes, number seven fifty-one," he said. "But the ABA won't accept it. They'll say it's a caged bird or something. That pisses me off."

"How would a bird like that get here?" someone asked.

"TWA," a joker suggested.

"It would get its compass turned completely around, a hundred eighty degrees," Banker said, assuming the role of authority. "I think that's certainly possible."

The grosbeak obliged the group for a couple of minutes, perching on a low branch. Then it flapped its wings, flew across the road and disappeared.

Back at the Mosmans, more birders had arrived. There was Marita Geerts, from Minneapolis.

"My husband thinks I'm absolutely crazy. He said, 'You're getting up at three? Be sure you tiptoe.' "

And there was a foursome from Rockford, Illinois, who had arrived just a few minutes too late.

Banker couldn't resist tormenting them with a report of the *fabulous* sighting they had just missed. The view of the bird had been so *clear*, and the light absolutely *purrrfect*.

"Oh, shut up, Louie," one of them shot back.

A short time later, as if to return the jab, she bragged to Banker, "I have hundreds of smews on my China list."

"I don't play this *international* game," he retorted.

It is one of the worst fears of a power birder to travel across the country only to miss the object of the hunt by moments.

Banker recalled a trip to Prescott, Arizona, where he'd glimpsed a Berryline hummingbird at 7:05 one morning. At 7:10, three people from California and Oregon showed up on the same mission. For hours they waited, to no avail. It surfaced that the trio had lingered for a second cup of coffee at breakfast.

"I never had the nerve to ask who suggested the second cup," said Banker, obviously pleased that he'd beat them.

While many rare birds are sighted on public lands, others stop on private land, which can cause problems for those who would watch them.

Banker recalled spying a blue bunting in a south Texas park once. The bird was eating cracked pecans next door to a mobile home. Early one morning, Banker and several others were observing the bird, through binoculars, from across the road. "All of a sudden a woman came out of her trailer, her hair in a net. She said, 'I want you peepers to know that I'm calling the police, the ranger and the sheriff!' "

Banker explained what they were after, and the next morning when they returned, there was a guest book and a pitcher of lemonade.

As the crowd in the Mosman garage grew larger, Diane — a pretty avid birder herself — invited them inside to raise their body temperature a few degrees. She fretted that the bird wasn't reappearing. "I like for people to see it, if they've come so far," she said.

"That's the only way you're going to get rid of us," someone joked.

"Pretty soon," said another, "you're going to want a headline that says, 'Rare bird leaves.' "

Iowa in the winter is a cinch to someone who's been to birding hell and back. Unbearable heat, numbing cold, dehydration, blizzard conditions . . . Banker's been through it all. "You have several birds on your list who stick out because of how hard they were to get to," he said.

For him, the dovekie is one of those. To be relatively certain of catching a glimpse of the elusive dovekie, Banker said, "You have to go to Newfoundland in the dead of winter."

Not a happy prospect.

When Banker and his friend Huntington arrived in the city of St. John's at the start of Presidents' Day weekend, the weather was "not quite a blizzard," as Banker recalls, "but close enough." The temperature was minus 5 degrees, and the snowflakes were large. The men had enough trouble coaxing their rental car up a snowy hillside to their hotel.

The next day the weather report warned of "frozen sea spray." The two men drove to the seashore, where they intended to board a ferry to the island where the dovekie had been reported.

Alas, although the birders were operational that day, the ferry wasn't.

Banker went off to smoke a cigarette, then heard a cry of victory from the wharf area, where his partner had taken a short hike.

"Right by the wharf, where the ferry comes in, was the dovekie," Banker said.

Unfortunately, many birds reside in places that humans find uninhabitable. One of those places, by the Mexican border in Arizona, is Sycamore Canyon, also known as the Bataan of birding.

The summertime temperature can reach 120 degrees. A birder must hike eight miles down the canyon, through a dry streambed, and over large rounded pebbles that are very tough on ankle bones. At least one birder broke an ankle there and reportedly had to be rescued by a helicopter dispatched from Tucson, 110 miles away.

According to Banker, the canyon is home to five or six pairs of black-capped gnatcatchers, making it "one of the better places to find the bird."

In competitive birding circles, at least one pilgrimage to Bataan is unavoidable.

"There are two things you have to worry about on that trip," Banker said as he headed to his kitchen for his fourth cup of coffee in ninety minutes. "One is dehydration. The other is, you're in this canyon, and if there's a sudden rainstorm, you can drown because you can't get out.

"It doesn't have to be overhead. It can be upstream. You have to be always aware of the next place, or last place where you can get up and out of it."

Between blistering Bataan and the freezing sea spray of Newfoundland, it's no wonder that Banker calls his the "Hannibal philosophy" of birding. "It's over the Alps and into Italy," the man roared in his brittle, Bette Davis voice, which dominates conversation and fills the room. Hannibal had the mountains and the Romans to face. Like the ancient general, Banker says that he, too, perseveres in spite of adversity.

If you wonder why he bothers, you raise a good question.

It seems the birds are really incidental here. "The only thing I can say is if you're a fisherman, hunter or collector of dolls, it becomes part of your life, an all-consuming passion," Banker said. "It's like a complusion to climb mountains. It's there, and these birds are there.

"A lot of it is the competition. I don't want to be just run-of-the-mill. There's some drive that comes from someplace. Perhaps it's in the family genes."

He theorizes that it may be the same drive that propelled one of his aunts to become the first licensed female embalmer in Missouri. The same woman joined the Order of the Eastern Star, set her sights on getting "to the top" and got there, according to Banker.

The point is, "Whatever you're going to do, do it well," he said.

In fact, it seems that the goal here is to win.

Banker has made noises to his friends about quitting birding to pursue one of the other goals he established for himself ten years ago — becoming fluent in Spanish and German, seeing the ancient Greek sites, attending Oxford University and becoming a master bridge player.

But his birding partner Huntington doesn't believe that for a minute. As of December 9, the score was Banker 751 species, Huntington 749.

"I'm snapping at his heels," Huntington said over the phone, glee in his voice. He's not gonna stop now."

MIKE KUPPER

Indy Visible

FROM THE LOS ANGELES TIMES

IT BEGAN, more than fifty years ago, with a couple of ambitious young hotshoes who thought nothing in life could be better than taming a rambunctious midget race car, making it go where only the brave dared go, faster than anyone else.

They didn't know it at the time, of course, but Tony Bettenhausen, whose first name wasn't really Tony, and Bill Vukovich, whose last name wasn't really Vukovich, were leaving tire prints that others carrying their names could not resist following.

In the beginning, Bettenhausen, who lived in Tinley Park, Illinois, then a sleepy farm town southwest of Chicago and now, for all practical purposes, a part of it, did most of his racing in the Midwest and the East. Vukovich, who lived in Fresno, ran in the West. Eventually, though, each discovered Indianapolis, its race track and its race, the Indianapolis 500. It brought them together, nourished what became a strong friendship, gave each a new focus for his life — and future generations' lives as well.

Vukovich won the Indy 500 twice in a row. Bettenhausen, recognized as one of the gutsiest, most determined drivers of his day, never won it, although he never quit trying. The Speedway rewarded their devotion and dedication by killing them. But then, from time to time, racing does that sort of thing.

Their sons picked up the torch, Gary, Merle and, later, Tony Lee of the Bettenhausen clan, and Bill Vukovich II. And his son, Billy III, took the racing Vukoviches into the third generation. Each of them staked a claim to success — by racing's standards, if not by popular acclaim — but the families have paid dearly for that.

Between them, Gary and Merle Bettenhausen have two good arms. A prosthesis extends from Merle's right sleeve, replacing the arm he left at Michigan International Speedway in his first Indy car race. And Gary's withered left arm works only to a point. He suffered nerve damage in a violent crash during warm-ups for a dirt-car race at Syracuse, New York.

To this day, no Bettenhausen has won at Indianapolis, and it will be a major upset if one ever does. Car failure cost Gary his one great shot, and although both he, at forty-nine, and brother Tony, thirty-nine, are still trying, there are younger drivers with faster cars and richer teams well ahead of them in racing's pecking order.

There will be no more Vukoviches winning at Indianapolis either, simply because there are no more racing Vukoviches. Bill II, forty-seven, has been retired from driving for several years, and Billy III, whose promising career was expected to take off this season, was killed in a sprint-car crash last November, practicing for a race at Bakersfield. His car went straight in a turn and hit the wall head-on. He was twenty-seven, unmarried, and Bill and Joyce Vukovich's only child.

So, after more than fifty years, the Bettenhausen-Vukovich influence on racing appears negligible. But the saga those racing families leave to racing is considerable. And, although there is sadness and grief to contend with, as well as intense pride, bitterness and regret are not big with the Bettenhausen brothers or the last Bill Vukovich. When you go racing, you bet your life. Every race driver knows that.

It was Tunney, not Tony, that a young Melvin Eugene Bettenhausen started calling himself. Tunney, after boxer Gene Tunney.

"I'm Jack Dempsey," one of the Bettenhausen farmhands called out at the start of free-time boxing sessions. "Who'll be Gene Tunney?"

"I'm Tunney," Tony answered, rising to the challenge. In time, Tunney became Tony, the first of many of Bettenhausen's nicknames.

And on the far side of the country, the original family name was Vucerovich, not Vukovich, although stories differ as to how and when the change was made. In any event, William Vukovich, too, had plenty of nicknames: "Vuky," "the Mad Russian" — he was really of Serbian descent — "Wild Bill."

Race promoters touted Bettenhausen as "the Tinley Park Express," but he was referred to more informally as "Flip," "Flippenhausen" and, often, "Cement Head," all reflecting the frequent consequences of his single-minded driving style — hard and fast, always. Tony Bettenhausen saw a lot of the world while he was upside down in race cars.

Old-timers still marvel that a friendship should have developed between two such disparate types: brash, confident, voluble, likable Bettenhausen and the quiet, introverted, almost reclusive Vukovich. But friends they were, Vukovich and his family once visiting the Bettenhausen farm.

It might not have been simply a case of opposites attracting. The link might well have been a shared approach to racing. Said Gary Bettenhausen of his dad, "He was almost just the opposite of Bill Vukovich — on the outside. But I think they were a lot alike on the inside. They both had that drive and determination."

There was, however, a distinct difference in style, both on and off the track. "He drove it flat-out, it didn't matter," Milwaukee racing historian Al Krause said of Bettenhausen. "Pell-mell, drive like hell." Vukovich, although he drove hard, was a bit smoother, although no less determined. Former 500 winner Rodger Ward said, "The thing about Bill, aside from an unbelievable talent, was his tenacity. . . . Bill Vukovich had the greatest degree of tenacity of anybody I ever saw. He just *never* gave up."

Off the track, they appeared to have little in common. Almost anyone who ever knew Bettenhausen describes him as a great guy. "I remember [an Indy car] win in 1950," Krause said of a race in Milwaukee, where Bettenhausen, with his Teutonic name and affable manner, was a great favorite. "[Afterward] he sat in the judges' stand, we brought him a cold drink, he lit a cigarette — 'O.K.,' he said, 'I'm ready. Let 'em in.' There were kids standing around [waiting for autographs]. Tony, sitting there in his stocking feet, baggy uniform on, he signed every one. Bettenhausen was his own best publicity man."

Vukovich was no such thing. "Vukovich was probably a very

nice guy, it's just that he was in a lousy mood for the last twenty-five years of his life," Krause said.

Ward, though, knew a different Vukovich. "Bill was a very unusual kind of individual," he said. "I don't know if I understand exactly what an introvert is, but Bill was the kind of guy that really avoided crowds. He also didn't make friends easily. If you became a friend, you were kind of in a special place."

The *Times*'s Pat Ray, who at one time worked in Vukovich's midget crew, recalls Vukovich as "almost a loner." "He came to race and that was it," he said. "When the race was over, he was gone. He was like a phantom."

He was a phantom, in fact, to his own son. "I didn't know him," said Bill II, who was eleven when his father died. "He never took me fishing, never took me hunting, we never talked about the stars. . . . I wish I knew [more about him]. In fact, I've fantasized that I could go back to 1952 and 1953. We used to live on Orleans Avenue [in Fresno] and I wish I could go back and walk by that house and walk into that garage and meet Bill Vukovich. Not as a son, just as a person, just to see what he was like. He's a mystery man. I wasn't close to him, even as a small boy." There is one thing, though, that he knows about the first Bill Vukovich. "He was the greatest — at Indy. . . . I know there's guys that have won more races, but I believe, throw 'em all together and my dad, some way, somehow, would come out on top."

There may be more than just family pride there. Vukovich *was* a master of the Speedway. He drove in the 500 only five times, won twice and, conceivably, could have won four times in succession.

He was leading the 1952 race, his second, when his steering failed on the 191st of the 200 laps. He led for 195 laps in winning in 1953, started nineteenth but still dominated again in winning the next year, and was leading yet again in 1955, when he was killed in a four-car pileup.

Bettenhausen, on the other hand, was tormented by the Speedway. A two-time national champion — he was as good as they came on dirt — he could never make all the pieces fit at Indy.

Sometimes he was the victim of circumstance, and sometimes he outsmarted himself.

In 1947, his second year at the big track, Bettenhausen had been promised one of Lou Moore's two new cars, each built specially for the 500. That year, though, there was strike talk and Tony joined a drivers' group that was threatening to boycott the race if the Speedway didn't increase the prize money. Moore was interested in winning the race and told Bettenhausen to choose. Tony elected to stay with the boycotting drivers, and Moore put Bill Holland into the car.

The dispute was solved before race time and Bettenhausen drove another car, but Moore's cars, with Mauri Rose and Holland driving, finished first and second.

Holland, driving the car originally assigned Bettenhausen, should in fact have won. He was leading — apparently he thought he was ahead by a lap — when his crew gave him the EZ sign and he let Rose pass him. Bettenhausen maintained ever after that had he been in Holland's car, teammate or not, Rose would not have gotten by.

In 1951, Bettenhausen gave up the seat in the car he usually drove for another crack at one of Moore's cars. Unfortunately for him, Moore's cars, by that time, were dated. More unfortunately for him, the car he had left behind turned out to be the class of the field, and Lee Wallard drove it to a convincing victory.

The best he ever did in fourteen tries at the Speedway was second, in 1955, the year his friend Bill Vukovich was killed. He finished fourth in 1959.

He might well have won in 1961 had he raced. He had the hot car and the top speeds in the early days of May that year and was planning to become the first driver to break the 150-mph barrier. He was killed testing a balky car for his friend Paul Russo before he could get that done.

"The tragedy of it is that both [Vukovich and Bettenhausen] lost their lives doing nothing wrong," Ward said. "They were victims, not involved in mistakes of their own."

Vukovich, in fact, died in a crash started by Ward's car, fifty-six laps into the 1955 race. "I exited turn 2 . . . and the car suddenly lurched and went out of control," Ward recalled. "We looked at it later and the right front axle had been cracked. I think the problem had developed through the race — the car was handling very poorly — but I'd made my mind up that I was going to stay out there till the s.o.b. fell apart. I wish I'd had the good sense to bring it in."

Ward's car spun, hit a fence there at the time and flipped down the track, involving cars driven by Al Keller and Johnny Boyd as well. Vukovich, blasting out of the turn and onto the back straightaway, tried to get outside the mess but ran up a tire on Boyd's car, got airborne and flipped over a guardrail, landing upside down, in flames, on some parked cars.

Whereas multicar wrecks like Vukovich's still occur in racing, Bettenhausen's accident would be highly unlikely today. Rarely do drivers ask other drivers to test their cars.

But they did in 1961, and Russo asked. He and Tony had been pals since back in the midget days, and Russo's star was not shining brightly. Lindsey Hopkins, who owned Bettenhausen's car, was against the idea but didn't say no, and Tony took the car out.

After several laps, the car suddenly turned right, into the retaining wall on the front straight. The car vaulted into the fencing atop the wall, rolling the wire mesh around itself as it went, finally landing upside down atop the wall.

A bolt that held the front axle in place had fallen out, and when Bettenhausen braked just past the start-finish line to slow for the first turn, the axle twisted and pulled the car into the wall.

"My dad never had the luck," Gary said. "[He] could have won the race several times if it hadn't been for car trouble. I think, without a doubt, that [in 1961] he would have won the race."

It was easy. It was what Gary Bettenhausen had been born to do. Finally, a Bettenhausen was going to win the 500. Easily.

A broken distributor rotor had taken Bobby Unser's pole-sitting Eagle out of the race after only thirty-one laps, and there was Gary, only twenty-seven laps from the end, tooling along nicely in Roger Penske's McLaren, winning the race in 1972.

And then he wasn't.

Debris on the track brought out the caution flag, and as Bettenhausen slowed in observance of it, his car emitted an ominous pop.

Two laps later the car was sounding ragged, and when Gary got the green flag on the 176th lap, it failed to respond. Jerry Grant breezed by him, and Mark Donohue, Gary's Penske teammate, eventually ran down Grant and won the race.

"I couldn't believe it," Bettenhausen said of the ignition problem that robbed him of racing's greatest prize.

If he needed convincing, though, he got it later that season. "The car broke while I was leading all three 500s that year, Indy, Pocono and California [at the now defunct Ontario Motor Speedway]. That was kind of frustrating."

Right in keeping with Bettenhausen luck, though.

Even to this day, the memory of that 1972 race can reduce brother Merle, forty-seven, to tears. "I was his board man, his radio man out on the [pit] wall," he said. "That night, we went to [a pizzeria] and I was so distraught."

After recovering his composure he said, "We've never won the race. I said that night it would never, ever happen. If it didn't happen then . . . I've had three terribly sad days in my life — when my dad died, when Gary didn't win at Indy, and when I had my accident.

"You look at the race drivers that've got their name on the Borg-Warner trophy and you look at the talent that my father and brother had, that's what's not fair. My arm is fair. But *that's* not fair."

No argument there from Vukovich, who said, "Justice hasn't been served because Gary didn't win that race and he should have. He was just a whisker away. It was his. It was *his*. . . . And that was his dream.

"So justice wasn't served. But it's that way in life an awful lot of times. Justice isn't served and you've got to get on. You can't let it destroy you. And it can. I've seen it destroy men."

But not these men named Bettenhausen and Vukovich, who embraced an uncaring sport that had already taken their fathers and, very often, would mock their own considerable talents, would hurt them, physically and otherwise.

"I wanted to be [a driver] from the time I was a little kid, but it was like a no-no," Gary said. "[Big Tony] wouldn't even talk about it. I remember as little kids, we had a bunch of little toy race cars and we'd sit out in the dirt for hours, a race track around us, just running those little race cars.

"When my dad got killed, I was pretty bitter toward racing for about a year. Then everything kind of gradually wears off and you realize that everything that we had came from racing, and how much he loved it."

Said Merle, "I remember the time Bill came to the farm and we had a bicycle race. It was about ninety-five degrees. . . . I remember Dad coming out, 'You'll have heat stroke!'

"But everything revolved around racing. I think that even when our dad died, the responsibility of winning Indy was left on our shoulders. No one forced that feeling, but that was it. It was almost like the first win would be for him. No one could claim the first win 'cause that was going to be our dad's. To get your own, you had to win the next one."

Vukovich, too, grew up pretty sure that he would become a driver. "There were years, there, after my father was killed, that I really wasn't sure. I still followed racing, but I really wasn't sure I wanted to do this," he said. "And then I got of age and was able to race, and in the back of your mind you're thinking, 'Yeah, one day I'll go to Indy.' But I really didn't get serious about it till after I started making a couple bucks.

"I thought, 'Wow! This is kind of easy.' It's not, but you think, 'This was an easy buck.' And then I started winning some races. And then I started winning a lot of races — midgets, modifieds, local stuff — and I got to thinking, 'Maybe I *could* go to Indy!' Then I got blinders on. That's all I thought about, just trying to get to Indy. That's the pinnacle."

Gary, too, came through the ranks — go-carts, stock cars, midgets — until he and Bill II arrived at the Speedway as rookies together in 1968.

"In fact, I took my rookie test in [Bill's] backup car," Gary said. "I came with [a] dirt car and could only run 150 mph with it. Well, the last phase of my driver's test had to be over 150. J. C. Agajanian [Vukovich's car owner] asked me if I wanted to finish my rookie test in his backup car. So now USAC made me take my rookie test all over again, right from the start, because now I was going to a rear-engine car.

"And then I actually ran faster in that car than Billy had been running in his new Brabham. So after I got my rookie test in, Billy decided he wanted the [backup car]. He ran it the rest of the month."

Vukovich not only ran it but finished seventh in it, for which he was voted Rookie of the Year.

By that time, he and Gary were on their way to becoming best friends. But it was a relationship long in developing. Some of that might have been brought on by the good-natured rivalry their fathers enjoyed but which their sons might have been too young to understand.

"[Big] Bill was a needle artist," Merle recalled. "He used to tell my dad, 'Hey, my kid's so tough he eats nails for breakfast.' This went on and on, so that by the time they came to the farm, they weren't there five minutes and I walked out in the garage, grabbed some nails about yea long, walked in the house and handed them to [Bill II] and said, 'Here, eat these first, will you!'"

Vukovich didn't much care for the whole idea of the family friendship. "When I first met Gary, I didn't like him," Bill said. "I didn't like him for a long time. I didn't like Merle, I didn't like Gary, I didn't like any of them. I thought Tony, the old man, was great because he was my hero. But we didn't get along [as kids]."

They didn't get along as young adults either, and although Bill and Gary eventually grew close, Bill and Merle still have only a casual relationship. Maybe it's because they never fought first, then talked later, as was the case with Bill and Gary.

"At a certain time in our little careers, we were coming up in the midgets, I had a better car and I was beating Gary," Vukovich said. "There was a lot of times he'd run second to me, and after the race he'd say, 'Well, if that thing would have been five or six more laps, I'd have won.' That used to piss me off. I said, 'Gary, this was a hundred laps, not a hundred five.'

"We used to do a lot of wheel banging. There was tremendous competition between us. Gary was the only guy I wanted to beat, and it was the same with him, 'cause we both had fast cars. It all came to a head at Manzanita Speedway [in Phoenix]. I was leading the race. I had him beat. Had him beat easy. Then the motor started seizing with about five or six laps to go, and Gary caught me on the [last] lap.

"There were some things I could do to other drivers and they'd give. Gary wouldn't do that. He wanted to beat me so bad. Anyway, we got together and it was a violent wreck . . . fire, cars in every which direction. Gary got loose and went on and won the race, [then] came around and stopped on the back straightaway to see if everybody was all right. I started hitting him. He still had his helmet on and every time I hit him, I hit his helmet. [Afterward,] we both got to thinking that we should start using a little more common sense [before] someone got hurt. We sat down and talked about it, gained a little more mutual respect and then everything was fine. Then slowly we became good friends."

Once, after Gary had flipped his Indy car on the backstretch at Milwaukee, Bill leaped out of his car, grabbed an extinguisher from a track worker and shot fire-suppressing foam into the cockpit of Gary's upside-down car, on the supposition that the car would burst into flames any minute. Gary, still belted in, was unhurt but couldn't move and didn't take kindly to the foam bath.

"I almost suffocated," he said, and he didn't find out until later that it was his buddy Bill Vukovich who had wielded the extinguisher.

Later, Gary laughed about the incident, understanding Vukovich's concern. "At that time, the Indy cars held eighty gallons of fuel, forty on each side, and the fuel cells were like rags," Gary said. "Why that thing didn't catch fire is beyond me."

There is much to be gained in auto racing — money, fame and kicks — that drivers say nondrivers simply can't comprehend. But if racing gives, it also takes away, sometimes in spades.

In 1974, Gary Bettenhausen was driving not only an Indy car for owner Roger Penske, but an AMC Matador for him as well, in major NASCAR stock car races.

"I'd driven it in four races — Daytona, Michigan, Atlanta, somewhere else — and the next one was supposed to be the Firecracker 400 at Daytona in July," he said. "A week before I was supposed to go down there, [Penske] informed me that [NASCAR veteran] Bobby Allison was going to drive the car."

Disappointed and angry, Gary decided to spend the long Fourth of July weekend dirt-tracking, in a sprint-car race at Reading, Pennsylvania, then in a championship dirt-track event the next day at Syracuse. He never made a worse decision. "That's the one thing I would like back," he said. "It was a hell of a big setback in my career."

At Reading, Gary was hit in the face by a flying chunk of the clay track, which broke his nose. "They wanted to take me to the hospital and set my nose, but I said, 'No, we got to get to Syracuse.' So we drove all night and got to Syracuse and had to be ready to hot-lap after no sleep. We fired the dirt car up and the thing had no turning radius. What had happened was, we had just moved the front axle back three inches and didn't shorten the drag link — a hurry-up deal. It prevented the front wheels from turning more than about 40 percent.

"The first [practice] lap, I ran down in the corner and the car popped the front end out on me. So I said, 'Next time I'll just run it in [the corner] a little bit harder and give it a bigger pitch.' So I ran down in there and gave it a pitch and that was as far as the steering wheel went. The car went into a big long slide, then just dug in.

"It was stupid of me. I remember the minute I [crimped the wheel] it all came back to me, 'No turning radius.' "

The car flipped wildly, soaring out of the corner, off the track and through the roof of an unused concession stand. Both of Bettenhausen's collarbones were broken, he had broken ribs, a broken thumb and a broken eye socket. And, of course, the broken nose from the night before.

"He was the saddest-looking . . . ," his brother Merle said. "I mean, his ears were black and blue."

It wasn't his ears, though, that bothered Gary. It was the lack of feeling in his left arm and hand. "The shoulder harness broke my collarbones because the car flipped so violently," he said. "It did nerve damage. It didn't sever the nerve but it stretched it and paralyzed my arm. After a few months, because of the nerve damage, I lost all the muscles in my arm. When the nerves did come back, there was no muscle for the nerve to grow into. But I did learn to live with it the way it is and, to me, there's absolutely nothing wrong with it.

"I won the first time I raced after that. Taped my hand to the steering wheel."

That horrible flip, though, cost Gary more than just the unrestricted use of his arm. It also cost him his Indy car ride with Penske, whose cars have since won the 500 six times. And Gary has not had a first-class Indy car ride since.

"I'm positive I would have won the Speedway at least once by now, had I continued to drive for Penske," Bettenhausen said. "He's certainly proved that his cars are capable, and I know I am. But I was just young and dumb at the time. I wanted to race every weekend if I could. I wasn't ready to settle down and race only nine or ten times a year."

In fact, Gary never did settle into that kind of routine, as is common now among top Indy car drivers. Even Bill Vukovich, Gary's buddy, put his dirt-track days far behind him once he established himself in Indy cars.

But as recently as last season, when again he was nearly killed in a dirt-car race at Sacramento, Gary was still power sliding through the corners in sprinters and dirt trackers. "Sacramento fairgrounds is a horse track, so they don't have any guardrail," he said. "What they did was get a bunch of these big concrete barriers, like they use on the highway, and set them around the track to keep you from getting into the light poles and the [infield] lake.

"My car just spun and got into one of those [barriers], backwards, at about 120 mph. The fuel tank ruptured immediately. I was just barely conscious enough to get out of the car, and I was on fire for twenty-eight seconds before the fire crew got to me. "I ended up with burns on my wrist and hands. . . . I had a ruptured spleen, three broken ribs and a broken shoulder, and I still managed to get out of the car. Then I got pneumonia in the hospital. I damn near died. For about a week it was touch and go. They thought maybe I was going to lose this [left] hand because it was burned so bad around the wrist. I lost all the circulation in my hand."

Even after that, Gary was planning to go back for more on the dirt this season. He changed his mind only after Billy Vukovich III was killed last fall while practicing for a sprint-car race at Bakersfield.

"When Billy got killed, I just said, 'That's it.' " From now on, he said, he will drive only in the 500, which he still thinks he can win.

"We've got brand-new cars for a change," he said. "I'm driving a 1991 Lola with a Buick [V-6] engine for John Menard, the same man I drove for last year at the Speedway. This is the first time since I drove for Penske that I feel like I've got a legitimate chance of winning this race, setting on the pole. We've definitely got the combination for qualifying fast, and if it runs all day . . ."

If Gary has been shortchanged at the Speedway, though, his dirt-track memories will carry him, in case he ever decides to retire. "I would have been a very unsuccessful race driver to this point if it had not been for sprint cars and champ dirt cars," he said. "I've been twice national sprint car champion and twice runner-up. And I've been twice dirt-car champion and twice runner-up. I won a total of eighty-three races in my career but only four in Indy cars. So it would have been a big part of my career missing if I hadn't been driving those things. And all of my wins in my champ dirt car, my championships, everything has come *since* my accident in Syracuse.

"Indy cars aren't really what you call fun racing. It's a business. I don't think anybody can say they really enjoy running 220 mph. Sprint racing and dirt cars, they were just fun. I loved driving a dirt car on a mile of dirt. Just something about running 140 mph and pitching that thing sideways and flatfooting it and doing hot laps. Hot laps, that's what's fun, when you back into the corner and throw dirt over the fence. It still gives me goose bumps.

"There's very few things I really like, as compared to automobile racing. It's going to be hard to find something to do that turns me on like racing, after I quit racing."

But then, he isn't planning to quit altogether. "There's no reason I couldn't run another five years [at the Speedway], anyway," he said. "As long as I take care of myself and stay out of the dirt cars and sprint cars."

If Gary's career has been long and bittersweet, Merle's was short and hardly sweet at all. He was already trying to prove that he could drive as well with one arm as most people can with two when Gary was hurt in 1974. And although he passed his rookie test at the Speedway, he never drove in the 500.

"Probably when all's said and done, I don't have the personality . . . the fierce competitive nature that it takes to be a race driver," he said. "But you grow up in [a racing] environment, and you see the excitement of it and you see the happiness of it, the winning, and the independence of it, not punching a time clock and not doing forty hours a week. You see the potential for financial gain and having the name to get you in the door, so to speak. I believe that drove me, more than anything.

"I always felt like I wanted to race, [but] I always wanted to be the guy that won the race at the slowest speed. Track records are nice if you want to see your name in the books. But to be able to run it at the slowest speed would be the safest speed. That was probably a bad habit, because it took [away] the aggressiveness. I wasn't aggressive enough.

What cost him his right arm, though, was not lack of aggressiveness. It might have been inexperience, or it might have been car failure. In any event on a Sunday afternoon in July of 1972, on the third lap of the Indy car event in the Irish Hills of Michigan, he crashed and burned.

"At the start of the race, with a full fuel load, the car just didn't feel right," he said a few days after the accident. "As I went into the second turn, it started to get away, so I corrected it and then the rear end stuck and I swung right around and went into the wall.

"I hit it hard and, somehow, the visor of my helmet ripped off. I felt it go, and when I looked up there was this big orange ball, so I knew there was fire. . . . It was getting pretty hot in there and I thought about getting out. I put my hands up on the side of the car and started lifting, because I didn't think I was going to hit the wall again. Then I said to myself, 'You're going too fast,' so I started to get back down and then felt this tug on my right arm.

"Finally the car stopped and I knew it was on fire, so I started to get out again. I couldn't figure out why I couldn't lift myself, and I looked over to the right and there was no arm. I said, 'Oh, my God! Oh, my God!' And then I started calling for help."

Besides losing the arm, he suffered serious facial burns and still carries the scars. Only days after the accident, though, Merle was talking about a comeback, and two years later he was locked in a battle for the national midget title with Mel Kenyon, who, coincidentally, drove successfully despite the lack of fingers on his right hand.

"What I wanted to do was win the midget championship and then quit," Merle said. "I really believe I would have won it, simply because Kenyon really had some disastrous times. I wasn't winning, but you looked over your shoulder, there I was. I had this goal. I wanted to [go out] as a champion, a one-armed champion.

"Johnson City, Tennessee, is still the benchmark for me. If I think things are tough or I think I can't do it, I think of that night that we won that race down there with one arm. The power steering went out about the ninth lap and I passed Bill Engelhart on the last lap, the last corner, beat him by six inches. That was the only feature I won with one arm."

But Merle didn't win that national championship. He pulled out of racing instead. "[At] the beginning of the 1974 season, I broke an axle and crashed at San Jose in one of the opening races of the year," he said. "And from that point on, every time I went to the race track, I worried about crashing. Never before had that happened. I'd be driving [to the track] and my heart would start pounding and I'd start thinking about crashing. I'd put it out of my head and think, 'No, no, no, you go out and you race.' " And so he did, until Gary flipped at Syracuse.

"I believe that things happen to give you warnings," Merle said. "Different things occur that are telling you something and you should take those messages. I almost think that had I not taken those messages, I would have been killed. The message of Gary getting hurt made me quit."

After learning of Gary's accident, Merle drove through the night from Indianapolis, where he was living at the time, to be with his brother. He decided on the way that he was through with racing.

He has never regretted racing, he said, but he has regretted quitting even less. "One night we were watching a race on TV and I said [to his wife Leslie], 'Honey, not only don't I miss it, now I wonder how I ever did it!'

"For every negative, there's a positive. Maybe this was a way God wanted to tell me, 'Merle, you shouldn't be doing this. I'm going to awaken you and get you into something you'd do better.' My forte [now] is communication. I do consulting work. I do motivational speaking and I love people. So, I gave my right arm to put my life in perspective."

Bill Vukovich II raced successfully for more than fifteen years and escaped the kind of serious injuries that Gary and Merle Bettenhausen suffered. "I was just lucky because I had my share of accidents — end over, the whole nine yards," Bill said. "I tore cars completely in half and walked away from them."

Racing had another kind of pain in store for him. It took his son. "It was just unbelievable," he said. "It's still unbelievable. It's devastating. . . . I force myself to do things, try to block it out. It pops into my mind, I think about something else. I wake up in the morning and the first thing that enters my mind is my son. And then I start thinking about golf, the last time I played golf. I go through every shot, for eighteen holes, to keep my mind off that.

"It happened to my dad. And when it happens to your son, well, not that it didn't affect me with my father, but it's nothing like your son. There's *nothing* like your son and the impossible happened. It was impossible. It can't happen. Not to my son."

Except that it did happen. And, deep down, he always knew it might. That's why he worried so. "It was horrible," he said. "There was times that I didn't want to go to the races. I didn't want to watch Billy race. I was happy for him and Billy won a lot of races but I didn't want to be there."

And often when he was there, he couldn't watch. "I'd go to Madera Speedway and they'd start a race and I'd get so nervous that I'd just turn around and go between some motor homes and wait till it was over," he said. "I was afraid. There was constant, constant fear and it's probably because we've been around this. I see other fathers out there and they just seem to enjoy this. Maybe they haven't seen it like I've seen it. I've seen my father, Tony Bettenhausen, Ed Elisian. I've seen too many, too many. I don't think it's fun and games. It's a very serious business and it's scary."

But Billy was a racer, and Bill had been a racer and he knew there was no steering his son into something else. Nor did he try. In fact, when young Billy let it be known that he wanted to follow in the family tradition — his grandfather on his mother's side was former driver Tommy Astone — Bill built him a back-yard go-cart track.

"There's such highs and lows in racing," he said. "Just the other day we were talking about Billy and I told my wife, 'You know, this young boy, at a young age, had more highs than probably ninety percent of men have in a lifetime."

Bill had his share of highs too — he was runner-up twice, for the Indy car national championship and finished second in the rain-shortened 1973 Indy 500 — but he always maintained that he was in it primarily for the money.

Now that he's out, though, he misses the highs more than the money. "[The things that go into everyday life] are minor challenges compared to racing," he said. "We [the company he works for as general manager] sell these racing trailers, and you sell a trailer and, 'Geez, that's kind of neat.' You're happy for fifteen minutes and it goes away. Where with racing, it lasted for *months*. Because winning a race, that was really, really what you wanted to do."

Vukovich never was a big winner in Indy cars — he won only one race in those cars — but he was a good finisher and his record shows five seconds, eighteen thirds and fourteenth fourths. "I believe that, well, for one thing, I never had the best equipment," he said. "I had it *almost*. It was just a step below the Penskes and the [Pat] Patricks and the [teams] like that. But, bottom line, I believe that I failed at racing. Indianapolis is the pinnacle, and if you don't win that, you've failed. It was my goal, and I didn't reach my goal. I'm not knocking myself as a racer, but still, you set out and you have a goal and if you don't reach it, well, what else would you call it?"

Vukovich figures he had two real shots at winning the 500. "I ran second [in 1973] and was about six seconds behind [winner Gordon] Johncock when the rain came," he said. "He had a faster car, but with a little bit of luck, maybe a mistake in the pits, a longer race . . .

"There was another year [1970], we were really fast. We started way back and I came right up to third. It was easy. I mean, we were fast. Al Unser won that race and we were faster than Al. The car broke. The rear end went out. What are you going to do? I wanted to win it bad. I think if I would have had the opportunity Gary had, driving for the Penske types, oh, yeah. It really doesn't bother me, though, because I think that I could have been smarter, and had I been smarter I could have had those opportunities. If I'd been smart, I think I would have got along with the car owners better, played golf with them, socialized with them.

"I didn't do that. I felt my job was to show up with a helmet and [drive], and I didn't have to do the rest of that stuff. That's not very good thinking, but that's how I felt. But I also know that there are drivers better than I was that never won that race, either. There's plenty of them, a lot of great drivers."

Tony Lee Bettenhausen — the Lee is for Wallard, the man

who won the 1951 Indy 500 in the car big Tony had hoped to drive — was nine when his father was killed. He grew up considerably different from his brothers. His mother eventually remarried and moved to the Southwest, Phoenix first, then Houston, where Tony Lee started racing.

He was more influenced by his brothers and by Gordon Van Liew, the businessman–race car owner who employed his stepfather, Webb Stephan, than he was by his dad when it came to racing. He is a second-generation driver, but not exactly. He came along ten years behind one brother, eight behind the other.

The original Bill Vukovich had been dead for eight years when Billy Vukovich III was born. So although he carried his famous grandfather's name, he was influenced by his racing dad, ultimately becoming the first third-generation driver to make the 500.

And he made it three times. He was voted Rookie of the Year when he finished fourteenth in 1988. His dad had earned that honor exactly twenty years earlier.

This year was to have been a breakthrough year for Billy. His car owner, Ron Hemelgarn, had nailed down solid sponsorship, had ordered 1991 Lolas for him and was figuring on fielding a competitive team. Coincidentally, Hemelgarn Racing shares the building Tony Bettenhausen — he doesn't use the Lee these days — had built recently near the Speedway for his Bettenhausen Motorsports team. He used his share of the proceeds from the recent sale of the family farm to finance the building. He is both owner and driver of his cars, now a rare combination.

He has been in and out of racing but says he is very serious about it these days. "I always tried to be serious. You can only be as serious as your budget allows you to be, though, unfortunately. That's been our restriction. This is the first year we've really got a budget and the equipment."

The budget is courtesy of AMAX, a diversified company with interests in aluminum, gold, coal and energy. It is Bettenhausen's primary sponsor.

The equipment is from Penske. Tony bought the 1990 Penske cars driven last season by Rick Mears and has a contract with Chevrolet for their state-of-the-art V-8s. "The cars, I think, es-

pecially on the ovals, are going to be very competitive," Tony
said. "The Penskes dominated the last half of the [1990] season.
So we're going into the 1991 season with the strongest car of
1990. I feel good about it. I think at Indy and Michigan and
those places [with oval tracks], we'll be right there."

If it seems that has been a long time coming, it has. Young
Tony was being touted as potentially the best of the racing Bettenhausens as far back as the early seventies. "But I can't com-
plain," he said. "There's a lot of good race drivers that never get
a chance to qualify for the Indianapolis 500 even one time. It's
not because they don't have the ability, it's because they don't
have the sponsorship. There's just a hell of a lot more race drivers than there are race cars.

"With the economy the way it is right now, you've got people
like Roberto Guerrero, Teo Fabi, Raul Boesel and Johnny Ruth-
erford, people like that, Tom Sneva, walking around without
rides. That's a tough deal.

"I don't particularly like having my own race team. I'm proud
of the team and I'm proud of the way the cars look when we get
to the race track. But frankly, if I was in a position where I could
just show up at the race track with my helmet bag, I'd enjoy that
more."

Tony has driven nine times at the Speedway, a seventh-place
in 1981, his rookie year, his best. He has yet to win an Indy car
race anywhere, and hopeful as he may be for this season, he obviously knows that last season's good cars aren't likely to be better
than this season's good cars.

And his hope to get off to a fast start this season hasn't been
realized. He finished tenth and twelfth in the first two events,
road races in Australia and at Long Beach, then was a disap-
pointing eighteenth in the first oval event, at Phoenix. But the
big race is still ahead. "There's going to be a lot of determination
[at Indy]," he said. "I hope next year we're more prepared and
going to be better off in 1992 than we are in 1991, but I'm assuming that this is the best chance for a Bettenhausen ever. We're
doing everything within our financial means to put every key
person in place and every part in place to go to Indianapolis very
aggressive.

"It's the biggest race in the world. It's the pinnacle of success for a race driver. We definitely would like to do it, for the whole family. But life will still go on if it doesn't work out."

Among the Bettenhausens, there are no prospective male drivers. Gary's children — his twin sons, Cary and Todd, grew up as good friends of Billy III — are in businesses other than racing. Merle has two teenagers, a girl and a boy. "From the time he was old enough to sit up, I've been throwing balls at him and doing everything else to . . . keep him out of race cars," Merle said of son Ryan.

Tony, whose wife, Shirley, is the daughter of former driver Jim McElreath, has contemplated what it would be like to have sons with the genes of two famous racing families coming up behind him.

"Bettenreath?" he said, smiling. "McElhausen?"

But he and Shirley have two daughters. "I've got one I wouldn't put it past, but she's only four years old," he said.

"She's got the name for it," Gary said of his niece. "Taryn. Taryn Bettenhausen."

But as much a part of their lives as the Indianapolis 500 has been, none of the brothers is sorry that the Bettenhausen-racing link probably will not be carried on. "It's naturally kind of sad but then again, I'm kind of relieved," Gary said. "All things must come to an end. At least I can hold my head up and know that I tried hard."

Said Merle, "From the time I was old enough to walk, I was worried about somebody driving a race car. The last thing I want to do is worry the next twenty-five years of my life about somebody in my immediate family driving race cars."

Bill Vukovich can identify with that. "Billy was a champion," he said. He was a [United States Auto Club supermodified] champion, he won the [California] state championship, he was a track champion. And not too many bad drivers get to the Indianapolis 500. I truly believe that Billy, given the proper amount of training and time, could have won that race. He was smart, fast and smooth.

"[But now] I don't have to worry anymore. This is a hard time and a tragic time and nobody knows this better than me and my wife. But in our little time of grieving, it's been brought up by both of us: We don't have to worry anymore, about anything. I can take on anything now."

MIKE LUPICA

Donfire of the Vanities

FROM ESQUIRE

THE BROWNSTONE on the Upper East Side of Manhattan is quiet for now, quiet the way a subway platform is before the train comes. You know the D is on the way, you can even feel the ground shake a bit, see some light way back in the tunnel. The train hasn't arrived yet. Don King has just left his office in another part of Manhattan.

On the table inside the front door there is a pile of books: *Hit Men, My Father Rudolf Hess, Winning Through Intimidation, Atlas Shrugged,* and the new novel by Sidney Sheldon. His dining area has a fax machine and a copy machine. On the desk in his study, he has the biggest bottle of extra-strength Tylenol you can buy. There is expensive sound equipment and a VCR, a Sergio Mendes tape, and a videocassette of the movie *Ball of Fire,* probably one of Tyson's. There is a red velvet crown and a glass jar filled with gumdrops and a smaller jar filled with hard candy.

An elderly maid steps from the kitchen. "He's comin'," she says. "Somebody called a few minutes ago." She disappears up the stairs, and the Manhattan home of Don King is quiet again. No shouting, no prison-yard rap, none of the "nigger" talk he had given Spike Lee on that HBO documentary before the Mike Tyson–Alex Stewart fight. Maybe this home is more like a theme park than a subway station, a theme park before the gates open in the morning.

Behind King's desk, four black-and-white television screens monitor security. This is no surprise. The owner of this place has not only made several fortunes in his life, he has made enemies too. Before he got into boxing, he was the numbers king of

Cleveland. He spent three years and eleven months in jail for manslaughter. Now, twenty years later, King is late for an interview because he has been busy making another kind of killing, closing out a $200 million deal with Showtime. He has taken Mike Tyson and Julio Cesar Chavez away from HBO. A few days earlier he told Spike Lee what a racist, oppressive society we live in. You're a nigger when you're born and a nigger when you die, he said. If you make a pile of money, you're just a rich nigger.

The front door opens now and the D train rumbles in. King is shouting at his longtime matchmaker and sideman, Al Braverman.

"Don't want any of them tellin' me about white folks, Al!" King shouts. "They gonna tell *me* about white folks?" He tries a laugh, but it comes out flat. "Shit," he says. "I've got a Ph.D. in Caucasianism."

Don King shouts for the next two hours. It is part prison-yard rap and it is part the rap of a Baptist preacher. It is angry, very angry, and funny, and brilliant, and completely ridiculous. He quotes Shakespeare and the Bible, and talks about Goebbels and Cosby and Oprah and Tyson and Evander Holyfield. Mostly he talks about Don King. He says he's been investigated by the IRS, the CIA, and Interpol.

"I beat all three!" King says. "Not even Spiro T. Agnew can say that!"

In 1972 he promoted an Ali exhibition for a black hospital in Cleveland. Ali fought four guys, two rounds each. Then King promoted the Ali-Foreman fight in Zaire. He was co-promoter for the "Thrilla in Manila."

"I watched the first Ali-Frazier fight in prison," he used to brag. "And I promoted the third one." In this brownstone now, fifteen years from Manila, after what seems like a million big boxing promotions, I say to King, "If this country is as racist as you say, they'd find a way to hold you back."

"They do," he says. "If I was white, I'd be on the cover of *Time, Newsweek, Life, Forbes.* I'd be on every magazine that was worth its salt; they'd have me there."

"If you were white, you'd probably be leveraged out like Trump is. You'd be one of those Murdoch guys."

"No, no, I would have been too good for that. You've got to

understand, I'm dealing with these guys without a formal education. The difference is my capability and my diligence and my ability to persevere. I've never used my blackness as an excuse. I've never got no fighter based on being black. My performance is the only thing that's carried me through. You've been told the nigger is worthless, that he's shiftless, lethargic, and sloppy. He lies and steals. Stereotype image of black folks. So I got me a new appraiser. An appraiser that tells me America is a great country. If you have faith in God and you persevere, you will overcome. So now I've overcome. I've been blocked out of many deals because I'm black. But I don't let that bother me. I want to deal with what is real and pragmatic. Everybody wants to make money."

King gives answers like this to the most innocent of questions. In an age when sports figures have been conditioned to talk in perfect sound bites, he is the first rap opera.

"What would happen if a controversial white man said the things about blacks you said about whites?" I ask him. "Do you think that moves us along? Or do you think it polarizes people even more?"

"The system has to be changed. The prevailing attitude of subordinating, demeaning, degrading, humiliating, dehumanizing black people hasn't changed. I try to explain what Hitler did, and the best way I can explain it is in my own humble opinion. . . . The Jew was the nigger of Germany. I live for the day when all people are clothed in dignity. But to prove my point I have to symbolize it with something dramatic enough to get people's attention. The Jew was the nigger of Germany. Hitler did what the white American did over here in racism. He did it with propaganda."

Larry Holmes once said that Don King "looks black, lives white, and thinks green." Holmes is one of a number of boxers who say that Don King cheated them. Tim Witherspoon is another. You can go all the way to junior welterweights like Saoul Mamby.

In boxing, it is illegal to be both promoter and manager, a conflict of interest where a fighter can only lose. King's way around that is to make his son, Carl, the manager. Witherspoon says he signed two contracts with Carl King. The one filed with boxing commissions, he says, had Carl taking 33 percent commission. The other, the real one, had Carl taking 50 percent.

Both Kings deny any improprieties in their dealings with boxers. Of course, the father does it at full shout.

"Larry Holmes is the best testimony in the world for me," he
says. "Here's a very nondescript, bland man, who just inciden-
tally happens to be black. Very talented boxer. Nobody would
fight against him. Don King's ingenuity brought him to the top
and left him with twenty million dollars."

"So why is he mad at you?"

"He's mad at me because he has an Oedipus complex."

"Larry Holmes is mad at you because he loves his mother?"

"No, no, Oedipus and his father. It's a parental thing. I've
done more for Larry Holmes and the Holmes family than his
father ever did. I've done more for Larry Holmes than he could
do for himself. . . . I taught him how to read and write. I'm talking about sitting up at night, trying to help this human being el-
evate himself. Now we find him being one of my condemners."

Don King is the same father figure to Mike Tyson that he says
he was to Holmes. Their relationship is very good for him. He
thinks the current heavyweight champ, Evander Holyfield, is a
fraud. He says he should be stripped of his title for fighting
George Foreman before Tyson because Tyson is the number one
contender and, in most people's minds, still the heavyweight
champion of the world.

"Evander Holyfield's a nigger. He's going to be a nigger till he
dies," King says. "If he's rich he's going to be a rich nigger, if he's
poor he's going to be a poor nigger. When he gets through running away from his commitment [to fight Tyson], he ain't going
to have nowhere to go. Big business spits on the name of Holyfield. . . . The people who like him like him 'cause he's docile.
Holyfield can be controlled. 'Run Johnny. Sing Johnny. Dance
Johnny.' "

King predicts that Foreman will win the title from Holyfield in
April, fight "bums" in Europe for a year or two, and retire without ever giving Tyson a shot at his title. I tell him that Tyson
shouldn't have to wait years for another shot at the title.

"You're the most brilliant man I've run across," he says. "You
touch my heart."

He is one of the most remarkable figures in the history of sports.
And he could have become the important black voice he desper-

ately wants to be. Up close with King, you see the brains, you see the charm, you see the passion. Ultimately, though, you have to see the hustler in him. The man is full of anger. It is more impressive than his whole range of thought, from Hitler to the Bible. King knows how smart he is. But he wants more. He wants respect. Unfortunately, he is trapped in this wild-haired character he created for himself. No one can see past it. King understands that, and it makes him mad.

"They try to vilify me," he says. "They try to make me the worst motherfucker that ever lived. Make everybody think I hate people. Try to make me a racist, but that's impossible because I've never used racism to get where I'm at. You go to my office, you'd think it's a white office, that I'm a token nigger."

King is at his best in his own courtroom, defense attorney and character witness and judge and jury all at once, asking and answering the questions, shouting down his accusers. But when all that is finished you have to ask yourself: Are they *all* lying? Holmes and Witherspoon and Tony Tubbs and Pinklon Thomas? Or is King a hypocrite, screaming about racism on one hand and preying on black fighters himself? He was supposed to be the impartial promoter of the Tyson-Douglas fight in Tokyo, but he tried to get the decision overturned in Tyson's favor as soon as the fight was over. It made him look like a fraud.

At 2:00 in the afternoon, I shut off the tape recorder and put it in my briefcase. King keeps shouting. I put on my sport jacket and then my overcoat. He does not acknowledge that I am leaving.

"They are trying to make the truth unbelievable and the untruth believable!" he shouts.

I stand there with my coat on and my briefcase in my hand and King shouts for another thirty minutes. There is something mesmerizing about it. I can understand how it happens, how a fighter like Witherspoon gets in the same room with him and signs his life away.

It is 2:40 in the afternoon when I get to the street. King is still shouting as I walk toward Third Avenue. I look back. A blond woman in running clothes is staring at him as if he were a spaceship.

LINDA ROBERTSON

What Made Bobby Run?

FROM TROPIC

BOBBY LESTER'S SMILE was like a blazing fire on a cold night. It pulled you close, kept you warm.

He was a baby-faced basketball and track star twelve years ago, the darling of Palmetto High School, my training partner on long, hot runs down Old Cutler Road. He was a shy, small boy, only five foot six. We'd gather before practice and gripe about the pain to come, and Lester would crack that grin, tell a joke, and have us all laughing.

When I visited Lester in jail in the spring of 1990, the first thing I noticed was how his smile had decayed. The upper right front tooth was chipped. A lower right tooth was missing. The formerly dazzling white teeth were discolored with brown smudges, like the diseased petals of a rose.

For police and a dentist, it was a clinically distinct smile, an unmistakable match: Bobby Lester was the Biting Bandit.

"These bites, I haven't seen anything like them," said Dr. Richard Souviron, a national expert in forensic dentistry who has handled hundreds of biting cases, including Ted Bundy's Chi Omega murders. "I've seen some heavy-duty bites, but I've never seen an appendage or ear bitten off. That takes a tremendous amount of power. This guy was really putting everything he had into the bite."

After Lester was arrested, Souviron took impressions of his bite. One day in his Coral Gables office, Souviron pulled out the plaster cast and several life-size photos of bite marks on victims. He placed the upper jaw and lower jaw on top of the red, cookie-

cutter shape of a bite on a man's shoulder. There was no indentation in the skin where the bottom tooth was missing, a lighter
indentation where the top tooth was chipped. He placed the
model on a photo of a man's biceps, then on a photo of another
man's upper back. Again and again, it fit.

"They come together like broken pieces of glass," Souviron
said.

His conclusion helped Homestead police wrap up one of the
most puzzling and grotesque cases in the city's history.

Lester was accused of being the elusive serial robber who —
during a crime spree in the fall and winter of 1989 — jumped
his victims from behind, clamping down on their flesh until they
surrendered their wallets.

When I saw Lester's mug shot in the newspaper on January 30,
1990, and the description of the crimes, I was shocked. I called
my sister Julie, who was in Lester's class of 1980. "Palmetto's
Bobby Lester?" she said. "The basketball star? He was such a
sweet guy."

People who never knew Lester might think his past as a star
athlete was an interesting twist to the story of the Biting Bandit.
But for those who knew him at Palmetto, it seemed a case of mis-
taken identity. "A lot of coaches heard about Bobby's arrest and
told me, 'Another one bites the dust,' " said Palmetto basketball
coach Jay Bouton. "But he wasn't your typical tale of an athlete
gone to waste. When you talked about what made teaching
worthwhile, Bobby Lester was the name you used."

Word spread through the Palmetto grapevine, through the
well-to-do southwest Dade neighborhoods. People shook their
heads and sighed, then went back to their tennis parties and
swimming pools. Lester had his opportunities, they said. He got
the breaks — three years at Palmetto High, a scholarship at Florida International University — and he blew it.

I couldn't let it go at that. I had lost touch with Bobby, but for
a time I had known him. At least I thought I had. The Bobby I
knew could not have disintegrated into the bizarre criminal in
the news stories. So I started to ask around. I discovered that
none of my old friends knew anything about Bobby beyond his
playing days at FIU — as if after he took off his uniform, he had
simply ceased to exist.

*

The police counted fifteen victims. One, Jesus Torrez, was a farm worker accosted while walking home at night. The bandit asked for 50 cents. When Torrez refused, the bandit bit him twice on the back, once on the left arm and once on the right shoulder. The take: $2 and a watch worth $9.

"Black male was also trying to bite victim's ears but met with negative results," the police report says.

Cornelio Ramirez lost $500 and small pieces of his cheek, shoulder and ear. Lawrence Sayers, an elderly homeless man, got bitten three times in four months; part of his ear was torn off. Lewellyn Thompson was out apartment hunting when a short man stopped him and struck up a conversation. He told Thompson he knew of some apartments and led him down an alley. The man jumped on Thompson's back, bit his right triceps and demanded money. Thompson handed over the $280 he carried for a security deposit. The bandit then did something strange — before fleeing, he gave back a twenty.

That much I learned from the police reports. But the stilted, just-the-facts narratives didn't begin to explain why a robber would bite. Was he sick? Was he crazy? I tracked down some of the victims in Homestead. They lived in grim, aging apartments in the center of town.

Lewellyn Thompson, a sixty-six-year-old man, was angry and bewildered. "He seemed like a smart boy, not crazed," he said. "Maybe he had a phobia or a weakness. I don't know. He was a coward, I guess. Biting was his style as a thief." Thompson rolled up his sleeve. The circular scar looked as though it was inflicted by a branding iron.

"That was a hell of an experience, let me tell you," he said. "To have someone attack you and bite you and say, 'Give me your money or I'll bite you again.' It hurt for days. It felt like someone stuck me with a knife."

Abel Ortiz, another farm worker, suffered the worst injury. He lived in a dilapidated wooden rooming house around the corner from the police station. Ortiz has returned to Nicaragua, but his roommates confirmed his description of the attack: Ortiz was sitting on the front stoop when a man came up and asked for money. Ortiz said no. The bandit threw him to the ground and bit off his right ring finger to the top knuckle.

"*Como una bestia,*" one of Ortiz's roommates said. "Like a beast."

Then the bandit spit out the finger, said the roommate, demonstrating by spitting on the ground.

While Ortiz was in the hospital, Homestead Detective Jim Pruneda returned to look for the finger. "It looked like a peanut shell," Pruneda said. "Then we shined a light on it and saw what it was." They rushed back to the hospital, but doctors couldn't reattach the finger.

Pruneda has Polaroid shots of the victims — sheepish, shirtless men exposing the ugly scarlet imprints. The case aroused horrible fascination. A local merchant sold Biting Bandit T-shirts. Reporters called from all over the world. "I got interviewed by Irish radio and the London *Times,*" Pruneda said. "They said it was the Florida vampire."

People were fascinated by the bestiality of the crime. Mad dogs bite. Snakes bite. Even cannibals first speared or shot their victims with poison-tipped arrows. We often talk of criminals as vicious animals, but here was one who actually acted the part.

To Detective Clayton, the biting was just a means to steal money. "Biting became his MO. He was going after migrants and other people he knew carried lots of cash." But others doubt the decision was entirely rational.

Souviron, the forensic dentist, said he sees biting crop up in cases where severe mental trauma has caused someone to "revert to instinctive behavior. Many biters don't even realize what they have done," Souviron said. "There was a guy who stabbed a woman multiple times, broke two or three knives on her, then skinned her, 'to cut the devil out,' he said. The cops asked him why he bit her too. He said, 'I didn't bite her. Do you think I'm some kind of freak?' "

Most of the Biting Bandit attacks happened near the Homestead police station on Krome Avenue. That makes sense in retrospect. But at the time nobody suspected Bobby, a neighborhood guy who wandered the streets and often slept in the station's lobby with the rest of the city's down-and-out.

"The victims stated that when he ran, he ran with a lot of power in his legs," Pruneda said. "Real fast — like a track star."

*

In the fall of 1978, Bobby was Palmetto High's top cross-country runner, among the best in Miami. He was a junior. I was a senior going after my third all-county season, getting ready to defend my title as Dade's fastest woman miler.

Cross-country and track were my only sports, and I pursued them year-round with a runner's obsessiveness. For Bobby, running was a sideline. He ran mostly on heart. His form was not graceful; pigeon-toed, head tilted too far back, he raced like he was running from something. But on a basketball court Bobby played point guard like Kenny Anderson, Georgia Tech's "Wizard of Ahs." He handled the ball like a yoyo, played the angles like a geometry professor. In 1980, his senior year, he led the Palmetto Panthers to the state Final Four, sinking the winning shot in a playoff against Carol City, a team whose front line was six foot eight, six foot seven, six foot five, the shortest nearly a foot taller than Bobby.

"That Palmetto team was the smartest team," said Bob Singer, a Miami attorney and 1965 Palmetto graduate who befriended Bobby at school. "It was a bunch of guys with three-point-eight averages going to Harvard and Dartmouth, and Bobby was the key."

Bobby was named Dade County Player of the Year. "Because he was a small kid he captured people's imagination," basketball coach Bouton said. "He had that little baby face, that little baby smile."

The basketball court — or at least a bucket on a pole — had been a refuge from the tin-roofed shotgun shack where Bobby grew up. He lived with some of his fifteen brothers and sisters and their children on a dirt road in Florida City, one of Dade County's poorest cities. There wasn't much furniture in the house. Mostly beds. Beds in the front room, beds in the kitchen. Three to a bed was common.

Bobby lived near a bar. Men drank out of paper sacks and dealt drugs on the corner.

None of Bobby's friends at Palmetto knew, or asked, much about his home life. Sometimes Bobby hung around the gym after practice, in need of a ride thirty minutes south. He didn't ask for one. He somehow gave the impression he'd be content to sleep in the gym — maybe out in the middle of the basketball court. But sooner or later, someone would offer him a ride.

I drove him home once. I barely noticed the neighborhood then. Once I turned around and headed back up the expressway, I gave it no further thought.

No further thought. How typical of high school. After college, when I returned to Miami, I discovered many things about Panther Territory I had missed or romanticized. The Bobby Lester case was just one of a series of disillusioning discoveries: in high school, my next-door neighbor had been a Haitian diplomat. I never realized he was part of Baby Doc's brutal regime. I didn't know his handsome, well-mannered son was in a car theft ring. One of Palmetto's star student athletes, an Ivy Leaguer, turned out to be a campus drug dealer.

Our friend's poverty passed us by too. We had other concerns — winning games and friends, getting a good date and into a good college.

Mardie Cooper Smith, a fellow athlete and classmate at Palmetto, now a Homestead teacher, came to the same uncomfortable conclusion when we talked about what Bobby had done. "It didn't occur to me until after he was arrested all he must have gone through in high school," Smith said. "His life was such a dichotomy. Palmetto and then home to a Florida City slum. We used to think he was kind of naïve, we the worldly big shots of Palmetto.

"I used to drive Bobby home in my Cutlass convertible and never really noticed the danger of the neighborhood. There was a girl on the team who got pregnant and I thought, 'How nice.' Hey, I was just concerned about what I was wearing Friday night."

Bobby brought up the subject of his background only once, in an offhand remark while we were running. I was griping about the way dogs chased runners. He told me how he had to dodge more than dogs. Once, he said, he was nearly hit by a bullet meant for a drug dealer.

Another time, I complained I had trouble sleeping the night before meets.

"Linda, Linda," he said, chuckling. "What do *you* have to worry about?" At the time, I had no idea what he meant.

After we were done running, I went home and jumped in the pool. Bobby lingered at the gym, waiting for a ride.

When I looked through old newspaper articles on Bobby in

the *Herald*'s library, I found a story from 1980, the year he won the Player of the Year award. "Nobody would want to raise their kids here," he said about his neighborhood. "I don't want to ever have to come back to a place like this once I leave."

I got Bobby's address in Homestead from the police reports. It was a small concrete-block house with a patchy yard surrounded by a collapsing chain-link fence. The house backed up to a mom-and-pop store on a corner the police had said was a notorious drug market.

Bobby's mother, Dallas Lovett, a woman in her late sixties dressed all in white, had just returned from church. She said she was tired, and she didn't want to talk about her son. "I don't hear from him," she said. But as she stood in the doorway in the heat, she reluctantly answered some questions.

Bobby's father left when he was four. She had worked in the fields since moving south from Porter, Georgia, in 1956. She picked tomatoes, cucumbers, squash. "I was pickin' anything I could find," Lovett said. "Sixty cent a hamper for beans, forty cent a box for limes." Bobby and the other children often worked alongside their mother on weekends. A day's labor paid about $10.

Bobby was nicknamed Boo-Boo, after Yogi the Bear's pint-sized sidekick, "because we saw it on the TV one day and Bobby was little too," Lovett said.

In his spare time, he played basketball. "He put a bucket up on a post," Lovett said. "He always had a ball, and he was always playing, until it was too dark to see."

Bobby was king of the playground at A. L. Lewis Elementary, where men and boys still gather every afternoon for pickup games. They remember Boo-Boo, how he'd score fifty points, how he made his teammates look good with perfect passes for easy lay-ups, how he was always there. "Anytime you wanted to find Bobby, you just listened for the sound of a bouncing basket-ball," said Ezzard Horn, a Homestead Parks and Recreation worker who started coaching Bobby on community teams when he was eleven.

Bobby lived in the school district for South Dade High. But when he was in ninth grade, the South Dade basketball coach told him he wasn't ready for varsity ball. So Bobby decided to go to Palmetto, in one of Dade's most affluent public school districts. It draws students from Pine Bay Estates, King's Bay, Pinecrest, Gables Estates, but is always ready to accept transfer minority students.

After Bobby became a varsity standout, South Dade coaches complained that Palmetto had engaged in forbidden recruiting. Bouton, the Palmetto coach, denies it. He says Bobby chose Palmetto on his own. "The perception is that Palmetto is a cut above, that more is expected of you," Bouton says. "Bobby made a lot of decisions with the idea of proving himself."

Most days, Bobby woke at 5 A.M., walked to the Homestead bus station, and took a Greyhound north on U.S. 1 for the forty-five-minute ride to Southwest 120th Street. He would do some cleaning on the buses and around the station, and the drivers would let him ride for free, waking him up when they reached a corner eight or ten blocks from the school.

As he walked to the pale blue school building, he passed the student parking lot, filled with Firebirds, Blazers, Monte Carlos. One girl used to be dropped off in a Rolls-Royce. Cars were important at Palmetto. Without a car, you couldn't skip school on Friday afternoons, drive to Crandon Park, and get a tan in time for weekend parties.

Palmetto had a harsh high school caste system. Bobby, an average student, wasn't in the honor society pack, destined for the Ivy League. He didn't have the looks or style to get into one of Palmetto's illegal but flourishing fraternities, or to be voted sweetheart of one of the sororities. He was a great athlete, but he didn't fit in with the golden-boy jocks.

But Bobby's unpretentious good nature, his combination of humility and talent, allowed him to rise above the cliques. I watched him mingle easily with one group and then the next, and thought, "Here's a good thing." The Palmetto snobs were accepting Bobby in spite of all the reasons they could have seized on to reject him. Students, teachers and coaches were enchanted by his simplicity, his quiet determination.

"He got along with everybody, black or white, and when we argued, he was the peacemaker," said Rose Borkowski, a star athlete who was close to Bobby at Palmetto.

During Bobby's senior year, he often stayed at the home of basketball teammate Mark Hollin. The Hollins don't want to talk about Bobby now, but Palmetto athletic director Yvette McKinney remembers that their kindness meant a lot to him. "They sort of took him in and made a big impression on him, a successful black family," McKinney said.

Bobby became something of a Palmetto project. Singer, the Palmetto alumnus, gave Lester odd jobs for pay. When Singer moved, he hired Lester to help carry boxes. "I found him going up and down the elevator in my four-story building," Singer said. "He had never been in an elevator before."

At the time Bobby made sure to express appreciation for any kindness. Now some of the people who took him out to eat or put him up for weeks in a spare bedroom feel betrayed. They say Bobby may have grown too dependent on favors. Maybe Bobby's problems started right there.

"People went out of their way to help him," said Irwin Adler, his junior high coach and a longtime friend. "He spent many evenings eating at my mother's house. He had knowledge of what a good environment was. You'd think that would have given him strength to persevere. It hurts me that he didn't make it. To find out all of a sudden that he's not a fine human being . . . it's devastating."

Bob Singer: "It broke my heart. He had fantastic guidance, and there was no exploitation behind the people who helped him. At some point it was like he bit the hand that fed him."

Visiting prisoners at the Turner Guilford Knight Correctional Center on Northwest 36th Street in Miami is a test of patience. There is usually a line at the front desk. Then calls to various guards and shift commanders to make sure you're on the visiting schedule. You turn over your driver's license, lock your belongings in a locker and walk through a metal detector.

One sullen corrections officer would stamp the back of my hand five times, mashing it hard, as if to tell me I was being temporarily incarcerated. Sometimes I'd wait up to two hours in the lobby. A guard would take me through two sets of electronic doors and up an elevator to the tiny visiting rooms, where a glass partition separates visitors from prisoners. Bobby and I talked on a phone. The jail was freezing.

"Kills germs," Bobby explained on the first of my many visits.

He wore a T-shirt and the red jumpsuit of inmates in Unit 8-1, a high-security section. His face was bloated, his eyes bloodshot. He had put on weight and muscle since I had seen him last, six years before.

He didn't get much exercise in jail: one hour of basketball five days a week on a small court against "pretty mediocre competition." He had invented a jail workout, running up and down the stairs with buckets of water.

It was a new jail, and Bobby had his own cell, his own TV and use of a phone. He watched a lot of religious programs and led a Bible study group. He was back in his old peacemaker role, acting as mediator between inmates and guards, who treated him as a pet.

His fellow inmates included a Colombian drug dealer, a man who had raped his daughter, and a murderer. He described the numbing routine of prison life and some of its tricks: how inmates burned their plastic shavers into knives, how LSD was smuggled in on letters.

Once I visited on a Saturday night, busiest night of the week. There was a long line at the front desk, mostly women dressed in high heels, short skirts and tight blouses. The guards looked them up and down to make sure they didn't violate the dress code. Some were turned away. It dawned on me that they were there on dates.

"One time I walked by the visiting area and saw a woman undressing in front of the glass and pressing her, you know, against it," Bobby told me.

"Her breasts?" I said. He nodded. We burst into laughter.

As the months passed, I kept prodding Bobby for answers. I checked court records for his criminal history. He made excuses, blamed his arrests on running with the wrong crowd, said it was hard for a black man to get a good job.

Fellow athletes from Palmetto, Rose Borkowski, Mardie Smith and I were the only people who visited Bobby in jail. He wrote to all of us and called often.

"I hope I'm not a burden to you," he wrote me. "Mistakes can be anchors that drag you down or stepping stones to greater levels of achievement."

He asked for money for stamps and snacks. I sent him $10

here, $20 there. When he asked Mardie Smith for money and she refused, he stopped writing.

"I felt I'd been manipulated," she said. "And I was a little skeptical about him finding religion. I was hysterical when Bobby was arrested, but I've talked to a lot of people and we concluded that he wasn't just a victim of society. We all have to grow up."

With time, Bobby's posture of denial softened. He admitted to drug use and "illegal activities." We danced around the Biting Bandit charges because he was awaiting trial. He never said he did it, but he never said he didn't. "I made a lot of mistakes," he said.

Through my often frustrating conversations with Bobby, and with those who had known him during his decline in Homestead, I pieced together those missing years.

Bobby's best days were behind him by the time he got to college. Coaches at major schools didn't want to gamble on Bobby because of his size, so they invited him to enroll and play his way to a scholarship, something Bobby couldn't afford to do. But Pensacola Junior College decided to take a chance. It paid off, for a while. In the one season he played there, he was dubbed "the little magician."

After Pensacola, he went to Miami-Dade Community College South, where he played one injury-plagued year, then transferred to Florida International University. At FIU, where basketball was a new sport and the team didn't win many games, Bobby played two years as a starter without any obvious problems. He wasn't a big scorer. His role was to feed the ball to the other players. But in his final college game, he decided to shoot as freely as he had in high school. He scored thirty-six points, still an FIU record.

Bobby majored in criminology. He said he was interested in law enforcement or coaching, but when his senior year ended and his scholarship ran out, he was seventeen hours short of a degree. It's a common phenomenon among scholarship athletes — less than 50 percent get a degree. FIU coach Rich Walker: "You try to transfer some of an athlete's energy into academics and a career, you provide that guidance, but you never know what really goes on inside a person."

Bobby drifted away from college and his Palmetto friends and moved in with his mother. He tried substitute teaching, but said it was like "babysitting for low pay." Then he sold cable TV subscriptions. "I found I was good dealing with people one-on-one," he said.

He also played basketball for an amateur team called the Push-Rods, coached by his old youth league coach, Ezzard Horn. Although the Push-Rods were among the best teams on the state amateur circuit, Bobby knew amateur ball didn't amount to much. He was already a has-been. All his life he had not allowed his height to become a liability, but he had reached the point in sports where heart could not overcome genetics.

"Bobby really wanted to be a pro basketball player," Horn said. "He used to say, 'If only I was six feet.' I told him if he was, he'd be in the NBA. A few inches — that's what separated him from an NBA contract."

Instead, Bobby moved from cable subscriptions to selling cars at Homestead Toyota. For a time, he seemed to thrive. "He had a lot of customers, and they all loved him because he was such a cheerful kid," said sales manager John Jameson. "He was doing above-average volume, making seven to eight hundred dollars a week. He wore a shirt and tie and ate like a horse. He used to eat two-foot-long subs from the Hungry Bear."

Bobby found something he liked in the job: competition among the salesmen. On weekends, he went fishing in a canal off Campbell Drive. He and Horn cleaned the fish, and Horn's wife cooked them.

Bobby was also quite the man about town. "He had a lot of girlfriends," Horn said. "One Thanksgiving he came over twice for dinner, each time with a different young lady."

But what looked to outsiders like the beginning of a comfortable middle-class life felt to Bobby like a charade. It was a feeling any high school star would recognize. "I finished my athletic career and sort of crashed, too," Rose Borkowski said when I told her about my conversations with Bobby. "But I had an economic net, in the suburbs, until I figured out I wanted to go to vet school. We used to think the toughest thing was winning a close game. But it's really the day-to-day living, the Joe Schmo job. Not being number one anymore."

Bobby had been number one for too long. "Coming from Palmetto I wanted something better. I felt I deserved something better," he said. He described standing in the Toyota showroom, watching the hours drip by, feeling like his life was swirling down the drain.

"When I scored fifty points against Coral Gables High, I felt like I was on top of the world," Bobby said. "Those feelings led me to trouble. You get this attitude that everything in sports will carry over into everyday life. Then you wake up one day and you're a regular nobody."

Bobby says now he was an addiction waiting to happen. Hanging out in his tough Homestead neighborhood, he didn't have to wait long: "It was at a party. I was more curious than anything. Being high gives you a feeling of relief. When you first begin to use cocaine you get that feeling of being on top of the world. You try to match that first high, but you never do. After a few months it goes away and it's just an addiction."

The people who knew Bobby the best could see the signs almost immediately — on the basketball court. Bobby was losing his touch. He was missing shots he used to make. His passes lost their zing. "He was losing weight, going through mood swings, letting sorry players beat him," Horn said. "During a tournament, this fat, stubby guy was talking trash to Bobby: 'I'm gonna take you, sucker.' He stole the ball from Bobby. That's when I knew something was wrong."

McKinney saw Lester at a Dade North game. His eyes were bloodshot. "I said, 'Bobby, you look like an old man,' " she said.

His job at Homestead Toyota was toast. "He did a one-eighty on us," said Jameson, his boss. "When they're doing coke, they don't eat. They drink a lot of coffee and call in sick. They don't care anymore. So I had to let him go."

Bobby got another job selling cars, this time at Expressway Toyota. In January 1988 he was arrested for stealing cars from the dealership. According to court records, a girlfriend tattled on him. She called Expressway to report that Bobby had several cars. Police found a missing 1987 Corolla next to the basketball court where Bobby played. The man driving the car, another member of the Push-Rods, said Bobby gave it to him. Police went to Bobby's house, and when his mother answered the door, he tried to run out the back.

Bobby confessed that during tent sales he would doctor the paperwork on trade-ins to hide the fact that some cars were missing from the lot. He was put on one year's probation and ordered to make restitution.

Around Homestead, the word was that Bobby was plunging deeper into addiction. Horn said drug dealers from Homestead and Miami set up games between players from their neighborhoods and then bet on them. "Bob was well liked by the dealers because they made money off him," Horn said. "They gave him cash and drugs when Homestead beat the hotshots from Miami."

Bobby's list of arrests grew: burglary, breaking and entering, loitering. Once, he and two other men tried to steal five-foot tractor tires from a farm equipment warehouse that was under a police watch. The two men got away, but Bobby was chased down by a police dog. Each time he sought help from his old Palmetto friends, Bouton and Singer, who was a lawyer. Time and again they bailed him out.

"There were some bozo crimes, like selling coke that was baking soda," Singer said. "He was an incompetent criminal. At some point I said, 'Sorry, Bobby, I can't help you anymore.' I figured if he kept being handled with kid gloves, he'd never learn to swim in the big sea by himself."

Bobby went to jail for six months. His friends hoped it would scare him straight. It seemed to be working. "He'd call me from jail and say, 'I was wrong, I'm getting my weight up and I'm killing these jokers on the court,' " Horn said.

But when he got out, even his Homestead friends lost track of him. Two months later, Bobby was hooked on crack. "People stopped me on the street and told me he was gone," Horn said. "He started ducking me, cutting through alleys when he saw me. When he stopped playing basketball, I knew that was it for Bobby Lester."

Bobby often smoked crack with neighbor Lolita Braggs. She has since put herself through rehabilitation. "We stole from our families," she said. "It controls you, makes you do mean things. It's like that crack is telling you, 'Get it, get it, get it.' "

Sometimes Bobby stayed with his mother, sometimes he slept on the streets. Or in the police station lobby.

"He is always walking around," night patrol officer Blake Wever said in a deposition. "Sometimes at two or three or four in the morning he crawls through the Dumpster at the Subway shop and makes himself a sandwich."

Homestead Detective Rodney Clayton, assigned to the Biting Bandit case, saw Bobby around town. As a boy, he had played with him at the A. L. Lewis basketball court. He felt no sympathy for his old playmate.

"He was looking just like a crackhead," Clayton said. "He'd say, 'I used to play with you, and look at how you're looking at me now.' He was ashamed, feeling sorry for himself, wanting a handout."

Bobby's Palmetto friend Mardie Smith ran into him at a Homestead Eckerd drugstore in November 1989, when the Biting Bandit was still at large.

"He was dirty and had an odor about him," Smith said. "I went to hug him and he gave me a little hug. He asked for five dollars for the bus, then asked for a ride home. I think my friendship was overriding my fear. His mood was really bad. He said his mother had died."

It was a lie. His mother was alive. But during all this time, his mother told me when I visited, she rarely saw him. "He never explained nothing to me," she said. "People get on that trash and don't care about nothing else."

True, says Bobby. "Cocaine screws up your thinking process. It changes you. You lower yourself to doing things you never imagined you could do. I felt like I was in a trap and there was no one to help me. I couldn't see a way out. I thought there was no way to get back to respectability. I would reflect back on my past and it seemed so far away, so long ago."

On November 19, 1989, Bobby and another man were arrested for a robbery at a Circle K convenience store, then released on bond. An odd thing about the robbery: in a scuffle, the cashier was bitten.

Nobody tied that to the biting incidents that began occurring on the street with alarming frequency. Police jailed one suspect, but the bitings continued. Bobby was finally caught on January 21, 1990, when one of the victims saw him walking on Third Avenue with a beer in one hand and five newspapers in the other. He often stole newspapers from vending machines and peddled them on the street.

Bobby was denied bond and stayed in jail for eleven months. That was the end of the Biting Bandit.

Bobby's class of 1980 held its ten-year reunion while he was in jail. My sister flew in from Dallas. "Reunions are mostly what you expect — kids, weight gain, hair loss," she said. "But nothing prepares you for those very strange deviations. You're ten years older, less self-centered, and you're sad not to see Bobby there."

I drove by Palmetto, walked into the gym. There on the wall were the Hall of Fame pictures: Rose Borkowski, Mardie Smith, myself, and Bobby Lester, holding a basketball.

"Kids asked me if I was going to leave his picture up," Coach McKinney said. "I said yes, because when I look at that picture I remember the Bobby Lester I taught. What's happening now, I just don't know."

Said Adler, Bobby's junior high coach, "Maybe it was amazing that Bobby was able to rise above the muck and mire for as long as he did before he was sucked back down."

Bobby never buckled under excruciating game pressure. He could bring the ball down as the seconds ticked off and the fans screamed and hit the winning shot. From everything I had learned, it seemed that as long as he had been leading a team down the court, all the problems of his past hadn't meant a thing; the kind of pressure that had sunk Bobby Lester was the kind that began when the games stopped.

And then I asked Bobby why he had played for Pensacola Junior College for only a year.

Bobby said, "I was homesick."

Considering what Bobby's home life had been like, and how well things had been going for him in Pensacola, that seemed odd and somehow disturbing. It was a lot more disturbing than I realized.

It seems the "little magician" had a big problem: things kept disappearing around him.

"Bobby was the last kid I would have worried about," said Pedro Peña, the team's assistant coach. "He was doing his schoolwork, playing awfully well for us, and he was the darling of our crowds. Everybody loved Bobby. He had that million-dollar smile. But certain things started coming up missing — a lot of what was missing was money. We were at a loss. It was tearing our team apart. Then it all began to come together and our suspicions focused on Bobby. We said we thought it might be better if he left Pensacola, and he immediately agreed."

Peña said that Bobby never admitted to anything in so many words. "But the circumstantial evidence was overwhelming. If you know Bobby, he came from a very tough background, and I don't think he even knew that what he was doing was wrong. To him it was a survival skill."

The team's coach, Chip Boes, thinks Bobby's problem was a little more complicated. "Bobby's talent and charm meant that he always had alternatives. And he knew it. If he had to leave Pensacola, he knew Miami-Dade would want him. And when he left Miami-Dade, there was FIU waiting for him," Boes said. "It was when he ran out of alternatives that things really went out of control."

Bobby never admitted to the trouble in Pensacola, or even to all the biting crimes he had been accused of. Even now, he still denies the whole truth.

But when it comes to the bottom line, Bobby is not so easy on himself.

"People owe me nothing," he said. "I was given an opportunity to be a role model. I let people down."

The two main monuments in the Florida panhandle town of Marianna honor the dead of a lost battle, the Confederate soldiers who "stubbornly resisted" but were defeated by Union cavalry in 1864. This is where Bobby chose to start over. He arrived on a bus in December, the same day he pleaded guilty to one count of strong-arm robbery and aggravated assault in the Biting Bandit case. Dade Circuit Court Judge Fredricka Smith sentenced him to time served and eighteen months' probation.

He left Miami with only the clothes on his back. He never went to Homestead to say goodbye. In Marianna he lived with a family he had met during his Pensacola junior college days, churchgoing people.

When I visited in March, I stopped at the post office to get directions. "You don't want to be going over there alone," the man said.

The neighborhood was actually better than his old one. When

we met, we shook hands and hugged. It felt strange to sit next to him and watch basketball on TV, after so many months of talking through a glass wall. I was appalled that Bobby had gotten no psychiatric help in jail. Still I was not scared of Bobby. I trusted him.

Not everyone does.

"He broke my glasses, stole my money and left a lifetime scar," said biting victim Thompson. "And he's out on holiday. They should have at least given him five years or sent him to a mental home to see if he's psycho."

Sitting beside me, Bobby did not seem deranged. He was working part-time at a grocery store. He talked about going to Kuwait when his probation ended, to work in the country's reconstruction. He was "witnessing" at various churches. He didn't tell the congregations the details of his past. Only that he had found God and the strength to learn from his mistakes.

We walked to three different houses on Bobby's street. He introduced me to the people who gave him a sofa to sleep on, a hot meal, a ride to church. One woman spat tobacco in a cup as we talked about how polite and helpful Bobby was. He called her Mom.

He showed me the positive-thinking cassettes he listened to, and a letter from his mother in Homestead. "You stay up there," she wrote. "The peoples here are too mean. I don't never know nothing about my children. I just love them."

A graveyard backed up to the little houses. "I walk by there and tell myself I could easily be dead," Bobby said.

He rarely plays basketball. Basketball was part of his past.

"When I thought about my past, it just added more pressure. I have an addictive personality, and I think I became dependent on basketball as an outlet," he said. "I'm trying to reprogram the child in me."

Finally, I asked him about the biting. Why didn't he just punch those people in the face or hold a gun to their heads? To close your teeth on a stranger's skin, tasting blood . . .

Bobby hesitated.

"I weighed a hundred twenty pounds," he said. "I couldn't overpower anybody. I couldn't buy a gun. Biting scared them. They were scared of me."

That still didn't answer the question. This had been the docile

Bobby Lester, the small kid his coaches said never fought, even when bigger players tripped or elbowed him.

"It wasn't the real me," Bobby said. "I was a tool of Satan."

I thought of the minister who strangled his wife, the stockbroker who shot his boss, the teenager who dismembered his grandmother. Bobby knew what I was thinking.

"Deep down, it's in all of us," he said.

After I last saw Bobby, he left Marianna and moved to the Rescue Mission in Panama City, where he helped with chores. He did not tell the Marianna family he was staying with where he was going. "His clothes are still here," the woman said.

Bobby and his probation officer agreed he might have a better chance of finding a job in Panama City, a bigger town. As for the family he left without explanation: "I figured I'd get back to them."

"I can grow spiritually here," Bobby said. "I can help people. I'm not as much of an imposition."

But the Rescue Mission has kicked Bobby out. Bobby called to explain: he had broken a house rule when he gave food to an old man after hours. He said he's now living with a pastor across the street and eats at the Mission.

The Mission superintendent, J. W. O'Daniel, said it wasn't that simple. Bobby had been shirking work assignments. They'd find him sitting off in a corner, reading his Bible. Bobby seemed confused, unable to figure out what to do with himself. He confided in the director that he had been thinking of asking his probation officer to send him back to prison. One time he came back to the Mission after he had clearly been drinking.

"He talks a good spiel," O'Daniel said. "But talking and doing are two different things. He certainly had an opportunity to get his life together here."

I couldn't help thinking: it's starting again. The excuses, the explanations for each failure, the slide back down.

But at least Bobby had called me. It's not easy to come back from where he has been. I think of the boy who ran beside me, mile after mile in the steamy heat of Matheson Hammock Park on our training runs — the strength, the endurance. I know he will need all that and more.

"The race has just started for me, and I won't quit," Bobby wrote me.

The last time I spoke to him he was going for a run on the beach.

Part of me wants Bobby to come back to Miami, to prove to everyone that he can beat the odds. But part of me doesn't want to know if he can't. Part of me wants him to run, and keep on running.

JOHN MARCHESE

The Man in the Mask

FROM GQ

GETTING ARRESTED in the parking lot of a T.G.I. Friday's on a cold Connecticut November night was a hell of a comedown for someone with Kevin Winn's career stats.

"Let's see," says Kevin, "I've been John Marzano." Sure enough, police say, the five-foot-eight, 190-pound, hazel-eyed Kevin *was* the five-foot-eleven, 185-pound, brown-eyed backup catcher for the Boston Red Sox. At least for one afternoon last fall, when he appeared at a movie casting call on a college campus, told jokes, signed autographs and regaled starry-eyed coeds with tales of life in the big leagues. Then he wrote down the girls' phone numbers. Later, police say, Kevin took off with $700 that wasn't his.

That was three months ago, and Kevin Winn has just been sentenced to jail, and now he's sitting in an empty courtroom in West Hartford, surrounded by courthouse guards. Not that they're guarding him, exactly. "He's a good kid," one of the policemen says. "He's not like the other sleazeballs we get in here." After all, cops like a good story, and Kevin Winn certainly has one.

"I was Scott Bradley," Kevin says. Yes, in the final days of the 1990 baseball season, Winn convinced a Boston woman that he was the journeyman catcher for the Seattle Mariners (lifetime batting average: .263). She stayed convinced, Kevin says, until they were in her Brighton bedroom, still sweaty from sex, and her mother called to tell her that Scott Bradley was on television.

The courthouse cops have started to chuckle. "I've been Peter Zezel," Kevin says. Zezel is a well-traveled hockey player now with the Maple Leafs of Toronto. As Zezel, Kevin says, he dated a thirtyish divorced mother *and* two of her college-age babysitters. He even moved into the home of one sitter's parents, golfing and drinking for more than a week at their country club as a guest of her father, a locally prominent attorney. When he left her, Kevin admits, he broke the girl's heart and stole her luggage. And Dad's Princeton ring.

Now, in the West Hartford courtroom, the police are starting to egg Kevin on. He runs through his bizarre roster: Terry Steinbach, Pat Borders, Tony Granato, Michael Stonebreaker. He's been them all. For his appearance as Kevin Winn before the judge today, he has worn a gray Brooks Brothers suit with a white shirt, a dark print tie and maroon braces, all of it paid for by a woman, he says. "Basically, since I graduated from high school, I've been . . . I've been, ah, flimflammin'."

He launches into a talk about the time a few years ago when he posed as an Olympic hockey player. Seems there was this group of nursing students and . . .

"C'mon, Kevin," says one of the cops, who can't stand such lack of detail. "Tell the man. Did you cook the macaroni or what?"

His ersatz sports career has come to an abrupt halt, but over the three years that Kevin Winn impersonated at least a dozen professional athletes — and even the occasional umpire or college coach — he cooked the macaroni with . . . well, he's not sure how many women. "Definitely in triple figures," he says. This despite the fact that he has yet to turn twenty-five and has thinning hair, a pudgy baby face and a short, husky body that looks as if he's spent more time catching pretzel nuggets than pop flies. A scout wouldn't look twice at Kevin Winn, but plenty of women did — and saw what they wanted to see.

But then, so did police, Secret Service agents, military officers, hotel workers and lots of other people. Kevin got more than sex by impersonating near-famous athletes: he got special treatment, attention, access — the caress of fame. Sure, on one level the story of Kevin Winn tilling his peculiar field of dreams simply proves a few shabby thing that we've always suspected — like, jocks get girls simply because they're jocks. But for those few brilliantly larcenous seasons, Winn also turned one of our cherished myths on its head, proving that in America you can grow up to be anything you pretend to be.

Who knows where the tale of Kevin Winn really begins, at what point he decided that he wasn't good enough as he was. Examining his life now that he's got some time to ponder (namely, two concurrent eighteen-month sentences), Kevin remembers that when he first posed as a pro, he was simply bored and a little lonely. A court-appointed psychiatrist who once interviewed Kevin thinks it will take years of intense psychoanalysis to sort out his motivations. And even then, you never know. But the best explanation may come from one of the women who fell for him.

"There's something in Kevin that's in every little boy," says Carolyn Houle, a twenty-five-year-old Connecticut bartender who dated Kevin just before his arrest, last fall, thinking he was Red Sox outfielder Phil Plantier — until she heard that he was also Plantier's teammate John Marzano. "Every little boy wants to be somebody famous."

Kevin Winn is now just barely infamous. In the sprawling prison camp in northern Connecticut where he resides, inmate number 170267, he is not even the most notorious prisoner. That honor belongs to the airline pilot in the next cellblock, Richard Crafts, who put his stewardess wife through a wood chipper. Convicted of four crimes and facing a raft of warrants for others after a binge of deception and larceny and, he claims, a hell of a good time all around, Winn is "a sleazeball" to some and "simply pathetic" to others. His guards seem to view him with hardened amusement. Soon after he arrived, one of them gave Kevin a John Marzano baseball card with prison bars drawn over it.

On Valentine's Day, 1989, Kevin Winn emerged from behind bars and walked into the bus station in Morgantown, West Virginia, feeling healthy and a little drunk. He'd just shot down a kamikaze and a Coors to celebrate his release from the country-club federal prison there, where he'd been sentenced to six months for violating probation. The probation was for "borrowing" an automobile from Andrews Air Force Base, in suburban Washington, D.C., where he'd spent more than a week telling student nurses and anyone else (including a military police-woman he slept with) that he was on the U.S. Olympic hockey team.

Despite that, the law enforcement folks at Andrews still have warm feelings for Kevin Winn. Lots of people do. Even the man who put Kevin on probation at Andrews laughs when he hears Winn's name, because Kevin had told guards at the federal courthouse that he was related to the judge. "I remember him well," says the Honorable James E. Kenkle. *"My son.* The hockey player."

"We were placing bets the day Kevin walked out of here," says former Air Force prosecutor Karl Koch. "The feeling generally was that Kevin wouldn't make it on probation. We all thought it would be sort of fun going around the country living for free and sleeping with women."

Sure enough, Kevin violated his probation very soon — for "borrowing" another car — and ended up serving four months of the six-month sentence. Now, as he boarded the bus to leave Morgantown, Kevin had about $100 in his pocket and a one-way ticket back to his hometown in Connecticut. When the bus stopped in Pittsburgh, Kevin gave the first indication that Morgantown Federal Correctional hadn't corrected him much.

He called Marlo, a Duquesne University student he'd met on a previous trip through town. On that layover, Kevin had convinced Marlo that he was Peter Zezel (pronounced *"Zeh-*zuhl"), who then played center for the Philadelphia Flyers. He also convinced her that his bags had been misplaced by the airline and that all his money and credit cards were somewhere else — his standard line.

Marlo was easy, Kevin says. "It's a power," says a detective, "that I guess we'd all like to have — to make women believe us so easily." Or as another policeman who chased him puts it, "A lot of these women *wanted* to believe him."

Marlo believed and believed. She bought Kevin a Brooks Brothers suit and a plane ticket to Washington, D.C., where she thought he had to play a hockey game, not make a court appearance. For the next several days, she paid for a hotel room, meals and many drinks. Finally, Kevin came back to their room to find her staring, stunned, at the television set, which was tuned to the video checkout, the ballooning bill coming up big and blue on the screen. He took off. But that had all happened more than a year ago, and he thought maybe he and Marlo could reunite. He popped a quarter into the phone.

"Wrong move!" says Kevin now. Marlo had obviously figured

things out and was, you might say, upset. So Kevin hung up and went to the Vista Hotel in downtown Pittsburgh, where he had first met Marlo. He liked to hang out at a club there called Motions, a perfect place to meet women and tell them lies.

People who have met Kevin Winn spend so much time telling you how little he looks like a professional athlete that it is remarkable he convinced *anyone,* let alone managed to leave behind what one police officer called "a string of broken hearts, jilted lovers and empty purses." But then again, keep in mind that places like Motions are teeming with people doing basically the same thing Kevin Winn did, only on a smaller and pitifully mundane level.

"The lines that people use to get laid are phenomenal," says Ed Norian, who used to be the bar manager at Motions. "There are a lot of people in bars like this who are telling everyone they meet that they're consultants, that they drive a Porsche. Then they leave — to go to their job at McDonald's or something — and get into their VW bug."

One of the keys to Winn's success was that he usually operated in that stratum of society where *USA Today* is the standard reference work and express checkout is the main social amenity. In the constantly shifting cast of characters at the bar of a mid-level business hotel, the only permanent thing is transience. Relationships are worked out around flight schedules, and your business card becomes your character. In this reputable demimonde of regional reps and vice presidents of sales, even a benchwarming hockey player is a glamour puss. Plus, Kevin Winn is a most charming young man.

"I'm super-outgoing," Kevin explains. "I could sit down next to Benno Schmidt — he's the president of Yale — and have a conversation with him. And I could sit down with Joe the garbage man and talk to him too."

But when Kevin Winn sat down in a place like Motions, he wasn't interested in talking higher education or sanitation engineering. He wanted to cook the macaroni. "When women found out I was a professional athlete, they usually wanted to go to bed with me right away," he insists. "The way I figure it, it's to impress their girlfriends. Who wants to say 'I went home last night with Joe who works at the bank' when they can say 'I went home with a hockey player'?"

Maybe. But of the half-dozen women who agreed to talk about Kevin Winn (all of them reluctant at first — two called *GQ*'s offices to check the legitimacy of my credentials — and all but one finally consenting only if her full name wouldn't be used), each said, "I wasn't impressed that he was an athlete," or words to that effect. They are hard-pressed, though, to say what *did* attract them.

"He had a sense of humor," says one Boston woman who took Kevin in, and was taken in. "He could make me laugh. He was upbeat. He wasn't blah." Says another, "I kind of liked the fact that he wasn't six-five and some hunk."

Besides being super-outgoing, Kevin was a sports junkie — someone who could rattle off the names of minor league players, pros' alma maters, even umpires. When he decided to become an athlete himself, his repertoire was at first limited to hockey players, who are padded and helmeted and who rank just above pro bowlers in terms of recognition. Later, he branched out to baseball, though even then he usually chose catchers, the men in masks. By the end, he was getting so out of control that if the police hadn't caught him, he might have tried some of the shorter white basketball players.

"Whenever I could," Kevin says, "I'd let other people introduce me. That gave me instant credibility." Once presented, he would start talking — about games and training, the personal problems of his teammates, his family in Canada, perhaps. He could even affect a credible Canadian accent. "He was *good*," says one of his victims. "Even after I found out he wasn't who he said he was, I thought he was an acting student practicing on me."

Kevin used all these tricks on Jan, the divorced mother, whom he spotted on a slow Saturday night in Motions. First the introduction: he simply asked a waitress to offer Jan a drink and ask her if she'd like to dance with a Philadelphia Flyer. Sure, Jan said. Then Kevin told her he was Peter Zezel, something she would believe for almost two years — until she found out that he'd also conned two of her babysitters. At first, Kevin says, "Jan didn't really know what a Flyer was." Soon enough, though, after the real Zezel was traded to St. Louis, she sent him flowers.

*

The real Kevin Winn grew up the youngest of five children in a pretty, middle-class neighborhood in Southington, Connecticut, a suburb of Hartford. His father was a high school athlete who'd served in the Air Force and then settled down to raise a family and work as a regional manager for the Friendly's restaurant chain. Both he and his wife were active in organizing youth sports, and as a kid, Kevin was always hanging around a ball field or a basketball court. Two older brothers followed their father into the Air Force, and later became policemen. Another brother is a television director who has worked for the sports network ESPN. Kevin's sister, a college athlete, now works for a Hartford insurance company. Kevin says he hung around with the "jocks and the preps" at Southington High and apparently has convinced himself that he played varsity sports, although no coach there seems to remember it that way. One of his former schoolmates describes Kevin as someone "who wanted to be a successful athlete but never had the talent. He was always the team-manager type."

After graduating in 1985, having rejected college and with no immediate goals, he bummed around and did some small-time umpiring in town. (Later, of course, Kevin told people that he'd gone to umpire school and would be working in the minors.)

Kevin Winn may not have much athletic ability, but he just may be the Dwight Gooden of schmooze. Once, while hanging out at the Vista Hotel in Pittsburgh, Kevin chatted up "two gorgeous girls" who were greeting guests for a sales convention. He told them he was Joey Mullen, a right wing for the Calgary Flames. Before long, he'd been introduced to the head of the company, who was a big hockey fan (but not big enough to know what Joey Mullen looked like), and the next thing he knew, he was stepping up to the dais at the convention banquet, pumping up storm-window salesmen with a little pep talk. "I talked for ten minutes," Kevin remembers, "about being a winner."

When Kevin Winn finally caught the bus back to Connecticut that spring two years ago, he was not exactly someone you'd call a winner. Though the details of his life at that time are difficult to pin down, Kevin says he held legit jobs for nearly a year: cooking at a truck stop, servicing automatic teller machines. Not terribly sexy stuff. So it wasn't long before he stopped being, as he says, "just Kevin Winn." He hadn't yet given up on Marlo, so he called her dorm at Duquesne. She wasn't there, so Kevin just started talking to the woman who answered. Her name was Michelle. His name, he said, was Kevin Deneen, and he played hockey for the Hartford Whalers.

"He started to call me all the time," Michelle says. A few days after their first conversation, an autographed picture of Kevin Deneen arrived from the Whalers. "I called the Whalers myself," Kevin explains.

"He was so believable," Michelle says. "He would call from a restaurant and put somebody else on — one of his teammates, he'd say — and say, 'Here, talk to Michelle.' Or he'd call and say, 'I'm on my car phone,' and it sounded like he was. [Kevin's trick was to pull rest-stop pay phones into his car and leave the motor running and the radio on.] He'd call and tell me he was in the locker room after a game, and it sounded like *that*. He must have been in his bathroom or something. He'd say he was at a hockey rink, and there would be rink noises. He did all these things; of course I believed him." Eventually, all her friends believed.

As the phone relationship developed, Kevin invited Michelle to come to Connecticut. "He told me he'd buy me gifts," she remembers. "You know, cheesy guy lines."

Kevin thought he was being suave. "I was always really romantic," he says. "I did things that normal guys don't do. Always champagne. I wrote them poetry. Cooked dinner. That kind of stuff." One of the women still has the baseball he autographed for her. "I used to buy them across the street from the stadium," Kevin admits.

Michelle didn't fall for Kevin's romantic approach and says that things got ugly when she refused to meet him. "He left scary messages on my answering machine," she says. "He told me he was in a hotel in Buffalo. I called there and asked to talk to Kevin Deneen, and they put me through. I still thought he was Kevin Deneen, only a really weird guy." She'd reached the real Deneen, who didn't know her. That's when Michelle called the police.

After weeks of phone calls, Kevin finally showed up at the Duquesne dormitory to see Michelle, dressed the way he figured a young jock should be — rugby shirt, khakis, a long black leather coat and a big diamond ring — and the university police were waiting. After being held for five days in the Allegheny County

Jail, Kevin emerged for his hearing, and, Michelle remembers, "he looked really sorry." His attorney and the prosecutor struck a plea bargain. Kevin admitted to what the Pennsylvania Crimes Code calls "harassment by communication." He was given a suspended sentence and told to stay away from campus.

Police say he violated that agreement the next day, by calling Michelle, and there are currently two warrants for his arrest in Pittsburgh.

When she finally saw Kevin for the first time, in court, Michelle says she was frightened, though "he didn't look like you'd expect a psycho to look.

"Even my mother said, 'He's a nice boy. It just seems like he made a mistake.' "

Soon, Kevin was back in Connecticut again, another mistake just waiting to happen. He took a job as a waiter at a Friendly's. The restaurant's manager knew a little of his past but says he liked him: "He was your basic guy who was full of shit." Kevin started dating a graduate history student (whom acquaintances describe as "very attractive"). She even knew his real name, since he had been her waiter. And she wanted to help him. Laura convinced Kevin he could get a better job. And he did: a job that seemed perfect for a young man of his abilities — selling cars. Kevin left his room at the YMCA and moved into Laura's apartment. "I want to spend the rest of my life with you," she says Kevin told her.

"The relationship soured," Laura says, "when he stole nine hundred dollars out of my bank account."

There's a spectrum that runs from fibbing to larceny, and most of us stay on the innocent end. Perhaps over time and telling, our role in the school play gets more important than it actually was. We inflate our résumés. "We all have to manipulate our environments to survive," says a prison psychologist who counseled Winn in Morgantown. "The thing that separates people whom we label 'antisocial' is the degree and the frequency." Kevin manipulated with a great degree of frequency.

After he and Laura parted, Kevin started dating a manager of a women's boutique in downtown Hartford, telling her he was Kay Whitmore, of the hometown Whalers. (She later saw the real

Whitmore signing autographs in a Hartford mall and demanded
to see his driver's license.)

Soon, he decided to become Peter Zezel again. Kevin had kept
in touch with Jan, the divorcée from Pittsburgh, who now lived
in upstate New York. He called her one day and talked to her
new babysitter, a college student named Katie, home on vacation. "There was something about her voice," Kevin says. "I had
to meet her." He persuaded Katie to come to Hartford for the
Fourth of July weekend, and, as it turned out, she was as pretty
as her voice. "I was worried, but she was gorgeous," Kevin says.

By her second night in Hartford, Katie thought she was engaged to Peter Zezel.

Going back to work at the car lot after that weekend, Kevin
Winn just couldn't be Kevin Winn again. He wanted to be Peter
Zezel and be with Katie. That was, he says, "the Big Fatal Day."
It would start a four-month streak that would take him through
more than a dozen cities, about that many different identities,
and eventually land him in jail. That July day, Kevin once again
"borrowed" a car, from his employer, bought a big stuffed bear
to surprise Katie and headed for New York.

Peter Zezel so charmed Katie's parents that they invited him to
stay with them. "Her father was a lawyer," Kevin says. "He did
tax law. He had one professional golfer that I know of as a client.
He wanted to talk about my investments. He gave me full use of
his country club. He took me on my first glider ride. This guy
was really taking care of me. He thought he had a future son-in-
law here."

The twelve idyllic days in New York with Katie, Kevin says,
were the longest stretch he'd ever spent with one girl as an impostor. The good thing started to fall apart, though, one morning when Kevin came down for breakfast. Katie's father was at
the kitchen table, and he knew something Kevin didn't.

"You were traded last night," he told Kevin. "I heard it on the
news."

Somehow, Kevin managed to bluff his way through. Zezel had
been traded to the Washington Capitals, so Kevin left New York
for a few days, supposedly on a trip to D.C. When he got back,
he didn't stay much longer at Katie's house. He packed his
things — in his hosts' Pierre Cardin luggage — and slipped on

Katie's father's Princeton class ring. Even after the family had discovered the theft, they didn't believe that Kevin was an impostor.

"These people called my parents in Toronto," says the *real* Peter Zezel. "They told them that they wanted me to return the luggage and some jewelry and stuff. My parents told them I was touring in Europe."

Katie's father the lawyer has only superlatives for Kevin Winn: "He's the world's biggest asshole." He hired a private investigator, who started to contact police and the sports leagues.

Security officials at the NHL and at Major League Baseball are reluctant to talk about the Kevin Winn case, or even to discuss how often men impersonate professional athletes. "There's really not much we can do about it," says an NHL security person. A few players would talk, and their reactions varied. Peter Zezel laughs off the whole affair now, although he was upset when he first heard from his parents. He remembers one woman approaching him in Pittsburgh and saying, simply, "So *you're* the real Peter Zezel."

John Marzano was not amused. He says someone used his name when he was still playing minor league ball. "It's disgusting," said Marzano when Kevin was still at large. "It must go on all the time."

"It's not *uncommon*," says the man from the NHL, "but it really isn't all that frequent." One thing that league officials and police agree on is that Kevin Winn did it more often, to more women, than anyone else they've seen.

On August 3, 1990, his twenty-fourth birthday, Kevin Winn headed for Boston. He was ready to cook the big macaroni.

"I saw Boston as a challenge," Kevin says. "It's probably the number one sports town. Doing it in Boston was like making it to the big leagues." Boston also might have more college-age women than any city in America, making it Mecca for someone with Kevin Winn's modus operandi. One young Boston woman who fell for his story says sadly now, "No one had ever lied to me before."

Kevin hung around Fenway Park so much that it got so he could walk in the employees' entrance, a sort of service-sector Zelig. He even talked his way into the umpires' locker room. Tony

Terzi, a sports reporter for the Hartford NBC affiliate and a high school classmate of Kevin's, remembers being on the field at Fenway doing pregame interviews during the American League playoffs and running into him. "What are *you* doing here?" Terzi asked Kevin. Kevin told him he was living in Boston and working for a car dealership.

Around Boston, where four different police departments have lodged warrants for his arrest, Kevin was telling women he was Pat Borders, the starting catcher for the Toronto Blue Jays. Or Scott Bradley, a catcher on the Seattle Mariners. (Even in a sports-crazy town like Boston, "nobody," Kevin says, "knows who played for the Seattle Mariners.")

Kevin decided to become Scott Bradley one day while shopping in the mall in Chestnut Hill, a tony Boston suburb. Stepping into an upscale men's clothing store, he was drawn to a young woman with long dirty-blond hair and a steady smile: Elizabeth, who Kevin says is the prettiest woman he seduced, a former beauty-pageant queen. Although no major Massachusetts pageant has any record of Elizabeth (did the con man get conned?), a Boston detective describes her as "a rather attractive-looking girl," a common description of most of the women Kevin duped.

When Kevin told Elizabeth he was a professional baseball player, he says, "her eyes got real big. She's a beauty queen. Finally, she met someone who was like her."

Their whirlwind romance ended a few days later, though, when, according to Kevin, they were interrupted in bed by a phone call from the woman's mother. She was reporting that Scott Bradley was on TV, and that she and her husband were coming right over. Kevin says he convinced Elizabeth it was probably a tape of an earlier game filling airtime during a rain delay. He suggested they clean up before her parents arrived. While she showered, he packed his things — along with a few of hers and her roommate's — and took off.

He didn't go very far. At the downtown Sheraton, Kevin soon met a woman named Marilyn, a pretty graduate of a small Boston college who was then working for the hotel. She had just broken up with her longtime boyfriend, and here was a baseball player named Pat Borders asking her to dinner during an elevator ride.

Of course, like all the other women, Marilyn was not impressed by Pat Borders and his fifteen home runs and .286 batting average and big league salary. It was just that she was single again. And "I was dating a professional baseball player all of a sudden."

Even in the face of overwhelming evidence to the contrary, the women simply *wanted* to believe. "In the beginning, I was convinced," says Marilyn. "But then he started doing things that just weren't right. He'd call and say he had just finished a game in Baltimore and he was going to fly back to Boston to be with me. Then he'd be at my door, like, twenty minutes later."

Finally, Marilyn's mother, who had been suspicious all along, faxed her a picture of the real Pat Borders. There is no resemblance. "Definitely," Marilyn told her mother. "That's him." She didn't want to upset her parents. "They still think I dated Pat Borders," she says.

By late October, Kevin had to leave Boston. Posters were up on the Boston University campus warning women to beware of him. Elizabeth, working with Boston detectives, had tried to trap him at a restaurant in her neighborhood. In Newton, where he'd spent a few days at a hotel telling people he was a federal marshal, Kevin had to dash away when the credit card he was using was reported as lost or stolen. So he went back to Connecticut and checked into one Waterbury hotel as Red Sox outfielder Phil Plantier and another as John Marzano. As Plantier, he hung out with some of George Bush's advance team, preparing security for a political fund-raising visit. As Marzano, he met the casting-company people who invited him to their call at Western Connecticut State, where he allegedly stole $700. The movie being cast: *Other People's Money*.

In the end, it was an off-duty police officer from his hometown, a family friend who knew his real identity, who saw him drinking in a bar and ended Kevin Winn's winning season. Even up to the moment he walked out to the parking lot and got arrested, Kevin was living his fantasy and letting others live theirs. In his last moments as a free man, that November Friday night, Kevin Winn spent happy hour telling everyone at the T.G.I. Friday's bar that he was a St. Louis Blues center-ice man named Michel Mongeau.

*

"I've been through a lot in the last three years," Kevin Winn is saying, sitting unshaven in his brown prison-issue uniform in a visiting room of the maximum-security cellblock where he will serve his time. After his many adventures, he has actually been convicted of larceny and forgery in a stolen-check scam. The charges were brought by his father.

Besides the numerous warrants for his arrest around Boston, most of them for stealing checks or cash from women who thought he was an athlete, Kevin is wanted for passing a bad check in Enid, Oklahoma, and on two charges in Pittsburgh.

Kevin says he is truly sorry for what he did. But what else would he say? A month into his term at the Connecticut Correctional Institution, it seems he still isn't fully corrected. "When I get out of here, we'll go out," he tells me in the prison visiting room, trying to counter my skepticism that women would fall for his lines so easily. "I'll show you. I'll *show* you."

A lot of people — even his victims — think Kevin Winn could be very successful in the straight world if only he would be himself. "I told him," says Leo Scully, the policeman who first took him into custody, at Andrews Air Base three years ago, " 'You're in the wrong business. You ought to be in sales. You'd make a million.' "

Police in several states think there are probably many other women out there who were fooled by Kevin Winn, women too embarrassed to come forward. "I know what the police would say," says the woman in Hartford who found out she hadn't dated Kay Whitmore, who never went to the cops. *"Another stupid girl."* Carolyn Houle, the Waterbury bartender who was the last woman to fall for Kevin, is still accepting his collect phone calls and may even wait for him. "All my friends and family are trying to convince me that I'm really stupid," she says.

Marilyn was not the only woman to catch on to Kevin Winn. He says several women in Pittsburgh and one in Boston discovered his real identity — or at least realized he wasn't who he said he was. A few women think Kevin really wanted to be found out. Maybe because he had a parting line just as good — better, in fact — than his pickup line, a line that would flatter the woman and evoke her pity at the same time. "I didn't think someone like you," he'd say, "would date me if I was just Kevin Winn."

LEIGH MONTVILLE

Citizen Ryan

FROM SPORTS ILLUSTRATED

THE LAST forty-five minutes of Texas twilight have arrived. The day has been gray anyway, cool, and now the colors begin to fade even further as the unseen sun dips toward the trees at the edge of the pasture. The birds know that night is coming. Hear them squawk? The horses have to be fed. They stand in a group, five of them, behind a brown three-board fence. Waiting. A car passes on the road in the distance. Another. Men coming home from work. Women bringing their children from late practices and meetings at the high school.

"Curveball," Nolan Ryan says.

He stands in the middle of the pasture. This is farmland. The horses have galloped across it and tractors and trucks have been driven across it, and the grass is all knobby and clumpy, certainly unmowed, and yet . . . He is at the base of a little grass-covered mound. Mound? His neighbor Harry Spilman, chewing a touch of tobacco, is crouched behind a patch of white that shows through the grass. A patch of white? Nolan tucks his left leg into his chest and accelerates off his right leg and throws the baseball. Harry does not have to move his mitt.

"Good one," Harry says.

There is a rusted chain-link fence, twelve feet high, a few feet behind Harry. Fence? There is the twelve-foot-high fence and the patch of white in front of Harry and the mound in back of Nolan and . . . yes, sure. The mind and the eye simultaneously bring out the recessed image of a diamond, as if they were solving a puzzle in the Sunday comics. "I built it for my son when he was in Little League," Nolan says. "Little Leaguers never have a place to practice. I built it and they used it for a couple of years. Then I let it all go back. Watch where you walk." He fingers the baseball in his hand.

"Straight," he says.

Nolan's three dogs are fanned out in what could be loosely called an outfield alignment. That is Buster in left and Suzy in center and fat old Bea in right. The fourth dog, tied in the back of the pickup in the driveway, the dog that is barking, is Harry's dog Sarge. Sarge simply can't control himself. Let him loose and he becomes too excited. He chases the ball wherever it goes. He tries to grab it straight out of Nolan's or Harry's hand. Sarge has had a million second chances. Had one just today. Can't control himself. Back in the truck.

"There was something on that pitch," Harry says a second after the ball arrives. "It was traveling."

The first time Nolan was in this field, let's see, he was with the Girl Scouts. Camping with the Girl Scouts. His mother, Martha, was a troop leader, and she wasn't going to let her youngest child, seven years old, stay home while she was taking those girls for a night of outdoor adventure at Mr. Evans's ranch. This was back in 1954, when the bayou over there wasn't straight, before the widening was done and the lake was formed at the other end and the tract development came. Let's see. There were more trees then. The road out there wasn't even a road. There was another road. Yes. Another road. Smaller. A back road. A further-back road.

"Change-up," Nolan says.

He still is here. How many years later? The land now is his, acquired thirteen years ago in a straight trade, a new house that Nolan owned for Mr. Evans's old house and the land. This is a Tuesday, late in February. The game of pitch and catch has been taking place almost every night for a month. Same time. Same place. Training camp is eight days away, and the fastballs are becoming faster and the curveballs are becoming curvier. A stranger, out on the road, might look and squint and see only a couple of middle-aged guys in the middle of nowhere trying to find a few Absorbine, Jr. memories, but there really aren't many strangers out there on the road. These are familiar people. A horn honks. Another. There's old Nolan, tossing with Harry. Getting ready.

"Looked good," Harry says.

"I don't know," Nolan says. "That one might have got hit."

The shades of gray darken, and Nolan is working just a little harder tonight. He has to miss the workout tomorrow. Has to go to the White House. To see the President. Up there in Washington. He will be back in Alvin, Texas, back here, Thursday.

"I don't know how he does it," says Kim Spilman, Nolan's secretary and Harry's wife. "The letters, the invitations, the demands. The businesses. There always is someone who wants him to be a grand marshal in a parade, to talk at Career Day. Something. The White House. How do you stay normal with all of these people pulling at you all of the time? And yet he does it. God, he does. He's everything a person would want to be. He talks with my kids and he's just so nice. They'll ask me, 'Is he supposed to be famous or something?' That's just how he is."

The White House is the latest thing. The White House. The war in the Persian Gulf is at its hottest stretch. The coalition airplanes are pounding Baghdad with their bombs. The ground war will start in four more days. The White House is on television seventeen times every day. The President is seen going from meeting to press conference to late night strategy session. In the midst of all this, the Queen and Prince Consort of Denmark are invited for dinner. Nolan and his wife, Ruth, also are invited for dinner. They are also invited to stay overnight. At the White House.

When will it all stop?

The drumbeat of celebrity always has been in the background — good pitcher, fastest fastball going, All-Star — but in the past two years, since Nolan went to the Texas Rangers, it has become louder and louder. The 5,000th strikeout was a jump in 1989. A record. The sixth no-hitter, spun in Oakland in June of last year against the then-world-champion Athletics, was another jump. Another record. The 300th win, in July, was a capper. How noisy can noisy be for an essentially quiet person practicing a physical craft? The line has shot off the graph paper. The White House.

"Nolan was here when the call came," Kim says in the office Nolan has rented in the Merchants Bank in Alvin to handle the increased demands on his life. "It's funny how that works. As soon as he gets here, the phone starts ringing off the hook. It's like people have antennae or something to tell them he's here. I took the call, and the message was something like, 'Please stay on the line for the President of the United States.' I was so excited I ran into the bank to tell everyone that Nolan was being invited to the White House."

There is the crazy thought that maybe George Bush is going to call this forty-four-year-old man into the Oval Office and ask him to take a quick trip to the Middle East. Let Saddam Hussein find an emissary to send from Iraq, a solid citizen, someone who represents all the best qualities of Iraqi culture. Let him talk to Nolan, the American representative, to straighten out all of this feuding and fighting. There is the crazy thought that this would not be so crazy.

Who would be better?

"I don't know how it is in the rest of the country," Jim Stinson, Nolan's longtime friend and business partner, says, "but in Texas he is bigger than John Wayne right now. And you will wear out a truck finding someone who's nicer than Nolan Ryan."

John Wayne?

"I talk with ad agencies about him," Matt Mcrola, Nolan's longtime agent from New York, says. "They will say, 'Well, can he talk?' I will tell them if they're looking for Sir Laurence Olivier, they'd better go to Central Casting. But if they're looking for someone who is honest, who is sincere, who can talk about things in his way — Jimmy Stewart. If they are looking for Jimmy Stewart, they want Nolan. He is someone who is really real."

Jimmy Stewart?

In the tie-a-yellow-ribbon Americanism of the nineties, Nolan somehow has become the perfect oak tree. The fact that he still can compete with the young and wild-eyed millionaires of his game and still can make them look silly is only the beginning. He is Citizen Ryan, a total package. Tired of the fatheads who spend their first paychecks on sports cars that run on airplane fuel?

Seen too much of the substance abusers and the late night ca-
rousers and the uncoachable prima donnas? Here is a family
man. Here is a businessman. Here is a cowboy. Here is Nolan
Ryan, cut from a good bolt of denim cloth and served with a glass
of milk and no apologies.

"Do you know what he has?" says Terry Koch-Bostic of the
Slater-Hanft-Martin advertising agency in New York, which
signed Ryan as the spokesman for Bic razors in 1990. "He has
the real stuff of real heroes, the kind of heroes that maybe we've
been missing for the last three decades. That's the kind of guy he
is. When we were making our deal, his first consideration was his
family. He said that money was not important, that he couldn't
be traveling around in the off-season. He wanted to be home. I
told that to Mr. [Bruno] Bich and he said, 'Well, yes, that's exactly
the kind of guy we want. A person whose family comes first. Absolutely.' "

After twenty-three years, the man still is married to his high
school sweetheart, and Ruth remembers when a big date simply
was watching him take target practice with his .22 pistol. They
still live in the same town and their kids attend the same schools
they attended. A big night still is a trip to Baskin-Robbins for ice
cream. A big Saturday night still is dancing the two-step with
friends at Eddie's Country Ballroom. Pretty good two-step too.

A workday is a workday. Vacations still are mostly for other
people, although there were three days at the end of last year in
Las Vegas for the National Finals Rodeo. There is no real "off"
in the off-season. Nolan is a rancher. Nolan owns three ranches.
The biggest, China Grove, in Rosharon, near Alvin, has 550
mama cows and 33 bulls and as many as 1,100 head, total, at the
end of calving season, which is just about now. Relaxation is riding a horse and penning the calves and doing a cattle rancher's
hard work.

"He's a hands-on owner, for sure," Larry McKim, the ranch
manager, says. "When he comes here, he gets right into it. He
helps us castrate the steers, dehorn 'em, everything. Nothing
fazes him. I'll see him reach into the chute with that million-dollar right arm and I'll say to myself, 'Are you sure you want to do
that?' But he'll never buckle. He'll go right in there."

"Nolan is as good a cattleman as there is in the state of Texas,"

Stinson, a partner in China Grove, says. "He's stride for stride with all of 'em. If he'd never picked up a baseball, he'd still be a great success as a cattleman. He's been doing it all his life. I remember his mother telling me once how he saved up enough money when he was a kid to buy four calves. He lived in town, so he had to raise 'em in the garage. Fed 'em all from a baby bottle."

The banking business is another long-term affair. Nolan made news last year when he purchased the Danbury State Bank, about ten miles from Alvin, but he had been on the board of directors of an Alvin bank for ten years. Again, he was not just a name on the letterhead. He worked. He sat in on loan meetings. He formulated bank policy. He preached moderation. He still is one of those guys who travel the extra mile for gas at $1.06 per gallon if the local station is charging $1.10. The word is frugal. He did not rush into a deal that translated into "dumb baseball player buys failing bank." He waited and learned, and moved at the proper time.

"I'd use another word for him, 'tight,' " Sonny Corley, president of the Danbury bank, says. "But that's all right, because I'm tight too. I think he got a great deal here, because under the bank's charter he can expand anywhere in the state of Texas. Nolan knows what he's doing. He's been in the banking business for a while, and he has a great ability to look at a situation and analyze it. He has what I'd call country smarts. Nolan has great country smarts."

His final off-season occupation is being Nolan Ryan. This has become the most demanding job of them all. Until the past two years, his endorsements mostly were local and regional — Whataburger and Bizmart office supplies — but now he shaves for Bic and takes Advil for headaches and wears Wrangler jeans over his Justin boots when he goes out for a western-wear night. He could sign baseballs forever for charity, especially across the "sweet spot" in the front of the ball, which immediately increases its value. He does not do the autograph shows, signing for money. He does not do speeches for money, but he does talk for certain charities he considers important. The requests are so numerous now that mail arrives at his office in tubs from the Alvin post office. He and Ruth used to handle the mail at home. The tubs began to take control. He has added the office and secretary in the past two years.

"Can you imagine that they did all this at home?" Kim says as Ruth arrives at the office with another tub. "The letters he gets. The requests — he could speak every night of the year if he wanted. Somewhere."

His strength is that he does not go somewhere every night. He usually goes home. The increase in Nolan's celebrity has come at a good time, because his oldest son, Reid, nineteen, is a freshman at the University of Texas in Austin, and his other children, Reese, fifteen, and Wendy, fourteen, are in high school, and his days are free. But he wants to be home for dinner. That is his base. He creates his own orbit around the base, and the orbit rarely leaves Texas in the off-season. He will travel to Arlington Stadium for a day, knock off a series of commitments there and come home. He will go to Abilene or Austin and come home. He works and then he comes home.

"He's just such an unassuming, fine guy," Stinson says. "I called him the day after he pitched the no-hitter last year. We talked for half an hour. He never mentioned the no-hitter. Finally, I had to mention it. He said, 'Yeah, I had it going pretty good.' That's it."

"We had to follow him around a bit during the season to complete the [Bic] commercial," Koch-Bostic at the ad agency says. "We finally did it in Los Angeles. He was coming off the disabled list with a bad back. I was thinking about his bad back. The next game, his second start, he's in Oakland, throwing the no-hitter. Reese is rubbing his back in the Ranger dugout between innings."

"The thing I like about him is not so much what he does but the way he does it," McKim says at the ranch. "The only thing fast about him is his fastball. He's so calm, so good-natured, so easy. He's the best rancher I've ever worked for. The other ones were pretty hyper, pretty nervous, always concerned with money. Nolan, he's a people person, not a money person."

The money matters, but it doesn't matter that much. Merola, the agent, tells clients they can have "the sizzle or the steak." Nolan is the steak, and steak is popular. He was asked to run for Texas agriculture commissioner last year, thought about it because he was opposed to what he considered the incumbent's anticattleman policies, but finally decided he didn't have the time. The candidate he endorsed, Rick Perry, beat the incumbent, Jim Hightower, in a surprise. The Texas Senate just passed a bill to have a stretch of Highway 288 near Alvin renamed the Nolan Ryan Expressway. There are plans in Alvin to build a Nolan Ryan Museum. Every day there seem to be offers from somewhere to do something involving Nolan. Every day Nolan gives them a look.

He takes his time. Always.

"The big thing with Nolan is that he's hard to pin down," Kim says. "He doesn't like to schedule things in advance because he never knows what's going to come up. Especially with the kids. If Reese or Wendy has a game or something, he'd like to go. If you do pin him down, though, he'll be where he's supposed to be. You can count on it."

The invitation to the White House was typical. Kim came back into the office, still excited at the news. Nolan said he couldn't go. He had looked at his schedule and found he had promised to speak to a cattlemen's civic group in Cotulla to raise scholarships. That was that. Kim told him he was crazy. He said he had turned down trips to the White House in the past. There always seemed to be something.

"Look," Kim said, "if you called the people in Cotulla and said you were invited to the White House, I'm sure they'd understand. They could just schedule you for another night."

"You do it," Nolan said.

The people in Cotulla understood. Duty called for Citizen Ryan. John Wayne, maybe Jimmy Stewart, had to be at the White House. He would appear in Cotulla the next week if he wasn't in the Middle East.

Nolan and Harry talk while they throw the ball back and forth in the pasture. Harry is not exactly the average next-door recruit, some accountant who bought himself a baseball glove just to help the famous pitcher get ready. Not at all. Harry played too, twelve years of scuffling on the fringes of four different teams in the major leagues and six in the minors. He is thirty-seven years old now, and he retired with bad knees at the end of the last season, which he spent with the Houston Astros' Triple A team in Tucson. He will be working this year as a roving hitting coach in the Cleveland Indians' minor league system.

"So Roger Clemens is getting five million dollars," Nolan says, shaking his head. "If Roger's worth five million, what's Wade Boggs going to be worth?"

Straight fastball.

Splat!

"What about Jim Deshaies?" Harry says. "He's making two million—something. He won seven games last year. Seven games and he's making two million. Isn't that something?"

Curveball.

Splat!

"I know one thing," Nolan says. "I'd like to be about twenty-five years old now and have about five thousand innings ahead of me."

Change-up.

Perfect.

Harry remembers the first time he saw Nolan pitch, in 1980. Harry was playing with the Cincinnati Reds, and Nolan, after eight years with the California Angels, had just arrived back in the National League with the Astros. It was an occasion, seeing the great fireballer for the first time. Harry had a great seat on the bench. He really wanted to see the first confrontation between Nolan and Johnny Bench. Everyone did. Bench dug in at the plate. Nolan stared from the mound. All the players moved to the far edges of their seats. Nolan threw a slow, lazy curveball that bounced about a foot and a half in front of the plate. Bench swung so hard that the temperature must have dropped 5 degrees in the ballpark. A curveball! Beautiful.

Harry soon moved along to the Astros himself, and that was where he became friends with Nolan. Harry is from Dawson, Georgia, so he is another small-town southern guy who talks with the accent. He has the same likes and values as Nolan. He likes to hunt. He likes to fish. He likes horses and riding and, of course, talking baseball. When it came time to decide where he would live in the off-season and the rest of his life, Harry picked Alvin, even though he had moved to the San Francisco Giants. Nolan worked out a deal for the land and house next door. What could be better? In the other years, when they were both playing, Nolan would throw batting practice to Harry down at the high school. Batting practice from Nolan Ryan. What could be better? Kim works for Nolan. Harry works with Nolan. Harry is one of ten current or former teammates who have named a son after Nolan. Everybody is friends.

In the big leagues, Harry faced Nolan twice. The first time, Harry hit a homer, a grand feat considering Harry had only eighteen homers lifetime. The second time, Nolan struck out Harry on a high, 3–2 fastball. Then, again, there is an argument about this.

"When Nolan got his five thousandth strikeout, *USA Today* ran a list of all the guys he'd struck out in his career," Harry says. "I looked for my name. It wasn't there. I remembered the strikeout and Nolan remembered it, but since my name wasn't there, I say it never happened. Nolan even checked with the Rangers public relations department. They said there must have been a mistake, because I pinch-hit. I say it never happened."

"It happened," Nolan says.

"Not if my name isn't on the list," Harry says. (It is now. The 1991 Rangers media guide lists Harry as one of Nolan's victims.)

Curveball.

Splat!

The workout began in the driveway. Nolan stretched and then started throwing a football with Harry, long and straight spirals. This is part of the conditioning process encouraged by Rangers pitching coach Tom House. Nolan had told House two years ago, his first day as a Ranger, that he hoped House wouldn't be upset if he didn't throw the football with everyone else. House said a sure-bet Hall of Famer could do what he wanted. One week passed and then two weeks and then Nolan suddenly was throwing the football. He did what he does with everything. He studied the concept. He decided for himself. He threw the football. No big deal. He liked the mechanics. He liked the way the motion loosened his arm and shoulder. Logic. He threw the football.

"We're finding it's harder than it looks," Nolan says.

"Maybe we remember ourselves being better than we were," Harry says. "I thought I could throw that thing in high school."

Nolan played two years of football in junior high and one year in high school. He was an end. His biggest memory is of an eighth-grade scrimmage down at Danbury, where he now owns the bank. The farm boys at Danbury were so poor they didn't even have shoes. Didn't have shoes! The Danbury coach said it wouldn't be fair if his team didn't have shoes and the other team did, so the Alvin coach had his players take off their shoes. No matter. Who couldn't beat a team that was so poor the players didn't have shoes? Danbury killed Alvin, 42–0. Nolan quit football after the next year. Stinson begged Nolan to stay because he thought Nolan would help the team. Help the team? Stinson says now that "Jim Thorpe couldn't have helped that team." Stinson and Nolan laugh about that.

"I liked basketball," Nolan says. "I could play a little. I could dunk."

After throwing the football, Nolan and Harry threw a baseball in the driveway for a while. Easy tosses. After that, Nolan put on his blue Rangers cleats to throw out in the pasture. Hard tosses. The workout began a little before five o'clock, and now the time is a little after six. The light is almost gone. The dogs have lost interest, running into the woods in what would be dead center field. Nolan says, "They're probably looking for yesterday's game ball." A pitcher's grim joke. Think about it. Nolan says this is the kind of light he wouldn't mind having for all baseball games all of the time. Think about it. He asks Harry if there is enough light for one more pitch. Harry says that there is.

"Straight," Nolan says.

Splat!

"The funniest thing, to me, is when we drive by the Bizmart billboards," Ruth Ryan says. "There's one on the Gulf Freeway and there's one on the freeway in Austin and one in Arlington. They're huge. You look up and there's Nolan. Thirty feet high. I look up, every time, and I say, 'This isn't real.' The kids always start to make fun of him."

There wasn't any grand plan for him to play this long. There wasn't any grand plan for him to become this famous. There wasn't even any grand plan for him to lead a life that would be held up as a model for family men everywhere. Everything sort of evolved. Happened. Nolan figured he would pitch for four years or five and then his arm would go dead and he would come home and maybe begin school and become a veterinarian. Or maybe not. Ruth remembers wondering fifteen years ago, when he was with the Angels and was having arm surgery, if he ever would throw a baseball again.

One pitch somehow was followed by another pitch and then another. One family crisis led to the next crisis. There was a balancing act that somehow led across a high wire to here. Twenty-six years of professional baseball. Twenty-six years of living. Twenty-six years?

"I was watching a television show the other night," Nolan says. "Carol Burnett was hosting a special about *The Ed Sullivan Show.* I remembered I was on *The Ed Sullivan Show.* With the Mets, when we won it in 1969. We all came on together and sang some song."

He has survived, he figures, on a combination of luck and work and those country smarts. He studied what he did, studied from the beginning. He remembers the first time he ever sat in a big league clubhouse, just a kid, up for a moment in 1966. The Mets were still an expansion team, filled with older rejects from established teams. He remembers the old-timers just coasting, taking the paycheck, gliding out the door as effortlessly as possible. He remembers thinking to himself that he would never do that. He never has.

"I figured things out for myself," he says. "I always wanted to keep in shape, especially after I turned thirty. I always had my workouts. I started lifting weights in 1972. Nobody was doing that back then. They told you not to lift weights. I thought it would help me. The older I got, the more I worked out . . . to the point now that I work out more than anyone on our team. I have to do it. To compete with kids who are half your age, you have to do a whole lot more than they do."

He stuck with three pitches. Fastball. Curve. Change. The fastball began to slow about ten years ago, but not enough to make hitters comfortable. The curve improved. The change-up improved a lot. He stayed away from the slider, a pitch he always has thought is a killer of arms. In California, Angel coach Marv

Grissom tried to get him to throw the slider. Nolan nodded, said he would try it out. He never really tried. Never wanted to take that chance.

The Rangers pitching coach, House, is sort of a New Age baseball experimentalist. He uses computers, tests pitching theories. He finds again and again that Nolan figured out this business in his head before the computers did. Nolan, for instance, will mention that he thinks if his back is loose and his left leg is extended just a little higher, his fastball will be better. House will test the proposition on the computer. Whir and hum. Nolan is right again.

"I sometimes think he's the only one who understands me," House says. "He's my translator. He takes what I'm saying in scientific language and puts it into English for the rest of the guys. He'll say, 'This is what he's saying . . .' Everyone else will start nodding his head."

The idea of staying in Alvin never really came to debate. Why not stay? Isn't this where everyone we know always has lived? The idea of staying married never came to debate. Why not? Isn't that what you're supposed to do? The idea of raising a family was ingrained. Wasn't that what our parents did? Raise families? One year has led into another. Last year, Nolan and Ruth went to the twenty-fifth reunion of the Alvin High class of 1965. Everyone hung out at Dairyland on Friday night, the way they had in school. There was a dance at the country club on Saturday night, a picnic on Sunday.

"He is the one who has kept everything together," Ruth says. "Him. It would be so easy for him to go off, to just say, 'You take care of the kids while I go do this business.' He never says that. He always tries to make us a part of everything. He is going to Abilene on business this weekend. He could just go. He doesn't want that. He wants us with him."

"I think you learn so much more from your parents than you ever thought possible," Nolan says. "It just comes through. I find it comes through again and again."

The lessons of long ago do not leave. How can he go to the gym early every morning of the year, to the free weights and torture machines inside a little room he built off his barn? How can he fight through the everyday soreness, refuse to stay in bed just once? How can he be strong when his body wants to turn soft?

How can he do all that work in the morning and then be throwing at night? He remembers delivering newspapers with his father as a boy. His father had two jobs. Nolan would have to get up at one o'clock in the morning, roll the papers for an hour, then deliver them around the back roads of Alvin, fifty-five miles of traveling, until four. Then he would go back to bed for a few more hours of sleep before school. Every day.

"You had the feeling that people were counting on you," he says. "If you didn't get up, they weren't going to get their papers. You just did it. You had a sense of responsibility. I guess I never lost it. There are a lot of mornings where I'd just like to keep my dead butt in bed. I just get up."

He says he is so old that he remembers when baseball wasn't the fast road to wealth that it has become. He says he made $7,000 in his first major league season. When the Mets won the World Series in 1969, his share of the winnings tripled his basic salary. He bought his first house. For ten years, playing baseball was an economic struggle. He remembers installing air conditioners in the off-season. Pumping gas. There weren't always ranches and banks and endorsement.

"I talk about some of this stuff sometimes and kids in the clubhouse look at me as if I'm sort of a codger," he says. "And I guess I am. I look at these kids on our team — we have a young team — and I'm the same age as most of their fathers. I'm like one of the coaches. That's how old I am. The one thing, I think, that age has given me is a sense of history. I see a lot of the young guys and the money they make, and they don't know what went into getting that money. That sort of bothers me. It makes you think about a lot of things we just take for granted."

He remembers a time when there was no television in his house, when he would stand in the dark of Dezo Drive and look through neighbors' windows at this miraculous invention. He remembers his grandmother had outdoor plumbing. Man walking on the moon? He remembers long before that. A bus was taking him to play some game in eighth grade in Houston. The coach pointed out the window and said that a thing called NASA was going to be built in a vacant field they were passing. Cows were in the middle of the field. NASA.

"You think sometimes about all the stuff that has happened,"

he says. "I was reading somewhere the other day that the Rural
Electrification Act is fifty years old. Fifty years ago, people were
just getting electricity. Thirty years after that, man was walking
on the moon."

He says he has no goals for how long he will pitch. The last few
years have been a wonderful bonus. He will pitch this year and
see what happens. His wife has a hunch that this will be his last
year, but it is only a hunch. His friends think he will pitch as long
as he is healthy and successful. House thinks, crazy as it sounds,
that Nolan is pitching as well now as he ever did. House thinks
Nolan will pitch as long as Nolan wants to pitch, as long as he
wants to make the physical sacrifices to fight the aging process.

After that, politics is always a possibility, but Nolan says he will
not go looking in that direction. He simply will listen if someone
talks. The ranching business always has been interesting. The
banking business is turning out to be very interesting. He has
plans for expansion. The Danbury bank has grown in less than a
year from a $9 million bank to a $13 million bank. Maybe he'll
do something in baseball. The baseball business certainly has
been interesting.

"I remember going to Houston to watch the old .45s play at
Colt Stadium," Nolan says. "I went with my dad, I guess. I remember saying, 'How about this? These guys get paid to play
baseball.' I said, 'Look at this guy over here, he doesn't even get
to play in the game and he still gets paid.' Then, that's what I did.
Played baseball for money. It's funny. I go to the career days at
high schools and I tell kids that playing baseball isn't a career. It
really isn't. How many players ever make the major leagues, and
how long do they stay if they make it? I think the average is something like five years. I tell kids they should plan to do something
else, really, with their lives . . . and yet, here I am. I've been in it
this long, and the last two years, I have to say, have been the
highlight."

"His age has brought him all this attention," Ruth says, "and I
really think he has earned it. I think people looked past him for
a long time. I remember being really aggravated back in 1973
when he didn't win the Cy Young Award and I really thought he
deserved it. I remember hearing some mean things that people
would say. About him being just a .500 pitcher. He would always
say that everyone is entitled to an opinion. I would get mad. So

now I get a lot of satisfaction from the accolades he's getting. He deserves them all."

Harry and Nolan walk out of the pasture carrying their gloves. Harry unties Sarge at last from the back of the pickup, and Sarge barks and runs around like the strange dog he is. Reese, who is in the ninth grade, is home from a baseball scrimmage. He drove the old farm-only truck to the lake and back to check his six trout lines. They were empty. Crabs had eaten the bait. He is talking, talking, a teenager in a rush. That is Reese. He picks up the football and starts throwing it with Harry.

"I'd be a great quarterback," Reese says. "I was the quarterback in seventh grade. You should have seen me. I was awesome. Just awesome. You should have seen me last year, eighth grade, when I was a Tower of Power free safety. Awesome."

"How'd practice go today?" Nolan asks.

"I got hit in the shin."

"You got hit in the chin?"

"The shin. It hurt."

"Did you pitch any?"

"Yes, sir. I pitched to five batters. One kid . . . I threw the ball behind him."

"Uh-huh," Harry says. "Like father, like son."

In the house, Ruth can be seen through the lighted kitchen window, moving around the cabinets. She went through the day in a buzz, picking up the tickets to Washington, packing the bags for the White House. She bought a new pleated shirt for Nolan to wear with his tuxedo because the old one looked a little too shabby for dinner with the Queen and Prince of Denmark, not to mention President Bush. She picked up her new dress, a long gown bought in Houston, from her mother's house. Her mother had sewn the hem.

Nolan still has to feed the horses and Harry will help him, but there is a moment here, a pause. It is the pause at the end of the normal working day. It is the pause at the end of a workout, the job done, the sweat still fresh. It is the reward. Night is here, and there is a fine sense of fulfillment. This is life. This is breathing. This is it. Friends and family and dogs and home and land. Dinner soon to arrive.

Nolan leans on the fender of his wife's car, resting. He is

wearing a cap from a feed company, a dark blue windbreaker and a pair of blue gym-instructor sweatpants. He could be any-body. Just a middle-aged, middle-of-the-road anybody. He looks across his pasture with its subliminal baseball field, and someone points out the similarity of the scene to ones in the baseball movie *Field of Dreams*. See the woods? Isn't that where Shoeless Joe Jack-son should emerge, ready to play baseball with the other immor-tals? What was the line? If you build it, he will come.

"I built it," Nolan says. "He never came. Maybe I should have put in lights."

Tomorrow, the White House.

DAVID HALBERSTAM

A Hero for the Wired World

FROM SPORTS ILLUSTRATED

IN SOME mysterious way the word has gotten out. The Chicago Bulls bus, the bus that *he* rides on (which is as close as most of these fans will ever get to the street where he lives), is to leave the Westin Hotel in Seattle at 5 P.M., and by 4:20 the crowd has begun to gather in the lobby, concentric rings of fans or, more properly, worshipers: they are more white than black, more young than old, more male than female, but they cut across every ethnic and demographic line. It seems almost ceremonial, a certain hum of anticipation rising each time the elevator opens. Finally at 4:50 — for he likes to be the last man on the bus — the door opens and out he comes, in his Michael Mode: his smile-and-sign-and move-and-smile-and-sign-and-keep-moving drill is flawless. He is the seigneur — swift, deft, graceful, never rude — in the splits of the second in which he at once enters and departs their lives. "I actually saw him *live*," a boy says. Fame is indeed fleeting for those whose closest connection to it is to stand and work the sixty yards from the Westin elevator to the team bus.

I have not seen fame like this in almost thirty years. I think of the time, in 1960, when I was the one reporter in the country allowed to ride the train bearing Elvis Presley back to Memphis from the Army, and I think of John Kennedy in that same year, when he campaigned in California, and I watched the teenyboppers and saw the first reflection that in a television age, politics had become theater. I do not cover rock concerts, but I presume Mick Jagger and others who play at his level deal with this all the time. In a pretelevision age, Joe DiMaggio had fame like this and

was comparably imprisoned, though his fame was limited largely
by the the boundaries of the forty-eight contiguous states.

There is an even greater dimension to the fame of Michael
Jordan. He is one of only two black American athletes who, almost forty-five years after Jackie Robinson broke into baseball,
have finally become true crossover heroes — that is, they receive
more commercial endorsement deals from the predominantly
white, middle-class purveyors of public tastes than do white athletes (the other is the pre-HIV Magic Johnson; the jury is out on
Bo Jackson now that he's a mere one-sport man). But unlike
Johnson, Jordan has created a kind of fame that exceeds sports;
he is both athlete and entertainer. He plays in the age of the satellite to an audience vastly larger than was possible in the past
and is thus the first great athlete of the wired world.

His good looks — indeed his beauty, for that is the right
word — are a surprise to older white Americans, who by cultural
instinct grew up thinking that Gary Cooper and Gregory Peck
and Robert Redford and Paul Newman were handsome but did
not see beauty in a young black athlete with a shaved head. Jordan has given us, then, among other things, a new definition of
American male beauty. Not surprisingly, in many households it
has been the children who have taught the parents about him
and about his fame, artistry and beauty.

About a year ago New York Governor Mario Cuomo gave a
speech bemoaning the disappearance of the athlete as hero in
America. Where have you gone Ted Williams and Joe DiMaggio?
he asked. A friend of mine named Dick Holbrooke, a former
U.S. State Department official, wrote him that comparable heroes still existed, but that their names were Michael Jordan and
Magic Johnson and that today's children were inspired by the
grace and ease with which they carried their fame. Cuomo called
back and said, I stand corrected.

Jordan, infinitely disciplined, product of a very strong, very
ambitious family, knows innately how to handle this staggering
role — to deal with the media, to know what to say and what not
to say and when to hide and when to go public, and to smile always. He is the first New Age athlete. And he is the right athlete
at the right time. He plays the right sport, for its purpose is easily
comprehensible even in a country where basketball has not yet

taken root. Had the satellite been pervasive twenty years earlier, Pelé, also playing an international sport — soccer — on a level above even the best players of his day and with a charm that radiated easily across national boundaries, might have been first. Perhaps Muhammad Ali might have been first, but he was politicized by his conversion to Islam and the Vietnam War. Besides, Ali's considerable charm notwithstanding, boxing was never the ideal sport for the young, with whom all idolatry of this kind must start. Ali, far more graceful than most boxers, conquered his opponents by stylishly punching them senseless; Jordan meets his opponents and conquers by gracefully soaring over them.

More, he does this for an audience that greatly exceeds that of the ballet. This is sports as ballet, something utterly new and modern, its roots African American, ballet as a contested sport. No one, after all, ever guarded Baryshnikov. When we talk in Jordan's hotel room, I talk to him about Baryshnikov and Nureyev and their beauty and grace and he listens, curious, patient, intrigued by these stories of potential rivals, and when I am through, he asks only one question about Baryshnikov: "How tall is he?" Short, I answer, quite short — low center of gravity. I detect a small smile, a category 4 smile, almost invisible, a smile of private victory: Michael's pleasure as he thinks about posting up Mischa.

Jordan's is the most original of performances. What thrills the fans — and the other players and his coaches — is that almost every night there is something unique in his moves. It is not, says Bulls coach Phil Jackson, that Jordan's hangtime is so great; there may well be others in the league with greater hangtime. What sets Jordan apart, Jackson says, is what he does in the air, the control, the vision, the ability to move his body after he has seemingly committed it. If Jordan, Jackson notes with a certain delight, is the lineal descendant of those great basketball innovators who went before — Elgin Baylor, Connie Hawkins and Julius Erving, each learning from and expanding upon the accomplishments of his predecessors — then the most exciting question is, What is the *next* great player going to be able to do?

Ever since the coming of the communications satellite, there has been an inevitability to all this — that there would be an athlete of Jordan's surpassing international fame, that he would most likely come from soccer or basketball, because they are the most readily understandable of international games, the games that essentially explain themselves. Since America is the home team in the wired world, it would likely be an American sport. But American football has too many rules and cloaks its players in uniforms that deny individuality. Baseball has complicated rules too and seems, in contrast with basketball, a languid sport to the uninitiated, building slowly over an entire season. That left basketball. It was therefore almost a given that the first athletic superstar of the wired world would be a black American basketball player who played above the rim.

The last great export of America in the postindustrial international economy may be entertainment and media. We as a country are now to the rest of the world what New York was to the rest of the nation when New York was merely a domestic media capital. (Consider the relative fame and success in endorsements of, say, Joe DiMaggio and Mickey Mantle of New York compared with Stan Musial of St. Louis and Hank Aaron of Milwaukee-Atlanta.) We do not, as a nation, merely reprocess the talents of others through our powerful communications system; like any good isolationist society, we tend to export, first and foremost, our own deeds, concerns and talents.

Jordan's fame is of a kind that builds on itself. Images in our world beget additional images. Having seen one dazzling image, we hunger for another. We fear only boredom. Because Jordan's athleticism is so great, the camera seeks him out every night. And because the camera singles him out, he in turn receives the endorsements, particularly the immensely skillful Nike commercials. What we finally come to is not merely the sale of sneakers but the creation of a myth, a movie in continuum, made up of brief commercial bites — the Michael Jordan story: chapter 1, Michael soaring into space; chapter 2, his palship with Mars Blackmon (even mocking Jordan's own lack of hair). In the end, he is a film star as well as an athlete.

The decision to broaden the story, year by year, was made by Jim Riswold, who writes the Nike commercials. He had heard early in Jordan's career that Bill Russell, not a man lightly given to compliments about other players, had told James and Deloris

Jordan that their son was an even better *person* than he was a basketball player. We will proceed, Riswold thought, to show that. And he has. The Michael Jordan story, as told by Nike, has become such a cultural event that the release of a new commercial is preceded by great secrecy. We are allowed to know only that a new Michael commercial is soon to appear on a television channel near you. Then there is a screening for journalists. *A screening of a commercial for journalists!* Of the next episode, to be unveiled at the Super Bowl, all we are allowed to know is that it portrays Michael with another American icon, someone older from outside sports. (The smart money is on a carrot-eating wabbit of cartoon ancestry.)

Jordan is a reflection of what the world has become and of the invisible wires that now bind it. CNN, the network of the satellite, has been in operation for little more than a decade; the rise of the NBA as an international sport has taken place largely in the past five years. Some seventy-five nations received some combination of regular-season and playoff games in 1990–91, and that figure is up to eighty-eight this season. The internationalization of the sport, of course, has dovetailed almost perfectly with Jordan's pro career. He had been half hidden in college in the controlled North Carolina offense. Nike had signed him in 1984, thinking it was getting one of the better players of the year. It did not know that it was getting the greatest athlete in the world. He was immediately able to showcase his abilities at the Los Angeles Olympics, while the world watched. From then on, the legend built.

When Nike bid to represent Jordan, his agent, David Falk, insisted that he not sign on as just another basketball player endorsing a sneaker, but that he have his own line. In time Nike agreed, and Air Jordan was created. Nike, which had come upon stagnant times in the sneaker wars, thought the Air Jordan line might do about $10 million in business the first year. Instead, despite the attempts of the NBA commissioner to ban the Jordan shoe, Nike sold $130 million worth of Air Jordans.

Thus began the legend (and the dilemma) of the young man who is the most talented athlete in basketball but whose fame and income transcend the game, making him entertainer as well as player. For everything in a media age must entertain; that Jordan can do so is his great value. He is not just the ultimate player; he is the ultimate show.

It is about more, of course, than scoring and smiling. Being a Pied Piper is not enough. He is a warrior, a smiling warrior to be sure, and that too comes through to the fan. There is an intensity to his game, a feral quality, and an almost palpable desire to win. Great athletes are not necessarily nice people, in the traditional definition of nice, which implies a certain balanced, relaxed attitude toward life. They are, at least in their youth, obsessed by winning, by conquering others. Jordan is, for all the charm and the smiles, the athlete personified, egocentric and single-minded, tough and hard — hard on himself, on teammates, on opponents — fearless and unbending, never backing down, eager to put his signature on an opponent, looking for new worlds and teams to conquer.

There are endless testimonials to this intensity: Michael wanting and needing to win at everything he does — pool, cards, video games; Michael staring for hours at a blank television set late at night after missing a crucial foul shot in the final seconds of a playoff game against Cleveland; Michael, in the Finals against the Lakers last spring, hurting his toe, which then swelled up badly, and trying to play in a special shoe that gave him more room but also limited his ability to cut, coming over to the Bulls bench early in the game and saying to the trainer, "Give me the pain," which translated meant, Give me my regular shoe, and I'll play in pain.

He had hated the reputation, which he bore in his early years in the NBA, that he was a great player, perhaps the greatest ever to play the game, but that he would never be able to win a championship ring. This was so, it was said, because the Bulls offense, like it or not, would revolve too much around him, and in the playoffs, at the highest level of the game, he would, in this most team-oriented of sports, subtract rather than add by playing into the hands of the defense. He became, year by year, a more complete player. But what also became clear about him — as it was clear about DiMaggio — was that he was the ultimate big-game player: the bigger the game, the better he played, and the better and tougher he played in the final quarter, and even more, in the last four minutes, when everyone else was exhausted. All of his skills came together last year in the Finals, giving him the championship some said he would never attain.

Now, with that championship under his belt, he pushes for a second and for wider victories. His teammates at Nike and Gatorade are thinking now of Europe. His teammate NBA commissioner David Stern is thinking of the rest of the planet. Their time is clearly coming. The phenomenon of the athlete as global figure grows at an accelerating rate. The Olympics loom ahead, and when Michael leads the U.S. team in the gold medal game just outside Barcelona on August 8, some 2.5 billion viewers in 170 countries will likely tune in.

And this is just the beginning. The stadium is now the world. Sports, particularly soccer and basketball, are ever more international (in soccer, only America lags behind the world, and that is partly generational; younger Americans are already more connected to the game than their parents were). The commercial impulse for more international competition can only grow — the shoe companies and the soft drink companies are increasingly international, and they hunger for this limitless audience.

As for Michael, he is contemplating other fields. We are sitting in Jordan's hotel room, and he is talking about playing another sport. It is hard to tell when he is entirely serious and when he is daydreaming. Sometimes the daydreams sound very real. Bo Jackson, he is saying, made it possible to be a two-sport man, opened it up for me. He clearly would like to compete against Jackson's achievement. Besides, all that jumping is hard on the knees. Football, he says . . . I could be a wide receiver. Almost nothing I couldn't catch. "But I won't go over the middle."

Then he goes on to baseball. He ponders a career there, for he loves the game and would still like to give it a try. At twenty-eight, could he hit the curveball? The question is tantalizing.

In the meantime, as his fame grows, his right to privacy shrinks. Almost everywhere he goes in the world now, he draws large, demanding crowds. Paris, cool to basketball, disdainful of Americans, was a surviving safe haven, a place where he could walk around with ease and relative anonymity. But the next Olympics, he knows, may cost him even Paris.

DONNA ST. GEORGE

The Hustler

FROM THE PHILADELPHIA INQUIRER MAGAZINE

A BAG OF bread crumbs snug under his arm, he shuffles out the
back door of the Hermitage Hotel and into a courtyard of
trimmed grass and budding flowers. In the shadow of Nashville's
downtown high-rises, a single tulip blooms in brilliant yellow.
Minnesota Fats is expectant from the moment the sun lights his
lined face.

He looks into the sky and whistles loudly. The sound is clear,
shrill, bird-like. Fats likes to tell people he's a champion whistler
who won two world titles in the 1920s; if they could hear him
now, he says, he'd be performing again. But for the moment, his
stage is the city square — and the birds hear him calling. Pigeons
descend, flapping and fluttering all around him: two dozen, then
two dozen more.

These are the same birds that perch in a shady tree outside the
suite where Fats lives. Every day he scrounges around the hotel
kitchen for scraps to feed them. Now he is winding a trail of stale
crusts and crumbs in a patch of grass near the tulip bed. He talks
to the pigeons as tenderly as his brittle New York English will
allow.

"Whaddya say, fatty?" he asks a plump bird.

The question echoes back to him.

For it's been thirty years since Rudolph W. Wanderone, Jr.,
became known to the world as Minnesota Fats, everybody's favorite pool hustler, the player who won big when the stakes were
high, and who talked such a good game that no one was sure
when fact crossed the line into legend. But with Fats, it didn't

really matter. His tales were smooth and colorful and irrepressible, and often as tall as Fats was wide.

These days, Minnesota Fats is not so fat. He doesn't play much pool, doesn't gamble at all. His money is no longer so big, and he's parted company with the woman he called Eva-line, his wife of forty-four years. His memory, once as sharp as his wardrobe, started slipping six months ago. Now Fats strains to recall a pool game just the week before — and he can't. "I had the greatest mind in the world for a hundred years and I can't remember what happened yesterday," he says, frustrated.

In his twilight years, Fats holds on to the glory of his time and the glow of celebrity. His imagination endures, right along with his stories. And he keeps up the hustle, even now. Only the stakes have changed.

He may be ninety-one years old. He may be seventy-eight. This is one of those occasions when you pick your own version of the facts, or decide the facts really don't matter. The story goes like this: In the early years of his fame, Fats said he was born in 1913; later, he said that was his "baseball age" and cited his actual birthdate as 1900. Later still, he wouldn't talk about age at all. Today Fats says he's ninety-one as if there were never any other way.

Whatever his age, Fats is up in years — and still looking for action, although he limits his travels to Nashville, his adopted home for six years, and the action is in many ways different. These days, Fats pays $400 a month to live in the Hermitage Hotel, a grand old Nashville institution where rooms usually go for $95 a night and Tennessee legislators often stay during session.

Afternoons, Fats waits on a well-stuffed couch in the hotel lobby, a regal room with polished marble columns, flowing drapes, brass lamps and an ornate stained-glass ceiling. His is the seat in the center, the one with the perfect angle on every door and table. The spot where he may be seen — and sought out.

If it's a good day, there will be visitors: the investor who wants to open a Minnesota Fats restaurant, the video producer who wants Fats on camera, tourists who ask for his autograph, people who recognize him, fans who remember.

Fats tells them all he's great, beyond compare, the best the world has ever heard of or known. He can string together more superlatives than a circus ringmaster: he's the best pool player, the greatest gambler, the champion whistler and world-class ladies' man — the man who has known every movie star and fighter and mobster, opened every Playboy Club, spoken five languages, traveled the world six times and survived three sinking ships.

"I know more about life than anyone living," he adds in one conversation, "even when I was a kid."

Four floors above the lobby is the carpeted suite where Fats lives with what is left of his hustling heyday: piles of tournament handbills and congratulatory letters, framed awards and autographed 8-by-10s. "I have so much junk, more stuff than anyone on earth," he says, considering his well-preserved collection. "A lot of that stuff goes out. I don't want it no more."

But there is no sign Fats will part with these attachments to the past. As he examines one after another — a 1978 pool-tournament poster, a kelly-green pool coat, a contract for an exhibition in Miami Beach — he is tuning in memories. Snapshots of his long waltz with fame.

Fats lingers with a note from Paul Newman, who starred with Jackie Gleason in *The Hustler,* the 1961 movie that made Minnesota Fats a household name. The message, telegrammed for his birthday this year, is: "Time to get back on the road and take everybody to the cleaners."

"I was known for that," Fats says. "I beat everyone."

The finer points often escape him. It started happening six months ago; he says he had a minor stroke, though no doctor has been able to establish that. Now he can't remember where he wore the green jacket, or why he's saved four decks of playing cards from the Four Seasons Hotel. But he can recall odd details, like the Bassett's ice cream sign in Philadelphia's Reading Terminal Market. And he savors his fame as much as he ever did, probably more.

In one pile, he has stacked framed letters thanking him for his kindness to children and animals. Fats has lent his persona to the Easter Seals Society, and he feeds every stray dog and cat — and pigeon — he encounters. Fats once agreed to shoot a pool match in Iowa to help a woman buy dog food for two hundred strays.

"I've done one hundred times more charity than any creature

on earth," he says. "I'm the greatest humanitarian the world has ever heard of or known. I would never let anybody go hungry or suffer, if I can help it."

As he closes the door on his suite of mementos, Fats tucks two pool-tournament leaflets into the breast pocket of his suit jacket. One calls him "the world's greatest pool player" and the other says he's a "living legend." They are reminders. They go where he does.

Minnesota Fats walks into the Stock-Yard like he's walking into his favorite poolroom: sure of his stature, familiar with the routine. He is wearing a navy jacket, taupe rayon trousers with cuffs and a pale yellow polo shirt buttoned to the neck; gleaming on his feet are caramel-brown alligator-skin shoes.

The Stock-Yard is a popular Nashville nightclub, an expansive, wood-paneled place with several lounges and a large and steady flow of country music and tourists. The first thing Fats does is mount the tall, clock-faced Toledo scale in the foyer. The needle jerks, but not as much as it once did; tonight it steadies at 183½ pounds. There is less of Fats than there once was — nearly 90 pounds less, in fact, than when he was dubbed Fats and Fatty and Fat Man.

"Livin' doll!" Fats calls out. "Gimme some skin."

Anita Allen hugs Fats and squeezes his lined, baby-soft hands. "He's a true southern gentleman," she gushes, "and he's not even from the South. He has great respect for women. He always makes me feel *good.*"

Allen, a Stock-Yard regular, strolls away smiling. "She's been trying to snatch me for years," Fats says. "People don't know I'm the greatest ladies' man on earth."

But Fats is wrong. Most people who know Fats for long know that he was so sought after that women used to "line up around the block with mattresses strapped to their backs." They assuredly know this in the Bull Pen, a cavernous basement lounge lit by a pink neon bull's head above the bar and red blinking lights near the dance floor. This is Fats' favorite spot at the Stock-Yard. He shows up a half hour before the first customer — every night the place is open, six nights a week.

"Livin' doll!" he says to one waitress. "Gimme some flesh."

She hugs him.

"What is it? What is it?" he asks a group of bartenders and waitresses with mock concern.

They laugh. Several surround him with chatter. In the Bull Pen, Fats is virtually a celebrity-in-residence. Everyone knows him. They know he drinks for free. They know that he tips $3 or $4 a night for his steady supply of Cokes and that he keeps the waitresses stocked in ballpoints that he's swiped from his hotel or his agent's office. "It costs a buck to buy a pen — this saves them a buck," Fats reasons. The waitresses are charmed, or at least they act charmed. For this is Fats. Fats — the only man who can get away with calling so many women "tomatoes."

On this night, as on every other, Fats claims the table closest to the stage and posts a Reserved sign on it. The place is empty. Fats turns down the ceiling fan that blows cool air at his table. He takes a stack of white cocktail napkins from the bar and a pile of Stock-Yard stationery from the lounge's gift shop; now he's prepared. Approach him with paper or without, Fats will give an autograph.

"Women never leave me alone," he says cheerfully one night as he sips a coffee. "It's the most amazing thing on earth. Every time I look, I got three, four, five girls sitting with me."

If Ginger Lynn is beside him, Fats has less interest in others. Lynn is a tiny country singer with big brown eyes, perfect fingernails and hands that glitter with diamonds; Fats calls her "Gingerale" (or his "tomato"). They've been close for several years. "That's my doll," he says.

Tonight Fats is disappointed when she sends word that she's singing late at another lounge; she won't be able to meet him. The Bull Pen is quieter than usual. Fats doesn't like that either. But the band starts playing and Fats starts whistling and in a trickle people come, asking for his autograph.

"Could you do me a favor?"

Fats looks into the face of a tentative man. When he shot pool, he used to shake a man's hand, and if it was the least bit damp, Fats knew the man was nervous. Then, as now, nervousness meant a man was impressed by Fats' reputation.

"I have a friend of mine who's a big pool player," the man continues. "Could you sign a twenty-dollar bill for me?"

Fats is prepared for this, more prepared than this man knows, more prepared than anyone on earth.

For years now, he's been carrying around his own signature stamper. It's the size of a lighter, a slender, silver-cased rubber stamp of his name in script that sits in a pad of ink. Fats remembers it the way most people remember their wallet. "I stamp everything," Fats tells the guy, a thirty-five-year-old from Connecticut. "It comes out like that," he says, looking proudly at his name. "See, that's the real joint. See, you could write 'Minnesota Fats.' But you ain't got that."

The man is satisfied with the stamp. But he has come in search of a memory, maybe a story to tell. "My problem is," the man begins, "I did this with another guy, with a hundred-dollar bill. Problem was, he wouldn't give it back to me." The man pauses. "It was Muhammad Ali."

What a perfect invitation.

"I knew Muhammad Ali when he was a baby," Fats says without missing a beat. "Jack Dempsey, Firpo, Carpentier, I knew them all. They had to come by me to be fighters. New York was my beat. Times Square."

"Oh, really?"

"I knew every fighter that ever walked, every movie star that ever walked. George Burns when he was looking for work, Milton Berle when he was looking for work."

Fats calls himself the world's greatest talker, and maybe he is. He once debated Muhammad Ali on Chicago television to determine who really should bear the title of "The Greatest." After a half hour of bottomless boasting, the match was declared a standoff. "I can talk on any subject, whether I'm familiar with it or not," Fats says proudly.

It's clear that Fats' favorite subject is himself. In the dark barroom, Fats tells how he grew up in the Washington Heights section of New York and began hanging out in taprooms when he was two years old. That's where he got his education, he says — including the lesson never to smoke or drink. "I learned everything I know not from intelligent people but from imbeciles," he says firmly. "You don't do what they do. It's automatic." In the same taprooms, Fats was introduced to pool.

"I was never brought up," he says. "I brought myself up. My

parents didn't have a match. They didn't have a match. My old man was lucky that he had a place to sleep.

"I could tell you a story. I had a racket when I was five, six, seven years old that Dillinger would like to have had. . . . At eight or nine in the morning, I'd go in the theater before the women came to clean and dig between the seats. In those days, everybody had pinch-penny purses and they would drop between the seats. Every day I grabbed fourteen, forty-eight, some days eight-three dollars. That was my racket. I always made it some way."

By the time he was eleven, Fats was breaking racks and banking shots, eyeing challengers and sizing up odds. His prowess earned him the name "Double Smart," and then, after he beat the poolroom hustler known as Smart Henny, "Triple Smart." By the time Fats took to the road, he was "New York Fats." His reputation grew as he crisscrossed the country.

Fats was a fine-suited, high-rolling hustler who could drop into town, find an empty pool table and create such a stir that half the town would get in on the wager. He changed his name to suit the locale: in Chicago, he was Chicago Fats; in Johnston City, Illinois, he was Johnston City Fats.

"He starts playing for two dollars a game, and pretty soon the butcher and the baker are playing for a hundred a game and they never saw a pool table before that," one hustler said of Fats in 1961. "If there's a hundred people in town, Fats had a hundred people at the pool hall, and then he would leave and it's a desert town again."

The legend of Fats may or may not have been told in *The Hustler,* a 1961 movie about a fictional character named Fast Eddie Felson (Newman) who aspires to conquer the unbeatable Minnesota Fats (Gleason). The movie generated a swell of interest in pool — and its characters. Walter Tevis, who wrote the novel on which the movie was based, said his Minnesota Fats was not based on the real New York Fats. But Fats insisted it was him, and appropriated the new name.

Thus the world got to know Minnesota Fats. And Fats never let the world forget. He started a pool-supply company called Minnesota Fats Enterprises. He took his stardom to television, shooting *Celebrity Billiards* with guests like Milton Berle, Mickey Rooney and Zsa Zsa Gabor. He appeared frequently on ABC's

Wide World of Sports. He did commercials, exhibition tournaments, instructional videos. He grew famous beyond compare, more popular than the world has ever heard of or known.

In the mezzanine of the Hermitage Hotel, framed pictures of Minnesota Fats hang on the wall beside a large pool table. The table is a perfect green, unscuffed and fitted with a fine leather slipcover. Seldom is the cover removed anymore. The hotel bought the table for Fats, and without him, no one else can play.

Every once in a while, when someone talks him into it, Fats will pick up his cue and hunch over the familiar rectangle of green. It's usually for a publicity event of some kind, because Fats now mostly avoids shooting pool. As he considers his pool days one evening at the Stock-Yard, he says he never had a best game. "That's for suckers and enthusiasts," he says. "I don't have no kinds of hangups. Every time I played was the greatest moment, 'cause I'm going to win anyhow.

"I'm the most unusual creature on earth; I don't miss nothing. Anything I want or like, I could have in one minute. None of them things bother me."

When Fats gets going about pool, he invariably brings up cards — and how at heart he was, above all, a gambler. But that is past too. "I don't have no occasion to gamble or nothing," he says. "I don't know what to say. I'm busy doing the things I do. You know. I was making videos and stuff. And I ain't traveling no more, so what the hell's the use of gambling? Ain't nobody here's going to play me. Nobody's going to play me nowhere, you understand. Nowhere on earth they're going to play me."

Fats sips a Coke — no cherries, please — in the dark country-western bar as he thinks about Willie Mosconi, who lives eight hundred miles away, in Haddon Heights, New Jersey. Mosconi set records in professional tournaments, while Fats' specialty was the down-and-dirty poolroom hustle. Mosconi was technical adviser on *The Hustler.* But after the film came out, Fats got the spotlight — and claimed he was best. When they finally shot pool on TV, Mosconi won. " 'Hustler' is another word for 'thief,' " Mosconi said in 1979, "and 'Minnesota Fats' is another word for 'phony.' "

Fats is reminded of this.

"Willie said that?" he asks. And for an instant Fats looks hurt.

He looks as if he'd forgotten the enduring hostility, the contempt. The look is fleeting, but it takes him a moment to regain his equilibrium. "He was just jealous," he says. "He always got second billing.

"Mosconi and [Ralph] Greenleaf — they're tremendous players, but they're nothing like me. I take charge of everything. Wherever I go on this earth, I take charge. See, Mosconi, a tremendous player, he's wondering if he's going to win; he's upset, uptight. I don't have no idea because I was always one-hundred-percent winner. Everybody looks like a joke to me."

This is the Fats that always was. And for Mosconi, time's passing has allowed for no new fondness, no forgetting yesterday's feuds and follies. Mosconi still insists Fats is all fiction. "He was a phony all his life," Mosconi, seventy-seven, said on the telephone. "He was a card hustler, a dice hustler, anything he could make a dollar on. . . . I've known this guy since he was a kid, and he was nothing but a hustler. If he could beat his uncle out of two dollars, he'd do it. . . . He stole the name from this picture [*The Hustler*]. He's probably never been to Minnesota."

The best Mosconi has to say is this: "I've tolerated him because he was just like a, a character — let's put it that way — in the billiard halls."

But really Fats was more than a character. Pool gained many more players and followers while Fats was talking it up. And Fats makes no apologies for his boastfulness. "I know what I can do. I can do ten things to any sucker. Suckers is a joke. I watched 'em all my life. They can't get out of their own way."

A business associate, Bill Norris, who said his father played pool with Fats, put it differently: "He's got a lot of bullshit, but so what? He's earned the right. He's kind to people, he's kind to animals. He grew up around the hustle and bustle of gangsters, and he never became one of them. That's the part of Minnesota Fats most people don't know about."

Fats indeed made his reputation in pool when money was on the table. He was a gambler of great gumption, endowed with the faith that if he lost it all today he could win it all back tomorrow. He disdains people who won't make a bet, who work from 9 to 5 and don't risk a nickel for what they know is true.

Still, he says he wasn't entirely the hustler he was made out to be. "I never really did hustle," he says. "Hustling is when you take advantage. I never took advantage or really wanted to take advantage. If a man wanted to get beat, that's his business. You understand, they know I'm great, what're they fooling with me for? Don't you understand? The situation was all a pact. I never went up and, seeing he had eighty dollars or something, wanting to play him and break him or something. I never wanted to fool with it. Not at all.

"I gave it back to a lot of people. It's all according. You beat someone gambling, you don't have to feel sorry for him. He wouldn't be gambling if he didn't know what the hell he was doing, you understand, or think he knows what he's doing. That's no crime or nothing."

And so maybe it is fitting that when Fats talks about why he is happy with his long life, he doesn't talk about pool. "I never had to worry about women and that's the main thing for a man: women," he says. "The women always made me feel like a million bucks."

The next evening at the Stock-Yard two men from Youngstown, Ohio, buy Minnesota Fats a Coke. Ginger Lynn shows up. Fats gives her his Coke until the waitress brings her one of her own. When the band starts, Fats and Lynn are first on the dance floor, sweeping and swirling, hands clasped, as the lounge fills with the twang and drawl of country music. People watch from all around the room. This is the way Fats likes it.

When they are back at the table, Fats is whistling. He whistles often, and at the Stock-Yard he whistles with the band. Lynn is singing softly, mouthing words as if she were on stage. Fats cleans Lynn's ashtray, then asks if she wants another Coke.

"Need a pen?" he asks a few minutes later.

"No."

"You don't need anything," he says, only partly playful. "You don't even need me, do you?"

Lynn shifts in her seat. "Yes," she says, "I need you."

In these later years, there are moments when Fats seems more grandfather than hustler, far more kind-spirited than cunning. There are moments when he feeds the birds, when he misses Ginger Lynn, when he delivers candy to the hotel desk clerk, when he eats ice cream with the enthusiasm of a child.

In these later years, too, the hustle has come back to Fats. A few times a week, entrepreneurs of various stripes approach him with deals; now, Fats turns many away, and when he doesn't, he's not always on the best side of the bargain. But he is comfortable with that. "I don't mind helping them," he says, even though it's been years since Fats had the money he once did. "I used to have unbelievable money," he says. "I ain't hurtin' or nothin', but I don't have unbelievable money."

And besides, he's still running some hustles of his own. When he wants his hands manicured or feet pedicured, the woman at the local salon charges him nothing. When he wants his shoe fixed, the owner of the shoe repair shop does it for free. He eats yogurt in the hotel kitchen, snacks on free happy-hour hors d'oeuvres at the Stock-Yard, rides in cars chauffeured by one of several aspiring country singers who are now his friends. "See, everybody looks after me. Because I look after everybody," he says.

For his part, Fats lends his name. He remembers to tip. He stamps his signature. He is for the most part agreeable, interested and endearing. He shares his celebrity — with the hotel, with the Stock-Yard, with his friends. For a couple of years now, one business associate and then another has been planning a Minnesota Fats restaurant and club in Nashville, just blocks from his hotel.

There, Fats could display his memorabilia and sit at a reserved stageside table. Ginger Lynn might sing on stage. And if the hopes of one friend are fulfilled, the man who no longer gambles might occasionally stand under the spotlight and whistle.

It's just after 9:30, and Gerry Pye is on stage singing her favorite song, "I Lie Myself to Sleep." The Bull Pen is packed. When her lost-love lament is finished, Pye glances at the nearest table. "The legendary pool player of all time," she announces to the crowd, "and the world's greatest whistler. I love him dearly. How 'bout a nice hand for Minnesota Fats."

Scores of surprised tourists applaud.

"Glad to be here," Fats tells them. He turns to Pye. "You are still fantastic. I know more about beauty than any living creature. I was a judge for fifty years of the Miss Universe and Miss America, and *you* could win it right now."

"Well, thank you," Pye says, laughing. "Meet my grandpa," she quips. "No, folks, just kidding. Minnesota Fats, thank you so much. Now you know why I love him," she tells the crowd. "He always has such nice things to say.

"You're having a good time, aren't you?"

"Always have a good time," he assures her.

"He's ninety-one, folks," Pye says. "I think that's wonderful. And he says the secret to it is ice cream."

What a perfect invitation.

"Come here," says Fats, "I'll tell you the secret."

But Pye has the microphone. And no one hears his secret except the three women sitting at his table. "Ice cream and sweets are the greatest things you can put in your body," he tells them. "Candy and ice cream and pie. Sweets!"

This is a good night. When the band takes a break, people approach Fats' table with awe. "It's an honor to meet you, sir," says Joe Froehle, forty, of Cincinnati. When Froehle walks away, Fats feigns despair. "My fans look at me like I'm a broad," he says.

On the way home, sitting in the car, Fats is talking about the birds. He remembers that the hotel hosted a luncheon that day and that he has gathered up several laundry bags full of leftover bread and rice. "They're going to feast tomorrow," he says happily, "beyond compare."

He steps out of the car and crosses the sidewalk. It is a warm night in Nashville and the street is quiet, no sign of even one pigeon. Minnesota Fats walks alone into the marbled lobby of the Hermitage Hotel.

JAN REID

Armed and Considered Dangerous

FROM TEXAS MONTHLY

IN AUSTIN, baseball season starts in early February with a game between the current University of Texas Longhorns and a team of UT alumni who are playing professional ball. It is an afternoon of nostalgia and yearning for spring. The alumni players wear their pro uniforms, chat with sports writers during batting practice, and sign autographs for swarms of kids. Nobody pays much attention to the score or takes things too seriously.

Except Roger Clemens. Although the two-time Cy Young Award winner from Katy has only a cameo role in these affairs — he pitches to the Longhorns' leadoff batter and then comes out of the game — it is enough time to make a statement. Last year Roger, a right-hander who is six-three and weighs 220 pounds, launched his first pitch directly at the head of heralded UT recruit Calvin Murray. What message was he trying to convey? Was it, *Welcome to the big time, kid?* Was it, *I make my own rules?* Or was it simply, *Don't mess with me?* The teenager didn't wait around to figure it out — he hit the dirt. Then, back to business, Roger struck Murray out. This year the game was Roger's first public appearance since umpire Terry Cooney threw the cursing pitcher out of the final game of the American League play-offs. With seventy-three hundred people wondering what he would do, he sailed his first pitch far over the head of the batter (Murray again), the catcher, and the umpire. All the way to the screen. This time the message was unmistakably clear: *I'm Roger Clemens, that wild and crazy guy. I'm on a different level than everyone else.*

But everyone in the ballpark already knew that, of course. Not only is Roger Clemens the best pitcher in baseball, but he is also the game's most celebrated enigma. He was only a few days removed from an ugly altercation at a Houston club called Bayou Mama's. Gary "Randy" Clemens had gotten into a tiff with a Houston cop who was moonlighting as a bouncer. Accounts differ as to what happened next — Dallas Cowboys running back Alonzo Highsmith was there and claimed that Roger and Randy ran into hotheads with badges — but both brothers ended up being charged with aggravated assault on a police officer, a felony that can get two to ten years.

Before the start of the alumni game, Roger's emergence from the clubhouse in his Boston Red Sox uniform had raised a loud, enthusiastic cry from the kids. He scribbled on baseballs and programs without much comment or eye contact and moved off abruptly when it suited him. He ambled to the bull pen with former UT teammate Calvin Schiraldi, who was wearing the brown pinstripes of the San Diego Padres. The catcher's mitts popped loudly as they warmed up. Returning to the dugout, Roger wagged a thumb a Schiraldi and told the other pros, "He is *gassed.*" Clearly first among equals — Roger's the only one who has achieved true stardom — he preens a bit among them. He struts.

Roger had declined requests for an interview regarding this article — his right and privilege, of course. As the players prepared to take the field, I approached Roger's friend and UT ex Mike Capel, a pitcher who has had brief stints in the majors with the Cubs and the Brewers. I hastily told Capel what I was doing and mentioned a few prior interviews with people recommended to me as Roger's friends, all of whom went to great lengths to cast him in a rosy light.

A moment later Capel appeared in the corridor between the dugout and the clubhouse with the man himself. Capel pointed at me. Roger did the same, then crooked his finger commandingly. Come here.

Could it be? An interview at last?

"What are you doing talking to Rich Hairston?" Roger demanded. Rich Hairston, an aspiring actor in Los Angeles, had been Roger's closest friend at Houston's Spring Woods High School. "I don't want you talking to no people like that. Rich

Hairston played baseball in *high school*. There's no reason to talk to people like that."

I was dumbfounded. In Roger's tidy little universe, nobody but professional ballplayers count?

"I knew you was going to be here today," he continued. "I been talking to my agents and my lawyers."

"Look, I don't want to offend you," I said, which seemed to help.

Roger tilted his head toward the locker room. "You can talk to these ballplayers. That's all right. But people like Hairston, they just want to get their names in the paper."

I thought back to my conversation with Hairston, whose days as an outfielder had ended with a knee injury at Rice University. "Other players get distracted — squabbles, family things," he had told me. "When Roger's out there, they don't exist. He gets this look in his eyes that's kind of scary. He gets so incredibly pumped. Maybe too pumped: you don't have control of your thoughts. It takes him a long time to come down. Last year I went to see him in Oakland. He's just beaten the A's, pitched a complete game. An hour and a half later, he's still on the exercise bike. There's Roger the person and Roger the baseball player. A total contrast, it really is."

Toward the end of the alumni game, Montreal Expos short-stop Spike Owen sat on a UT clubhouse rubdown table, giving the kind of authorized interview Roger had in mind. "It's hard to understand why some of these things are happening to Roger," Owen told me. "It's sad to see a good guy — and he really is a good guy, not a troublemaker at all — get a bum rap. I know Roger too well. He's not the kind of guy he's been made out to be. I know that for a fact."

Roger strolled up, abruptly leaned across me, and talked to Owen about their evening plans on Austin's Sixth Street entertainment strip. Though he didn't address me, his air was civil. I was doing what I was supposed to do. The moon and stars were correctly aligned. For the moment, everything was peachy. Just fine.

On a raw April night in Boston in 1986, Roger Clemens transformed himself from a twenty-three-year-old prospect with a history of arm trouble into an instant superstar. He struck out twenty Seattle Mariners in nine innings, a major league record. Spike Owen led off for Seattle. The first fastball was a strike. The second sailed near enough to Owen's helmet to drop him spinning to one knee. The third one passed six inches from his chin. Roger knocked his old Texas chum down, then struck him out.

Roger's specialty is "going up the ladder." The high fastball looks big. Hitters think they can catch up with it, but it keeps rising, and they keep flailing, up and up, striking out. He also has a quick-breaking curve and an 88 mph slider — the velocity of an average big league fastball. And that night against Seattle, he worked low and in, low and out, shaving the rectangle of air with the touch of a razor. The radar gun timed Roger's fastball at 97 mph. Of 138 pitches, the Mariners got a bat on only 29, and 19 of those were fouls. Roger didn't walk a batter that night in Boston. Not one.

Most great fastball pitchers fight for years to gain control. A jerk of the head shoots the ball wide. A jolting stomp of the foot disrupts the follow-through. When the pitcher's motion is fluid, then coaches delve into the mental process. Some teach control in images: the hollow of the catcher's mitt, the lines of his shin guards. Stand on the rubber and read the writing on the mitt. Total focus. Shut the world out.

Roger Clemens never needed much of that. From the day he walked onto a high school field in West Houston, he could throw strikes; he just couldn't get them there fast enough. Fastballs are supposed to be God's gift, if you happen to be a pitcher. "I don't care if you can't hit the backstop," one big league scout put it. "If you can throw the ball 93 mph, you're going to be a number one draft choice." Everything else can be taught and learned. Roger arrived at San Jacinto Junior College in Houston with a mediocre fastball clocked in the low eighties. But in three years he somehow willed, worked, and forced himself into the power range of the New York Mets' Dwight Gooden and the Texas Rangers' Nolan Ryan — without losing his uncanny control.

With the Red Sox, he has won twenty or more games three times. Last season he had an earned run average of 1.93, the best in either league. He won twenty-one games and lost only six. He tied for the lead in shutouts, with four. Only six pitchers threw more complete games. He struck out 209 batters and walked 54 — by far the best ratio in the game. Gooden and Oakland's

Dave Stewart are the only pitchers who are even close to his standard.

But stardom is a somewhat different proposition. As a public figure, Roger Clemens projects an image that consistently spins *out* of control. In 1985, suffering torn shoulder cartilage, he threatened a Boston sports writer with bodily harm after the columnist called him a head case. In 1987 he whirled and raged off the mound, screaming at Kansas City's Willie Wilson, who had reached second base. Well, Roger, it's the ninth inning, and Wilson's team is down 2–0 in a three-hitter in which you've struck out sixteen — of course he's trying to steal your signs.

"Who does he think he is?" Wilson said later. "He struts around out there like, 'Hey, man, I'm God. I'm Roger God Clemens, and nobody's going to hit me.' "

Last year in the American League Championship Series against Oakland, Roger sat in the corner of the Red Sox dugout on the two days he didn't pitch, mouthing a stream of invective toward the plate. In the fourth game, with Boston embarrassed and all but swept, he meant to put on a one-man show. It scarcely got beyond the credits. Trailing the A's 1–0 in a second-inning jam, Roger scowled at Terry Cooney, the home plate ump, and started shaking his head. Cooney appeared to speak first. Roger told him to keep his mask on — he wasn't talking to him. But Roger kept talking, profanely. Without so much as a warning, Cooney ejected him.

In a big game of sorts, Roger got into a baiting match with an umpire he rubbed the wrong way. He used foul language in a most public setting. So what? Ty Cobb and Babe Ruth had an advantage — no instant replays, no zoom lens. More alarming were reported threats by Roger that he would get Cooney, find out where he lived. In the off-season, Roger pursued a doomed appeal of his league punishment — a five-game suspension, which amounts to one lost start, and a $10,000 fine; no big deal for someone who makes $48,000 a week.

A January wire story promised a mellowed and matured Roger, a team leader. One week later, he left Bayou Mama's in handcuffs. Nonetheless, in February the Red Sox management made him the richest player in the game, with a four-year contract extension that pays an average annual salary of $5,380,250.

Head case or no head case, if the Red Sox executives had

balked at Roger's demands and allowed him to leave the team as a free agent, the fans would have howled for *their* heads. New Englanders and their team have made an art form of losing. The Red Sox have had sluggers like Babe Ruth, Jimmie Foxx, Ted Williams, Carl Yastrzemski, Jim Rice, and Wade Boggs — yet haven't won a World Series since the end of World War I. Pitching has to be the prime suspect.

To baseball fans in most parts of the country, Cy Young is a remote and patriarchal figure. Over beers in New England, fans still talk about Cy Young's years with the Red Sox: he led the league in strikeouts in 1901, went 28–9 two years later.

Roger Clemens has heard boos in Boston's Fenway Park, but deep down the fans don't mean it. The ghosts in those venerable stands haven't seen one like him in ninety years.

Born in Dayton, Ohio, in 1962, Roger came to Texas in the midseventies, during the Houston boom. His eldest brother, Rick, a Vietnam vet, led the migration to Houston. Except for one unpleasant phone conversation, Roger never knew his dad, and his stepfather had a fatal heart attack when Roger was nine. In Houston, Roger's mother managed a convenience store. They had little money. As a teenager he never had a car, so he jogged everywhere he went. From Little League on, he had been talented and encouraged to think that he was a future star. When Roger was in high school, his brother Randy, who was ten years older, took charge of Roger's career development. Randy had been a basketball star in high school and college; he had had two unsuccessful tryouts with NBA teams. Roger pitched in Sugar Land as a sophomore, but Randy thought Roger needed a more demanding league and program, so he found the family a condo near Spring Woods High.

At Spring Woods, coaches, scouts, and friends referred to Roger's bulk as baby fat. And life had dealt him a real-world jolt: with a fastball clocked at 82 mph, he simply didn't have the arm. In despair after graduation, he talked about going to North Texas State to play football.

Finally, a baseball offer came from San Jacinto Junior College. There, his baby fat began to turn into muscle, and he learned to lengthen his pitching delivery, which increased the velocity of his fastball. After one year he won a baseball scholarship to UT, a

program that has been an assembly line of big league pitchers —
Burt Hooton, Jerry Don Gleaton, Jim Acker, and more. In the
spring of 1982, few would have picked Roger to be the best of
them, but he was always running, throwing, lifting weights —
inching up his marks on the all-important radar gun.

As a sophomore at UT, Roger missed most of the conference
games with bursitis, then pitched thirty-five consecutive shutout
innings in the postseason tournaments, helping the Longhorns
to a third-place finish in the College World Series. He lived in a
dorm and then in a student apartment ghetto beside Town Lake.
He had a green Pinto that was always breaking down. His social
life was so unremarkable that his teammates were hard-pressed
to remember anything except his addiction to the video games at
a Riverside Drive arcade. "He'd find a game that challenged him
and play it till it smoked," says one, "and then move on to another when he had that one beat. Roger knew what he was here
for: Get the big money. Be a first-round draft choice."

During his junior year, more than Roger's muscle and talent
were developing. The closer he got to his goal, the more in-
tensely he pursued it. On the mound, he talked to himself and
taunted opposing hitters, especially in late innings. In a meaningless game against UT-Arlington, Roger didn't like the strike
zone of Randy Christal, an Austin umpire good enough to have
been invited to work the Olympics and the College World Series.
Nor did Texas catcher Jeff Hearron, who started holding the ball
on every close pitch. Christal finally had enough of it and threw
the catcher out. Roger avoided ejection, but after the game he
popped off in the presence of an Austin sports writer, calling
Christal "a choker who's so scared of making a call for us that he
chokes. It's time for him to move on." Christal declined to work
any more Texas home games that year.

Suddenly, Roger went into a tailspin. Calvin Schiraldi, another
fast right-hander, became the ace and an All-American. Roger
gave up a game-winning homer to Texas Lutheran and looked
like a batting practice pitcher against Texas A&M. Shelled in
Tulsa by Oral Roberts, he tore up his uniform and swore that he
was quitting the game.

In June 1983, at the end of his junior year, the Red Sox
drafted Roger in the first round. The New York Mets chose
Schiraldi a few picks later. The same week, in the College World

Series in Omaha, Roger started the national championship game against Alabama. That game ranks among his most arresting performances on TV. Roughed up early, he hung in and kept throwing strikes until Texas took the lead. As the game progressed, he got so excited that he couldn't breathe between innings. In the ninth, he gave up a leadoff double to Dave Magadan, now with the Mets, and found himself in danger of blowing Texas' lead. UT Coach Cliff Gustafson trotted out to calm him down.

The game ended with a pop fly; near ESPN's on-field camera, Roger disappeared, grinning, cap askew, under a pile of exultant players. The camera worked closer, along with a directional mike. Schiraldi pulled Roger up. Roger thrust a fist at the sky and yelled upward, distinctly, though he disputes it in his autobiography: "You tested me, you motherfucker!"

Schiraldi was grinning. Pat, pat, pat. Roger backed up, unfinished, with an emphatic look of wild anger. "Don't test me!"

Who, viewers wondered, was he talking to?

A moment later, Roger was on the screen being interviewed. "Coach came out there, and I said, 'I ain't coming out of this one, Coach. I don't wanna come out.' The man upstairs was testing me." Roger's eyes rolled upward. "It's been an up-and-down season all year for me, and Alabama's a good-hitting ball club. . . . I was hyperventilating in the eighth inning, and I settled down a little bit. The man upstairs was testing me . . ." — the eyes rolled up again — "I said, 'Coach, I don't wanna go nowhere. I want this one. I ain't coming out.' "

Bonkers. Put a rope on him. Walk him around.

A year after leaving UT, Roger went 9–4 as a Red Sox rookie. He got his first shutout against the White Sox, his first three-hitter against the Indians, and struck out fifteen Royals while walking none. He also pulled a muscle in his forearm. In 1985 a new pain was diagnosed as tendinitis, then as torn shoulder cartilage. In *Rocket Man*, his autobiography co-written with Peter Gammons, Roger described his revelation that the injury was serious:

> I grabbed that heavy metal door that goes from the clubhouse to the dugout runway and tore it off its hinges. Somewhere in the run-

way I must have torn my jersey off, for there were buttons everywhere. I kicked off one shoe somewhere down there, then kicked the
other one across the clubhouse. I fired my glove into one trash can,
my pants and socks into another trash can, and picked up the chair
and fired it into my locker. . . .

I went up the flight of stairs, walked out into the parking lot, and
took off. It was a hot July afternoon in Anaheim, about ninety degrees. As I ran, I thought about playing with the broken ankle or
breaking my nose three of four times or what pain tolerance really is.
I ran about as hard a pace as I could, with tears in my eyes from frustration. *Junkball,* I thought.

But arthroscopic surgery repaired the ailing shoulder. In
April 1986 Roger mowed down Spike Owen and all the other
Mariners in the twenty-strikeout game. He was off on a four-
teen-game winning streak, on his way to his first Cy Young
Award. After the All-Star break, the Red Sox called up Calvin
Schiraldi, whom they had obtained from the Mets as a relief
pitcher. With a spectacular 1.41 ERA, Schiraldi emerged as Boston's fireball closer. Then in August, Boston traded for short-
shop Spike Owen. When the Red Sox won the pennant and
pounded the Angels in the final game of the League Championship Series, Roger pitched seven innings with the flu. Out of the
bull pen, Schiraldi struck out five of the last six. At the plate,
Owen went two for four and drove in one run and scored another. Hook 'em, Horns!

Boston's 1986 season propelled Roger toward the Hall of
Fame. In the end it ate Calvin Schiraldi's lunch. In the infamous
sixth game of the World Series against the Mets, Roger went to
the bench after the seventh inning with a torn blister on his finger. Then Schiraldi was out there, throwing a bunt away, giving
up a sacrifice fly, letting the game go into extra innings. In the
tenth, with two outs and a two-run lead, he gave up three straight
singles and let the dream slip away. Schiraldi had the Red Sox
one strike away. Another New York single. Another Boston nightmare. A new man to blame.

Schiraldi spends off-seasons in Austin. Roger often drives up
from Katy and plays golf with him at Barton Creek Country
Club. Schiraldi was in Roger's wedding. They've been friends for

a long time now. But after the 1986 Series, Roger made some comments that must have stung. He complained about being pulled with the bleeding finger. In *Rocket Man,* Roger categorized Schiraldi: "He's basically a three- to six-out pitcher." Schiraldi hated the bull pen. He wanted to start — go the distance, just like Roger. Trades moved him on to the Chicago Cubs and the San Diego Padres, where last year he was 3–8 with a 4.41 ERA and just one save. (This March, in spring training, San Diego gave the former first-round draft choice his unconditional release.)

Schiraldi is tall, with sleepy eyes and Italian features. He sat in the Barton Creek dining room in cutoff jeans and a tattered Cubs T-shirt. Schiraldi doesn't like talking to reporters and said so flatly.

"Yeah, I had a real good year," he said of the 1986 Boston experience. "And it's been fucking downhill ever since. I'm not much for relief. A reliever's got to be able to forget a game he didn't do his job in, and I have a tough time doing that." He yawned. "It's a living."

Schiraldi seemed a little damaged by baseball. The subject of his famous friend made him kind of tired. "No comment," he said when asked about the Red Sox fans. "That gets you in trouble, talking about fans."

All right. Boston sports writers?

A very long pause. "They treated me all right," he said. "Most of them. You had a couple of jerks."

How did Roger get so crosswise with them?

Another long pause. "Always up there, they like controversy. Roger had some things misquoted, and it pissed him off. Then in 1986, they kept saying, 'When are they gonna fold, when are they gonna fold?' That tends to grate on you — when the team's winning, whenever you're going good. Roger knows he's good enough; he's gonna be around. He doesn't have to sit and take all the bullshit. He's gonna voice his opinion, and if you don't like it, screw you."

One off-season, veteran magazine journalist Pat Jordan flew to Houston and drove out to Katy. Jordan had been engaged by *GQ* to write a spring cover story about Roger. In Katy, he found a

Tudor house expensively furnished and strewn with children's toys. Roger was passing the time with a friend, another pitcher. Jordan, who had played minor league ball in the fifties, dropped some names Roger would recognize, trying to draw him out. No response. Outside he watched the athletes lift weights and throw a football around. They ignored him. Back in the house, Roger perked up only when he inserted a cassette into his VCR.

The TV set played a scene recorded, they said, at a car lot owned by the other pitcher, and now he was being sued. Two stringy-haired youths climbed a fence and were attacked by guard dogs. One burglar reached safety. While the pitchers laughed and Jordan stared, the other kid was torn apart, killed. Roger finally told the writer what he was watching. It was a scandalous purported documentary composed of real moments of human destruction, certain of which had been arranged, some said, not simply observed. A kind of snuff film, the allegations went. Some joke. Roger gave Jordan a copy of *Rocket Man*, autographed it, and then began writing a list of his achievements. Cy Young Award. American League MVP. End of interview. Some days, Jordan thought, driving away, this is a wretched way to make a living.

The *GQ* cover story never ran. Roger couldn't make the photo sessions in New York. Nor did he call to cancel. He wasn't going to fly to New York for some photographer; send the guy to Houston. The stiffed photographer — as famous in his profession as Roger Clemens is in baseball — was Richard Avedon.

On the pitcher's mound, Roger Clemens has few equals. In the real world, he often comes across as a big baby. In late 1988 he received the crew of a Boston TV station on his lawn in Katy; he meant to rip into Red Sox executives for letting pitcher Bruce Hurst get away in free agency. "Playing major league baseball is not all fun and glory," he rambled instead. "Traveling on road trips, carrying your luggage — that's not my idea of family-oriented. There are certain things going on there in Boston that make it a little bit tough on your family." Nobody has ever accused Roger of being articulate. He was trying to be a labor spokesman. Among other grievances, he blamed Red Sox management for allowing Fenway fans to jeer and curse the players' wives in the stands. But Boston is a proud working-class town, and on opening day in Fenway Park the following spring, several thousand Bostonians booed their ace.

Red Sox fans have always had a love-hate relationship with their stars. Ted Williams would spit on Boston fans and shoot them the finger. In batting practice, he would take aim and whack line drives at groups of his tormentors in the outfield bleachers. New Englanders know their baseball, and they love to hate the experience of being let down. "It's hard to be a great player in Fenway Park," said former Red Sox infielder Marty Barrett, in recent years Roger's closest friend on the team. "The fans have had their hearts broke too often. Come through for them one day, that's nice. Blow it the next, and you're a bum all over again."

Strangely, though, Roger's recent comic opera — the ejection and tirade in Oakland, the professional lip-reader summoned to testify at his suspension hearing, the barroom rumble in Houston — has solidified his standing with Red Sox fans. Hey, the guy's a jock. Leave him alone. He produces. Roger's $21 million contract was perceived as an emotional commitment. He'll put up with sarcastic sports writers and Fenway's hooligans. The fans' elusive dream is his own crusade. New Hampshire resident Eric McDowell was schooled in this quixotic art by a grandmother who started pulling for the Sox at the turn of the century. His outlook on Roger is representative: "The only way we'll ever get to that Holy Grail is with him. But we've all made him out to be a king or god. When somebody that young receives that kind of treatment, it's just human nature: tell him no, and he's going to throw a tantrum."

Lordly airs may come easier to an athlete when success is won by total focus and unrelenting effort — not by birthright, not through some lucky draw of the genes. Roger Clemens is consumed with baseball. He runs and lifts weights constantly. At home, his Jacuzzi is equipped with a special jet that soothes and conditions his shoulder. He sifts and clenches his hand in a bowl of uncooked rice to strengthen his grip. His sons are named Koby and Kory — spelled with a *k* because that's the scoring symbol for a strikeout.

"Roger's had to feel his way," said Barrett. "But there's no question about him on the field. 'Put the blinders on' — that's his favorite expression. I'll tell you what he's like as a player. On the television replay, watch his eyes. It's like a mad dog has his little boy by the leg, and if Roger doesn't throw a baseball through that dog, it's gonna eat his kid."

Rich Hairston, the high school friend turned actor whose interview annoyed Roger, once played Tom Sawyer to Roger's Huck Finn. Two years younger than Roger, he met him in biology class at Spring Woods. I had gone to see Hairston when he returned to Houston for the Christmas holidays.

At one point he exclaimed, "We never drank. We didn't do drugs. We never got in trouble!" That was the tenor of the forbidden interview. Stardom has made Roger just a tad paranoid, if you ask me.

Hairston's mother, Martha, a handsome woman, came home from the psychiatric hospital where she works. She pointed at the sofa where Roger met Debbie, his wife. Debbie and her mom had come over to give the Hairstons a cat. Not long after that, Roger popped the question. Martha Hairston crossed her arms, leaned against the kitchen cabinet, and sifted further back in her memories. "They were good kids," she said. "I'd come home and say, 'Roger's been here, right? The milk's all gone.' 'Rich! How many times do I have to tell you, Roger can't drive my car!' 'He doesn't, Mom.' 'Then why's my seat set back for somebody six feet four?' "

"No matter what," Rich Hairston said, "Roger always had to get his workout in. He'd come in huffing all the time. Our house was between theirs and the high school, and his girlfriend's was beyond that. He'd run back and forth at night and hang out on the baseball field. Do his sit-ups. Lie on the mound and dream."

Wait. You saw him do that?

"No, I just knew. Everybody did. One time he and I were out driving around. He was seventeen, I was fifteen. Two-thirty in the morning, big perfect moon. I'll never forget it. He said, 'Rich, I really think I can be a baseball player.' He said, 'Don't you think we can be *bigger than life?*' "

CRAIG MEDRED

Alone Across the Burn

FROM WE ALASKANS

SOMEWHERE IN THE FAREWELL BURN — Alone in the cold, the
dark and the blowing snow, Tom Daily was hunting the Iditarod
Trail. The reflective markers that had moments before pointed
the way safely through rolling hills and ravines reminiscent of
the extreme western edge of the Great Plains had disappeared,
and Daily was lost. The beam of his headlamp swung back and
forth across the darkness, probing for the glint of a reflector, the
hint of an old sled track on the wind-packed snow, the flap of a
ribbon of surveyor's tape tied to the hulk of a charred spruce
tree.

His dog team waited patiently. Several times that night they
had been through this drill. Lead dogs Diamond and Bertha had
come to trust that sooner or later Daily would gee them right or
haw them left toward some sign of trail he thought worth investigation. Faith in Daily held strong within the team. Every time
their driver lost the trail in the dark, he quickly found it again.
There had been none of the mindless wandering back and forth
that drives a dog team first to distraction, then frustration and
finally revolt.

Many a dog team competing in the Iditarod Trail Sled Dog
Race has gone that route on the long, tiresome ninety-three-mile
trip from the checkpoint of Rohn through the Post River valley,
past Farewell Lake and out into the desolate Burn. The trail here
is sometimes difficult to follow, and the land itself can prove in-
timidating. This is some of the wildest country in wild Alaska. A
man or woman doesn't have to wander around aimlessly for long

out here before the little hairs on the small of the back stand up and try to crawl away. It is a bad place to get lost.

From here to anywhere is a long, long way, and help is hard to find.

Only one trail, the Iditarod, runs through this country, and it is the thinnest strand of contact with civilization. For eleven months of the year the trail is unused. No regular traffic exists to keep it open. No bush villagers travel this trail, as they do most trails in Alaska. There are no villages to the north, and the nearest to the south is more than ninety miles away. At Farewell Lake, about halfway from Rohn to Nikolai, there is a lodge, but most winters it is deserted. Farther west, at Farewell Station, is a landing strip, but it is a long way from the Iditarod and there is no connecting trail.

Get lost out here, and you might stay lost for a long, long time.

Rookie musher Brian O'Donoghue of Fairbanks admitted the thought of traveling the Rohn-to-Nikolai section of the Iditarod Trail by himself made him nervous, and rookie musher Urtha Lenharr of Eagle River was worried enough to turn back to Rohn when he lost his way.

The day before Daily was to depart the Rohn checkpoint — a lonely log cabin in a deserted valley deep in the heart of the Alaska Range — Lenharr went an hour out in the dark on the South Fork Kuskokwim River and turned back. By then he was lost and not sure he could find where the trail left the rock patches, driftwood snags, sand bars and glare ice of the broad river bottom for the climb up the short, dense spruce forest toward Post River.

Nothing upsets a musher or frustrates a dog team more than retracing trail, so Lenharr stayed at Rohn until other mushers were ready to go. They could help him find the trail, lead the team back out on the long journey to Nikolai and provide the simple security of companionship.

Behind this group, Daily waited. He was still completing his mandatory twenty-four-hour Iditarod rest stop at Rohn. He would not be clear to leave until the next afternoon. Then he would face a decision: set out on the trail alone or wait hours for the last three mushers at the end of the race to complete their twenty-four-hour stops.

An Iditarod rookie with years of dog sense but no knowledge of the trail, Daily pondered that thought as he sat around the checkpoint nursing dogs, chatting with other mushers and drinking a strange brew of maple syrup, lime and cayenne pepper. He offered some to musher Barry Lee, parked nearby.

"It was popular for a while for losing weight," Daily said. "Girls in Hawaii were drinking it."

The two men squatted in the snow that blankets the thick, quiet forest at Rohn and drank. Their dogs were curled in balls on piles of snow. Daily studied his tenderly.

"They're sick," he said. "You're supposed to push in this race. The idea is to push them and to push yourself, but we can't now. I'm just nursing them along, hoping I can get them to Nome. It's interesting how you become a total slave to them in this race, like having a little teeny baby. You watch guys who would never even think of changing a diaper, out here babying dogs. It's kind of funny, actually."

Since early in the race, Daily had been caring for sick dogs, giving the team lots of rest, seeing that they ate and drank well, tending to the merest hint of a foot problem, traveling mainly at night because that was when the leaders were most eager to run.

All the way up into the Alaska Range he mollycoddled the team, and then down on the wild roller-coaster ride through the Dalzell Gorge.

"I wouldn't say I'd be ready to do that again," he said afterward. "It was scary going downhill and not being able to slow down the sled. Kayaking is what it is. You're kayaking down the hill, bouncing off the rocks. I wouldn't want to be the dogs.

"But the worst thing was the anticipation coming around the corners. The not knowing what's ahead is the hard part, and now another difficult part [of the trail] is coming up. It just drains you of energy."

Every Iditarod rookie learns that feeling sooner or later. There is no way to really understand the perils and pitfalls of the trail without experiencing them, though many praise a book written by four-time-winner Rick Swenson that at least offers some advice on hazards. Few think that is preparation enough.

"I'd sure caution anyone who just jumped into this," Daily said. "I wouldn't take it lightly. I'm surprised no people have died. It's probably just a matter of time."

A dog driver for twelve years, Tom Daily had come into this race with some knowledge of what was ahead. He knew how to care for dogs; he knew something about winter wilderness travel; and he thought he was in pretty good condition.

The flaws of his assessment quickly became evident. "I'm still amazed at how physical the Iditarod is," Daily said. "I jogged in the summer. I did a little weight training. But I'll do a lot more if I do this again next year. Heavy weight training, and I'd have my head examined. I didn't realize I'd be bouncing into so many trees, and I didn't realize I'd be the last one [in the race]. I'm amazed the sled makes it."

He said these things near Farewell Lake when he stopped to snack his dogs in a dense forest of spruce and aspen about a third of the way into the run from Rohn to Nikolai. Ahead awaited the Burn and a night of wandering in the dark, but now it was still and quiet in the forest with the snow falling heavily, as if in a scene on a Christmas card.

The dogs were chewing chunks of meat, and Daily had taken off his soaked boots to study his pink and wrinkled feet. He was trying to decide whether to put on dry mukluks or a pair of Mickey Mouse boots that had been found along the trail, debris from someone else's sled crash. He had given up hope on the expensive, foam-insulated, state-of-the-art boots that had worked for him so well in the dry cold. They were useless at least until Nikolai, where the dry heat of a cabin would help.

"They work under most conditions, but not these," Daily said. "Now these are gonna freeze up into big chunks of ice." He mashed around in his sled bag trying to find room for the bulky boots. He joked about the size of his load, aware that he was carrying much more equipment than needed. "I bet Susan Butcher travels with a tenth of what I've got," Daily said, and he was right. Butcher, like all top competitors, travels as light as possible.

Daily was learning the value in that. Less gear allows a musher to pack and unpack the sled easily, saving hours of time and effort. Lighter sleds are easier to manhandle around the trees, along the cliffs and over the bumps on the trail. Daily's sled was too heavy, and he was paying a price.

"I just get [physically] whipped on every one of these runs," he said, "and I've been lucky because the dogs have needed a rest every time I've been really tired, so I've been getting plenty of sleep. Still, this is quite the experience. Free torture. I'll tell you, I was wondering a few times on the trail. But I'm sure, as the trail gets more safe, I'll forget about how tough this was."

Behind him were the worst stretches of the Iditarod: the crazy, crashing route down steep, tree-lined hillsides into the Happy River valley; the snaking, tree-bashing climb up to Rainy Pass; and then the uniquely crazy stretch of trail from Rohn through the Post River valley to Farewell Lake. That was the worst section of trail in the 1991 race.

From Rohn the trail headed out onto the glare ice of the broad and desolate valley of the South Fork Kuskokwim, wound its way around driftwood snags and across windblown gravel bars and then entered a stand of black spruce no more than twenty feet tall but as thick and friendly as the hair on the back of a wolverine.

Here the snow was brown from the wind-driven grit that flies down off the mountains of sand and rock. Young mountains, they are sheer-sided with no sign of vegetation above two thousand feet, where the last of the spruce and alder cling tenaciously to stone.

The trail fights its way through a three-foot opening in the dense spruce on a small beach along the southwest side of the South Fork Kuskokwim. This trail is too narrow for easy riding, and many of the trees on either side are scarred at the base from sled runners. The sleds bang through here, and a musher must be constantly on watch for eye-level branches.

Some places along this trail there is snow, but in many others there is not, and the trail crosses bare, dry lichen and stunted willow brush as it climbs and winds toward the Post River. On those rare occasions the trail opens into muskegs there is glare ice where the snow has been blown away and layer after layer of overflow has frozen in temperatures that fall to 50 degrees below zero.

At Post River, the trail ventures again into a large, barren valley marked with the flagging of surveyor's tape tracing an intricate route around driftwood snags and over gravel bars and onto glare ice before it starts a climb into a land of spruce forests and meadows bare of snow. In one of these meadows there is a naked, grassy area full of frozen overflow on a hillside that has become a slick, slippery glacier hard for the dogs to navigate. Beyond that lie bare muskegs and bare, frozen tussocks that offer a pounding, miserable ride on the sled.

Crossing this country on a partly sunny day almost too mild for running dogs reminded Daily of Colorado. He had come here from that state — a less than perfect place for running dogs, he said — and the Post River country had stirred strong memories that were not altogether fond. "That's why I left there," he said. "The trails were too wacky. I'd never think of running a dog race through there."

He left Crested Butte, Colorado, anticipating the better trails and the snow of Alaska. He'd been running dogsled tours in Crested Butte with his Saudi Arabian wife, Fidaa, when the opportunity to enter the Iditarod presented itself. Daily said the couple had been surviving on a business that offered tourists two-hour sled rides for $180 when they accidentally hit the mushing jackpot. It took shape from a ride the Dailys gave two members of the Suechting family.

The Suechtings — Barbara, David, David Junior and Debbie — own Track 'N Trail, a shoe store chain. The Suechtings, through connections with the Timberland Boot Company, had become interested in the world's longest and best-known sled dog marathon. Timberland is the Iditarod's major sponsor.

Track 'N Trail asked Timberland about joining in its Iditarod promotion, but couldn't reach an agreement with the manufacturer. "So they said, 'Heck, we'll just sponsor our own musher,' " Daily said. "So they took a chance on a rookie. They were really generous, and I needed it. I was almost totally broke, and when you start training you're quickly broke."

"We had thought about [the Iditarod] before," Fidaa said, "but we never had enough money to do it."

The appearance of Track 'N Trail was almost a miracle. No musher could have dreamt of more. "I was incredibly lucky financially on this race," Tom said. "This happened a year ago, and I immediately moved back up here."

The couple spent the winter training at Trapper Creek. It was a strange new experience for Fidaa, who had met Tom only two years before. Their love affair started, naturally enough, on a dogsled.

"He gave me a dogsled ride in Colorado," Fidaa said. She was just another tourist on that first ride, but that changed quickly. Soon Fidaa found herself out of the sled basket and on the runners. She learned to drive the sled, and the next thing she knew she was involved in Daily's business, helping run the sled dog trips for tourists. Then came the agreement with Track 'N Trail and the big move to the bizarre new world of Alaska. "We lived quite primitively in the bush," Fidaa said. "Being with Tom was quite helpful."

Daily had the experience. He'd been kicking around Alaska since fleeing Michigan State University in the early 1970s. Three years of college biology had been enough for a boy from Illinois who drove west and got a look at Colorado one summer. "I didn't want to spend my life looking through microscopes all day," Daily said. "Just seeing Colorado did it. Somebody told me Alaska was even better than Colorado, and that was it.

"I was fortunate to show up [in the state] right before the pipeline construction started. I didn't come up for the pipeline, but I sure did work on it. I worked really hard for three or four years. That's how I could have dogs."

He started running dogs with Bruce Johnson of Atlin, British Columbia, in 1978. A well-known Canadian musher, Johnson would eventually go on to win the one-thousand-mile Yukon Quest International Sled Dog Race from Whitehorse, Yukon, to Fairbanks. From Atlin, Daily moved to Haines, where he met up with Bruce Denton of Juneau, an eventual top-ten finisher in the Iditarod. Denton moved to Nenana, in the Alaska interior, to get better training one winter, and Daily went along. "What I learned about the Iditarod, I learned from him," Daily said.

It helped, but nothing that he learned from Denton or anyone else could prepare him for the reality of the race, with its miles of unknown and energy-sapping trail.

*

On the seventh day of the race, Tom Daily would find himself all alone in the fabled Farewell Burn, dealing with a classic rookie mistake. He would leave the last, thick stand of spruce before the Burn, and mush less than a mile out into the desolation before realizing it was time to rest and snack the dogs.

The night was deathly black and the wind was blowing the snow horizontal at speeds of 20 to 30 mph. The snow infiltrated the coats of the dogs as each curled into a protective ball to rest along the gang line. A shivering Daily cut them round steak. "Dogs eat better than people any day," he said.

He knelt in the snow with his back to the wind. The fingers on his bare hands fumbled like so many thumbs. Snow swirled around his face. The dogs' eyes glinted in the beam of his headlamp when he swung the light down the team to make sure all were resting. He shook his head at one team dog still pulling in his harness. "I got one knucklehead who wants to go no matter what," Daily said. "Dogs."

For an hour, then, the team rested in the cold. Daily got no rest. After feeding the dogs, he took to trying to hack away the ice balls that had accumulated on the footrests of his sled runners. Then he ate a granola bar from a sack of munchies he kept in the back of the sled. The night was growing colder and grimmer by the minute. "It's starting to get sort of nippy here," he said. "All I got to do is change a few booties, and I can get going."

He admitted to being nervous about the trail, but he planned to press on. "If I get lost, I'll stop," he said.

He drove on. By midnight he was well out into the Burn. His headlamp played over two-foot-tall willows and the hulks of old trees. Sometimes there were reflectors to mark the trail. Sometimes there were not.

Much of the trail was blown in, but parts of it could be found where it climbed up and over the desolate, rolling hills that sometimes provided protection from the wind and sometimes exposed him to its full force. Again and again he got lost. Always he searched about, found the trail and drove on, following at times the tracks of a fox that seemed to be the only other living thing moving in the Burn this night.

He lost the fox markings where the trail passed out of the hills sprinkled with burnt-over trees and onto a broad, flat plain where there was only grass and willow.

Years ago, Alaska's largest-ever wildfire had roared through there with an intense heat, and there was nothing left. It has been more than a decade since the fire, and still nothing has come back. This part of the Burn belonged to the wind and the grass, but it was here, ironically, that the trail was best marked.

On tripods scattered in a row across the flatlands were reflective markers. Daily followed them straight and true for hour after monotonous hour, traveling first from one reflector to the next and then reaching stretches so well marked that the reflectors could be seen stretching out in long rows ahead.

"They make all the difference," Daily said. "Sometimes there were so many they make you feel like you're cheating."

For a while there it seemed almost too easy. Sullivan Creek, on the north end of the Burn, twenty-two miles out of Nikolai, changed that. The creek was thirty feet of wide-open, flowing water crossed by a sorry imitation of a bridge made from some spruce trees. Daily's dogs balked.

"That bridge was worthless," he said. "Usually I can make the dogs go through creeks, but not that one. They hated that."

The musher ended up ferrying the dogs across the creek himself, one at a time, wading back and forth through the cold water in his once dry mukluks. It was miserable work, and it took two hours. Near dawn, Daily finally got back on the trail to Nikolai.

He had passed most of the night in the Burn. Ahead he had the still-long ride to Nikolai, but the wind had died and the sun was starting to lighten the sky. By daybreak he was coming into the Nikolai checkpoint, tired and moving as stiffly as an old man but happy to be there.

"We're here, guys," he said to the dogs. "You can relax.

"It's nice being in this town," he said to a small group of people. "I started to not like it when my feet got frozen out there. I was dreaming of the community center [and its warmth]. The main thing was my feet hurt after going in the water."

It was an observation, not a complaint. Despite his appearance, he was a happy man. He knew the worst of the Iditarod was behind him. He praised his dogs. "It was good to have a command leader. We spent a lot of time lost out there. Everything was drifted in. I'm sure glad for my leaders. You'd be sunk on this trip if you didn't have at least one good one."

Despite the horror stories, he added, the Burn had not been horrible. The trip had been long and arduous, but at no point was it particularly scary. "It's hard to get lonely with my pack of idiots," Daily said. "It [the Burn] wasn't as bad as I thought, but I'm sure it could be. It is good to have it over with in one shot, but it didn't scare the hell out of me or anything. It's all mushable."

Almost anything is mushable for people and dogs who are crazy enough. Joe Redington and Susan Butcher proved that by taking a dog team to the 20,320-foot summit of Mount McKinley, North America's highest peak. The question for the Burn is, How mushable?

The answer, Daily admitted, depends on how you look at the question.

The Daily family plan was for Tom to run the Iditarod this year and for Fidaa to run next year. Track 'N Trail liked the idea of sponsoring the first Saudi Arabian woman to make the 1,100-mile run from Anchorage to Nome. But Tom, with his newfound experience, was having second thoughts in Nikolai. "I'm not sure I'd want her to run it," he said. "It's too dangerous. You could get killed out there."

DAVE BARRY

Why the NBA Isn't as Offensive as You Think

FROM TROPIC

IT'S A TUESDAY night in January, and somewhere in America
some guys who consider themselves to be Knowledgeable Sports
Fans are sitting in a bar, talking. One of them is saying, "You
know what's wrong with pro basketball? They don't play *defense*.
All it is is big goons running up and down the court scoring
whenever the hell they feel like it."

And the other guys nod.

Meanwhile, in the Miami Arena, the Heat are playing the Sacramento Kings. The Kings are quite possibly the worst team in
the NBA. This means that the Heat, who are not exactly a dy-
nasty themselves, have a good chance to win. It's the second
quarter, and Sacramento, which is trailing but gaining, has the
ball.

Grant Long, the Heat's starting power forward, six feet eight
inches tall, 230 pounds — this is considered *small* for an NBA
power forward — is getting back on defense. He plays in the
middle where the tall timbers hang out. He's guarding Sacramento forward Antoine Carr, a major load of lumber, arms bigger than your legs, legs bigger than your recreation room. Tacti-
cally, what's happening is that Carr is trying to establish position
near the basket so he can accept a pass and maybe take a close-in
shot; Long is trying to deny Carr the position, and the pass. In
concrete terms, this means that they're banging on each other
like enraged buffalo. Their leg tendons bulge as they lean

against each other, their huge bodies forming a triangle with the floor as a base. Long keeps one hand on Carr, sometimes two. This is, technically, a violation of the rules, but it's also such a fundamental part of NBA big-man defensive play that no ref will call it. Carr retaliates by jerking his big arms back, shooting elbows into Long, pounding, pounding, sending sweat drops flying. This is also, of course, against the letter of the rules, but refs usually ignore it, too, unless they see actual teeth on the floor.

This intense little war is going on near the center of a swirling, ten-man mass of violently fast motion — "small" men, who are actually big, darting around the perimeter, changing direction so quickly that you expect their sneakers to leave scorch marks on the floor; bigger men inside, grunting and trying to muscle their way to the right places, the places that were so easy to get to in practice when the coach would simply point to spots on the floor and say, O.K., now you move over here, and the players would just trot over. But now they fight for each inch.

Antoine Carr lunges away from Grant Long, toward the middle. A Sacramento guard, seeing this — NBA guards see everything — instantly fires the ball inside. Carr grabs the pass and whirls to his right, driving to the basket — this is happening faster than you can think about it — and Long leaps to the right, trying to get in the way, and *WHUMP GRUNT* they slam into each other, a collision that would hospitalize normal people — they'd be telling their grandchildren about it twenty years from now — and *WHAM* Long is on the floor, skidding backward ten feet on his butt, and *TWEEE* the ref is blowing his whistle. Both Carr and Long look at the ref with that injured, puppy-dog-eyed "Who ME?" expression that NBA players adopt reflexively, sometimes with their elbows still deep in an opponent's gut. The ref points at Long, on the floor. "That's where it's at," he says. Long shakes his head, gets up, ready to bang some more, because the game goes on with you or without you, and nobody has time to dwell on a routine foul play that took maybe two seconds.

Meanwhile, back in the bar somewhere in America, the Knowledgeable Sports Fans are deciding to have another beer.

I should stress that I'm not at all knowledgeable myself. I just like pro basketball a lot, and I wanted to do a story about Grant Long because (a) I love the way he plays, and (b) this would give me a chance to hang around Miami Heat practices and, with professional coaching, develop a potentially lethal outside jump shot.

I need a strong jumper to compensate for my weak inside game. I haven't been able to slam-dunk a basketball for the past five years. Or for the thirty-eight years before that, either. I'm not physically gifted, which is why I'm a fan of Grant Long, because he's not gifted either, by NBA standards. Ask ten basketball people to describe him, and they'll all say the same things, often in the same words: *He's a blue-collar player. A great attitude. Great work ethic. A much better player than he should be. He doesn't look pretty out there, but he always gives you 110 percent. A heckuva nice guy. He's done a tremendous amount for a guy with limited physical gifts.*

Of course all this is relative. Compared with Godzilla, King Kong had limited physical gifts. Even the most marginal NBA player is an absurdly better athlete than an ordinary person. When basketball people say that Grant Long can't shoot, can't pass, can't dribble, what they mean is: He can shoot, pass and dribble better than you, better than anybody you know, better than all but a few hundred people in the world. Long's jump shot is so bad, by NBA standards, that his team never runs a play designed to set him up for it; but you could practice *your* jump shot every day forever and still never beat him in a game of horse.

One day Long and I were standing on the floor of the Miami Arena, talking. I was bouncing a basketball, and suddenly Long flicked his hand out, stole the ball, and started dribbling it. I tried to steal it back. I tried *hard* to steal it back, for about thirty seconds, and I never once touched it, despite the fact that Long, nearly a foot taller than I, was bouncing it to the height of my chest, and was making no effort to back away from me, or use his body as a shield. The problem was that I was operating in Normal Person Time, which is slow motion for an NBA player. Long would be bouncing the ball so that it passed a foot from my hand, and I'd make my craftiest, slickest, lightning-quickest move for it, and Long — looking at me, not the ball — would casually alter the dribble, flick the ball through his legs, pick it up on the other side, leaving me lunging at air, time and again. But in the NBA, this is a guy whose ball-handling skills are considered to be zero. This is a guy who, if everything went according to the Heat game plan, would not dribble the ball *once*.

"Offensive plays aren't run for me," Long says. "So I have to do everything I can do with my own strengths. One of my strengths is to play good post [near the basket] defense — to beat up guys, body them really hard. By the end of the night, I have the advantage, because they're running around, trying to score, getting tired, and I don't have to score. (He laughs.) All I have to do is beat up on them."

I asked Ron Rothstein, the Heat's head coach, what a power forward is supposed to do.

"He's supposed to kill people," he answered, only partly kidding.

Long is one of the NBA's top foulers. In 1988–89, his rookie season (and the Heat's), he led the league in fouls, with 337, and was disqualified from thirteen games (you're disqualified from a game when you commit six personal fouls); last season he committed 300 fouls and led the league in disqualifications, with eleven. In one game last year, the Arena crowd actually gave him an ovation for getting all the way to the fourth quarter before committing his first foul.

Long commits fouls because that's part of his job. Unfortunately, fouling is not the route to glamour and fame and lucrative product endorsements. The Wheaties people pay big bucks for the image of Michael Jordan soaring to the basket at cruise-missile speed and altitude; there's no demand for Grant Long playing grunt defense, planting his body inside Antoine Carr's shorts.

But watch Long closely in a game and you won't be bored. If the NBA kept a statistic for floor burns, he'd lead the league; he's constantly colliding, falling, diving, skidding. Nothing looks easy for him. Other players flow gracefully around the court; Long flails his body violently from place to place, running with such obvious effort that he seems to have several extra knees and elbows, shooting out in random directions. Also his shirttail is always out and his shorts always seem to be almost falling off. This is why he wears a pair of tight, knicker-like, knee-length white shorts under his uniform shorts, sticking out the bottom, creating a semi-comical look. These are called "compression pants," and I always thought they served some medical purpose, but in Long's case they don't.

"In college, I always feared that my shorts would come off," he says. "I feared I'd be breaking away for a lay-up and somebody would be behind me, and he'd trip and fall and grab my waist, and my shorts would come down and I'd just be standing there naked. That was one of my biggest fears."

"So now you wear those knickers," I say.

"Exactly," he says.

"They look goofy," I say.

"That's my protection," he says. "At least if my shorts come down, I'll be standing there looking sexy."

Still in the second quarter against Sacramento: Antoine Carr is out of the game, and Long is now guarding Anthony Bonner, another side of beef. Bonner gets the ball down low and *WHUMP GRUNT* . . . Surprise! Long is on the floor *again*. Both players immediately shoot sincere, hurt looks at the ref, who, this time, calls traveling on Bonner. No blood, no foul. Heat ball. Long, happy that he's not being charged with anything, is up instantly, churning down the court. Coach Rothstein is running up the sideline after his team, yelling instructions. At least I *assume* they're instructions. What it sounds like he's yelling is totally random nouns. He does this all game long.

"MOTION!" he'll yell.

Or: "FIST!" He yells this a lot.

Sometimes, mysteriously, he'll yell: "X!"

Occasionally he'll yell something less technical, such as: "WHERE THE FUCK IS OUR DEFENSE??"

Rothstein virtually never looks happy during a game. Even when things are going well for the Heat, he looks like a man being informed by surgeons that at least one kidney has to go.

Much of the time Rothstein yells his instructions to Sherman Douglas, the Heat's starting point guard. Douglas doesn't look like a pro basketball player: he's only six feet tall, if that; he has a baby face and a squat, lumpy body. But he has the eyes of a predator, and he's an amazing athlete. He has to be. An NBA point guard must be able to simultaneously (1) dribble the ball quickly up the court while an opposition player with world-class quickness tries to steal it; (2) watch the clock, because his team has only twenty-four seconds to get off a shot; (3) analyze the other team's defense; (4) keep track of all four of his teammates, sometimes directing them with his free hand; and (5) glance at his coach, who is yelling seemingly random nouns at him. Above all, the point guard must always be ready to *act* — to whip the ball instantly when a teammate breaks for the basket, creating an opening, lasting maybe a tenth of a second before the defense adjusts, during which a perfectly thrown pass will result in a score. So point guards are *extremely* decisive. You put point guards on the Supreme Court and they'd hand down a landmark decision every five minutes.

The best point guard in the NBA now, and maybe ever, is the Los Angeles Lakers' Earvin "Magic" Johnson, who regularly throws seemingly impossible passes, without looking, to teammates in a perfect position to score. These passes are so sudden, so deceptive, that they sometimes surprise even Johnson's teammates, bouncing embarrassingly off their bodies. It would be scary to be a Laker. You'd never be able to really relax. You'd have this recurring *Psycho*-style nightmare where you're in your hotel room, taking a shower, feeling safe, and suddenly CRASH the shower door explodes and a laser-beam Magic pass breaks your nose.

Magic Johnson, who starred at Michigan State before turning pro, was Grant Long's idol when Long was growing up in Romulus, Michigan, the second-oldest of four brothers.

"My father left when I was . . . to tell you the truth, I don't remember at all," he says. "I guess it just didn't faze me at all. That's probably why I don't remember it. It just never fazed me at all when he left. It seemed like the family just pulled together." His mother, Dorothy Long, worked for an airport catering service. "She worked so hard. We had our struggles, but you couldn't tell that we didn't have a lot. The things we had were precious. For Christmas, we might get one or two things, but it would be the best Christmas ever.

"To this day, she works on Christmas. She works *so* hard. I think that's where I get it from. What they always say about me is, 'He works hard.' But you're *supposed* to work hard. That's why they *pay* you."

Long makes $300,000 a year now. His teammates, who like to

kid him, claim that he has not spent any of these dollars. He does not have a lavish lifestyle. He drives a Chevy Blazer, eats at Wendy's. He wears jeans and T-shirts, which is unusual in the style-conscious world of pro basketball. "I don't put a lot of value on clothes," he says. "I've always worn jeans, and I'm not going to stop just because I'm in the NBA. I think that's part of me that says, 'You're still Grant Long, from Romulus.' "

Long is popular with his teammates, his coaches, the press. He's funny, articulate and incongruously gentle for a guy who makes his living killing people. He's your basic nice guy, a guy who actually married his high school sweetheart (they have an eight-month-old son). Nobody has anything bad to say about him, and he doesn't have anything bad to say about anybody else, except . . .

"The drivers in Miami are terrible. That's the only thing I don't like about Miami. The drivers are *terrible*." Long is getting worked up now, showing far more emotion than he does when he gets flattened by Antoine Carr. "I'm watching the TV news, and they have this statistic: over 75 percent of Miami drivers don't have licenses or insurance. They *know* this. So why are they *telling* us this? Why aren't they getting these people off the *street*? And the drivers are so noncourteous. They don't let the other drivers merge. They're saying, 'I'm not letting *anybody* in,' and they go bumper-to-bumper so nobody can merge, and it makes me sick. Then you got people who drive the *whole way* with their blinkers on, never turning. They *never turn*. They're crouched way down, got both hands on the wheel, driving about 25 mph. In the *fast lane*. I don't think there *is* a fast lane in Miami."

Long's favorite recreational activity is bowling. Yes. Also, like most Heat players, he plays Nintendo.

ME: Are you any good at Nintendo?

LONG: I'm pretty good.

ME: What board can you get to on Super Mario Brothers III?

Note: I'm asking this penetrating question because my son plays this game a lot, and I'm wondering if he has reached NBA caliber.

LONG: I got to the Dark World. I haven't rescued the Princess, though.

ME (triumphantly): My son did.

LONG (skeptically): No he didn't.
ME: Yes he did.
LONG: No he didn't.
Note: I checked with my son, and it turns out he didn't.

Back in the Sacramento game: Sherman Douglas, with the ball, is scuttling up the court, watching everything, including Long, who is churning up the right sideline. The man guarding Long looks away for an instant, and as he does *SQUEAK* Long plants his right sneaker and blasts to the basket and launches himself into the air, reaching the rim at the same moment as a long, high, arcing pass, which was thrown by Douglas in the nanosecond that Long started his move, before anybody else in the Arena saw it. This is the alley oop, the most fun-to-watch play in basketball. As Long sails past the rim he grabs the ball and with the same motion *WHOOM* hurls it through the basket. The crowd explodes, but Long is already churning hard back up the court, because if he pauses to bask in the glory, *his* man will score an easy basket at the other end, and that's the one that Rothstein will remember.

Long's basket produces a burst of words from my right on the press table, where Jose Pañeda is doing the play-by-play in Spanish for radio station WRFM. To me, it sounds like this:

Derechelosimplemadoamos SHERMAN DOUGLAS *esteisquierdalamenteierdoasos* GRANT LONG *erdamentalastalamentemenclavar* ¡PERFECTO!

I met Pañeda earlier that day, when I challenged him to a game of one-on-one on the Arena floor after the Heat practice. I lost pathetically because of an Invisible Force Field that kept popping up around the basket whenever I took shots at it.

Pañeda said doing basketball play-by-play in Spanish takes a lot of energy. "I have to use about eight words for every English word," he said. "In English you say, 'ALLEY OOP!' I have to say, 'HE THREW THE BALL AND IT GOT TO THE BASKET AT THE SAME TIME AS THE OTHER GUY AND THE OTHER GUY SCORED!' "

At halftime the Heat are trailing, 42–40. The PA announcer informs the crowd that the halftime entertainment will be "one of the premier freestyle cyclists in the world." A young man comes out riding a small bicycle and does some premier freestyle tricks such as: The Front Pogo, The Rear Pogo, The Grasshopper, and of course The Front Infinity Roll Into A Side Glide. The crowd, enthralled, heads for the restrooms.

You never know what you're going to see at the halftime of a Heat game. Bizarre, mutant halftime acts roam the country, going from arena to arena, and sooner or later they all come to Miami. Last year there were two guys who did trampoline tricks while wearing water skis. Also there's a guy who comes out with a frame attached to his body, and life-size Michael Jackson dolls attached to the frame, so that when he dances, the Michael Jackson dolls dance in perfect unison. You have to see it to truly appreciate it, especially when one of the dolls' heads or arms comes loose from the frame and starts jerking around spasmodically, as though that particular Michael Jackson has a neurological disorder.

So far this year at halftime I've seen a guy who balanced a spinning basketball on top of what looked like a skinny, scraggly, thirty-foot-tall dead tree; a group of men who did precision drill formations with lawn chairs; and — this was the best — a man who used a vacuum-cleaner-like machine to slowly inflate a large balloon, after which he somehow got his entire body *inside* the balloon, after which he hopped to the other end of the court, still squatting inside the balloon, looking like a hyperactive disease germ magnified several million times, after which he popped the balloon and leaped up, thrusting his arms out triumphantly, as though he had just won the Tour de France. I watched this act in rapt fascination along with many other spectators, and I know I speak for them all when I say that my reaction was: *Huh?* I mean, at parties, when other people ask this guy what he does, does he come right out and say that he hops around basketball courts inside a balloon? Or does he just say that he's in show business?

Also appearing regularly on the Arena floor are Burnie, the Heat mascot, who wears a very big costume and engages in comical antics, and the Miami Heat Dancers, who wear very small costumes and cause the guy fans to chew their pretzels more slowly. I asked Shaun Powell, who covers the Heat for the *Herald,* how the Heat Dancers stack up against the rest of the league. He frowned thoughtfully, a trained journalist offering an informed opinion. "I'd say that the Heat Dancers are probably in the top thirty percent of the NBA dancers right now," he said. "I would say that Burnie, as a mascot, is second only to the Gorilla of Phoenix."

The actual Heat basketball team has not yet reached this level of performance.

"Every city we go to, you see the same headlines in the sports pages," Powell said."LOCAL TEAM COOLS HEAT. Or LOCAL TEAM CHILLS HEAT. Or ICES HEAT. Or FREEZES HEAT. In the stories, they're always the 'hapless Heat.' The hapless Heat did this, the hapless Heat did that. It's like they're from Hapless, Florida."

Nevertheless, in the third quarter the Hapless Heat come out strong, thanks to hustle, determination and the fact that WRFM's Jose Pañeda has switched to his Lucky Green Scoring Pen. "Green for go!" he informs me, holding it up, in between shouting "*¡PERFECTO!*"

Also helping out is Grant Long, who puts the Heat ahead, 49–48, by making two foul shots, which is a good example of performing under pressure, inasmuch as the foul consisted of Long's getting kneed in a Highly Sensitive Area.

I ask him later if this kind of thing every makes him angry.

"No," he says, "I never take it personally, because it's part of the game. You leave it on the court."

I ask him if he ever talks to opponents, or if they talk to him.

"I never have time to talk," he says. "What could I say? 'Hey, I got a rebound!' Some of the other players talk, but when they talk, it's just in fun. They've done it since they were on the playground, and it's always in a joking manner. Like, one of Larry's [Larry Bird's] favorite things is, you know how he just sits there and shoots the jumper, and you come running out at him, and he'll say something like, 'Just in time.' Or: 'You're too late.' But you know Larry's a great player and a great competitor; he's not trying to be a smartass or anything, so you don't take it personally."

I myself was shocked to learn that Larry Bird, the Great White Basketball God, was making snide remarks out there. He always looks so businesslike, so clinical, so *in control*. If you were in a 747 with the Boston Celtics, and the entire flight crew keeled over dead, you'd say, "No problem! We'll have Larry land it!"

Long shakes his head at the aggrandizement of athletes. "It doesn't make sense," he says. "I mean, think about it. A professional athlete has achieved success *athletically*, but then suddenly he's supposed to know everything. That's ridiculous. He knows no more than he did before; he just makes a lot of money. Why should his opinions have weight? You've got doctors out there who've been to school for twelve years. *Those* are the role models. We're just basketball players. I don't mind people coming to me for advice, and I'll tell them what I think, but I don't know any more than the next guy knows."

A game-day Heat practice has just ended on the floor of the Arena, and the team has left, except for Long, who's taping a public-service TV announcement for a program called CHARLEE, which aids abused and neglected children. In the script, a CHARLEE official, Ray Porredon, is supposed to announce a horse shoot-out tournament to benefit the program, and then Long is supposed to come on camera and say, "Be there, and see who has the best shot in south Florida. Please support our children with special needs." Then he's supposed to turn and make a jump shot. It takes quite a few takes to get everything right. Both men appear as relaxed and natural as utility poles; they eye the camera warily, as though at any moment they expect snakes to come shooting out of it.

In the first few takes, Porredon tries to act as though he's surprised to see Long. "Hey!" he says, his face reflecting either surprise or terror. "It's my friend Grant Long of the Miami Heat!" The director decides that, dramatically, this is not working. He observes that, logically, Porredon wouldn't be surprised to see Long, because (a) he's on a basketball court, and (b) Long is a large individual who has clearly been standing right next to him.

"So you don't need to act surprised," the director says.

"No surprise," Porredon says.

"Ax the surprise," Long says.

Both men have some trouble delivering their lines. At one point, Porredon announces that the event will be a "horse-out"; at another point, as Long is finishing his lines, a highly visible fly, left over from the circus, lands on his face. But finally they get through everything flawlessly, and all that remains is for Long to turn and sink a twenty-foot jump shot. The irony here is that, when he attempts these in games, a giant involuntary cringe sweeps the crowd, accompanied by the occasional half-whispered "Noooooo . . ."

"Please support our children with special needs," Long says, then he turns, cocks the ball, shoots and . . . SWISH. Yes! The crowd (me) goes wild, pumping their fists, performing The Wave.

"Makeup!" shouts Long, suddenly a star.

Speaking of jump shots: a bit earlier I was working on mine when up walked Tony Fiorentino, who is one of Rothstein's two assistant coaches and also the runner-up in the NBA Coaching Staff Omar Sharif Look-Alike Contest. (The winner is Rothstein's other assistant coach, Dave Wohl.) Fiorentino spent a moment watching me take my shot, which goes like this:

Shot . . . CLUNK

Shot . . . CLUNK

Shot . . . CLUNK

The "CLUNK" is the sound of the ball banging off the rim. This happens frequently when I shoot because of wind shear.

"You're holding the ball wrong," Fiorentino says. "Try holding the ball with the seams like this." It turns out that you're supposed to hold the ball with the seams running horizontally under your fingertips. Good players, when they get ready to shoot, automatically align the ball so the seams are right.

This is a revelation for me. In all the years I've been clunking the ball off the rim, nobody has ever told me that you're supposed to grip the seams a certain way. This is significant. I can feel it. This is the turning point in my game, and it's happening on a real NBA court, in front of a real NBA coach. I grab the ball, dribble out fifteen feet, and . . .

Shot . . . CLUNK

Shot . . . CLUNK

Shot . . . CLUNK

"Maybe you should stand closer to the basket," suggests Fiorentino.

Now we're back to the Sacramento game, and you'll never guess where Grant Long is. Right! The floor! I'm not sure exactly how he got there, because all my notes say is, "GL on floor again," but while he's lying there the ball, miraculously, *rolls right to him,* so he grabs it and fires a pass. The game is going well for the Heat. They're more than ten points ahead and playing well with only a few minutes to go. They're definitely going to win, and Rothstein looks like a man whose surgeons are now telling him they need to remove *both* kidneys, plus at least one major limb.

The Heat call time-out; they set up a play, the players gathering around Rothstein, frowning down at him while he talks. The time-out over, they head back onto the court. Sherman Douglas takes the inbounds pass, dribbles the ball on the perimeter. "Grant!" he shouts.

Long comes out, but not to get the ball. The ball is for scorers. Long's job is to set a pick, which means plant his body in a spot so that Douglas can run past, running his defensive man into Long and thus breaking free.

"You ready?" yells Long, planting himself. There is nothing subtle about this. This play does not have an element of surprise. Everybody on both teams knows what is about to happen. Out in space, orbiting Russian spy satellites are picking this up, sending the word back to Moscow: Long is about to set a pick for Douglas.

ZIP Douglas makes his cut and *WHUMP* the defensive man hits Long and *ZOOM* Douglas is skittering into the middle, a water bug among sequoias, and *BANG* he collides with somebody and stumbles and *TWEEE* the ref calls . . . traveling. Sacramento ball. Rothstein is enraged.

"GIVE US A CALL!" he shouts to the ref, and then, turning away, he says some other things that would not be wise to say to an NBA referee.

Later, I asked Rothstein how come he's so intense, even when it seems as though the game is over.

"Anybody who thinks the game is over doesn't know anything about the NBA," he said. "I've seen teams lose with the ball, up by six, with ten seconds left."

But not this time. This time the Heat win, 95–83. Long walks off the court, dripping sweat. Also walking off the court, not sweating at all, is Sacramento player Ralph Sampson, a seven-foot-four-inch center. He'll make $2 million this season, and, under his contract, he'll make $2 million more for each of the next two seasons. He didn't play *one second* in this game. He hardly ever plays. Bad knees.

After the game, some reporters are in the hall outside the Heat locker room, waiting to talk with Rothstein. He emerges from the locker room, looking tired and much more relaxed. He pauses next to me.

"I watched you play today," he says, his voice becoming soft, almost fatherly. "You were awful."

Before I can explain about the wind shear, he's talking to the reporters about the game.

"It wasn't real pretty," he says, "but we'll take it and run."

Meanwhile, in the locker room, assistant coaches Wohl and Fiorentino, the dual Omars, are doing paper work. I decide to ask them an informed, technical, savvy basketball question.

"What's an informed, technical, savvy basketball question I can ask Wohl and Fiorentino?" I whisper to *Herald* columnist Bob Rubin.

"Ask them if they were pleased with the defensive rotation," Rubin suggests.

"So," I say to Wohl and Fiorentino. "Were you guys pleased with the defensive rotation? Or what?"

Wohl looks up. "Oh yes, pleased," he says. "Definitely."

"We squeezed the traps well," notes Fiorentino, adding, "but then the game started."

"Here's what I want to know," I say. "When Rothstein is yelling things like 'fist,' is he just making up random nouns?"

"Yes," says Wohl. "He yells random nouns, and we yell random verbs back. We hope they'll connect and make a sentence."

"The idea," explains Fiorentino, "is that the other team will listen and become confused."

Meanwhile, all around us, large wet men are giving quotations naked. The players were making a lot of noise in the shower, laughing, shouting, whooping, but when they get to their lockers, where the press is waiting with note pads and microphones, they shift into Quote Mode, adopting somber expressions and using phrases like "putting forth a good effort" and "playing with intensity," which I doubt is what they were saying in the shower.

The striking exception is Grant Long, who is not remotely somber. Striding from the shower, he grabs a cold bottle of Evian Natural Spring Water and, without hesitating, pokes it into the naked butt of Sherman Douglas, who is speaking into a radio microphone. Fortunately Douglas, with a point guard's presence of mind, is able to swat the bottle away without interrupting his quotation. Next Long strides over and sits down next to forward Billy Thompson, who's being interviewed by a TV reporter. Long leans over, listens a second. "He's lying," he informs the reporter.

A couple of reporters ask Long questions, but most of the attention is focused on the scorers — Douglas, Thompson, Glen Rice, Kevin Edwards. In the next day's *Herald* story, only one sentence will be totally devoted to Long. It comes at the end, in a section called "Odds and Ends." It says:

UNSUNG HERO: Who else? Grant Long had a double-double with 10 points and 10 rebounds, and spent lots of time diving for loose balls — as usual.

In the locker room, the press finally gets its quota of quotations and goes off to write stories. I go home to practice gripping the seams. Grant Long pulls on his jeans and T-shirt, goes home to his wife, Nikki, and son, Garvis.

Somewhere in America, Knowledgeable Sports Fans are watching the late sports on the TV over the bar. On the screen are some NBA highlights; a player is making a spectacular dunk shot.

"Look at that," a fan is saying. "No defense at all. A million dollars a year and they don't play defense. Bunch of overgrown spoiled babies."

"Being a dad is great," Long says. "Except lately he doesn't want to sleep at night. It's three o'clock in the morning and he's standing up in his crib, screaming, making a noise like somebody's in there burning his foot. So I go in there, and he has snot all over his face, and he sees me, and he just starts smiling. He's *laughing*. He wants to *play*. So I finally brought him into our bedroom and laid him on our bed, and he played with his toys for about ten minutes and fell right off to sleep. Three in the morning, I had practice the next day, had to get up at nine, but it was great.

"The fathers don't know what they're missing out on, the ones that leave home. They just don't know what they're missing."

It's ten nights after the Sacramento game, and the Heat, to the delight of the Miami fans, are slaughtering the New York Knicks. Even Rothstein would probably admit, under torture, that the game is out of reach. This is what's known as Garbage Time, because play gets sloppy and players can score easy baskets. Rothstein's lineup now includes Alan Ogg, a rookie center who has had little playing time. Ogg is not considered to be highly talented. What he is considered to be is seven feet two inches. He moves with a slow, lumbering gait, but he works very hard. In the Heat practices I watched, every chance he got he slamdunked the ball. It was as if he knew he wouldn't get many chances to do it in games, so he was determined to do it when he could. They'd run a little drill, and at the end somebody'd feed the ball to Ogg, and *WHOMP* he'd stuff it hard through the hoop, then look at the floor kind of bashfully, because after all, it was only practice. Sometimes the other players would smile. They've affectionately nicknamed Ogg "Ogglajuwan," after Akeem Olajuwan, the very gifted center of the Houston Rockets.

Ogg is a cult figure among Heat fans. They go nuts when he comes into a game. "Oggggg!!" they shout. "OGGGGGGGG!!!!" It sounds like thousands of people simultaneously getting sick.

There are just a few seconds left in Garbage Time, and the Heat have the ball. In fact Grant Long has the ball, and he's actually *dribbling* it, an indication that things are very loose indeed.

Now Long is in the lane, close to the basket. The defense is slack. This is an easy shot opportunity, a chance to pad his statistics in a meaningless moment, to indulge in a little self-gratification, and so Long . . . passes off to Alan Ogg, standing under the basket. Ogg rears up — he doesn't really have to jump — and *WHOMP* jams that mother home.

"OGGGGGGGGGGGG!!!!" goes the crowd, high-fiving, insane with joy.

Grant Long, unsung hero, churns back up the court.

Biographical Notes

Notable Sports Writing of 1991

Biographical Notes

DAVE BARRY of the *Miami Herald* is a nationally known syndicated columnist and best-selling humorist. His books include *Dave Barry Slept Here, Dave Barry Turns Forty,* and, most recently, *Dave Barry's Greatest Hits.*

MICHAEL DISEND has written for numerous publications, including *GQ, Details,* and *Sport.* He is also an actor and appears as a serial killer in the film *Fathers and Sons,* starring Jeff Goldblum and Roseanne Arquette.

TIMOTHY DWYER lives outside Philadelphia and is a graduate of Northeastern University. He joined the staff of the *Philadelphia Inquirer* in 1983, following five years as a general assignment reporter with the *Boston Globe.* He has worked on the sports staff of the *Inquirer* since 1990.

PETER GAMMONS has worked for *Sports Illustrated* and the *Boston Globe,* for which he is a frequent contributor. He is the author of *Beyond the Sixth Game* and is ESPN's major league baseball analyst. He lives in Bourne, Massachusetts.

WILLIAM GILDEA will soon have a memoir published by Ticknor & Fields about growing up in Baltimore as a Baltimore Colts football fan. He is a former Nieman Fellow and currently lives in Bethesda, Maryland.

DAVID HALBERSTAM, who has won the Pulitzer Prize, is the author of many books, including *The Breaks of the Game* and *The Summer of Forty-nine.* He served as guest editor of *The Best American Sports Writing 1991.*

JAMES KILGO teaches English at the University of Georgia and lives in Athens, where, he reports, he is still looking for the big brown trout. His unique nonfiction narratives have appeared in *The Gettysburg Review*, *The New England Review*, and other publications. He is the author of *Deep Enough for Ivorybills*.

MICHAEL KUPPER is assistant sports editor of the *Los Angeles Times*. A native of Wisconsin, Kupper attended Marquette University. He lives in Agoura, California.

SYDNEY LEA founded *The New England Review* and *Bread Loaf Quarterly*. He is the author of a novel, *A Place in the Mind*, and a collection of poetry, *Prayer for the Little City*.

MIKE LUPICA is an award-winning columnist for the *New York Daily News* and *Esquire*. He is also the author of *Dead Air*, a mystery novel. He lives in New Canaan, Connecticut, and Jupiter, Florida.

THOMAS MALLON is the author of two novels, *Arts and Sciences* and *Aurora 7*, as well as several books of literary criticism. A collection of essays, *Rockets and Rodeos*, will be published this winter. He lives in New York, where he is literary editor of *Gentlemen's Quarterly*.

JOHN MARCHESE was born in Scranton, Pennsylvania, and now lives in Brooklyn, New York. He is a graduate of Temple University, has been a professional trumpeter and worked on the staff of *Atlantic City* magazine, *Philadelphia* magazine, and *7 Days*. His only previous sports story was a feature on girls' basketball, which appeared in the *Denton* (Texas) *Record Chronicle* in 1976.

CRAIG MEDRED moved to Alaska nineteen years ago after getting caught in a traffic jam on the first day of fishing season in his native Minnesota. He is a past recipient of the American Society of Newspaper Editors award for deadline reporting, and outdoors editor for the *Anchorage Daily News*.

LEIGH MONTVILLE was a sports reporter and columnist for the *Boston Globe* before joining *Sports Illustrated* in 1989. During his tenure with the magazine Montville has produced both features and columns, and he is a regular contributor to *Sports Illustrated*'s "Point After" section. He lives in Newton, Massachusetts.

WILLIAM NACK's story "Pure Heart," which appeared in *The Best American Sports Writing 1991*, also collected an Eclipse Award. Nack, a senior writer for *Sports Illustrated*, has covered everything from politics to court cases to horse races during his career. A Chicago native, he is a graduate of the University of Illinois. After serving two years in the army, including a stint in Vietnam, Nack was a reporter and sports columnist for *Newsday* for eleven years. He joined *Sports Illustrated* in 1979, and lives in Washington, D.C.

GEORGE PLIMPTON pioneered participatory sports journalism in the now classic *Paper Lion*. He is a frequent contributor to numerous publications and is the editor of *The Paris Review*. His most recent book is a collection of his work, *The Best of Plimpton*.

JAN REID has been a contributing editor at *Texas Monthly* since 1973. He has written for *Esquire* and *Inside Sports* and is the author of two nonfiction books, *The Improbable Rise of Redneck Rock* and *Vain Glory*. His novel *Deerinwater* was published in 1985. He lives in Austin, Texas.

LINDA ROBERTSON's story "Pride and Poison," about ex–football star Ted Hendricks, appeared in *The Best American Sports Writing 1991*. She has written for the *Miami Herald* since 1983.

DONNA ST. GEORGE, a national reporter based in New Orleans, covers the South for the *Philadelphia Inquirer*. She attended the University of Illinois and served as managing editor of the *Daily Illini*. She began her career at the *Los Angeles Times* and was a reporter for *Newsday* before joining the *Inquirer* in 1986.

JOE SEXTON lives in Brooklyn, New York, where he spent his childhood playing roller hockey. A graduate of the University of Wisconsin with a degree in English literature, Sexton worked for UPI before joining the *New York Times* in 1987. He is a contributor to numerous publications, including *Sport* and *Interview*.

GARY SMITH is a special contributor to *Sports Illustrated*. His profile of boxer James "Buster" Douglas appeared in *The Best American Sports Writing 1991*. "Shadow of a Nation," which appears in this year's edition, was selected in the feature-writing category for the 1991 National Magazine Awards. A graduate of La Salle University, Smith has written for *Rolling Stone, Inside Sports*, and the *Philadelphia Daily News*. He joined *Sports Illustrated* in 1982, and lives in Charleston, South Carolina.

PAUL SOLOTAROFF is a graduate of the State University of New York, Stony Brook, and the University of Iowa Writers' Workshop. He was a staff member of *The National Sports Daily*. A frequent contributor to *GQ*, Solotaroff lives in New York City.

KAREN UHLENHUTH grew up in Baltimore and Chicago before graduating from Northwestern University with a degree in journalism in

1976. She worked as a stringer for *AP* and *Time* before joining the *Lawrence* (Kansas) *Journal World*. She is now a feature writer with the *Kansas City Star*.

DAVID VON DREHLE is a Denver native and graduate of the University of Denver and Oxford University. He joined the *Miami Herald* as a city desk reporter before becoming a national correspondent. In 1991 he became the *Washington Post*'s New York bureau chief, and is at work on a book on the death penalty.

BRYAN WOOLLEY's study of shuffleboard hustler Billy Mays appeared in *The Best American Sports Writing 1991*. He is the author of two non-fiction collections, *Edge of the West* and *The Bride Wore Crimson*, published by Texas Western University Press. He lives in Dallas.

Notable Sports Writing of 1991

SELECTED BY GLENN STOUT

ROGER ANGELL
Ninety Feet. *The New Yorker,*
    December 9.

CHARLES ANZALONE
Bingo. *Buffalo Magazine,* February 3.

MARK ARMIJO
Weighing In Is Jockey's Nightmare.
    Arizona Republic, May 12.

CHUCK BARNEY
Forever a Yankee. *Contra Costa Times,*
    April 7.

PHIL BERGER
Body and Soul. *The New York Times
    Magazine,* March 24.
Brutally Beaten, a Boxer Still Dreams
    of Title. *New York Times,* July 14.

MICHAEL BIALAS
Golf's Angry Young Man Awaits
    Senior Years. *Denver Post,* April 7.

THOMAS BOSWELL
John Thompson Lightens Up. *GQ,*
    January.
Fields of Dreams. *The Washington Post
    Magazine,* March 24.

MIKE BOWDEN
The World's Worst Team. *Philadelphia
    Inquirer,* May 12.

BILL BRUBAKER
Tyson Maintains Innocence, Lifestyle.
    Washington Post, September 15.

AMBY BURFOOT
Slice of Life. *Runner's World,* May.

BRUCE BUSCHEL
Fastballs from the Edge. *The New York
    Times Magazine,* June 2.

GERRY CALLAHAN
Vic Goes for Broke. *Boston Herald,*
    October 16.

GARY CARTWRIGHT
The Real Deal vs. the Real Meal. *Texas
    Monthly,* June.

DAVID CATTAU
So, Maybe There Really Is Such a
    Thing as "the Natural." *Smithsonian,*
    July.

RAAD CAWTHON
Baseball's Biggest Flake. *Atlanta
    Journal and Constitution,* July 28.

GAIL CIAMPA
A Grand Slam of Fenway. *Providence
    Journal,* June 30.

JONATHAN COLEMAN
Little League. *Albemarle,* August–
    September.

MIKE CONKLIN
Scaling Mt. Hood Well Worth the
Effort. *Chicago Tribune*, July 25.

JEFF COPLON
Headstrong. *The New York Times
Magazine*, March 17.
Air Apparent. *Playboy*, June.

JOHN CRUMPACKER
The Day Ryun Ran into History. *San
Francisco Examiner*, July 14.

GEORGE DIAZ
Field of Dreams. *Florida Magazine*,
April 7.

JOSEPH D'O'BRIAN
The Business of Boxing. *American
Heritage*, October.

JIM DOHERTY
Seventy Years in Packerland.
Smithsonian, August.

JOHN DORSCHNER
Requiem for a Middleweight. *Tropic*,
July 7.

DUDLEY DOUST
Going the Distance. *The San Francisco
Examiner Magazine*, February 10.

MIKE DOWNEY
All Heart. *Los Angeles Times*, May 12.

CHRIS DUFRESNE
Crimes of Passion. *Los Angeles Times*,
May 19.

JONATHAN EIG
Goal Tending. *Dallas Life Magazine*,
January 6.

LOREN FELDMAN
Strikeouts and Psych-outs. *The New
York Times Magazine*, July 2.

LUIS H. FRANCIA
Peckerheads. *The Village Voice*,
September 17.

NORM FRAUENHEIM
Legends of the Land Are Long-
Running. *Arizona Republic*, June 16.

LEW FREEDMAN
When 2nd Doesn't Count. *Anchorage
Daily News*, July 7.

KEN FUSON
The Final Season. *Des Moines Register*,
July 14.

DAN GERSTEIN
Baseball's Roughriders. *Hartford
Courant*, July 7.

BIL GILBERT
The Twists of Fait. *Sports Illustrated
Classic*, Fall.

WILLIAM GILDEA
Lancelloti Logs 15th Year on Road to
the Show. *Washington Post*, August
11.

FRED GIRARD
Pulling Plug on Bookies. *Detroit News*,
March 31.

MICHAEL GOODMAN
Caged Animals, Wild Hunters. *Los
Angeles Times Magazine*, November
10.

HERBERT HADAD
Kelley's Run. *Northeast/Hartford
Courant*, April 14.

STEVE HEIMOFF
Muscle Man. *Express*, November 22.

ED HINTON
The Last Ride of A. J. Foyt. *The
National Sports Daily*, May 7.

JENNIFER HOWE
Old Soles. *Kansas City Star Magazine*,
June 2.

SCOTT HULER
Shoot to Thrill. *Philadelphia Magazine*,
October.